The Catholic Biblical Quarterly
Monograph Series
39

The Lord
Has Saved Me

A Study of the Psalm of Hezekiah
(Isaiah 38:9–20)

BY

Michael L. Barré, S.S.

The Catholic Biblical Quarterly
Monograph Series
39

Produced in the United States of America

Library of Congress Cataloging-in-Publication Data

Barré, Michael L.
    The Lord has saved me : a study of the Psalm of Hezekiah (Isaiah 38:9-20) /
by Michael L. Barré.
        p. cm. — (The Catholic Biblical quarterly. Monograph series ; 39)
    Appendix contains text of Isaiah XXXVIII, 9-20 in Hebrew and English.
    Includes bibliographical references and index.
    ISBN 0-915170-38-8
    1. Bible. O.T. Isaiah XXXVIII, 9-20—Commentaries. I. Bible. O.T. Isaiah
XXXVIII, 9-20. Hebrew. 2005. II. Bible. O.T. Isaiah XXXVIII, 9-20. English.
2005. III. Title. IV. Series.
BS1515.53.B37 2005
224'.106—dc22

                                                                    2005005066

To the memory of

Rev. Michael H. Gosselin
(1947–2001)
dear friend, who loved poetry

and

Rev. Dr. A. Vanlier Hunter
(1939–1992)
esteemed colleague, who loved the Hebrew Scriptures

לזכר עולם יהיה צדיק
(Ps 112:6)

Contents

Acknowledgments

This book has been long in production—in fact, from a certain vantage point, too long. It began with an idea I had some twenty years ago about the last verse of the Psalm of Hezekiah (Isa 38:20). From that seminal insight my interest gradually spread to the entire poem, and at some point I decided to write a monograph on it. But although I worked on the text during the better part of several sabbaticals, and even between sabbaticals to a lesser extent, and although progress was made during each of these periods, I was never able to finish it until now. From another perspective, however, it is probably all for the best that things turned out this way. What I would have written twenty or fifteen years ago would have been the result of less mature scholarship than—hopefully—appears here.

I am grateful to many different publics and individuals who, during this rather lengthy period of time, gave me encouragement, motivation, and support toward the completion of this project. In most cases the encouragement came in the form of "tough love" from friends and colleagues in heartening exhortations such as, "Are you *ever* going to finish that book?" Blunt though this kind of encouragement was, it was this more than anything else that gave me the necessary motivation to bring this project to completion.

I would like to thank first of all the Society of St. Sulpice for its encouragement and support in my work on this book. The support came in many forms, including financial aid and time away from teaching to work on the monograph. I would also like to mention the two institutions at which I taught while this project was in progress, whether on paper or in my head: St. Patrick's Seminary, Menlo Park,

CA, and my *alma mater*, St. Mary's Seminary & University, Baltimore, MD, the first seminary in the United States. I want to express my gratitude to the many brothers in the Society of St. Sulpice, faculty members at both seminaries, and many friends who supported me in innumerable ways as this undertaking slowly moved along.

I must also express a particular word of gratitude to Richard J. Clifford, S.J. and John S. Kselman, S.S., who were involved in the final phase of the project. Being first-rate Old Testament scholars in their own right, as well as sharp-eyed proofreaders, both provided invaluable suggestions and corrections on the original draft of this book. I would also like to thank the excellent work of the reviewers of this book in manuscript form, for their many suggestions and corrections. Finally, I owe a debt of thanks to Mark S. Smith, editor of the Catholic Biblical Monograph Series, for the great deal of time and work he put into bringing this study to publication in the Catholic Biblical Quarterly Monograph Series.

Michael L. Barré, S.S.
Baltimore
May, 2004

Introduction

A. Begrich and Beyond

The present monograph represents the first major treatment of the Psalm of Hezekiah (hereafter PsHez) since J. Begrich's 68-page monograph published in 1926,[1] which to this day is the standard work on the subject.[2] Begrich was the pupil of Hermann Gunkel. He lived in a period during which contemporary scholarship regarded the MT with some degree of mistrust, but he tried to adhere to it whenever possible in his translation of this psalm. Nevertheless, he did make use of the versions, particularly the LXX. Begrich proposed twenty-two emendations to the text of PsHez, many of which have been widely accepted. He gave priority in his study to determining the literary form and meter of the psalm. As to the former, he judged that it was a thanksgiving psalm, and this view has won the day in terms of the form-critical classification of PsHez. As regards meter, Begrich determined that the poem consists almost entirely of "Fünfers" (3 + 2 accents per bicolon).

Begrich's commentary on PsHez was a milestone in its time and set the course for the interpretation of this poem for the last century. Despite some advances that it made over previous studies, many of

---

[1] J. Begrich, *Der Psalm des Hiskia: Ein Beitrag zum Verständnis Jesaja 38 10–20* (FRLANT [Neue Folge] 25; Göttingen: Vandenhoeck & Ruprecht, 1926).

[2] For a brief review of treatments of the Psalm of Hezekiah from the sixteenth century to the 1980s, see A. van der Kooij, *Die alten Textzeugen des Jesajabuches: Ein Beitrag zur Textgeschichte des Alten Testaments* (OBO 35; Göttingen: Vandenhoeck & Ruprecht, 1981) 3–7.

which have stood the test of time the test of time, it has a number of limitations, especially when viewed from a twenty-first century vantage point. I list below some of the principal ones.

(1) Although the majority of interpreters since Begrich have accepted his classification of PsHez as a thanksgiving psalm, some of his argumentation that led to this conclusion is flawed. Perhaps the parade example is his emendation of *ʾddh* in v. 15c to *ʾdkh*, "I shall give you thanks/praise you."[3]

(2) The reigning view of Hebrew metrics in Begrich's day counted accents within cola or half-lines. Like many of his German contemporaries, he was not loath to eliminate material that did not fit into this view of what the meter of a line should look like. For example, he shortened the "overlong" colon v. 14d *metri causa* to make it a "Fünfer" (3 + 2 accents) like most of the bicola in the poem (according to his scansion), hardly an expedient emendation methodologically.

(3) Begrich's dating of the psalm as post-exilic depended largely on his claim that it contains a fair number of "Aramaisms." This claim needs to be reconsidered by means of an investigation of each of the terms in question as well as an overview of modern approaches to the criteria for determining what features classify a given passage as Standard or Late Biblical Hebrew.

(4) Begrich's monograph was published just over twenty years before the discovery of the Dead Sea Scrolls, some of the first of which to be found were the two Isaiah scrolls from Cave I. Thus he was unable to make use of these important witnesses to the text of Isaiah, specifically to the text of PsHez.

I mention here two other twentieth-century studies that deal with the PsHez as a whole. The first is the article by P. A. H. de Boer, which appeared in 1951.[4] He was the first to discuss PsHez in the light of the recently discovered 1QIsa^a. He makes a comparison of the differences between the MT and 1QIsa^a in their readings within PsHez. In view of the variety of traditions behind PsHez, made even more varied by this

---

[3] *Der Psalm des Hiskia*, 42.

[4] P. A. H. de Boer, "Notes on the Text and Meaning of Isaiah xxxviii 9–20," *OTS* 9 (1951) 170–86.

newly discovered manuscript, he takes a pessimistic view of the possibility of arriving at an "Urtext" of PsHez, calling such an endeavor "guess-work." He opts for translating and explaining the MT as it now stands. The translation he gives is quite idiosyncratic—not to mention unidiomatic at times—and as a whole does not cohere too well. Some of his linguistic work is also open to criticism. His derivation of the verb *tašlîmēnî* in v. 12e from the alleged *šafel* form of the root *l-w-y/l-m-y*, "to surround, besiege," strikes one as a bit of a stretch. For reasons not explained in the article he refers to the psalm as "a magic text" that fathers must teach to their sons. Finally, he makes the apodictic statement that the psalm bears no direct association with the narrative within which it is situated.

In 1973 the Swedish scholar H. S. Nyberg published a treatment of PsHez[5] that was more optimistic than de Boer's about the use of ancient versions, including the Dead Sea Scrolls, for a critical reading of the text. His discussion of the text draws upon the various versions as well as 1QIsa[a], concluding that 1QIsa[a] offers several readings superior to the MT, though in other places its readings are inferior. In his presentation of the text he reads *lw* for MT's *ly* in v. 15a, *ʾdwdh* for MT's *ʾddh* in v. 15c, and *ʾlwh* for MT's *ʾl* in v. 19d—all based on 1QIsa[a]. Nyberg was one of the few twentieth-century authors to maintain the secondary character of v. 20 as a "liturgical conclusion." The study spends only a few lines on the structure of the poem and its arrangement of the text reveals no careful investigation of this important aspect of the poem. Finally, it is noteworthy that Nyberg parts company with Begrich and his followers on the issue of the alleged Aramaisms in PsHez, expressing doubt as to whether any are to be found in PsHez.[6]

The fact that the last major study of PsHez was published almost eighty years ago and before the discovery of the Dead Sea Scrolls

---

[5] H. S. Nyberg, "Hiskias Danklied Jes. 38, 9–20," *ASTI* 9 (1973) 85–97.

[6] Other comprehensive twentieth-century studies on PsHez include J. Linder, "Textkritische und exegetische Studie zum Canticum Ezechiae: Js. 38, 9–20," *ZKT* 42 (1918) 46–73; R. D. von Legelshurst, *Die Hiskiaerzählungen: Eine formgeschichtliche Untersuchung der Texte Js 36–39 und 2R 18–20* (Basel: Basileia Verlag, 1969) 38–46; J. P. van der Westhuizen, "Isaiah 38:10-20: Literary Devices and Exegesis," in *Studies in Isaiah* (ed. W. C. van Wyk; Ou-Testamentiese Werkgemeenskap in Suider Africa 22, 23; Hercules, South Africa: Nhw Press, 1982) 198–212. See also D. Barthélemy, ed., *Critique Textuelle de l'Ancien Testament: Rapport final du Comité pour l'analyse textuelle de l'Ancien*

argues for the need of a new, comprehensive study of this important OT poem. Beyond this, almost none of the earlier studies have given adequate attention to the poetic character of the psalm. The study of the structure and literary devices in this poetic text is a worthy pursuit in its own right, but it is also important for the task of interpretation. In the present work I shall make use of textual criticism, rhetorical criticism, and other methods to arrive at the clearest understanding of PsHez that is possible given our current understanding of Biblical Hebrew poetry at the beginning of the twenty-first century.

B. The Focus of the Present Work

It is important to state at the outset the focus and limitations of this work. Its first aim is to establish insofar as is possible the earliest recoverable text of PsHez. Anyone who has spent any time looking at the Hebrew text of this poem knows that it contains a fair share of textual difficulties, to say the least. Over the centuries in the pre-masoretic period various scribal errors obscured the pristine text, a situation analogous to a painting by one of the great masters that has deteriorated over the centuries through discoloration, peeling, etc. and has been retouched by various well-meaning artists, covering over and compromising the master's original work. Analogously, in this book it is my intention and hope, through the judicious use of textual and rhetorical criticism and other methods, to attempt to resolve the textual difficulties in this poem and to restore it to something close to the "original text."

A second, equally important aim is to look at this psalm as a work of poetry. This investigation will be at times separate from the task of textual reconstruction, but not entirely so. It is axiomatic that in poetry form and content are intimately related. An understanding of a poem's structure, its literary artistry, poetic devices, and so forth is *necessary* to a full understanding of the text itself. It is significant that almost no earlier treatments of this OT literary masterpiece have given any attention to its poetic features.[7]

Testament hébreu institué par l'Alliance biblique universelle (3 vols.; OBO 50; Fribourg: Éditions universitaires; Göttingen: Vandenhoeck & Ruprecht, 1982-) 2. 263-77.

[7] A noteworthy exception is van der Westhuizen, "Isaiah 38:10–20."

After having given primary attention to these aims I shall deal with several other aspects of the poem. I will deal with the three issues of literary genre, date of composition, and authorship. The question of the literary form of PsHez was one of the primary aims of Begrich's monograph. Although some agreement now obtains in the scholarly community as to the literary genre of PsHez, it will be important to revisit this topic after a fresh look at the entire composition. It is extremely difficult to establish the date of any of the OT psalms, either those within the Psalter or those outside of it, such as the Prayer of Habakkuk. Begrich's dating had relied mainly on what he considered to be Aramaisms in the poem. Is PsHez to be dated to the pre-exilic, the exilic, or the post-exilic period? And on the basis of the latter investigation, is it possible to identify the author of this poem or at least to narrow down the possible candidates for this distinction?

Finally, I shall give some attention to the issue of PsHez within its context in the Book of Isaiah. Because this is not the principal focus of this work, I shall limit the context to Isaiah 36–38.

I should also indicate here what I will *not* be treating in this work. It is only understandable that scholars will point out that certain legitimate areas of investigation and certain valid hermeneutical approaches are not taken into consideration in this study. But no monograph-length treatment, such as the present work is, can possibly take into consideration all aspects of a particular passage, important though these other areas may be. My intention is to treat only the aspects of PsHez indicated in the above paragraphs. My hope is that future investigations of this important text will profit from the groundwork laid in this monograph.

C. Working Assumptions and Methodology

1. Texts and Versions of the Book of Isaiah

Recent studies in the text of the OT, specifically those that make use of the latest textual evidence from the Dead Sea Scrolls, have profoundly changed the way that scholars look at—or should look at—the "text" of the OT. Prior to this, in part because no earlier copies of OT books were available in Hebrew, the dominant view in the OT scholarly community regarded the MT as a text superior to all other ancient witnesses. The view that is emerging from this newer research, however, based largely on evidence from the Scrolls, insists that the MT is one of a number of text-types circulating in the Jewish world in the last several centuries B.C.[8] This research has also established as fact that textual traditions reflected in the LXX, the Samaritan Pentateuch, and the writings of Josephus go back to more ancient Hebrew sources. No longer can one validly regard these or the ancient Hebrew witnesses such as 1QIsa[a] and 1QIsa[b] as inherently inferior to the MT or as "vulgar" text-types. Nevertheless, because of its important place in the history of biblical interpretation, it is fitting as a general rule to use the MT as the starting point for the study of an OT passage. Hence in this study, in those chapters dealing directly with textual matters, the vocalized MT will be set forth at the beginning.

In line with the foregoing remarks, the witness of other versions will regularly be brought into the discussion of the text of the Psalm of Hezekiah. In a thorough examination of a passage, all ancient evidence must be taken into consideration: the MT, other ancient Hebrew texts, the LXX, the Vg, the Syriac, the *Targum of Isaiah*, and the translations of Aquila, Symmachus, and Theodotion (where extant). At times one of the ancient Hebrew texts of Isaiah will be judged to contain the best reading of a given word or phrase, at other times the LXX or another ancient version. In some cases one ancient text or version will contain part of the more original reading and another ancient version another part. At still other times the argument will be made that neither the MT nor any of these ancient witnesses appears to preserve the earlier text. Of particular importance here is 1QIsa[a], the oldest virtually complete copy of the Book of Isaiah that has come down to us to date. Whereas fifty years ago H. M. Orlinsky termed it "worthless"[9] and E. Y. Kutscher described it as "a later textual type than the Masoretic Text",[10] recent studies have rendered such evaluations of this manuscript untenable. As a result of a textual comparison of the

---

[8] See, for example, the excellent volume by E. Ulrich, *The Dead Sea Scrolls and the Origins of the Bible* (Studies in the Dead Sea Scrolls and Related Literature; Leiden: Brill; Grand Rapids: Eerdmans, 1999), esp. chap. 6, "Multiple Literary Editions: Toward a Theory of the Biblical Text," pp. 99–120.

[9] H. M. Orlinsky, "Studies in the St. Mark's Isaiah Scroll, IV," *JQR* 43 (1952–53) 340.

[10] E. Y. Kutscher, *The Language and Linguistic Background of the Isaiah Scroll (1QIsa[a])* (STDJ 6: Leiden: Brill, 1974) 2–3.

MT, the LXX, and 1QIsaᵃ in ten passages, E. Ulrich concludes: "This evidence contradicts the prevailing view of 1QIsaᵃ: the scroll witnesses to the 'original text' most frequently, i.e., eight out of ten times."[11] By my calculation the MT and 1QIsaᵃ differ on twenty-six readings in the PsHez, and in fourteen of these 1QIsaᵃ preserves a reading superior to the MT.

2. *Comparative Philology*

In this section I shall summarize several previous publications of mine that illustrate my application of the comparative method. These will give the reader a preview of how I will use cognate languages in this study.[12]

A Hebrew term whose meaning eluded interpreters until recently was the *hapax legomenon happaršĕdōnâ* in Judg 3:22. Some commentators had pronounced the word hopelessly corrupt. The standard etymology was based on a rare Akkadian term (*parašdinnu*) that occurred only in a lexical list, not a solid basis upon which to establish an etymology. Despite the warnings of the eminent Assyriologist W. von Soden that those who proposed this etymology were not reading the source word correctly (it should be *paraštinnu*), the two recent editions of Koehler-Baumgartner's lexicon continued to support it. Some years ago I proposed as the etymon the common quadriliteral Akkadian verb *naparšudu*, "to escape, exit," whose root (*p-r-š-d*) is the same as that of the Hebrew term.[13] A term with this meaning fits well in the context of Judges 3, where it denotes either an escape hatch or something "exiting" from the body.

Ps 116:15 is one of those texts with which commentators find themselves uncomfortable: "Precious in the sight of the Lord is the death of his saints" (*RSV*). There is a natural sense of revulsion at the thought

---

[11] E. Ulrich, "The Text of the Hebrew Scriptures at the Time of Hillel and Jesus," in *Congress Volume: Basel 2001* (ed. A. Lemaire; VTSup 92; Leiden: Brill, 2002) 90; see idem, "The Developmental Composition of the Book of Isaiah: Light from 1QIsaᵃ on Additions in the MT," *DSD* 8 (2001) 305.

[12] On the comparative method in Semitic languages in general, see J. Barr, *Comparative Philology and the Text of the Old Testament* (Oxford: Clarendon Press, 1968), esp. chap. IX, "Late Hebrew and the Loss of Vocabulary," 223–37.

[13] M. L. Barré, "The Meaning of *pršdn* in Judges iii 22," *VT* (1991) 1–11.

that God derives pleasure from their death. The usual explanation is that *yāqār* in this passage means "too costly" (*NAB*). But this interpretation flies in the face of the clearly attested meaning of the idiom "precious in the sight of X is Y" in all its occurrences in Hebrew, Aramaic, and Akkadian, where it means that X *is pleased with, delights in* Y. I suggested reading the Aramaic term *hmnwth*[14] (*hēmānûtāh* = *hēmānûtāʾ*), "faithfulness," for the MT's unusual term for death, *hmwth*.[15] Despite the fact that this necessitates adding an extra letter, *nun* (*nun* and the preceding *mem* were very similar during most of the history of the Hebrew alphabet), "faithfulness" fits the context better and is justified by structural elements in the poem. The two main parts of the psalm (vv. 1–9, 10–19) break down into two subsections: IA (vv. 1–4) and IB (vv. 5–9) and IIA (vv. 10–14) and IIB (vv. 15–19). The first cola of IA and IB are connected by the root *ḥ-n-n*: *tḥnwny* (v. 1) and *ḥnwn* (v. 5). There is a corresponding connection between the first cola of IIA and IIB if one accepts the proposed emendation: the root *ʾ-m-n*: *hʾmnty* (v. 10) and *hmnwth* (v. 15). The fact that Psalm 116 also contains several Aramaic pronominal suffixes (vv. 7, 12) gives further support to the hypothesis of an Aramaic loanword here.

The interpretational issue in Hos 6:2 is not so much the meaning of the terms themselves as the Sitz im Leben of this passage. Is it resurrection? medical diagnosis? covenant renewal? I noted the likelihood of a connection with Akkadian medical diagnostic texts, which also use the verbs "to live" (*balāṭu* = *ḥ-y-y*) and "get up" (*tebû* = *q-w-m*) in the sense of "recover" and "get up (from a sickbed)," and temporal expressions including "in two or three days" to denote when the patient could be expected to recover.[16] Thus the Sitz im Leben of this passage is medical diagnosis. I later published a discussion of a hymn to Gula, the Akkadian goddess of healing, which also contained these two verbs in a poetic context (in parallelism as in Hos 6:2), as well as references to the medical practice of "binding up" wounds (as in Hos 6:1).[17]

---

[14] Note the spelling *hymnwth*, identical to the one proposed here except for the vowel-letter *y*, in the sayings of Ahiqar (see J. M. Lindenberger, *The Aramaic Proverbs of Ahiqar* [JHNES; Baltimore/London: The Johns Hopkins University Press, 1983] 126).

[15] M. L. Barré, "Psalm 116: Its Structure and Its Enigmas," *JBL* 109 (1990) 69–73.

[16] M. L. Barré, "New Light on the Interpretation of Hosea vi 2," *VT* 28 (1978) 129–41.

[17] M. L. Barré, "Bulluṭsa-rabi's Hymn to Gula and Hosea 6:1-2," *Or* 50 (1981) 241–45.

Comparative philology is not about ransacking Semitic dictionaries to find a cognate for a given Hebrew term. It should be apparent from the foregoing examples that the proper application of this method involves the judicious use of cognates and potential parallels, and in particular a sensitivity to the *context* and *structure* (the latter especially in the case of a poetic text) of the Hebrew passage.

3. Textual Emendations

From my earlier remarks in this section it should be clear that I reject the view that the MT is without error or that it is superior to all other text-types. *Some* emendation is inevitable in *some* passages and in such cases one should consult the versions and ancient Hebrew manuscripts. When the text appears to be corrupt, one should steer a prudent course between the Scylla of reckless emendation and the Charybdis of treating the MT as if it were infallible.

Some commentators believe on principle that the MT should never be emended.[18] The MT is always correct, and if we cannot make sense out of it is because the apparently corrupted lexeme or idiom in question has yet to be correctly interpreted by modern scholarship. Such a position is in the view of most contemporary critical scholars untenable. Scribal error in a book copied by hand for centuries is virtually a certainty. To illustrate the fallibility of the text I cite here the case of Pss 31:3b and Ps 71:3b. Only the most adamant Masoretic fundamentalist could deny that 71:3b is partially corrupt and as a whole makes little sense. In this case one does not have to propose one's own emendation to arrive at an earlier, uncorrupted text of this colon, because we are fortunate to have that text in a doublet of this psalm passage—viz., in Ps 31:3bβ.

Ps 31:3b: *hyh ly lṣwr mᶜwz // lbyt mṣwdwt   lhwšyᶜny*
Ps 71:3:   *hyh ly lṣwr mᶜwn // lbwʾ tmyd ṣwyt lhwšyᶜny*

Aside from the common confusion of *māᶜôz* and *māᶜôn* in the first colon, the textual problem is obviously the beginning of the second

---

[18] Note the judgment of G. R. Driver ("Two Forgotten Hebrew Words," *JTS* 28 [1927] 287): "The time has come to lay down the rule that no word, and especially no verb, in the Hebrew Bible, if only it presents a truly Semitic form, may be emended."

colon. One notes immediately that in Ps 31:3 the second colon makes good sense (unlike in Ps 71:3): "Be for me a rock of refuge // a secure dwelling-place to keep me safe." It is unreasonable to deny that Ps 71:3b represents a corruption of this original form of the colon. *KJV* makes a noble but unconvincing attempt to make sense of it: "(a strong habitation) whereunto I may continually resort: thou hast given commandment to save me." One can immediately see how close the two passages are with respect to their lettering. It is instructive to notice here that the corruption is not a simple one but must have involved several stages.[19]

What is more, it is important to note that changes to the text were not always involuntary on the part of scribes. While many textual errors can be chalked up to scribal inattention, some were deliberate. The best known of these in Jewish tradition are perhaps the so-called *tiqqûnê sôpĕrîm*, a series of eighteen textual emendations known to the Masoretic tradition made to avoid objectionable expressions referring to the deity.[20] But the scribes also made other sorts of "improvements" to the text. We can see in the scrolls, for example, instances of

---

[19] It is usually recommended procedure in dealing with a textually corrupt passage to convert the text to one with less than "full" orthography. Now it is a fact that the term *mṣwdh* (*mĕṣûdâ*) appears a number of times in the MT with the *û*-vowel unexpressed in the orthography: *mṣdh*, *mṣdty*, etc. This would yield *lbyt mṣdwt* in Ps 71:3b. It is now easier to see how Ps 31:3b could have become *lbwʾ tmyd ṣwyt*. (1) The first error that occurred is most likely that the *yod* of *lbyt* was misread as a *waw*, one of the most common graphic errors in the MT. (2) As a result the first three letters were interpreted as the infinitive of the verb *b-w-ʾ* with prefixed *l-*, *lbw*, which was then (3) "corrected" to *lbwʾ* with the addition of an *alep*. (4) Then the left-over *t* was affixed to the following, but this would make no sense without first (5) switching the order of *ṣade* and *dalet*. This yielded *lbwʾ tmd ṣwt*. Finally, (6) the last two words were supplied with *matres lectionis* (two *yod*s), resulting in the MT's *lbwʾ tmyd ṣwyt*. In other words, the corruption in Ps 71:3b was not the result of a simple scribal "accident" but a complex series of changes. The above analysis was done before looking at S. Talmon's solution of this crux—his differs only slightly from the one given here ("The Ancient Hebrew Alphabet and Biblical Text Criticism," in *Mélanges Dominique Barthélemy: Études bibliques offertes à l'occasion de son 60e anniversaire* [ed. P. Casetti et al.; OBO 38; Fribourg: Editions Universitaires, 1981] 508; and "The Ancient Hebrew Alphabet and Biblical Text Criticism," in *Mélanges bibliques et orientaux en l'honneur de M Mathias Delcor* [ed. A. Caquot et al.; AOAT 215; Kevelaer: Butzon & Bercker, 1985] 394). I am indebted to J. S. Kselman for bringing these publications to my attention.

[20] See E. Würthwein, *The Text of the Old Testament: An Introduction to the Biblia Hebraica* (2d ed.; Grand Rapids: Eerdmans, 1995) 17.

"modernizing" the text, such as replacing an archaic or little known term with what the scribes behind this manuscript believed to be an improved reading, replacing obsolete grammatical forms with current ones, etc.[21]

When one encounters a term or phrase in a biblical poem that does not make sense in Hebrew and is satisfied after sufficient investigation that there is some disturbance in the text, three steps are necessary in my opinion to establish a plausible emendation.[22]

(1) Textual emendation should propose *the least amount of change to the consonantal text*, whether of the MT, of an ancient Hebrew manuscript (e.g., 1QIsaᵃ), or of the reconstructed LXX *Vorlage*. In general the proposed emendation should also follow the lettering very closely.[23] Emendations that propose deleting entire words from the text, adding words, or radically changing the lettering of the text in question rarely result in a plausible earlier reading, except when haplography or dittography is arguably evident. Moreover, the one proposing the emendation should be able to give a plausible textual history of the word or words within the passage in question, showing how this allegedly earlier (or original) reading came to be corrupted into the reading that appears in the MT or *Vorlage*.

(2) The emendation should make sense in terms of ancient Hebrew grammar and lexicography. Forcing a term into a particular grammatical category where it does not appear to belong or forcing it to bear a nuance that is not attested in Hebrew or the cognate languages is not good methodology. An example of this would be de Boer's treatment of Isa 38:10. He derives the MT's *bdmy* from the root *d-m-m* II, "to wail, mourn." This in itself is not problematic, but then he proceeds to translate the word as though it could mean "to fear death," whereas there is no evi-

---

[21] See B. K. Waltke, "How We Got the Hebrew Bible: The Text and Canon of the Old Testament," in *The Bible at Qumran: Text, Shape, and Interpretation* (ed. P. W. Flint and T. H. Kim; Studies in the Dead Sea Scrolls and Related Literature; Grand Rapids: Eerdmans, 2001) 45: "Scribes sometimes modernized archaic features of a verse."

[22] For an example of this methodology, see my article, "'Tarshish Has Perished': The Crux of Isaiah 23,10," *Bib* 85 (2004) 115–19.

[23] For an example of an emendation based on the LXX *Vorlage*, see ibid.

dence in Hebrew, Ugaritic, or Akkadian that the root can be translated this way.

(3) The emendation should respect the passage as poetry. For example, does the emended word or phrase fit the colometry of the poem? Does it lop off various words or syllables to fit some preconceived notion of Hebrew metrics? Does it introduce a prosaic element that is rarely found in poetry? Other aspects of the poetry such as structure, parallelism, word-pairs, alliteration, and assonance must also be taken into consideration when emending a poetic text.

(4) Above all, the proposed emendation should fit well into the *context* in which the problematic term lies, as far as the translator is able to determine that context. Earlier I mentioned Begrich's emendation of *ʾddh* in Isa 38:15c to *ʾdkh*, "I (shall) praise/thank you." In a lament situation, one does not perform the action of *y-d-y* (*hiphil*)—to give thankful praise to God—until God has granted the deliverance the sufferer has asked for. The deliverance does not take place in this poem until v. 17, a fact which renders Begrich's emendation highly unlikely.

D. Some Principal Characteristics of Hebrew Poetry

1. Metrics and a Sense of Symmetry

In the study of Hebrew poetry in the last several centuries various systems have been proposed as the basis of meter in Hebrew poetry. Some have counted beats or accents on words. Another system, which came into vogue in the twentieth century, counts syllables. Still others count more easily quantifiable units such as words or colometric units (cola or various aggregates of cola such as bicola, tricola, etc.). It is undeniable that some Hebrew poets counted colometric units in some of their poetry. The most obvious example are the alphabetic psalms. In Psalm 119, for example, each "letter-section" (*ʾalep*, *bet*, *gimel*, etc.) has eight bicola; in Lamentations 1–3, each has three bicola; and in Lamentations 4, each has two. Beyond the alphabetic psalms, Psalm 88 has 20 cola in its first half (vv. 2–9) and 20 in the second half (vv. 10b–19).[24]

---

[24] I.e., the colon beginning with *qĕrāʾtîkā*.

Like masterworks of architecture, many Biblical Hebrew poems display a marked sense of symmetry or proportion between their parts. Sometimes this is manifested in mathematical exactitude. I shall say a few things here about word-count. I do not believe that all Hebrew poets counted words in composing their poems. But it is difficult to deny outright that at least *some* poets counted words in *some* of their poems. Clearly this was not the only quantum counted by poets, but it was certainly one of them. Several Biblical Hebrew poems have the same number of words in their major sections (with a variation of one word in some cases). Psalm 91 has fifty-six words in each of its two major sections (vv. 1–8, 9–16). Psalm 116 has sixty-three words in its first major section (vv, 1–9) and sixty-four in the second (vv. 10–19). Other indications of word-counting are found in Psalm 101, where the key word *lēbāb*, "heart," occurs in only three places in the psalm: as the fifteenth word (v. 2b), the thirtieth word (v. 4a), and the forty-fifth word (v. 5b). In Psalm 23 the colon that is literally and thematically central—*kî ʾattâ ʿimmādî*, "for you are with me" (v. 4cα)—is preceded and followed by nine cola. But its centrality may also be determined by word-count: these three words are preceded and followed by exactly twenty-six words.

2. Structure

The first object of inquiry into an ancient Hebrew poem should be its structure. Form and meaning are inextricably linked in poetry, and thus to pay scant attention to the poetic features of the object of study is to miss important information about the meaning of the poem, whether in part or as a whole.

Serious errors in interpretation can occur when the interpreter either does not see or misjudges the structure of a poem. This is particularly true in poems which have a kind of "narrative," i.e., relate a particular sequence of events. PsHez is such a poem, containing as it does passages that refer to the psalmist's suffering, his cry for help, his deliverance, his thanksgiving, etc. Ideally the commentator must have a good grasp of precisely where each of these "events" occurs within the poem. Otherwise, for example, he or she may misread a passage referring to suffering as referring to deliverance or thanksgiving, and so forth.

Hebrew poems come in all sizes and "shapes," one might say—i.e., they are of different lengths and have different structures. In the case of some poems various stylistic devices help the interpreter to see dividing lines and structural units more clearly. Others make the task more difficult by lacking—as far as modern scholarship can detect—these important clues.

3. Stylistic Devices

Structural and stylistic devices within a poem have an aesthetic value in themselves and are thus worthy of inquiry for their own sake. As a side benefit, such aspects of the poem are often helpful for establishing the text. Below I shall list a number of these, to which I shall allude in the body of this work.

Inclusion (or *inclusio*) not only creates an aesthetically appealing structure within the poem but is often important for determining boundaries. It is the repetition of a word, phrase, or theme at the beginning and end of a (sub)unit. It usually indicates a major or minor juncture in the poem. The word or phrase may be identical in both locations or involve the break-up of word-pairs. Such a usage is usually termed "distant parallelism." Examples of this usage in Hebrew poetry are the beginning and ending bicola of Psalms 8 (vv. 21, 10), 20 (vv. 2, 10), 26 (vv. 1, 11–12), etc.

Chiasmus (also called "envelope construction") is actually a series of inclusions, one within the other, arranged in a palindrome pattern usually designated by letters—A, B, C, C', B', A', etc. The number of components may be even or odd. In the latter case there is a central component which is often emphasized. There is no rule in Hebrew poetry for the distribution of the members of a chiasmus.[25] Being a variation of the inclusion, the chiasmus also usually indicates struc-

---

[25] Although the members of a chiasmus are usually distributed more or less evenly throughout a poem or section thereof, they may also be tightly clustered in one part and arranged loosely in the other. For example, the central stanza of Psalm 22 is marked off by a chiasmus consisting of three types of threatening animals: bovine, leonine, and canine. The first three are distributed throughout the first half of the stanza (vv. 13, 14, and 17) but in the second half occur in three cola in rapid succession (vv. 21b, 22a, 22b), no doubt to give the impression of breathless haste as the poet desperately pleads to God for his life.

tural seams in a poem. In a recent study of Isa 2:12–17 I identified this as a self-contained poetic unit. That this is the case is apparent from the chiastic structure throughout the whole composition. In particular, the first and last members (vv. 12 and 17) contain four elements arranged chiastically:

A	v. 12a	*yôm*		D'	v. 17a	*gabhût*
B	v. 12a	*layhwh*		C'	v. 17b	*rûm*
C	v. 12b	*wĕrām*		B'	v. 17c	*yhwh*
D	v. 12c	*wĕgābah*[26]		A'	v. 17d	*bayyôm*

Although there has been some question as to whether v. 17 is part of the poem, since it appears elsewhere in Isaiah, the chiasmus indicates that as the passage now stands it is clearly integral to the poem.[27]

Repetition of terms at the beginning or end of a unit is another way of indicating the structural divisions of a poem and is an alternative to inclusion or chiasmus. In this case a word or series of words at the beginning of one unit are repeated at the beginning of the following unit, and/or similarly with words at the end of a unit. For example, in Psalm 91 *ʿelyôn* in v. 1a and *(la)yhwh maḥsî* in v. 2a at the *beginning* of Part I (vv. 1–8) are repeated (in reverse order) at the beginning of Part II (vv. 9–16), i.e., in v. 9. The poem contains only two instances of the root *r-ʾ-y*, which appear at the *end* of Part I (v. 8b: *tirʾeh*) and the end of Part II (v. 16b: *wĕʾarʾēhû*).

Change of mood, whether grammatical or emotional, is frequently used to signal the beginning of a new (sub)section in the poem. For example, the change from declarative to interrogative mood is often used in this way. In addition, the change from a lament "tone" to a bright mood of joy and praise functions similarly. In Psalm 22, the beginning of the final stanza of the psalm is marked by the abrupt change from lament to praise in v. 23, which continues to the end of the poem.[28] Note also the abrupt upswing in mood at the very center of

---

[26] Based on textual emendation (cf. LXX: καὶ μετέωρον [= *wgbh*]); see M. L. Barré, "A Rhetorical-Critical Study of Isaiah 2:12–17," *CBQ* 65 (2003) 523–24.

[27] Ibid., 527–28.

[28] In addition, this juncture within the poem is also indicated by the tripartite chiasmus delimiting the second stanza, vv. 13–22 (see n. 25 above). See M. L. Barré, "The Crux of Psalm 22:17c—Solved at Long Last?" in *David and Zion: Biblical Studies in*

Psalm 119. The *kap* stanza (vv. 81–88) is cast in somber tones, but it is unmistakable that a change in mood begins with the *lamed* stanza (vv. 89–96). As for grammatical mood, note the beginning of second stanza of Psalm 49 signaled by the change to interrogative mood (*lāmmâ* [v. 6]) and other examples.[29] Also, a *change of speaker* within a poem can also indicate the beginning of a new subdivision. For example, in Ps 91:13 the "narrator" ceases to speak and in vv. 14–16 (the last subdivision of the psalm) Yhwh is the speaker.

Terminal variation is a deliberate change in an ongoing pattern to mark the conclusion of a series.[30] This can be achieved by altering part of a refrain-like phrase or by discontinuing the phrase. In the poem in Isa 2:12–17 the anaphoric (*wĕ*)ʿal-kol, repeated ten times in the poem, ceases just before v. 17, indicating that the latter begins a new subunit. Verse 17 is also marked off by its chiastic relationship with v. 12. Another instance of this in the same poem is the appearance in v. 17, the last verse, of verbs denoting lowness (*š-ḥ-ḥ* and *š-p-l*), marking an abrupt change from a series of images denoting height in vv. 12–16.[31] Another form of terminal variation is effected by colometry. In this case the relative length of cola within bicola is changed. In Jonah 2, for example, the word-count pattern in the bicola is 3 + 2 or 3 + 3 (once 4 + 2), i.e., the second colon is always shorter. But in v. 7bc, the end of the first major division, it is 2 + 3. In Exod 15:5b the second colon is longer than the first; the word-count is 2 + 4. This bicolon comes at the end of the second subsection, just before the dividing chorus (v. 6).

But stylistic devices in Hebrew poetry are also used to join certain segments. The clearest example is *parallelism*, which is (in most cases) but a specialized form of repetition, as are inclusion and chiasmus. Synonymous and antithetical parallelism are built upon *formulaic*

Honor of J. J. M. Roberts (ed. B. F. Batto and K. L. Roberts; Winona Lake, IN: Eisenbrauns, 2004) 295–97.

[29] See also Pss 4:3 (ʿad-meh), 39:8 (mah), 60:11 (mî), 89:47 (ʿad-mâ), 94:16 (mî), 108:11 (mî), 139:7 (ʾānâ).

[30] The phenomenon has been noted by A. Berlin, *The Dynamics of Biblical Parallelism* (Bloomington, IN: Indiana University Press, 1985) 87; R. Alter, *The Art of Biblical Poetry* (New York: Basic Books, 1985) 7; D. N. Freedman, "Deliberate Deviation from an Established Pattern of Repetition in Hebrew Poetry as a Literary Device," in *Divine Commitment and Human Obligation: Selected Writings of David Noel Freedman* (ed. J. R. Huddlestun; 2 vols.; Grand Rapids: Eerdmans, 1997) 2. 205–12.

[31] See Barré, "Isaiah 2:12–17," 533.

word-pairs, many of which are shared by other Semitic languages. Many of these have been catalogued[32] and more are being discovered as time goes on. The interpreter of a passage of Hebrew poetry must be familiar with these pairs and alert to the possibility that one member of the pair may have been obscured or lost through textual corruption.

The *repetition of words, phrases, or sounds* is one of the most common techniques used in Hebrew poetry to establish connections between sections of a poem. Frequently a word is repeated in a different context so as to effect a contrast. For example, in the Song of Moses (Exod 15:1–18) the enemy boasts, "*my hand* shall destroy them" (v. 9). Of course, Yhwh wins the day and the poem concludes with a reference to "the sanctuary, O Yhwh, which *your hand*[33] established." There is an artful repetition of sounds in Psalm 26, again from one section of the psalm to another, which also forms a phonetic inclusion. The psalmist begins by averring, "I shall not slip (from the path of righteousness)" (v. 1) and concludes, "My foot has stood firm" (v. 12). The two verbs here, with opposite meanings, have the same root letters but in different sequence—*m-ᶜ-d* and *ᶜ-m-d* respectively. One would thus be ill advised to emend the former verb, though it is rare.[34] It is hard to deny that the poet deliberately chose it because of its phonic connection with and opposite sense to the common verb *ᶜ-m-d*.

E. Overview of the Book

Chapter 1 will consist of an overview of the structure of PsHez insofar as that is discernible from the unemended MT. Not all of the aspects of the structure will be apparent until after the text-critical work is done, but enough are evident to serve as a guide at the outset. The chapter will present the primary, secondary, and tertiary divisions of the poem.

[32] See Y. Avishur, *Stylistic Studies of Word-Pairs in Biblical and Ancient Semitic Literatures* (AOAT 210; Kevelaer: Butzon & Bercker; Neukirchen-Vluyn: Neukirchener Verlag, 1984).

[33] I read here *ydk*, "your hand" (sg.), attested by the Samaritan Pentateuch and 4QExodᶜ, which is likely the original reading. The MT has *ydyk*, "your hands."

[34] The verb occurs only in poetry: 2 Sam 22:37; Job 12:15; Pss 18:37; 26:1; 37:31; 69:24; Prov 25:19.

The content of the subsequent chapters (Chapter 2 up to and including Chapter 7) is determined by the structure set forth in Chapter 1. Each will treat one of the primary divisions of the poem plus the superscription, six chapters in all. A certain procedure will be followed here. First, **The Masoretic Text**[35] of the section to be discussed will be given, vocalized and arranged according to the Masoretes' punctuation as indicated by the disjunctive accents. To show the Masoretic division of the verses I insert the disjunctive accents at the end of each segment as a superscript letter, after the word over which it appears in the MT.[36] The accents indicated, in the order of their disjunctive power, are: ^{s} = *sillûq*, the major divider, which occurs just before the *sôp pāsûq* (:); ^{a} = *ʾatnāḥ*, the principal divider within the verse; and then further subdividers: ^{z} = *zāqēp*, ^{t} = *ṭipḥāʾ*, and ^{p} = *paštāʾ*. Even though this section presents the MT according to its own versification, only one system of sub-verse labeling will be used, in order to avoid confusion. This will be the system represented in the emended text in the Appendix. For example, the body of the poem begins with the words (in the MT) *ʾănî ʾāmartî bidmî yāmay ʾēlēkâ bĕšaʿărê šĕʾôl puqqadtî yeter šĕnôtāy* (v. 10). The MT of this verse will appear as follows:

    10a   *ʾănî ʾāmartî* b *bidmî yāmay ʾēlēkâ*^{t}

       c   *bĕšaʿărê šĕʾôl*^{a}

            puqqadtî d *yeter šĕnôtāy*^{s}

Here the "b" and "c" represent v. 10b and 10c respectively. But as a result of my study of this passage (Chapter 3) I divide the subverses differently:

    10a   *ʾănî ʾāmartî*

       b   *bidmî yāmay ʾēlēkâ*

       c   *bĕšaʿărê šĕʾôl puqqadtî*

       d   *yeter šĕnôtāy*[37]

---

[35] Here and elsewhere throughout this book, the subdivisions of the chapters are indicated with bold print, since they are printed in bold in the chapters themselves.

[36] The insertion of the disjunctive accents will be omitted in Chapter 2, which deals with the superscription, since this verse is prose, not poetry.

[37] I do not give here the emendations I propose in this passage, as to do so before a thorough examination of the text would be premature. See Chapter 3 on vv. 10–11.

The use of these lower case letters (a, b, c, etc.) allows me to present the Masoretes' subdivision of the verses in question while retaining a single system of verse labeling that will be used throughout this work. These verse-dividing letters (a, b, c, etc.) should be ignored, of course, when reading the MT.

The second section in these chapters dealing with the text I have entitled **Textual Remarks**. Here verses and subverses of the MT are given in a lemma. Immediately following this the readings of the lemma in nine ancient witnesses are given: 1QIsaᵃ, 1QIsaᵇ, the LXX, Aquila, Symmachus, Theodotion, Vg, the Syriac, and the *Targum of Isaiah*. What is presented here does not aim to be a full textual apparatus but an abridged apparatus giving the basic reading of the various witnesses. The readings are taken from photographs (in the case of the Hebrew manuscripts) or critical editions of the respective versions.³⁸ Where the equivalent text or translation is lacking, this is indicated by square brackets: [ ]. In the case of Aquila, Symmachus, and Theodotion, the text is prefaced by an asterisk (*) if it is marked with the asterisk in Ziegler's edition. A small superscript circle above a letter means that it is not clear on the photograph. A small superscript question-mark after a *yod* means that it might in fact be a *waw*.

This is followed by a discussion of the text—i.e., whether it is to be regarded as correct as it stands or is in need of emendation. Here will be discussed questions about individual words and phrases—e.g., whether the MT has the best reading in this case—as well as issues of syntax and definition of words. At times poetic aspects of the verse or

---

³⁸ The readings from 1QIsaᵃ are based on the photographs in J. C. Trever, *Scrolls from Qumrân Cave I* (Jerusalem: The Albright Institute of Archaeological Research; The Shrine of the Book, 1972) 79 (pl. xxxii). Those from 1QIsaᵇ are based on a transparency of the plate of this scroll containing part of Isa 38:9-20 from the Ancient Biblical Manuscript Center (SHR 4354). Those from the LXX are taken from the text of J. Ziegler, ed., *Isaias* (Septuaginta: Vetus Testamentum Graecum Auctoritate Societatis Litterarum Göttingensis editum 14; Göttingen: Vandenhoeck & Ruprecht, 1939) 262–64. The readings from Aquila, Symmachus, and Theodotion are taken from Ziegler's critical apparatus (ibid.). Those from Jerome's Vulgate are taken from R. Weber et al., eds., *Biblia Sacra Iuxta Vulgatam Versionem* (Stuttgart: Deutsche Bibelgesellschaft, 1983) 1135–36. The readings from the Peshitta are taken from the critical edition by S. P. Brock, ed., *The Old Testament in Syriac, according to the Peshitta Version: Part III Fascicle 1. Isaiah* (Leiden: Brill, 1987) 67-68. The readings from the *Targum of Isaiah* are taken from J. Stenning, *The Targum of Isaiah* (Oxford: Clarendon Press, 1949) 127-29.

term in question will be brought to bear that play some role in determining the best reading of terms within the verse as well as their interpretation. This section, of course, will be the longest in each chapter.

The third section is **Emended Text and Translation**. As the title implies, here I present the Hebrew text of the section under discussion with any emendations and rearrangements of the subverses that were argued in the foregoing section. This is followed by a translation of the emended text. In addition, each stanza subdivision is given a heading describing its contents.

The fourth section is **Rhetorical-Critical Observations**. Here the focus will be on the poetic aspects of PsHez, which, as I indicated above, is a major concern of this work. These include poetic devices (inclusion, chiasmus, parallelism, sonant connections, etc.), structured arrangements of various parts of the poem, as well as interconnections within the poem, and so forth.[39]

The final section in these chapters is **General Comments**. This will be in the nature of a general "commentary" on the section discussed in the chapter.

Chapter 8, "Form, Date, Authorship," deals with three questions concerning PsHez that are of interest to critical students of this poem. To what form-critical category should it be assigned? To what period of ancient Hebrew is it to be dated? And to what author is it to be ascribed? The areas here are arranged in the order of answerability.

Chapter 9, "The Psalm of Hezekiah in Its Context," will explore the relationship between PsHez and its immediate context, namely Isaiah 36–38, the Isaian parallel to 2 Kgs 18:13–20:11. Both are divisible into two major sections, Sennacherib's military campaign against Jerusalem in 701 B.C. (Isaiah 36–37) and Hezekiah's illness (38:1–8). Earlier studies have pointed out some connections between this narrative context and the psalm. This chapter will provide further investigation into the possible connections.

The textual-rhetorical discussion of the poem, the issues of form, date, authorship, and its situation within chaps. 36–37 are concluded by a brief **Summary**.

Finally, as noted above, the Appendix will contain the emended text and translations of PsHez repeating the translation from the **Emended**

---

[39] Again, this section will be omitted in Chapter 2, which deals with the superscription, because a superscription is by definition a prosaic element, not poetry.

Text and Translation section of Chapters 2 through 7. To the technical translation already given I add a freer, non-technical rendering of the text. This section will be a useful reference for the reader, enabling him or her to follow references to subversification and structural divisions more easily, and also to get a better overview of the psalm as restored by the present writer.

CHAPTER 1

Structure

A. The Limits of the Poem

The first task that confronts the interpreter in treating a biblical poem is to determine its parameters, viz., where it begins and where it ends. In the prophetic books this can be difficult. For example, sometimes what seems to be a single poem is really several independent units of poetry in succession. At other times poetry and elevated prose are interspersed in such a way as to make it difficult to decide where one ends and the other begins.

Fortunately neither is the case with PsHez. Here the boundaries of the poem are clearly delimited. The abrupt appearance of the superscription (v. 9) after the narrative section of vv. 1–8 clearly marks the beginning of something new. Because this superscription is very similar in form and wording to others in the Psalter, its presence announces that a psalm of some type follows immediately. Hence v. 10 must be the opening verse of PsHez. Isaiah 38 ends with an abbreviated form of two incidents (vv. 21–22) that are obviously taken from or at least are parallels of the 2 Kings narrative (20:7–8) and were not part of the original chapter.[1] They unmistakably signal a return to the narrative form with the words *wayyōᵓmer yěšaᶜyāhû*, "And Isaiah said. . . ." The previous verse, v. 20, however, is not part of this prosaic addition and thus is the final verse of the psalm.

---

[1] On the secondary character of these verses, see Chapter 9, pp. 232-33.

The boundaries of PsHez, then, are vv. 10 and 20. As we shall see, there has been some discussion (mainly in the nineteenth century) as to whether or not v. 20 is a secondary, "liturgical" addition to the poem, but it is nonetheless part of the poem as it now stands in the MT and will be treated as such in this work.

B. The Primary Divisions

Earlier studies of PsHez paid little attention to structure. Specifically, little if any consideration was given to rhetorical devices indicating structural divisions in the poem. The assumption underlying the present study reflects a methodological approach to Hebrew poetic texts that is becoming commonplace among interpreters of Hebrew poetry, namely, that the structure of a poem and its meaning are closely related. No investigation of a poetic passage is complete without some attention to how its various sections are delimited, the interrelation of parts, verbal and thematic repetitions throughout, and so forth. In the case of the present text consideration of structure is all the more crucial, given a number of *cruces* and exegetical problems. Attention to structure is also relevant to the question of the poem's integrity and unity.

The relationship between the structure (or form) and content of poems is something like the proverbial "chicken or egg" question. Is it possible to speak of a logical priority of one over the other? On the one hand, should one attempt to determine structure first, and then using that information proceed to the analysis of a poem? On the other, is it not true that the structure can be divined only from a critical reading of the text of the poem followed by a careful analysis of its vocabulary and themes? The fact is that interpretation involves a consideration of both of these factors at every stage of the process. A grasp of the overall structure is a great help in understanding the components of the composition, even to the correct reading and interpretation of individual words in some cases. And yet a valid analysis of the structure should be based on a reading of the text as free from textual corruptions as possible. This may necessitate some emendation, with the realization that such restorations are always to some extent hypothetical. In what follows I shall present an overview of the structure of PsHez, based on a prior analysis of its components. The intention here is to present a plausible division of the text based on strong indications from literary devices. Of course, the overall division of the poem presented in this chapter is not based on a cursory reading of the text but on the author's thorough study of the entire passage. However, this preliminary view of the structure will be based on the MT of the poem. In the course of the present work I shall have occasion to point out many other structural aspects that can be seen only after the restoration of the earliest recoverable text of each section.

The working hypothesis adopted in this study vis-à-vis the structure of PsHez is that its primary divisions are a superscription (v. 9), a body composed of two main sections (vv. 10–19), and a coda (v. 20). I shall designate the two main subdivisions of the body of the poem as Part I (= vv. 10–14) and Part II (vv. 15–19). In what follows I shall present some of the reasons for this particular division of the text. Further corroboration for this division will be given in the detailed discussion of the various (sub)sections. Whenever possible I shall base the divisions on the MT, though it contains a number of corruptions, some of which have already been noted in scholarly discussion of this poem. The reader is here referred to the Appendix, which contains the versification of PsHez that will be used in this work.

Verse 9 is clearly a superscription. It is almost identical in form to a number of superscriptions in the Psalter[2] and is easily distinguishable from vv. 10–20 as a prosaic introduction to the psalm. Thus it is not part of the poem itself.

The first question to be settled as regards the body of PsHez (vv. 10–20) is where its major divisions occur. Despite the fact that a number of translations make v. 16a (ʾǎdōnāy, "O Lord") the beginning of Part II[3] and some v. 17c (wĕʾattâ, "But you"),[4] the division should be made between vv. 14 and 15.[5] J. Begrich recognized this in his monograph, correctly noting that the *Klagelied*, which constitutes the first part of the poem, ends with v. 14.[6] Several other considerations support

---

[2] Compare, for example, the superscription at the beginning of Psalm 52 (v. 1).

[3] E.g., *RSV, NRSV, NJB, TEV*; see also O. Kaiser, *Isaiah 13–39: A Commentary* (OTL; Philadelphia: Westminster, 1974) 406.

[4] See most recently J. H. Coetzee, "The 'Song of Hezekiah' (Isaiah 38:9–20): A Doxology of Judgement from the Exilic Period," *Old Testament Essays* 2 (1989) 23.

[5] For example, *NJPSV, NAB, NIV*.

[6] Begrich, *Der Psalm des Hiskia*, 41. The translation of the complete psalm at the end of his monograph has a small line between vv. 14 and 15, evidently meant to be taken as the major dividing line (p. 52). See also Linder, "Canticum Ezechiae," 71; G. Fohrer,

the view that a major break occurs after v. 14: (1) the climactic nature of the brief *Stossgebet* or ejaculatory prayer at the end of v. 14 (the first time in Part I that the poet addresses God in direct speech); (2) the abrupt change to the interrogative mode (*mâ*, "What . . . ?") in v. 15; (3) the reappearance of the verb *ʾ-m-r* in v. 15, which occurs elsewhere in the poem only at the beginning of Part I (vv. 10–11).

The chiastic word-pair *yāmîm // šānôt*,[7] "(my) days" // "(my) years," is one of the most important structural indicators in the poem. For one thing, it indicates that a new section begins with v. 15. These terms occur at the beginning and end of v. 10. They appear again in vv. 15 and 20 (preceded by *kol*), to form a chiasmus spanning the entire poem:[8] *yāmay . . . šěnôtāy* in v. 10, *kol-šěnôtay* in v. 15, and *kol-yěmê ḥayyēnû* in v. 20. In the last mentioned passage *yāmîm* has been expanded by the synonymous term *ḥayyîm*, "life":[9] *kol-yěmê ḥay-yênû*, "all the days of our life."[10]

The subject matter of vv. 10–14 and 15–19 provides another reason for taking these sections as distinct, major units. Textual difficulties that

---

Das Buch Jesaja (3 vols.; ZBAT; 2d ed.; Zurich/Stuttgart: Zwingli, 1960–67) 2. 185; G. R. Castellino, "Lamentazioni individuali accadiche ed ebraiche," *Salesianum* 10 (1948) 153.

[7] For this word-pair, see Avishur, *Word-Pairs*, 601–2, who notes that the pair is attested in five Semitic languages (Hebrew, Phoenician, Ammonite, Ugaritic, Akkadian).

[8] The phenomenon of the parallel terms being close together in the first instance (separated by five words) but relatively far apart in the second (separated by fifty-six words) is attested in other examples of chiasmus in Biblical Hebrew poetry. The second or central major section of Psalm 22 (vv. 13–22) is marked off by a chiasmus made up of three types of animals: bovines, lions, and dogs. The first reference to bovines (*pārîm*) appears in v. 13; the first reference to lions (*ʾaryeh*) in v. 14 is separated by seven words from *pārîm*; and the first appearance of "dogs" (*kělābîm*) comes twenty-three words after this. In contrast, in their last occurrence the members of the trio appear close together: "dog" in v. 21b, "lion" in v. 22a after three intervening words, and a different term for bovines (*rēmîm*) in 22b after one intervening word. See M. L. Barré, "The Crux of Psalm 22:17c," 295–97. The change of the term used for the bovines (from *pārîm* to *rēmîm*) within the chiasmus is further way of indicating the ending of the subsection.

[9] As a rule parallel terms (such as *yāmay // šěnôtay* here) may be expanded only by a synonymous term, which also forms a paratactic pair with one or both of the other terms (see my article, "The Formulaic Pair טוב (ו)חסד in the Psalter," *ZAW* 98 [1986] 104). Note "my life" // "my days" (or vice-versa) in Job 7:16; Ps 39:4; "my life" // "my years" in Ps 31:10; and "days . . . years . . . life" in Gen 25:7; 47:8, 9(3x), 28; Prov 3:2; 9:11.

[10] In Chapter 7 I shall argue that the last word in v. 20b was originally *ḥayyay* (see the LXX).

beset certain sections of the MT (especially vv. 15–17b) make it impossible with certainty without further investigation to speak about the subject matter of every line of this composition. But one is on fairly safe ground in maintaining that vv. 10–14 constitute the *Klagelied* proper, whose main theme is the poet's untimely fate.[11] Certainly the first half of the poem (vv. 10–14) gives no hint that the fate of imminent death will be reversed. Only the last colon in Part I alludes to this possibility, by means of a cry to God to do something about the present distress: *ʾădōnāy ʿāšĕqâ-lî ʿorbēnî*, "O Lord, I am in straits, be my surety!" (*NAB*). Verses 15–19 appear to contain only a passing reference or two to the subject of the poet's troubles. The difficult vv. 15–17b probably contain some allusion to this theme, but there is no indication that they signal a reopening of the subject of personal afflictions. When we emerge from the obscurity of vv. 15–17b and come to v. 17c–f, some clarity returns. The subject of the latter is unmistakably deliverance and forgiveness. From here the scope of the poem broadens to a celebration of the fact that only the living can praise Yhwh (vv. 18–19) and that the psalmist and others (according to the MT) will praise God with music for the rest of their days in the temple precincts. Here again there is no return to the plaintive subject matter of vv. 10–14.

The division of the body into two equal parts, which I shall support with further arguments in subsequent chapters,[12] also supports the contention that the final verse (v. 20) is not part of the second half of the body but to some extent a separate section. I have entitled this section the "coda." That is, it is formally separate from the body of the poem and yet echoes several of its major themes. The fact that v. 20 is circumscribed by the divine name *yhwh* (an inclusion) further argues for a degree of structural independence from the preceding verses.

Not only does v. 20 tie together a number of thematic and structural threads in the poem but in addition it exhibits a number of connections with the beginning of the psalm, thus forming a kind of inclusion with the beginning of Part I. The divine name *yhwh*, which begins and

---

[11] Begrich, *Der Psalm des Hiskia*, 41.

[12] A word-count of vv. 10–19 (MT) shows that vv. 10–14 contain a total of sixty words, matched by sixty words in vv. 15–19. This computation is based on the unemended MT with the exception of v. 13d, which together with a number of commentators I take as secondary (see Chapter 4). In arriving at this figure I ignore *metheg*s and count each morphological unit as a separate word.

ends the coda, occurs elsewhere only in v. 11b, in the odd double form *yāh yāh* in v. 11.[13] And if, as I have argued elsewhere, *ʾereṣ haḥayyîm* (v. 11c) can in certain passages refer to the temple,[14] it finds an echo in *bêt yhwh* in v. 20c; there are no other references to the temple in the poem. Note too that structurally v. 20 is most likely to be scanned as a tricolon. In this respect too it echoes the first unit in the poem, v. 10b–d, the only other example of a tricolon in PsHez. Finally, note that both of these units (vv. 10 and 20) contain exactly ten words.[15]

C. The Secondary Divisions

The foregoing is a preliminary overview of the basic division of Isa 38:9–20 into its primary components. But Parts I and II may be further subdivided.

Part I may be subdivided into IA (vv. 10–11) and IB (vv. 12–14—minus the intrusive v. 13d). In IA the monocola *ʾănî ʾāmartî* in v. 10a and *ʾāmartî* in v. 11a introduce the tricolon v. 10b–d and the two bicola v. 11b–e respectively and establish a connection between them. This subsection voices the poet's realization that he is about to die. IB continues the theme of dismay at the prospect of imminent death developed in IA. But these verses, comprised of six bicola, contain something not found in vv. 10–11 nor indeed in the rest of the poem: a series of similes.[16] The particles *kĕ-* and *kēn* occur seven times in these verses (*kĕ-* five times, *kēn* twice). This high density of comparative particles within the space of a few verses marks off these lines as a distinct subunit.

As for Part II, we have already seen that its overall size matches that of Part I—sixty words. The content of these subsections provides the major indication of the primary dividing line in Part II. In vv. 18–19 the poet makes the point that Yhwh cannot be praised in the world of the

---

[13] The accuracy of this observation does not depend on whether accepts the MT's unusual reading *yh yh* or emends to *yhwh*. Clearly *yh* is a shortened form of the Tetragrammaton.

[14] M. L. Barré, "*ʾrṣ (h)ḥyym*—'The Land of the Living'?" *JSOT* 41 (1988) 37–59.

[15] This overview of the connections of v. 20 with the rest of the poem also argues, against some earlier exegetes, that it is integral to the poem, not a "liturgical addition."

[16] The only other simile in the poem is v. 19b: *kāmônî hayyôm*, "As I (give you praise) this day."

dead; only the living can do this. This thought is not present in vv.
15–17, however. Although vv. 16–17b are obscure, v. 17c–f is rather
straightforward. It tells of the author's restoration to health in two
images: his deliverance from the netherworld (v. 17cd) and the forgiveness of his sins (v. 17ef), which for people of the ancient Near East was
closely linked to physical healing. Thus Part II divides into two subsections: IIA (vv. 15–17) and IIB (vv. 18–19).

The beginning and end of Part II are linked by references to speaking. The unit opens with the two primary verbs of speech, *dibbēr* and
ʾāmar (v. 15a). It ends with two verbs similar to each other in sound
denoting speech, *yôdekā* and *yôdîaʿ* (in v. 19).

As regards word-count, the overall structure of the major sections of
the prayer (Parts I and II) is chiastic in several respects. First, it is chiastic with regard to the number of words in each subunit. IA and IIB
have twenty-four and twenty-three words respectively, and IB and IIA
have thirty-six and thirty-seven words respectively.

Subsection	Word-Count	
IA	24	A
IB	36[17]	B
Total	60	
IIA	37	B'
IIB	23	A'
Total	60	

Secondly, the contents of these major sections also exhibit inclusion.
For example, only IA and IIB (i.e., the first and last subsections) contain the negative particle *lōʾ*. In both subunits this word comes at the
beginning of each bicolon. Only IA and IIB refer to the netherworld;
specifically, only here does the word *šeʾôl* appear in the poem. Thematically IIB reverses IA. In the latter the speaker had been preoccu-
pied with the thought that his life was at an end, that he was to have

---

[17] Not counting the secondary v. 13d.

no further relationship with God or human beings, that he had no future. By contrast, in IIB he is aware that having been healed of his affliction he too is a living person, able to praise God and to hand on to his descendants the message of Yhwh's saving faithfulness.

D. The Tertiary Divisions

Each of the two subunits IA and IB may in turn be further subdivided. IA (vv. 10–11) can be broken down into v. 10 and v. 11, which I shall designate as IAa and IAb. As already noted, anaphoric *ʾănî* *ʾāmartî* and *ʾāmartî* in vv. 10a and 11a are best taken as monocola which introduce the material that immediately follows them—vv. 10b–d and 11b–e. The distribution of the word-pair *yāmay* // *šĕnôtay* at the beginning and end of the ensuing tricolon (v. 10b–d) forms an inclusion that marks this verse as a self-contained subunit, IAa. Following *ʾāmartî* in v. 11a are two closely connected bicola (v. 11b–e). These are connected by the fact that each begins with an anaphoric *lōʾ* (vv. 11b and 11d) and each is followed by a member of the word-pair *r-ʾ-y* // *n-b-ṭ* (*hiphil*).[18] The objects of these verbs are *yāh yāh* and *ʾādām* respectively, denoting meristically the divine and human worlds. Finally, *ʾereṣ haḥayyîm* and *yôšĕbê-ḥādel* also appear to be related terms.[19]

The second subunit of Part I, IB (vv. 12–14), consists of six bicola and also breaks down into two subsections, IBa and IBb. In the case of these lines the dividing line between the subsections is not as easy to see. One clue is the distribution of the seven comparative particles that characterize IB. These particles are not distributed evenly throughout these bicola but appear only in four of them, namely, the first and second (v. 12a–d) and the fourth and fifth (vv. 13b–14b). The third and sixth bicola have in common the fact that each lacks similes and contains a 2d sg. object suffix *-ēnî* (*tašlîmēnî* in v. 12e, *ʿorbēnî* in v. 14d), a morpheme that appears nowhere else in Part I:

IBa	12ab	simile (human)	*kĕ-*
	cd	simile (human)	*kĕ-*
	12e–13a	no simile	2d sg. verb + *-ēnî*

[18] See Avishur, *Word-Pairs* , 659.

[19] Actually, the two expressions are not very well matched as they stand now in the MT. In the discussion of v. 11e (Chapter 3) I shall argue for a widely accepted emendation of the second word that is a much closer match to *ʾereṣ haḥayyîm*.

IBb	13bc	simile (lion)	*kě-* . . . *kēn*
	14a	simile (swallow)	*kě-* . . . *kēn*
	b	simile (dove)	*kě-*
	cd	no simile	2d sg. verb + *-ēnî*

The subdivision of Part IIA is somewhat more challenging, in large measure because of the textual and interpretational difficulties in this section. There can be little doubt that vv. 15–17b are the most difficult lines in our passage. In particular, vv. 16–17b have been called "an exegete's nightmare."[20] The difficulty touches not only on how the individual words in these verses are to be translated—which is problematic enough—but also on how they are to be arranged in poetic lines. Thus before discussing them we should take note of certain colometric patterns elsewhere in the poem that may have a bearing on this troublesome passage.

PsHez contains a consistent colometric feature: *the last colon* in every poetic line (i.e., in every tricolon or bicolon) save one[21] consists of either two words or three words only. More specifically, in the examples of three-word terminal cola one of the words is always a monosyllabic preposition, usually in first position.[22]

Verse Last Colon in Bi- or Tricolon

10d	*yeter šěnôtāy*
11c	*bě'ereṣ haḥayyîm*
11e	*'im-yôšěbê ḥādel*
12b	*kě'ōhel rō'î*
12d	*middāllâ yěbaṣṣě'ēnî*
13a	*šiwwîtî 'ad-bōqer*
13c	*kol-'aṣmôtāy*
14b	*'ehgeh kayyônâ*

---

[20] H. Wildberger (*Jesaja: 3. Teilband: Jesaja 28–39: Das Buch, der Prophet, und seine Botschaft* [BKAT 10/3; Neukirchen-Vluyn: Neukirchener Verlag, 1982] 1444) describes this passage in these words ("ein Alptraum der Exegeten").

[21] The exception to this pattern is v. 14d: *'ădōnāy 'āšěqâ-lî 'orbēnî*. This colon forms the conclusion to Part I. The fact that it is longer than the other final cola in PsHez (which have two or three words) is deliberate, serving to draw attention to its structural significance as the conclusion of the first half of the poem.

[22] I published this observation in my article, "Restoring the 'Lost' Prayer in the Psalm of Hezekiah (Isaiah 38:16–17b)," *JBL* 114 (1995) 387–88.

15b	*wĕhû* *ʿāśâ*
15d	*ʿal-mar napšî*
17d	*miššaḥat bĕlî*
17f	*kol-ḥăṭāʾāy*
18b	*māwet yĕhallĕlekkā*
18d	*ʾel-ʾămittekā*
19b	*kāmônî ḥayyôm*
19d	*ʾel-ʾămittekā*
20d	*ʿal-bêt yhwh*

On the other hand, the other cola contain either three or four words, with the exception of the monocola in vv. 10a (*ʾănî ʾāmartî*) and 11a (*ʾāmartî*).

This information provides some tentative guidance in scanning IIA. Verse 15 consists of two bicola; as expected, the final cola in these are quite short: *wĕhû* *ʿāśâ* in v. 15b and *ʿal-mar napšî* in v. 15d. The last part of the subsection is also composed of two bicola (vv. 17cd and 17ef), which likewise conclude with short cola: *miššaḥat bĕlî* in v. 17d and *kol-ḥăṭāʾāy* in v. 17f. Provisionally we may identify *mar-lî mār* in v. 16d as the second member of a bicolon,[23] though it is not clear without detailed study how vv. 16–17b as a whole are to be organized. However, it seems possible if not plausible that these verses also contain two bicola. Thus the tentative conclusion at this point is that IIA contains a total of six bicola, like IB (for further details, see the discussion in Chapter 5).

Like Part IB, IIA also consists of six bicola. But unlike it, IIA seems to be best divided into three subunits each with two bicola rather than two subunits each with three bicola. The subunits would be IIAa (v. 15), IIAb (vv. 16–17b), and IIAc (v. 17c–f). One of the observable themes in IIA is that of "bitter(ness)" (*mar*), a word that appears only in this section according to the MT. The boundaries of IIAa are indicated in part by the assonant interconnection between *ʾāmar* in v. 15a and *mar* in 15d. The vocative *ʾădōnāy* in v. 16a marks shift from 3d to 2d person, and is thus the beginning of a second subsection, IIAb. It is probably structurally significant too that the root *ḥ-y-y* occurs three times in vv. 16–17b, tying these two bicola together. If we are correct in tentatively

---

[23] In the MT these words do not and cannot form a colon, as they are grammatically linked with the preceding two words. See the discussion of v. 17 below.

identifying *mar-lî mār* as the concluding colon of IIAb, then this sub-unit ends with the theme of "bitter(ness)" as does IIAa (v. 15d). IIAb seems to be the speaker's prayer to Yhwh, anticipated by v. 15a ("What shall I say?"), and appears to be in essence a request for healing. Finally, *wĕʾattâ* in v. 17c appears to signal the beginning of another sub-unit. In laments it sometimes marks the turning point from the speaker's suffering to divine deliverance.[24] Moreover, IIAc appears to acknowledge that the prayer in IIAb has been answered—that is, that the psalmist has been delivered from his suffering.

The last section to be considered is IIB. Subdivision in this case is a rather simple matter. IIBa is v. 18, which consists of two bicola, each being a negative statement—that the dead cannot praise Yhwh. The first colon of each begins with the negative particle *lōʾ* (preceded by the connective *kî* in the case of v. 18a). The first three cola each contain a designation of the netherworld or its inhabitants: *šĕʾôl*, *māwet*, and *yôrĕdê-bôr*. IIBb continues the thought of IIBa but in positive language: it is the living who alone can praise God, as the psalmist is doing now. In both subunits of IIB the verb *y-d-y* (*hiphil*) with the suffix *-kā* concludes the opening cola and *ʾl*[25] begins the last colon of each.

In summary, the structure of PsHez may be schematized as follows:

Part	Verses		
	Primary	*Secondary*	*Tertiary*
Superscription	9		
Part I	10–14		
IA		10–11	
IAa			10
IAb			11
IB		12–14	
IBa			12–13a
IBb			13b–14d

[24] See, for example, the use of *wĕʾattâ* in Pss 3:4; 22:20; 55:23; 102:13.

[25] In Chapter 6 I shall argue that this word is not the preposition *ʾel*, as the MT reads it, but rather the divine name *ʾēl*.

CHAPTER 2

A *Miktam* by Hezekiah

The Superscription (v. 9)

The Masoretic Text

[9] *miktāb lĕḥizqiyyāhû melek-yĕhûdâ baḥălōtô wayḥî mēḥolyô*

Textual Remarks

miktāb:
1QIsaᵃ: *mktb*; 1QIsaᵇ: [ ]; LXX: προσευχή; Aquila: γραφή; Symmachus: *ditto*; Theodotion: *ditto*; Vg: scriptura; Syriac: *kbtʾ*; *Targum of Isaiah*: *ktb ʾwdʾh*.

The most widely discussed term in the superscription is the first word. The MT has *miktāb*, lit., "a writing, something written." The term properly denotes the act of writing or its result and can therefore refer to any type of writing, irrespective of the medium (i.e., whether on papyrus, stone,[1] metal,[2] etc.). It probably occurs in one of the Arad letters, where it means "a report."[3] In 2 Chr 21:12 (*RSV*) and in Mish-

---

[1] The tablets of the covenant: Exod 32:16; Deut 10:4.
[2] On gold: Exod 39:30.
[3] D. Pardee (*Handbook of Ancient Hebrew Letters: A Study Edition* [SBLSBS 15; Chico, CA: Scholars Press, 1982] 63–64) restores the line in which this term appears as

naic Hebrew it can mean a "letter."[4] In several late biblical passages it seems to denote a "proclamation" or "edict."[5] The Syriac cognate can denote "a written narrative."[6]

A number of commentators opt for retaining the MT here, interpreting *miktāb* in various ways. Noting that the term can mean "letter" in late Hebrew, W. H. Hallo wonders if the superscription has connections with Sumerian "letter-prayers" as a literary antecedent to PsHez.[7] Although he mentions "numerous verbal correspondences between the prayer attributed to Hezekiah and the comparative Sumerian material,"[8] he provides no examples. To be sure, there are parallels between the two genres, but these lie almost exclusively on the general level of themes and expressions common to the language of Near Eastern laments. More striking are the differences between the two genres. Whereas Sumerian letter-prayers begin with an epistolary address to a deity (e.g., "To Nin-isina, beloved daughter of lofty An, mistress of Egalmaḫ, speak!"[9]), PsHez contains no such introduction; in fact the poet does not invoke Yhwh until the end of the first half of the poem, in v. 14d.

Nowhere else in ancient Hebrew literature does *miktāb* appear in the superscription to a poetic composition. For this and other reasons a number of interpreters have opted for an emendation to *miktām*. The close formal similarity of v. 9 to superscriptions in the Psalter, where the paleographically similar *miktām*[10] does occur a number of

follows: *wḥ*ᵖ. *hmktb.bqš* [*wlᵖ ntt*]*y*, "And he tried to obtain the *report* [but I would not give (it to him)]."

    [4] M. Jastrow, *Dictionary of the Targumim, Talmud Babli, Talmud Yerushalmi and Mishnaic Literature* (New York: Jastrow, 1967) 785.

    [5] 2 Chr 36:22; Ezra 1:1.

    [6] J. Payne Smith, *A Compendious Syriac Dictionary* (Oxford: Clarendon Press, 1903) 273.

    [7] W. H. Hallo, "The Royal Correspondence of Larsa: I. A Sumerian Prototype for the Prayer of Hezekiah?" in *Kramer Anniversary Volume: Cuneiform Studies in Honor of Samuel Noah Kramer* (ed. B. L. Eichler et al.; AOAT 25; Kevelaer: Butzon & Bercker; Neukirchen-Vluyn: Neukirchener Verlag, 1976) 209.

    [8] Ibid., 213.

    [9] Ibid., 214–15.

    [10] *Bet* and *mem* were at times confused in Hebrew orthography, suggesting that *miktāb* could be a corruption from an original *miktām*. See F. Delitzsch, *Die Lese-und Schreibfehler im Alten Testament* (Berlin/Leipzig: de Gruyter, 1920) §114b; P. Kyle McCarter, Jr., *Textual Criticism: Recovering the Text of the Hebrew Bible* (Philadel-

times, suggests that the latter was the original reading. Below I give a schematic of the structure of the superscription together with that of Psalms 52 and 63 and also—for comparative purposes—that of a late psalmic composition found in Qumran Cave IV.

Isa 38:9		*miktāb lĕḥizqiyyāhû*	*melek yĕhûdâ*
Ps 52:1	*lamnaṣṣēaḥ*	*maśkîl lĕdāwīd*	
Ps 63:1		*mizmôr lĕdāwīd*	
4Q381 33:8:		*tplh lmnśḥ*	*mlk yhwdh*

Isa 38:9	*baḥălôtô*	*wayḥî mēḥolyô*
Ps 52:1	*bĕbôʾ dôʾēg haʾădōmî*	*wayyaggēd lĕšāʾûl . . . .*
Ps 63:1	*bihyôtô bĕmidbar yĕhûdâ*	
4Q381 33:8:	*bklw ʾtw mlk ʾšwr*[11]	

Isa 38:9		A *miktab*	by Hezekiah, king of Judah,
Ps 52:1	For the *mnṣḥ*;	A *maskil*	by David,
Ps 63:1		A *psalm*	by David,
4Q381 33:8:		A *prayer*	by Manasseh, king of Judah,

Isa 38:9	when he had been ill	and recovered from his illness.
Ps 52:1	when Doeg . . . went	and told Saul . . . .
Ps 63:1	when he was in the desert of Judah.	
4Q381 33:8:	when the king of Assyria imprisoned him.	

PsHez lacks the *lamnaṣṣēaḥ* but otherwise follows the superscriptions of Psalms 52 and 63 very closely as to form. That is, all three contain the following elements in the same order: (1) the "category" of the composition (*miktāb/maśkîl/mizmôr*), (2) *lĕ-* (the *lamed auctoris*) followed by the alleged composer of the psalm (PsHez and 4Q381 33:8 add the royal titulary), (3) a "when"-clause consisting of (a) the preposition *b-* + infinitive construct in the first part and (b) a *waw*-conversive construction in the second (PsHez and Psalm 52).

---

phia: Fortress, 1986) 44. Both authors express the opinion that *miktām* was the original reading in Isa 38:9 (see also E. Tov, *Textual Criticism of the Hebrew Bible*, [Minneapolis: Fortress, 1992] 247–48).

[11] E. M. Schuller, *Non-Canonical Psalms from Qumran: A Pseudepigraphic Collection* (HSS 28; Atlanta: Scholars Press, 1986) 146, 151.

The Greek translation of *miktām* in the superscriptions of LXX Psalms 15, 55–59 is στηλογραφία, "an inscription on a stela,"[12] a term otherwise unattested in ancient Greek. In the opinion of several contemporary commentators this translation is the key to understanding the meaning of *miktām*. P. D. Miller, for example, following H. L. Ginsberg, believes that *miktām* may indicate that the psalms in whose superscriptions this word appears were published by being inscribed on a stela or the like.[13] It is true that this term is used for the "inscription" of the commandments on the stone tablets (Exod 32:16). Yet there is no ancient Near Eastern inscription on stone by a king that is a poetic composition like PsHez dealing with divine deliverance from illness. The closest thing to this is the Prayer of Nabonidus (4Q242 f1). The opening lines of this "prayer" do bear some resemblance to the superscription to PsHez. But the speaker in this apocryphal composition describes it as a "prayer" (ṣltʾ)," not an inscription or writing on stone. Moreover, what is preserved of it is clearly not a poem but a narrative relating the king's healing from this disease by a Jewish "exorcist."

Ginsberg points to the fact that ʾal-tašḥēt, "Do not destroy," appears in three of the superscriptions containing *miktām* (Pss 57:1; 58:1; 59:1), suggesting that such an injunction would be appropriate to include with an epigraphic psalm.[14] But this reasoning is far from persuasive. First, in Psalm 60, which likewise contains *miktām* in the superscription, a different phrase occurs after *lamnaṣṣēaḥ*: ʿal-šûšan ʿēdût. In Psalm 75 ʾal-tašḥēt does occur after *lamnaṣṣēaḥ*, but without *miktām*.[15] Second, it has long been noted that whenever ʾal-tašḥēt occurs in psalm superscriptions it appears immediately after *lamnaṣṣēaḥ*[16] (viz., in Psalms 57, 58, 59, and 75) like the more common prepositional phrases beginning with ʿal. Of particular importance is

---

[12] Cf. *Targum Pseudo-Jonathan's glypʾ tryṣʾ* with the same meaning.

[13] P. D. Miller, "Psalms and Inscriptions," in *Congress Volume: Vienna 1980* (ed. J. A. Emerton; VTSup 32; Leiden: Brill, 1981) 313.

[14] H. L. Ginsberg, "Psalms and Inscriptions of Petition and Acknowledgement," in *Louis Ginsberg Jubilee Volume* (ed. A. Marx; New York: American Academy for Jewish Research, 1945) 171 n. 49.

[15] Besides Psalms 57, 58, and 59, the only other psalm heading containing *miktām* is Psalm 16:1: *miktām lĕdāwīd*.

[16] This phrase occurs in the superscriptions to Psalms 4–6, 8–9, 12, 22, 39, 45–46, 54–62, 68, 75–76, 80–81, 84, 88.

the fact that in all superscriptions containing both *ʾal-tašḥēt* and *miktām* the two are separated by the "authorial" *lĕdāwīd*.[17] Hence the close connection of this phrase with the foregoing *lamnaṣṣēaḥ* and its separation from *miktām* by the authorial "slot" make it doubtful that that latter has any connection with *miktām* and thus that *ʾal-tašḥēt* has any real bearing on the meaning the term under consideration.

A more significant argument against the alleged "epigraphic" nature of the *miktām* is indirectly provided by the psalm superscriptions and similar forms. In four of the six titles containing this term (Psalms 56, 57, 59, 60) it is followed by *b-* + infinitive construct, which is found after other "category" designations as well. These constructions could be translated, "A *miktam* by David, when/after he. . . ." In each case *a predicate* is implied. What is this predicate? It could theoretically be something like "wrote" or "composed," which would fit well with the supporters of the stela hypothesis: "A *miktam* by David, (which he inscribed on a stela) when/after he. . . ." But such a predicate never appears in the MT. More than likely the predicate to be supplied is "uttered" or "sang," for which there is abundant biblical attestation. Terms in the "category" slot imply an interest in the fact that the subject uttered or sang the composition to (or in the presence of) Yhwh in response to some event in his life, and no interest in the medium on which the composition was preserved. This means that *miktām* (like the other terms in this slot) would be expected to impart some information that has to do with the *recitation or performance* of the composition rather than with what it was written on.[18] Evidence for this claim comes from one psalm heading and the introductions of several poems that appear in a narrative context. Ps 7:1 reads: *šiggāyôn lĕdāwīd ʾăšer-šār layhwh* . . . , "A shiggayon by David, *which he sang to Yhwh* . . . ." Compare the following introductions to biblical poetic texts situated in a narrative context:

Exod 15:1 (in response to the deliverance at the Red Sea):
ʾāz yāšîr môšeh ûbĕnê yiśrāʾēl ʾet-haššîrâ hazzōʾt layhwh . . .
Then Moses and the children of Israel *sang this song to Yhwh* . . .

---

[17] I.e., in Psalms 57, 58, 59.

[18] This information could have to do with some aspect of the accompanying music, a particular style of singing or recitation, specific gestures employed in its performance, etc.

Josh 10:12 (in response to the victory over the Amorites):
ʾāz yĕdabbēr yĕhôšûaʿ layhwh bĕyôm tēt yhwh . . .
Then Joshua *said to* Yhwh when/after Yhwh had given . . .

Judg 5:1 (in response to the victory over Sisera):
wattāšar dĕbôrâ ûbārāq ben-ʾAbînôʿam bayyôm hahûʾ . . .
Then Deborah and Barak, son of Abinoam, *sang* on that day . . .

2 Sam 22:1 (in response to David's deliverance from foes and death):[19]
wayyĕdabbēr dāwīd layhwh ʾet-dibrê haššîrâ hazzōʾt bayyôm . . .
And David *uttered* the words of *this song to* Yhwh when . . .

Jonah 2:2 (in response to being delivered from the belly of the fish):[20]
wayyitpallēl yônâ ʾel-yhwh ʾĕlōhāyw . . .
And Jonah *prayed to* Yhwh his God . . .[21]

These data make it even less likely that LXX's στηλογραφία is an accurate interpretation of *miktām* in psalm superscriptions, since information about how or on what medium the psalm was written down has

[19] As the MT now reads, the introduction appears to run contrary to the narrative context. The section immediately preceding (21:15–22) relates the exploits of certain "giant-killers" among David's men, including one who rescued the king from almost certain death (vv. 15–17)—although the last verse of the narrative ascribes these acts of valor to David as well (v. 22). But the expanded introduction connects the poem with David's deliverance "from the hand of all his enemies and from the hand of Saul." A plausible solution, put forth by M. Dahood (*Psalms I: 1–50* [AB 16; Garden City, NY: Doubleday, 1966] 104), is to read *šĕʾôl* (" Sheol") for the MT's *šāʾûl* ("Saul"). Note the reference to Sheol in the poem (22:6).

[20] In this case the narrative mentions the act of deliverance after the prayer itself (vv. 2b–9)—i.e., in v. 10.

[21] Even when the psalm in question is not a thanksgiving hymn (as the passages cited above can be generally classified), the superscription still seems to refer to the performance of the psalm. Note, for example, Ps 51:1: *lamnaṣṣēaḥ mizmôr lĕdāwīd bĕbôʾ-ʾēlāyw nātān hannābîʾ kaʾăšer-bāʾ ʾel-bat-šābaʿ*—"For the leader: A psalm of David, (which he recited/sang) after the prophet Nathan had come to him after he had relations with Bathsheba." Here it could not be more obvious that the superscription situates (the recitation of) the psalm *after* the event(s) referred to. The superscription to Psalm 51 thus suggests a sequence of three events: (1) David's sin with Bathsheba; (2) Yhwh's reprimand of David through the prophet Nathan; (3) David's recitation of this penitential prayer in response to Yhwh's reprimand.

nothing whatsoever to do with the performance of the composition, which seems to have been far more important to ancient Israelites.

It is surprising that discussions of *miktām* and other psalm categories do not take into account the available evidence of the classification of hymns and prayers elsewhere in the ancient Near East. Sumerian and Akkadian prayers are consistently supplied with a subscription which imparts such information. What is relevant to our discussion is that none of the categories listed over a period of several millennia has to do with the written form or medium of the composition. Rather, they are concerned with some aspect of the *recitation* of the prayer or psalm. These category-names variously relate information about gestures of the one praying, accompanying musical instrumentation, the purpose of the prayer, etc. For example, a šu íl-la is a psalm prayed "(with) the hand raised."[22] A balag is a lament accompanied by the *balag*-drum. An eršemma is a poem sung to the "wail of the *šem*-drum."[23] An ér-šá-ḫug-gá is a "lament to appease the heart (of an angry god)."[24] Some Akkadian "psalms" are classified simply as *unnīnu ša* DN, "a prayer of (= to) DN,"[25] like *tĕpillâ* in several psalm superscriptions.[26] If we look at attested Hebrew psalm categories that are understandable, we also find that they never impart information about the writing of the composition—e.g., *mizmôr* ("a hymn accompanied by [stringed] instruments"), *šîr* ("a song"), *tĕpillâ* ("a prayer"), etc. Even the term *maśkîl*, whose meaning is still not completely understood, most likely relates to something about the content of the psalm-prayer or perhaps its skillful execution. It would be difficult to see how such a designation relates to the medium on which this type of psalm was written. Moreover, the technical, quasi-liturgical character of psalm superscriptions in the MT also shows that their composers were

[22] See W. Mayer, *Untersuchungen zur Formensprache der babylonischen "Gebetsbeschwörungen"* (Studia Pohl: Series Maior 5; Rome: Biblical Institute, 1976) 7–8.

[23] See M. E. Cohen, *Sumerian Hymnology: The Eršemma* (*HUCA* Supplements 2; Cincinnati: Ktav Press, 1981) 18.

[24] A category with similar meaning is the dingir-šà-dib-ba incantation, an abbreviation of a longer phrase which means "incantation for appeasing an angry god." See W. G. Lambert, "Dingir.šà.dib.ba Incantations," *JNES* 33 (1974) 267.

[25] W. G. Lambert, "Three Literary Prayers of the Babylonians," *AfO* 19 (1959–60) 60.

[26] Pss 17:1; 86:1; 90:1; 142:1; Hab 3:1; 4Q381 33:8.

not interested in the kind of surface on which the psalms they prefaced were written.[27]

As regards the LXX's στηλογραφία in the superscriptions of LXX Psalms 15, 55–59, one has the suspicion that the LXX translators, having no clue as to the meaning of the obscure *miktām*, "read" the more familiar *miktāb* in these superscriptions. That is, whether the word in their Vorlage ended in -*b* or -*m*, they translated in every instance as if the text before them read *miktāb*, no doubt since this word was more familiar to them.[28] A Greek term ending in the root γραφ-, "to write," is a logical translation of a Hebrew word ostensibly based on the synonymous Hebrew root *k-t-b*. Finally, it is significant that in Isa 38:9 the LXX has προσευχή, not στηλογραφία. If the LXX *Vorlage* had a Hebrew term clearly based on the root *k-t-b*, it is difficult to see why the translator would not render it with a Greek term containing the same idea—that is, with a word containing the root γραφ-. Hence it is more likely that προσευχή is a free rendering of (an original and) unintelligible *miktām* than a translation of *miktāb*.

At present, then, no attempt to elucidate *miktām* has been successful and the term remains obscure.[29] In all probability it has something to

---

[27] It is true that in Akkadian there was a subclass of inscriptions known as "*narû* literature." The term *narû*, from Sumerian na-rú-a (lit., "erected stone"), meant "stele." A *narû* in the literary sense was a royal poetic autobiography. But any similarities to *miktāb* end here. These *narû* compositions contained a prologue, narrative, and epilogue, a message for future kings in the form of a blessing, oracle, or curse, and were didactic in character. Formally speaking they were not psalms, prayers, or any other type of religious composition. See J. G. Westenholz, *Legends of the Kings of Agade* (Winona Lake, IN: Eisenbrauns, 1997) 16–24.

[28] The hypothesis that the translators "read" *miktāb* for *miktām* in six psalm superscripts is not far-fetched. Note that for *every* occurrence of the name "Sennacherib" in the MT (Hebrew *sanḥērîb*) the LXX has Σενναχηριμ—that is, twelve times (4 Kgdms 18:13; 19:16, 20, 36; 2 Par 32:1, 2, 9, 10, 22; Isa 36:1; 37:17, 21). It would be preposterous, of course, to claim that the LXX translator(s) "misread" the final *bet* as a *mem* twelve times!

[29] See H.-J. Kraus, *Psalms 1–59: A Commentary* (Minneapolis: Augsburg, 1988) 25. A recent attempt to shed light on the term is that of C. T. Hodge "Miktam," in *Semitic Studies in Honor of Wolf Leslau on the Occasion of his Eighty-fifth Birthday, November 14th, 1991* (ed. A. S. Kaye; 2 vols.; Wiesbaden: Harrassowitz, 1991) 1. 634–44. Basically, he proposes that *miktām* actually derives from the root *k-t-b* and that the -*m* phoneme derives from a "dialectal" variation of the sounds /b/ and /m/ in the language (pp. 640–1). I am not convinced by his explanation of *miktām*.

do with the "category" of a composition or some aspect of its performance or musical accompaniment. I would consider the latter the most likely probability. It is interesting to note that three of the major medieval Jewish exegetes—Rashi, Ibn Ezra, and Kimhi—concurred that *miktām* was a *musical* term of some sort.[30] There is now some evidence that a derivative from the root *k-t-m* was so used in ancient times. Within the last fifty years elements of an arcane Akkadian technical vocabulary pertaining to the lyre has been discovered. Of the six terms that designated various "tunings" or intervals of the lyre, one was *kitmu*, which is used elsewhere in Akkadian to denote a "covering." The term designated "a musical interval sounded by strings 6 + 3" or a particular string on the lyre.[31] Hence it is possible that Hebrew *miktām* is related to the Akkadian term[32] and has a similar meaning (i.e., a particular interval or tuning on the lyre). It would thus designate a psalm sung in this particular "key," to use modern musical terminology.

One must keep in mind that the superscriptions to the psalms and passages such as Isa 38:9 and Hab 3:1, 19b[33] represent the principal repository in the MT of technical terminology for the performance of the psalms they are associated with. If only a handful of texts containing this kind of technical terminology have come down to us from an ancient language like Akkadian, whose texts number in the tens of thousands and cover three millennia, it should not be surprising that even fewer terms from such a highly specialized area of Hebrew vocabulary—and no elucidating texts whatsoever—would have been preserved in the much smaller corpus of the Hebrew Bible. Hence we may never know the meaning of *miktām* for certain.

---

[30] Ibid., 636.

[31] J. Black, A. George, and N. Postgate, eds., *A Concise Dictionary of Akkadian* (SANTAG: Arbeiten und Untersuchungen zur Keilschriftkunde 5; Wiesbaden: Harrassowitz, 2000) 162. See also *CAD* K, 466; A. D. Kilmer, "The Musical Instruments from Ur and Ancient Mesopotamian Music," *Expedition* 40 (1998) 12–19.

[32] Both terms are clearly derived from the root *k-t-m* and both are noun formations of this root, *kitmu* being of the *qitl* pattern and *miktām* of the *miqtāl* (< *maqtāl*) pattern.

[33] In the case of Habakkuk 3 we have the unique situation of a poem with both a superscription (v. 1) and a "subscription" (v. 19b), which when put together would read like many of the psalms superscriptions in the MT.

In summary, it is likely that *miktām* is the original reading of the text in Isa 38:9 rather than the MT's *miktāb*. The latter term probably reflects the fact that already in antiquity the meaning of *miktām* had been forgotten and was at some point replaced by the more familiar word.[34]

lĕḥizqiyyāhû:

1QIsaᵃ: *lyḥwzqyh*; 1QIsaᵇ: [ ]; LXX: Εζεκιου; Aquila: [ ]; Symmachus: [ ]; Theodotion: Εζεκιου; Vg: Ezechiae; Syriac: *dḥzqyʾ*; *Targum of Isaiah*: *lḥzqyh*.

The position of this term in the superscription exactly parallels that of the authorial slot (marked by the *lamed auctoris*) in psalm superscriptions. Unlike the superscriptions in the canonical Psalter, where most psalms appear without a context strictly speaking, the literary context of Isa 38:9 (cf. Hab 3:1) leaves no doubt that the function of the *lĕ-* is to ascribe authorship of the ensuing poem to Hezekiah. One still might translate "of Hezekiah," but "by Hezekiah" is certainly what was intended by whoever created the superscription.[35] The Syriac version of several other psalm-like compositions discovered among the Dead Sea scrolls contains a superscription attributing these psalms to Hezekiah: "A prayer by Hezekiah, (which he recited/sang) when. . . ."[36]

---

[34] Wildberger, *Jesaja 28–39*, 1442. B. Duhm also read the term in question as *miktām* (*Das Buch Jesaja* [4th ed.; HKAT; Göttingen: Vandenhoeck & Ruprecht, 1922] 279) as did Kaiser (*Isaiah 13–39*, 398).

[35] "In the Chronicler's day . . . it can scarcely be doubted that the meaning of *ldwd* was 'by David.' . . . Any attempt to distinguish *lĕdāwīd* from the others, or to say that none of them refers to authorship at all, is unsupported by the early evidence and flies in the face of all that we know of early rabbinic methods" (J. F. A. Sawyer, "An Analysis of the Context and Meaning of the Psalm Headings," *Glasgow University Oriental Society Transactions* 22 [1970] 26). See also B. K. Waltke and M. O'Connor, *Introduction to Biblical Hebrew Syntax* (Winona Lake, Ind.: Eisenbrauns, 1990) 207 (§11.2.10d).

[36] 5ApocSyrPs 3: "The prayer of Hezekiah when the Assyrians were surrounding him and he was asking God for deliverance from them." The Hebrew version of this psalm from Qumran (11QPsᵃ 155) has no superscription. 5ApocSyrPs 2 contains an expanded version of this psalm-title: "The prayer of Hezekiah when the Assyrians were surrounding him and he was asking God for deliverance from them so that the people might receive permission from Cyrus to return to their land. And they asked God to fulfill their expectation." The beginning of the Hebrew text of this psalm preserved at Qumran (11QPsᵃ 154) is lost. The attribution of the prayers to Hezekiah is probably

The name "Hezekiah" is written several ways in the MT: *ḥzqyhw* (as here), *ḥzqyh*, *yḥzqyhw*, and *yḥzqyh*. On the many bullae discovered in recent years bearing the official emblem of Hezekiah and three bullae belonging to three different courtiers (*ᶜbd*) of his, all display only the first spelling.[37] The Annals of Sennacherib also mention Hezekiah, spelling his name ᵐ*ḥa-za-qi-a-ú* and ᵐ*ḥa-za-qi-ya-(a)-ú*.[38] This means we can be certain that the spelling *ḥzqyhw* dates from as early as the eighth-seventh century B.C., whereas we can have no such certainty with regard to the others.

melek-yĕhûdâ:

1QIsaᵃ: *mlk yhwdh*; 1QIsaᵇ: [ ]; LXX: βασιλέως τῆς Ἰουδαίας; Aquila: [ ]; Symmachus: [ ]; Theodotion: βασιλέως Ιουδα; Vg: regis Iuda; Syriac: *mlkʾ dyhwdʾ*; *Targum of Isaiah*: *mlk šbṭ dbyt yhwdh*.

There is no example of the epithet "king of Judah" in superscriptions in the Psalter, either in the MT or the LXX. The epithet is attested, however, in headings of psalms or prayers dating from the Second Temple period. Among the scrolls from Qumran Cave IV, 4Q381 33:8 preserves the complete superscription *tplh lmnśh mlk yhwdh bklw ʾtw mlk ʾšwr*—"A prayer by Manasseh, king of Judah, (which he recited/sang) after the king of Assyria had imprisoned him."[39] This is the closest parallel to Isa 38:9 known to date. 4Q381 31:4 preserves a fragment of what is apparently a similar superscription: [*tplh? l-X m*]*lk yhwdh*[40]—"[A prayer(?) by X, ki]ng of Judah." *mlk yhdh* is Hezekiah's royal epithet that appears on the many bullae that

---

quite late and not based on a Hebrew *Vorlage*. See J. H. Charlesworth and J. A. Sanders, "More Psalms of David (Third Century B.C.–First Century A.D.)," in *The Old Testament Pseudepigrapha: Volume 2: Expansions of the "Old Testament" and Legends, Wisdom and Philosophical Literature, Prayers, Psalms, and Odes, Fragments of Lost Judeo-Hellenistic Works* (ed. J. H. Charlesworth; Garden City, NY: Doubleday, 1985) 618–23, esp. pp. 620 and 623.

[37] See R. Deutsch, "Lasting Impressions: New Bullae Reveal Egyptian-Style Emblems on Judah's Royal Seals," *BAR* 28 (2002) 42–52, 60–62.

[38] See D. D. Luckenbill, ed., *The Annals of Sennacherib* (OIP 2; Chicago: University of Chicago Press, 1924) 31:76; 32:18; 33:37; 69:29; 70:27, 30; 86:15. As regards the unusual spelling ᵐ*ḥa-za-qi-ya-a* (77:21), the scribe may simply have forgotten to add the final *ú*. Note the variant ᵐ*ḥa-za-qi-ya-a-ú* in 31:76.

[39] Schuller, *Non-Canonical Psalms from Qumran*, 146, 151.

[40] Ibid., 128, 134.

have been discovered in recent years, each bearing one of several of his official seals.[41]

baḥălōtô wayḥî mēḥolyô:

1QIsa[a]: *bḥwlywtyw wyḥy mḥwlyw*; 1QIsa[b]: [ ]; LXX: ἡνίκα ἐμαλακίσθη καὶ ἀνέστη ἐκ τῆς μαλακίας αὐτοῦ; Aquila: ἐν τῷ ἀρρωστῆσαι αὐτὸν καὶ ἔζησεν ἀπὸ τῆς ἀρρωστίας αὐτοῦ ; Symmachus: [ ] καὶ ὑγίανεν [ ]; Theodotion: ἐν τῷ ἀρρωστῆσαι αὐτὸν καὶ ἔζησεν ἀπὸ τῆς ἀρρωστίας αὐτοῦ; Vg: cum aegrotasset et convaluisset de infirmitate sua; Syriac: *kd ʾtkrh wḥyʾ mn kwrhnh*; *Targum of Isaiah*: *kd mrˁ wʾtsy mmrˁyh*.

After the authorial slot a number of psalm superscriptions contain a temporal clause (introduced by *b*- + infinitive construct) that refers to some event in the psalmist's life. All psalm headings containing this construction name David as the author (*lĕdāwīd*). The closest parallels to Isa 38:9 are the superscriptions of Psalms 59 and 60:

Ps 59:1:
lĕdāwīd miktām bišlôaḥ šāʾûl . . .
A *miktam* by David, (which he recited/sang) after Saul had sent . . .

Ps 60:1:
miktām lĕdāwīd lĕlammēd bĕṣwōtô ʾet ʾăram nahărayim
A *miktam* by David, for instruction(?), (which he recited/sang) when he struggled/after he had struggled with Aram-naharaim . . .

The *b*- + infinitive in many if not most cases should be translated "after" rather than "when," since in most cases we are hardly meant to think that the psalm is recited during the event described.[42] Similarly Isa 38:9 refers to Hezekiah's having recited this psalm not while when he was still sick but when he had recovered. In any case, the poem purports to be something that Hezekiah both composed and recited/sang in response to his recovery. Within the larger context of Isa 38:1–8 this could only be understood as the illness alluded to in v. 1. It is quite probable, though not certain, that the editors who affixed

---

[41] See Deutsch, "Lasting Impressions."

[42] "Sometimes it [*bĕ*-] has in appearance the force of *after that* . . . ; but as a rule this is really due to the action denoted by the inf[initive] being treated as extending over a period *within* which the action of the principal verb takes place" (BDB, 91). In the case of superscriptions, as noted earlier, the main verb is not explicitly stated.

the superscription to this psalm understood his "illness" in the same way.

Emended Text and Translation

miktām lĕḥizqiyyāhû melek yĕhûdâ baḥălōtô wayḥî mēḥolyô

A *miktam* by Hezekiah, king of Judah,
(which he uttered/sang) after he had been sick
and had recovered from his sickness.

General Comments

PsHez is a rare example outside of the Psalter of a poem supplied with a superscription. The reading and interpretation of this superscription are fairly straightforward, with only one term being the subject of controversy. Nevertheless, the presence of a superscription within the narrative of Isaiah 38 raises some questions.

One issue that calls for comment is the fact that the superscription appears in a narrative context. One might have expected some kind of a narrative lead-in, as in the case of other poems inserted within such contexts—e.g., the "Song of the Sea" (Exod 15:1a), the song of Moses (Deut 31:30), the blessing of Moses (Deut 33:1–2a), the Song of Deborah (Judg 5:1), the psalm of David in 2 Sam 22:1 (cf. Ps 18:1),[43] and the prayer of Jonah (Jonah 2:1–2a).

The only other OT composition outside the Psalter provided with a superscription is Hab 3:1. In the case of this poem, which also contains a subscription as well as several *selah*s, T. Hiebert has convincingly argued that an already existing poetic composition has been appended to a corpus of poetic material.[44] This example is quite instructive. Hiebert maintains that what he calls the "liturgical notes" in

---

[43] Compare the narrative introduction to David's song in 2 Sam 22:1 with the psalm superscription to the same poem in Ps 18:1. The canonical psalm title appears to consist of an original superscription (*lamnaṣṣēaḥ lĕ‘ebed yhwh lĕdāwīd*) plus a longer clause modelled on the material in 2 Sam 22:1. See G. Schmuttermayr, *Psalm 18 und 2 Samuel 22: Studien zu einem Doppeltext: Probleme der Textkritik und Übersetzung und das Psalterium Pianum* (SANT 25; Munich: Kösel, 1971) 31–32.

[44] I find this explanation of the facts more plausible than the view that the poem was an integral part of the Book of Habakkuk from the beginning and originally lacked

Habakkuk 3 "had become so firmly fixed as part of the text of this poem that they could not be disregarded when the poem was added to the writings of Habakkuk."[45] By "liturgical notes" he is referring not only to the "subscription" (3:19: *lamnaṣṣēaḥ binĕgînôtāy*) and the three *selah*s (3:3, 9, 13), but presumably to the superscription as well (3:1: *tĕpillâ laḥăbaqqûq hannābîʾ ʿal šigyōnôt*, "A prayer by Habakkuk the prophet; on [?] the shigiyonoth"). The most probable explanation as to why these were taken over together with the text of the poem is that at the time this prayer was appended to the body of Habakkuk such "notations" had come to be considered an integral part of the poem and thus could not be eliminated. They had as much of a "canonical" status as the body of the poem and thus could not be removed when the composition as a whole was relocated to new context.[46] G. H. Wilson makes the same observation with regard to the superscriptions of the biblical psalms.[47]

This explanation probably holds true for the superscription to PsHez. The fact that this poem is supplied with a superscription—which could hardly have been the creation of the Isaian editors, since the superscription causes the poem to fit awkwardly in the narrative context—argues compellingly that it had already become a fixed part of the composition by the time it was excerpted from a (now) lost collection of poems by the editors of Isaiah and inserted into chap. 38. The superscription obviated the need to supply a prose lead-in to join PsHez to the preceding narrative, yet at the same time its retention by the editors made for a poor fit in its new literary context.

---

a superscription, postscript, and *selah*s. J. J. M. Roberts, for example, claims that these were added to the poem "when the text came to be used in communal worship" (*Nahum, Habakkuk, and Zephaniah* [OTL; Louisville: Westminster/John Knox Press, 1991] 148).

[45] T. Hiebert, *God of My Victory: The Ancient Hymn in Habakkuk 3* (HSM 38; Atlanta: Scholars Press, 1986) 142.

[46] Similarly B. S. Childs, "Psalm Titles and Midrashic Exegesis," *JSS* 16 (1971) 142: "The title in Isa. xxxviii reflects a stage in the transmission of poetic tradition in which its literary fixation as an independent composition made it difficult to incorporate within a larger narrative setting."

[47] G. H. Wilson, *The Editing of the Hebrew Psalter* (SBLDS 76; Chico, CA: Scholars Press, 1985) 144: "Certain indications suggest that, at the time of the editorial arrangement of the Psalter, these [superscriptions] had already become fixed parts of their compositions with which the editor(s) could not freely tamper."

If this view is correct, PsHez was not first ascribed to Hezekiah by the editors of the Book of Isaiah. It had already been ascribed to the Judahite king prior to its insertion into Isaiah 38. In theory this ascription could have come ultimately from the author of the poem himself—though this is doubtful—or from the editors who added the psalm to the poetic collection from which it was later taken by the Isaian editors. It would have been these earlier editors who produced the superscription.

In its present setting v. 9 announces that the psalm is intimately connected to the events of Isa 38:1–8. It also indicates that the psalm was composed after the king's recovery from his sickness. While this is not precisely confirmation that the poem belongs to the form-critical category of a thanksgiving hymn, it comes close to being such.

The interpretation of the superscription given here accords with the dominant view that describes the psalm as having been composed *after* Hezekiah's recovery from his illness. C. R. Seitz has argued against this line of interpretation, claiming that the superscription does not "fix [the psalm] at one point in time."[48] He proposes to translate *baḥălōtô wayḥî mēḥolyô* "when he was sick and lived beyond his sickness."[49] But this interpretation is unlikely. First, what evidence is there to justify Seitz's *ad hoc* rendering of this phrase as "*lived beyond* his sickness"? It is true that the preposition *min* can mean "beyond" in some contexts, but hardly in this phrase. All other occurrences of the verb *ḥ-y-y* with *mēḥoly-* in the MT refer straightforwardly to *recovery from* sickness: 2 Kgs 1:2; 8:8, 9. Furthermore, the equivalent expression appears in Akkadian with reference to healing from illness: *innana-ma ištu murṣiya abtaluṭ*, "But now I have *recovered from* my sickness,"[50] where *balāṭu* (lit., "to live") is the interdialectic equivalent of *ḥ-y-y* as is *murṣu* of *ḥŏlî*. But even if one accepts Seitz's translation, which he proposes in order to avoid the conclusion that the king had recovered, it proves nothing because "to live beyond" an illness implies that one has recovered from it. Second, as noted earlier in this chapter, one must supply a phrase such as "which he recited" or "which he sang"

---

[48] C. R. Seitz, *Zion's Final Destiny: The Development of the Book of Isaiah: A Reassessment of Isaiah 36–39* (Minneapolis: Fortress, 1991) 171.

[49] Ibid., 170.

[50] *CAD* B, 53.

after "A *miktam* by Hezekiah, king of Judah" in order to understand it correctly. It would be most unusual if the psalmist were singing a psalm about his deliverance from life-threatening illness (v. 17c–f) and giving thanks for it (v. 19ab) before that deliverance had definitively taken place.[51]

---

[51] Seitz maintains a "distinction between thanksgiving for a death sentence being removed and actual healing" and claims that "the psalm contains no explicit reference to healing" (ibid., 168). I shall discuss his position in further detail in Chapter 5 under the treatment of v. 17c–f.

CHAPTER 3

Departure and Separation

Part IA (vv. 10–11)

The Masoretic Text

IAa 10a   *ʾănî ʾāmartî b bidmî yāmay ʾēlēkâ*^{t}
    c   *bĕšaʿărê šĕʾôl*^{a}
        puqqadtî d yeter šĕnôtāy^s

IAb 11a   *ʾāmartî b lōʾ-ʾerʾeh yāh*^{z}
        yāh c bĕʾereṣ haḥayyîm^a
    d   *lōʾ ʾabbîṭ ʾādām ʿôd*^{t}
    e   *ʿim-yôšĕbê ḥādel*^{s}

Textual Remarks

[10a] *ʾănî ʾāmartî:*

1QIsa^a: *ʾny ʾmrty*; 1QIsa^b: [ ]; LXX: ἐγὼ εἶπα; Aquila: ἐγὼ εἶπα; Symmachus: ἐγὼ εἶπον; Theodotion: ἐγὼ εἶπα; Vg: ego dixi; Syriac: *ʾnʾ ʾmrt*; *Targum of Isaiah*: *ʾnʾ ʾmryt*.

The MT links these words syntactically to what follows: "I said in the . . . of my days, 'I must go / to the gates of Sheol.'" There are instances in which *ʾănî ʾāmartî* is closely bound with the word that immediately follows, as for example in Pss 31:23; 116:11: *ʾănî ʾāmartî bĕḥopzî*, "I said in my trepidation . . . ."[1] On the other hand, it is

---

[1] On Ps 116:11, see Barré, "Psalm 116," 75.

51

hardly possible to accept M. Dahood's arrangement: *ʾănî ʾāmartî bidmî // yāmay ʾēlēkâ*, "I said in my sorrow, 'I have marched my days'."[2] "To march (one's) days" is an idiom unattested in Hebrew. It is therefore preferable to parse *bidmî* as a construct with *yāmay*: "In the X of my days."

The two opening words of the psalm could be scanned as a mono-colon, introducing the section that follows.[3] W. G. E. Watson notes that one of the characteristic uses of the monocolon is to open a poem or stanza.[4] Further evidence that this is the correct scansion of *ʾănî ʾāmartî* is the fact that the second *ʾāmartî* (i.e., in v. 11a) cannot be con-nected syntactically with what follows it, and so can only be taken as introductory to and independent of v. 11b–e. Such a beginning is unusual for OT psalms. Apart from PsHez only Psalm 39 begins with *(ʾănî) ʾāmartî*.

Biblical Hebrew lacks a verb that specifically denotes "thinking"— i.e., "speech" that is interiorized—and uses the verb "to say" (*ʾ-m-r*) to express this concept. In such cases the verb is usually followed by *bĕlēb(āb)*, "in (one's) heart." But the noun may be omitted (ellipsis). It is evident that in vv. 10a and 11a the psalmist is not addressing a specific person. Therefore the verb is best taken here as expressing not some-thing that he said orally but something he thought: "(This is what) I thought."

In a number of instances, "I said" or "I said in my heart" (= "I said to myself") introduces a wrong way of thinking that the text goes on to correct—"I thought . . . (but). . . ." There are two common varia-tions of this pattern. In the first, the speaker is in a situation of security and thinks all is well, but the text goes on to speak of disaster—e.g., Ps 30:7–8:

> As for me, *I said* in my prosperity,
> "I shall never be moved."

---

[2] M. Dahood, "Textual Problems in Isaia," *CBQ* 22 (1960) 401. B. A. Levine rejects the syntax proposed by Dahood ("Silence, Sound, and the Phenomenology of Mourn-ing in Biblical Israel," *JANES* 22 [1993] 98–99).

[3] As in Ps 41:5; Jonah 2:5.

[4] W. G. E. Watson, *Classical Hebrew Poetry: A Guide to Its Techniques* (JSOTSup 26; Sheffield: JSOT Press, 1984) 170.

By your favor, O Lord, you had established me as a strong
   mountain;
[*but* then] you hid your face; I was dismayed (*NRSV*).

The other variation expresses the opposite situation: the speaker is in
some desperate situation and therefore thinks all is lost, but the text
goes on to speak of deliverance. A good example is Ps 31:23:

> *I had said* in my alarm,
>   "I am driven far from your sight."
> *But* [then] you heard my supplications
>   when I cried out to you for help (*NRSV*).

Isa 38:10a, 11a is an example of the latter variation. Here *(ʾănî) ʾāmartî*
functions as an introduction to the psalmist's frame of mind *before his
deliverance*, narrated in v. 17c–f. Therefore in this context *ʾāmartî* in vv.
10a and 11a is best translated as a pluperfect, "I had thought,"[5] as in Ps
31:23. In the latter this is immediately followed by a past tense relating
that Yhwh "heard" (i.e., answered, granted) the psalmist's prayer for
deliverance.

[10bcd] *bidmî yāmay ʾēlēkâ běšaʿărê šĕʾôl puqqadtî yeter šěnôtāy:*
1QIsaᵃ: *bdmy ʷʸymy ʾlkh bšʿry šʾwl pqwdty wmr šnwty*; 1QIsaᵇ: [ ];
LXX: ἐν τῷ ὕψει τῶν ἡμερῶν μου ἐν πύλαις ᾅδου καταλείψω τὰ ἔτη τὰ
ἐπίλοιπα; Aquila: (in infirmitate/silentio)[6] τῶν ἡμερῶν μου [ ]; Symmachus: ἐν τῷ κατασιγηθῆναι τὰς ἡμέρας μου [ ]; Theodotion: (in infir-
mitate/silentio) τῶν ἡμερῶν μου; Vg: in dimidio dierum meorum vadam
ad portas inferi quaesivi residuum annorum meorum; Syriac: *dbplgwt*

---

   [5] So *NJPSV*. At this point a general observation is in order about the verbs in PsHez.
The poet is remarkably consistent in the way he expresses *aspect*. Verbs denoting completed action (i.e., perfect or future perfect), like *ʾāmartî* in the present verse, are always
qtl. Incomplete action (present or future) is consistently expressed by verbs in the *yqtl*.

   [6] This is from Jerome, who noted that Aquila, Symmachus, and Theodotion had "in
infirmity and silence" in their respective translations (see F. Field, *Origenis Hexaplorum Quae Supersunt* [2 vols.; Oxford: Clarendon, 1875] 2. 506, n. 26). Since we have
Symmachus' reading, it is clear that his reading had to do with "silence," though he
read an infinitive rather than a noun. Thus it is not clear from Jerome's statement which
translator read which—whether Aquila "in infirmity" and Theodotion "in silence" or
vice-versa. But in any case it is evidence that they both probably read some form of the
root *d-m-m*.

ywmy ʾzl btrᵓ dšywl šbqt šrkᵓ dšny; Targum of Isaiah: bdwwn ywmy ᵓhk btrʿy šᵓwl ʿl dwkrny lṭb ᵓytwsp ʿl šny.

The key to understanding this subunit is the word-pair *yôm* // *šānâ* together with their construct nouns. For this reason I will treat vv. 10b and 10d first, and later the intervening material. The meaning of the first of these construct nouns with this word-pair, *bidmî*, has been the subject of some controversy.

The plural nouns *yāmay* and *šĕnôtāy*, "my days" and "my years," denote the lifetime of the speaker. The second of these is preceded by the noun *yeter*, forming a construct chain that can only be translated "the rest of my years." The function of this expression in the verse depends to some extent on how one translates *puqqadtî*. But in any case the general import of these final words of IAa seems to be that the remainder of the psalmist's years—i.e., presumably the remainder of a normal lifespan—has been taken away from him. In other words, they refer to his untimely demise.

A widespread, usually unstated assumption in the interpretation of v. 10 is that *yeter šĕnôtāy* and *bdmy yāmay* are similar in their ultimate import. Thus if *yeter šĕnôtāy* is associated with the idea of death before one's time, one would expect the same of the corresponding *bidmî yāmay*. The most widely accepted interpretation of the latter fits this expectation, which is quite likely how MT understood the phrase. The psalmist rues the fact that his life has suddenly come to an end before he has lived out half of his allotted days. But is this what *dmy* means in v. 10?

The MT reads the first word presumably as a noun from a root *d-m-y* I. *d-m-y* I means "to be (a)like," like Akkadian *mašālu*. A nominal derivative from the Akkadian root is *mišlu*, meaning "half, middle point" (since halves are "like" or "equal" each to the other) and frequently occurs with time designations.[7] Based on this analogy, *bdmy ymy* would mean "at the half-way point of my days"—i.e., "before my time." This interpretation could appeal to parallels such as Ps 55:24, *lōʾ yeḥĕṣû yĕmêhem*, "They shall not live out half their days," and has been defended by interpreters like F. Delitzsch.[8] Such a reading has

---

[7] *CAD* M/2, 126–29; *AHw*, 661 (cf. *HALAT*, 217).

[8] F. Delitzsch, *Assyrische Lesestücke mit den Elementen der Grammatik und vollständigem Glossar* (Assyriologische Bibliothek 16; 5th ed.; Leipzig: Hinrichs, 1912). 175.

support in the versions[9] and the majority of modern English translations follow this line of thought.[10] But significantly, neither *d-m-y* nor
d-m-m—nor any of their homophones—refers to time. As ingenious as
this interpretation is, one should be wary of accepting a meaning
attested in only one text, though it cannot be dismissed out of hand.
Begrich is no doubt correct in rejecting it.[11]

A derivation from *d-m-y* II ("to come to rest, end; be silent") is also
theoretically possible.[12] Both *d-m-y* II and *d-m-m* can sustain meanings like "perish, come to an end," and the like. In this case the first
colon could be translated, "At the cessation/end of my days I must
depart." An objection that may be raised against such a translation is
that, interpreted at face value, it removes the poignancy of the poet's
lament. To say "At the cessation of my days I must depart (= die)"
seems tautologous, equivalent to saying, "When my life is over I must
die."

But the root could be *d-m-m*, of which several homophonous roots
are attested: *d-m-m* I, "to be silent," and *d-m-m* II, "to mourn, wail."
If so, *bdmy ymy* would represent a scribal error, a dittography of the
yod. In this case the original phrase would have been *bdm ymy*. Two
ancient versions witness, one directly and one indirectly, to a *Vorlage*
with *bdm*. First, such a reading is indirectly attested by the LXX,
which reads: ἐν τῷ ὕψει τῶν ἡμερῶν μου, "at the height of my years."
Jerome recognized that the Greek text assumed the root *r-w-m* (i.e.,
reading *bĕrūm* in the *Vorlage*). But the latter could be a misreading of
bdm,[13] given the common confusion of *dalet* and *resh* in the MT.
Second, and more directly, the *Targum of Isaiah* points to *dm* in its

---

[9] *Hoi heteroi* translate MT's *bdmy ymy* ἐν ἡμίσει τῶν ἡμερῶν μου, "in the midst of
my days" (cited from Field, *Origenis Hexaplorum Quae Supersunt* 2. 506 n. 26), which
agrees with Vg's "in dimidio dierum meorum" and the Syriac's *bplgwt ywmy*.

[10] E.g., *NAB*: "in the noontime of life"; *RSV* = *NRSV*: "in the noontide of my
days"; *NJPSV*: "in the middle of my days"; *NJB*: "in the noon of my life."

[11] Begrich, *Der Psalm des Hiskia*, 21-22.

[12] For an insightful discussion of the similar roots *d-m-m*, *d-w-m*, and *d-m-y* in Biblical Hebrew, see Levine, "Silence, Sound," 89–106.

[13] "[Hoc verbum] LXX *excelsum* interpretati sunt, ob litterae similitudinem RAME
pro DAME legentes" (cited from Field, *Origenis Hexaplorum Quae Supersunt* 2. 506 n.
26). Begrich opts for the LXX reading as original (i.e., *brm*), translating, "Auf der Höhe
meiner Tagen" (*Der Psalm des Hiskia*, 51–52). The translation "in the prime of (my)
life" (*NIV, REB*) might also be based on an emendation to *brm*. This reading is highly
unlikely, however, since the root *r-w-m* never refers to time in Biblical Hebrew.

Hebrew text with the translation, *bdwwn ywmy*, "in grieving for my days."[14] The root *d-w-y* can mean "to mourn" in Syriac.[15] In Samaritan Aramaic *dwwn* clearly denotes *grieving for the dead*, as when this word is used to translate Hebrew *yāgôn* in Gen 42:38; 44:31 in the expression, "to bring down (someone's) grey hairs *běyāgôn* to Sheol."[16] In the context the reference is to an aging father's grief over the untimely death of one of his children. Hence it is highly probable that the *Targum of Isaiah's Vorlage* had *bdm*, from the root *d-m-m* II, "to mourn, grieve," for the MT's *bdmy*. Finally, Jerome notes that the translations of Aquila, Symmachus, and Theodotion reflect the sense of "sickness" or "silence": ". . . ut Aq. et Sym. et Theod. interpretati sunt, *in infirmitate* et *silentio dierum meorum*, pro quo LXX *excelsum* interpretati sunt, ob literae similitudinem RAME pro DAME legentes."[17] This statement indicates that these three translators understood the root in question to be *d-m-m* II instead of *d-m-y* (as in the MT). G. Fohrer, O. Kaiser, M. Dahood, and P. A. H. de Boer also support this derivation in Isa 38:10.[18]

I believe that the MT's *bdmy ymy* does in fact represent a dittography and the correct reading is *bdm ymy*, the first word being derived from *d-m-m* II. But what does "In the grief/mourning of my days" mean? A note of explanation is needed here with regard to how to translate the construct phrase in this case. Although the preposition *ʿal* is commonly used in the sense of "for, over" with expressions referring

---

[14] This is the translation of B. D. Chilton, *The Isaiah Targum* (The Aramaic Bible 11; Wilmington: Michael Glazier, 1987) 75.

[15] See Payne Smith, *A Compendious Syriac Dictionary*, 84, and K. Brockelmann, *Lexicon Syriacum* (2d ed.; Halle: Straus & Cramer, 1928) 143. Payne Smith notes this nuance in the *ethpeal* and the *aphel*, and Brockelmann in the *ethpaal* ("planctus est").

[16] See A. Tal, *A Dictionary of Samaritan Aramaic* (HdO 50/1–2; Leiden: Brill, 2000) 172, where he translates *dwwn* as "grief."

[17] Field, *Origenis Hexaplorum Quae Supersunt* 2. 506 n. 26.

[18] Fohrer, *Das Buch Jesaja* 2. 183; Kaiser, *Isaiah 13–39*, 398 n. c; Dahood, "Textual Problems in Isaia," 400–402; de Boer, "Isaiah xxxviii 9–20," 178. Because he cannot accept Dahood's interpretation of the syntax of v. 10ab, in particular his dubious translation of *yāmay ʾēlēkâ* as "I have marched my days," Levine rejects the derivation of the word in question from *d-m-m* II ("Sound, Silence," 99). Unfortunately, part of his reason for doing so is his linking together the syntax of v. 10ab and the derivation of *dm(y)*. But these are separate issues, and the negation of one does not necessitate the negation of the other.

to "mourning, weeping," it may be dispensed with when the term denoting mourning is a noun rather than a verb. In such a case the noun is in construct with the object of the act of mourning[19]—e.g., *ʾēbel yāḥîd*, "(the) mourning for/grief over an only child (who has died)."[20] Recently B. A. Levine has suggested reading this construction in Ezek 24:17, i.e., with *dm* from *d-m-m* II—*dōm mētîm*, "lament over the dead."[21] Hence I parse *bdm* in Isa 38:10b as the preposition *bĕ-* followed by *dōm* in construct with *yāmay*, an emendation earlier suggested by O. Kaiser.[22] The construct phrase here denotes attendant circumstance and could be translated, "in (the act of) mourning for my days." A smoother English translation would be simply "mourning for my days." The presupposition is that the poet considers his lifetime to have virtually come to an end. For this reason his days—i.e., his lifetime up to now—can be mourned in the same way that one can mourn for a deceased loved one, i.e., *because it is now virtually lost to him forever.* This is the only instance in the MT of someone mourning for his (virtually terminated) lifetime.

An objection that might be raised to this interpretation of *bdm ymy* is that when examined more closely it does not fit well with its complement—i.e., the construct phrase containing the second member of the word-pair—*yeter šĕnôtāy*. As noted earlier, the latter can only mean "(for) the rest of my years." Yet such an expression is problematic. In Biblical Hebrew and other languages of the ancient Near East (e.g., Akkadian)[23] one's "days" or "years" are synonymous designations of one's life span. Since "life" is exclusively existence in the present world—existence in the netherworld is never called "life"—it is impossible to speak of someone's "days" or "years" *in the netherworld.* Therefore the poet cannot be consigned to Sheol "for the rest of [his] years." By the very fact of being there, his days and years are over. Despite the occasional commentator who dismisses this problem with

---

[19] Jer 6:26. Cf. Amos 8:10; cf. Gen 27:41; Deut 34:8; Ps 35:13.

[20] Jer 6:26; Amos 8:10.

[21] Levine, "Silence, Sound," 100. See also M. Greenberg, *Ezekiel 21–37* (AB 22A; New York: Doubleday, 1997) 508.

[22] *Isaiah 13–39*, 398 n. c. But Kaiser translates, "In the misery of my days."

[23] Cf. *ittatlakū ūmēya // i[qtat]û šanātūa*, "My days have gone away, my years have come to an end" (E. Ebeling, *Die akkadische Gebetsserie "Handerhebung"* [Deutsche Akademie der Wissenschaft zu Berlin, Institut für Orientforschung 20; Berlin: Akademie Verlag, 1953] 10).

the assertion that one should not interpret this kind of expression too literally,[24] the fact remains that reference to being in the netherworld for the remainder of one's lifetime is totally lacking in ancient Near Eastern literature.

The Great Isaiah Scroll from Qumran (1QIsaᵃ) provides a significant variant to *ytr*, namely *wmr*.[25] It is likely that the MT's *ytr* is a corruption from *wmr*.[26] De Boer claims that the latter "does not make any sense."[27] But this is not true; *mr* may be plausibly interpreted as the noun *mar*, "bitterness." Here *mar šĕnôtāy* forms an inclusion in this stanza with *dōm yāmay*, and thus should have a similar meaning. It is important to note that the concept of "bitter(ness)" contained in the root *m-r-r* has various connotations. The most significant for our passage is extreme sorrow or depression,[28] which can be seen from the close association of this root with *b-k-y*, "to weep," as well as with "to mourn" such as *ʾ-b-l* and *s-p-d*.[29] In the *hiphil* the verb can mean "to weep bitterly, be bitterly sad," as in Zech 12:10:

---

[24] Coetzee, "The 'Song of Hezekiah'," 14; see also K. Seybold, *Das Gebet des Kranken im Alten Testament: Untersuchungen zur Bestimmung und Zuordnung der Krankheits- und Heilungspsalmen* (BWANT 99; Stuttgart: Kohlhammer, 1973) 153.

[25] There is some difficulty with the reading of the second letter. M. Burrows had transliterated the word as *y.r* (*The Dead Sea Scrolls of St. Mark's Monastery* [New Haven: American Schools of Oriental Research, 1950] pl. xxxii). Nyberg ("Hiskias Danklied," 86) claimed that 1QIsaᵃ actually reads *ytr*, but that the *taw* is blurred or indistinct ("verwischt"). But computer enhancement of the word shows beyond question that the second letter is a *mem*. The first letter too is somewhat unclear, though it is almost certainly to be read as *waw* rather than *yod*. In his critical edition of the text of Isaiah, M. H. Goshen-Gottstein also reads the word in question as *wmr* (*The Book of Isaiah* [The Hebrew University Bible; Jerusalem: Magnes Press, 1995] 167) as do D. W. Parry and E. Qimron in a new edition of the Great Isaiah Scroll (*The Great Isaiah Scroll (1QIsaᵃ): A New Edition* [STDJ 32; Leiden: Brill, 1999] 65).

[26] The change *w > y* is easy to explain. The confusion of *mem* and *taw* is much less frequent but is attested. See Delitzsch, *Lese- und Schreibfehler*, §129b.

[27] De Boer, "Isaiah xxxviii 9–20," 172.

[28] The roots *d-m-m* II and *m-r-r* may also be paired in Ps 4:5. A number of commentators propose an emendation of the first word as a derivative from *m-r-r* rather than *ʾ-m-r*. Hence read: *hēmārû* (MT: *ʾimrû*) *bilbabkem* // *ʿal-miškabkem wĕdōmmû*, "Weep within your hearts // wail upon your beds." See M. L. Barré, "Hearts, Beds, and Repentance in Psalm 4,5 and Hosea 7,14," *Bib* 76 (1995) 53–62.

[29] Jer 6:26; Lam 1:4; Ezek 27:31; Amos 8:10; Zech 12:10.

wĕsāpĕdû ʿālāyw kĕmispēd ʿal-hayyāḥîd
wĕhāmēr ʿālāyw kĕhāmēr ʿal-habbĕkôr

And they shall *mourn* for him like the mourning for an only child,
and they shall *weep bitterly* for him[30]
like the bitter weeping for a first-born.[31]

This facet of the semantic range of *m-r-r* suggests that at times the noun *mar* itself can be translated "bitter weeping." D. R. Hillers has drawn attention to this meaning in Lam 1:4: *wĕhîʾ mar-lāh*, lit., "and as for her (Zion), bitter weeping is hers" = "she weeps bitterly."[32] Such a meaning is probable also in Amos 8:10:

wĕśamtîhā kĕʾēbel yāḥîd
wĕʾaḥărîtāh kĕyôm mar

And I will make it ("that day") like the mourning for an only child, and its aftermath like a day of bitter weeping.[33]

Thus *wĕmar*[34] *šĕnôtāy* is synonymous with *bĕdōm yāmay* in v. 10b. Like the latter, it refers to grieving for one's lifetime, now seen as gone, as if it were a departed loved one—"bitter weeping for my years." The one minor difficulty is the precise nuance of the *waw*. A copulative force is hardly appropriate here. The *waw* could be analyzed as

[30] Another example of the collocation of the roots *s-p-d* and *m-r-r* is found in Jer 6:26: *mispad tamrûrîm*, which *RSV* translates, "make . . . most bitter lamentation."

[31] The use of the *hiphil* with *m-r-r* with the meaning "to weep bitterly" may be explained in one of two ways. (1) It could be an ellipsis, in which one is to supply *bĕkî*, "weeping"—lit., "to make bitter (one's) weeping." Cf. Sir 38:17: *hmr bky whtm mspd*, "Weep bitterly and wail thoroughly" (lit., "Make [your] weeping bitter and make [your] wailing fulsome"). On this reading of the text, see P. W. Skehan and A. Di Lella, *The Wisdom of Ben Sira* (AB 39; New York: Doubleday, 1987) 439–40. (2) It could be taken literally to mean, "to produce (that which is) bitter" or "to cause (that which is) bitter to be"—i.e., tears or the bitter taste associated with weeping. On this concept, see T. Collins, "The Physiology of Tears (Part I)," *CBQ* 33 (1971) 35–37.

[32] D. R. Hillers, "The Roads to Zion Mourn," *Perspective* 12 (1971) 129–30. I am indebted to J. S. Kselman for bringing this reference to my attention.

[33] Note the parallelism of *ʾēbel* and *mar* and compare the association of *ʾābēlôt* and *mar* in Lam 1:4a,c, the passage where Hillers proposes to translate *mar* as "bitter weeping."

[34] This is almost certainly the earlier vocalization of the copula before the labial, and accords with the Babylonian pronunciation rather than the Tiberian (GKC §26a).

emphatic, with the preposition *bĕ-* in vv. 10b and 10c governing *mar* as well: "Yea, in bitter weeping for my years."[35] Again, as with *bĕdōm* above, a smoother English translation is achieved by translating *wĕmar* as an English participle: "Weeping bitterly (for my years)."[36]

The term *ʾēlēkâ* presents no textual problems. But is it to be taken in an absolute sense or does it go with *bĕšaʿărê šĕʾôl*? In the OT one almost always "goes down" (*y-r-d*) to the netherworld. The expression "to go (*h-l-k*) to the netherworld" is unknown in pre-exilic Hebrew.[37] A syntactic connection with "to the gates of the netherworld" is therefore unlikely and the word is to be taken in an absolute sense, "to go away, depart = die" as in Ps 39:14; Job 10:21; 14:20.[38] In this context the cohortative probably has overtones of necessity: "I must go (away), I have to go (away)." The fact that it is not connected syntactically with what follows also indicates a caesura after *ʾēlēkâ*. This word marks the end of the first colon in IAa after the introductory monocolon.

At this point we shall discuss the central colon of this tricolon, *bĕšaʿărê šĕʾôl puqqadtî* (v. 10c). The first point of discussion with regard to *pqdty* is whether it is a verb or a noun. 1QIsaᵃ has *pqwdty*, which is most easily explained as the nominal form plus the 1st sg. suffix.[39] But the line does not yield good sense with *pqdty* parsed in this way and few commentators have followed this interpretation.[40]

---

[35] It is possible that *wĕ-* is a corruption from an original *bĕ-* that resulted from an auditory error. (In v. 13a I shall point out an example of an original post-vocalic spirantized labial corrupted to a *waw*.) The same thing may have occurred in v. 10d, where the *waw* is intervocalic, between the /î/ of *puqqadtî* and the vowel preceding *mar*. If this is correct, a spirantized *bet* at some point could have been "heard" as a sound close to /v/ and wrongly written as *waw*. But in the final analysis I judge it best to read *wĕmar šĕnôtāy* with 1QIsaᵃ.

[36] For further evidence of this interpretation of *bdm* and *wmr* in v. 10, see **Rhetorical-Critical Observations** below.

[37] Only once in the MT is *h-l-k* associated with Sheol, in the post-exilic book of Qoheleth: *bišĕʾôl ʾăšer ʾattâ hôlēk šammâ*, "in Sheol, to which you are going" (Qoh 9:10). On the dating of Qoheleth, see C. L. Seow, "Linguistic Evidence and the Dating of Qoheleth," *JBL* 115 (1996) 643–66, who dates Qoheleth "between the second half of the fifth century [B.C.] and the first half of the fourth" (ibid., 666).

[38] So Begrich, *Der Psalm des Hiskia*, 22. On *h-l-k* as "to die," see *HALAT*, 237.

[39] So Kutscher, *The Language and Linguistic Background of the Isaiah Scroll*, 322. On the other hand, 1QIsaᵃ's *pqwdty* might be a scribal error for *pwqdty*, with *plene* writing of the vowel typical of Qumran texts (see de Boer, "Isaiah xxxviii 9–20," 171).

[40] So G. André, *Determining the Destiny: PQD in the Old Testament* (ConBOT

Almost all recent studies agree in taking *pqdty* as a verb, specifically, as a *pual* form. But there is lack of consensus as to its precise nuance. Because the root can mean "to miss, lack," some connect *puqqadtî* with the following colon and translate, "I am deprived of the rest of my years" (i.e., "I have been made to lack/miss the rest of my years").[41] This is the purport of Vg's *quaesivi*. But in only one text is it possible to translate *p-q-d* (*qal*) "to miss"—1 Sam 20:6. From this one might theorize that the *piel* could have a causal force, "to cause to miss," and on the basis of this logic to translate "to be made to miss." But there are no clear examples of the *piel* with this meaning. In fact there is only one occurrence of the verb in this conjugation (Isa 13:4), and from the context its meaning in that passage is "to be counted." In sum, there is no attestation of this hypothetical meaning ascribed to the root in the *piel* and therefore little if any basis on which to posit a *pual* meaning, "to be made to miss." G. R. Driver has rightly characterized this rendering of the verb as "very doubtful."[42]

The majority of commentaries and translations posit a connection between this verb and the preceding phrase, *bĕšacărê šĕʾôl*. One of the most common renderings is, "I am/have been consigned (to the gates of Sheol)."[43] This meaning of *p-q-d* makes good sense in the context, though it is not well attested in Biblical Hebrew.

The only other example this root in the *pual* (Exod 38:21) means "to be counted,"[44] which does not fit well with the context of Isa 38:10. The form in question, however, could be a *qal* passive.[45] Now in the

---

Series 10; Gleerup: CWK, 1980) 228: ". . . my *pĕquddāh* will be within the gates of Sheol for the rest of my years." He concludes that the *pual* stem of *p-q-d* is not represented in MT (ibid., 225; see also 152 n. 89, 167 n. 96). Yet his translation makes no sense.

[41] Cf. *NIV*: "robbed of the rest of my years."

[42] G. R. Driver, "Isaiah i–xxxix: Textual and Linguistic Problems," *JSS* 13 (1968) 56.

[43] *JPS, NAB, NEB, REB, RSV, NRSV*; Kaiser, *Isaiah 13–39*, 398; cf. Wildberger, *Jesaia 28–39*, 1440: "entboten."

[44] Given the military context of this passage, the verb here is best translated, "muster" (cf. *HALAT*, 901; E. Jenni, *Das hebräische Picel: Syntaktisch-semasiologische Untersuchung einer Verbalform im Alten Testament* [Zurich: EVZ Verlag, 1968] 228–29).

[45] On the *qal* passive, see R. J. Williams, "The Passive *Qal* Theme in Hebrew," in *Essays on the Ancient Semitic World* (ed. J. W. Wevers and D. B. Redford; Toronto Semitic Texts and Studies; Toronto: University of Toronto Press, 1970) 43–50. Evidence for this form may be found in Ugaritic and Amarna Akkadian as well as classical Arabic; Arabic probably reflects the original vocalization of this theme: perfect /qutila/ and imperfect /yuqtalu/ (ibid., 42–45). The Masoretes doubled the consonant after the *u*

qal p-q-d can signify, "to deposit (something) in a place," as in 2 Kgs 5:24. This usage is also attested with the *hiphil* (Isa 10:28; Jer 36:20). The modern English verb "to warehouse," though usually used with things, can also be used with persons as objects. In such a case the verb bears a negative sense. Perhaps it is possible, therefore, that the poet, for dramatic effect, is deliberately applying to himself an expression usually predicated of objects.[46]

More likely, however, this apparently uncommon usage is a calque from Akkadian, especially given the connection with the netherworld here.[47] Relevant to our discussion of *p-q-d* are a number of Akkadian curse formulae with *p-q-d* (G stem = *qal*) requesting that some god hand over the accursed to a netherworld deity[48] or to the netherworld itself. The following formula is particularly close to v. 10c:

Šamaš bēl elâti u šaplâti ana māt lā târi lipqissu[49]

May Shamash, Lord of the upper and lower regions, consign him to the Land-of-No-Return (the netherworld).[50]

---

to preserve the vowel, which in many cases made the form indistinguishable from the *pual* (ibid., 50). Originally *pqdty* would have been vocalized as /puqadtī/. It was probably later pronounced /pōqadtī/ (ibid., 50). Because it is difficult to be certain how it was vocalized in Biblical Hebrew, I retain the Masoretic vocalization of the *qal* passive form, which would be /puqqadtī/ in the case of the verb in question (ibid., 46–47).

[46] See also Driver, "Isaiah i–xxxix," 56.

[47] See most recently C. Cohen, "The Meaning of צלמות 'Darkness': A Study in Philological Method," in *Texts, Temples, and Traditions: A Tribute to Menahem Haran* (ed. M. V. Fox et al.; Winona Lake, IN: Eisenbrauns, 1996) 300 n. 43.

[48] Cf. rituals asking that the individual in question be handed over (*p-q-d*) "to (the power of) Namtar, the vizier of the netherworld" (E. Ebeling, *Tod und Leben nach den Vorstellungen der Babylonier* [Berlin: de Gruyter, 1931] 128 line 5*, 129 line 3, 130 line 24, 131 line 43).

[49] O. R. Gurney and J. J. Finkelstein, eds., *The Sultantepe Tablets I* (Occasional Publications of the British Institute of Archaeology at Ankara 3; London: British Institute of Archaeology at Ankara, 1957) 215 III 9; see also T. Bauer, *Das Inschriftenwerk Assurbanipals* (2 vols.; Assyriologische Bibliothek [Neue Folge] 1–2; Leipzig: Hinrichs, 1933) 1. 87.

[50] This is a standard Akkadian designation of the netherworld (= Sumerian kur.nu.gi₄.a). The closest parallel in Biblical Hebrew is Job 16:22: *'ōraḥ lō'-'āšûb*, "the path of no return" (lit., "the path [from which] I shall not return").

A slight variation of this curse has the condemned handed over to the gatekeeper(s) of the netherworld:

[*ana* NE-GAB NI.]GAB.GAL *ša erṣetim lū paqid*[51]

Let him be consigned [to Negab] the chief [gate]keeper of the netherworld.

lipqidkunū ši ana 7 atê [ša] Ereškigal[52]
Let him consign you (pl.) to the seven gatekeepers [of] Ereshkigal (the queen of the netherworld).

These last two texts raise a question about the reading of *šᶜry* in Isa 38:10c. Is it to be read *šaᶜărê*, "gates," or *šōᶜărê*, "gatekeepers"?[53] In theory either is possible here. In fact, in the present context consonantal *šᶜry* may be polysemous and thus mean either (poetic ambiguity). On the one hand, in favor of the translation "the gates of the netherworld" is the fact that nowhere in the MT does *šᶜry(m)* occur in a netherworld context where it must mean "gatekeepers" rather than "gates." Further evidence is the existence of an equivalent expression, "the gates of Death" (*šaᶜărê māwet*), in a number of passages in the OT and related literature.[54] "The gates of the netherworld," however, appears only here in the MT, although it is attested several times in later biblical and related literature.[55] In both cases the figure of speech depicts death/Sheol as a city, a phenomenon attested in Ugaritic and Akkadian literature as well. On the other hand, in favor of "the gatekeeper(s) of the netherworld" is the attestation of this image in Akkadian (see above) and also in Ugaritic. In the ritual text RS 12.061 the god Reshep is called *ṯǵrh*, "her gatekeeper," i.e., the gatekeeper of Shapash, the sun-goddess.[56] In Ugaritic religion Shapash was also the god-

[51] Ebeling, *Tod und Leben* I. 141 line 15.
[52] CAD A/2, 517.
[53] The latter reading is endorsed by Cohen, "The Meaning of צלמות 'Darkness'," 300 n. 43.
[54] Pss 9:14; 107:18; Job 38:17 (// *šᶜry ṣlmwt*); 1QH 6:24.
[55] Wis 16:13; Sir 51:9; 3 Macc 5:51; *Pss. Sol.* 16:2; Matt 16:18.
[56] See D. Pardee, *Ritual and Cult at Ugarit* (Writings from the Ancient World: Society of Biblical Literature 10; Atlanta: Scholars Press, 2002) 132–33.

dess of the netherworld, because she descended into the nether regions every night. Hence Reshep, a god whose name appears in the Hebrew Bible, was considered the gatekeeper of the netherworld at Ugarit and may have been known as such to Israelites.[57] According to some, reference to netherworld gatekeepers may be present in Job 38:17b.[58] But "the gates of the netherworld" seems to fit with Biblical Hebrew usage, and thus is perhaps the more likely of the two translations. (See also **Rhetorical-Critical Observations** below.)

[11a] *ʾāmartî*:

1QIsaᵃ: *ʾmrty*; 1QIsaᵇ: [ ]; LXX: εἶπα; Aquila: [ ]; Symmachus: [ ]; Theodotion: [ ]; Vg: dixi; Syriac: *ʾmrt*; *Targum of Isaiah*: *ʾmryt*.

The monocolon is repeated from v. 10a but without the *ʾănî*. Here it is clearer than in v. 10a that there is no syntactic relationship between this word and what follows. It serves a strictly introductory function.

[11de] *lōʾ ʾabbîṭ ʾādām ʿôd ʿim yôšĕbê ḥādel*:

1QIsaᵃ: *lwʾ ʾbyt ʾdm ʿwd ʿm ywšby ḥdl*; 1QIsaᵇ: [ ]; LXX: οὐκέτι μὴ ἴδω ἄνθρωπον ἐκ τῆς συγγενείας μου. κατέλιπον; Aquila: οὐκ ἐμβλέψω ἄνθρωπον ἔτι μετὰ κατοικούντων [ ]; Symmachus: *ditto*; Theodotion: *ditto*; Vg: non aspiciem hominem ultra et habitatorem quievit; Syriac: *lʾ ʾḥzʾ ʾnšʾ ʿm ʿmry ḥprʾ*; *Targum of Isaiah*: *lʾ ʾplḥ qdmwhy ʿwd bbyt mqdšʾ dmtmn ʿtyd lmpq ḥdwʾ lkl ytby ʾrʿʾ*.

I shall treat the two parts of IAb in reverse order, i.e., v. 11de before v. 11ab. The reason for this is that v. 11de contains a textual error that must be cleared up before we can properly understand the relationship of this bicolon to v. 11ab, and thus the meaning of the subunit as a whole.

Verse	Verb	Object	Preposition	Object of Prep.
11bc	*ʾerʾeh*	*yāh yāh*	*bĕ-*	*ʾereṣ haḥayyîm*
11de	*ʾabbîṭ*	*ʾādām*	*ʿim*	*yôšĕbê ḥādel*

There is a mixture of synonymous and antithetical parallelism in IAb, but not between the cola of each bicolon. These cola are related

---

[57] On Resheph in the OT, see P. Xella, "Reshep רֶשֶׁף," *DDD* (rev. ed.) 700–703.

[58] *REB* supports this interpretation of *šʿry* in Job 38:17, where it translates *šʿry ṣlmwt* as "the door-keepers of the place of darkness," parallel to *šaʿărê māwet*.

to each other by "synthetic" parallelism; the second colon completes the thought of the first rather than repeating it in different words. The synonymous/antithetical parallelism, rather, is between the two bicola themselves. The first sign of this is the appearance of the common synonymous word-pair *r-ɔ-y* // *n-b-ṭ* (*hiphil*)[59] in the first colon of each bicolon, each negated by *lōɔ*. The objects of these verbs, *yāh yāh* and *ɔādām*, also display parallelism, but here antithetical: divine versus human. The prepositions in vv. 11c and 11e are also in synonymous parallelism.[60] But are the terms they govern in synonymous parallelism, viz., *ɔereṣ haḥayyîm* and *yôšĕbê ḥādel*?

The chief obstacle to resolving this question is the MT's *ḥādel*. It is a *hapax legomenon*, here in the pausal form, presumably from an absolute form **ḥedel*. The LXX and Vg misunderstood this term, translating it as if it were from the verb "to cease." But since it follows what must be a plural construct in Hebrew, *ywšby*, it has to be parsed as a noun. The Syriac and the *Targum of Isaiah* take it as a noun—"the grave" and "the land" respectively.

Dahood took it to mean "the land of cessation," adding it to his list of terms for the netherworld.[61] Since the verb *ḥ-d-l* does mean "to cease," it is not impossible that **ḥedel* has this meaning. But more likely it is in fact a "ghost word."

First, this lexeme is nowhere attested in Northwest Semitic. Second, those who favor emending the expression to *yôšĕbê ḥāled* can point to Ps 49:1, where this expression occurs. Third, although *yôšĕbê ḥāled* only occurs once in the MT, the synonymous *yôšĕbê tēbēl* occurs four times[62] and the equivalent *tēbēl wĕyôšĕbê bāh* three times.[63] These

---

[59] Avishur, *Word-Pairs*, 639, 659.

[60] Of the four parts of these two bicola, indicated in the schema above, the first and third are attested as synonymous word-pairs. The synonymity and parallel usage of the prepositions *bĕ-* and *ɔim* can be seen from poetic passages such as Pss 36:9; 78:37; Job 10:13; 25:2; 28:14; 29:20. The most striking of these is Job 28:14: *tĕhôm ɔāmar lōɔ bî-hîɔ* // *wĕyām ɔāmar ɔên ɔimmādî*, "The Deep says, 'It is not *in* me,' and the Sea says, 'It is not *with* me.'" See also Ps 36:9.

[61] M. Dahood, "*ḥadel*, 'Cessation' in Isaiah 38:11," *Bib* 52 (1971) 215. Dahood's student, N. J. Tromp (*Primitive Conceptions of Death and the Nether World in the Old Testament* [BibOr 21; Rome: Pontifical Biblical Institute: 1969] 84), follows this view.

[62] Ps 33:8; Isa 18:3; 26:9, 18.

[63] Pss 24:1; 98:7; Lam 4:12.

expressions are parallel to (X-)ʾereṣ in five of these passages.[64] Finally, ḥeled is parallel to ḥayyîm, "the living," in Ps 17:14:

> mĕmîtām [MT: mimĕtîm] yādĕkā yhwh
> mĕmîtām [MT: mimĕtîm] mēḥeled
> ḥallĕqām [MT: ḥelqām] baḥayyîm

(May you be) their exterminator by means of your hand,[65] O Yhwh, (may you be the one to) exterminate them out of the world; eradicate them from among the living![66]

In Isa 38:11 ʾereṣ (ha)ḥayyîm // ḥeled is an expansion of the word-pair ḥeled // ḥayyîm in the psalm passage.[67]

[11b] lōʾ ʾerʾeh yāh yāh bĕʾereṣ haḥayyîm:
1QIsaᵃ: lʾ ʾrʾh yh bʾrṣ ḥyym; 1QIsaᵇ: [ ]; LXX: οὐκέτι μὴ ἴδω τὸ σωτήριον τοῦ θεοῦ ἐπὶ τῆς γῆς; Aquila: οὐκ ὄψομαι ια ια ἐν γῇ τῶν ζώντων; Symmachus: οὐκ ὄψομαι τὸν κύριον ἐπὶ γῆς ζώντων; Theodotion: οὐκ ὄψομαι ια ια ἐν γῇ τῶν ζώντων; Vg: non videbo dominum dominum in terra viventium; Syriac: lʾ ʾḥzʾ lmryʾ bʾrʿ dḥyʾ; Targum of Isaiah: lʾ ʾytḥzy ʿwd qdm dḥylʾ dyhwh bʾrʿ byt škyntʾ dbh ʾrykwt ḥyʾ.

---

[64] Isa 18:3 (// šōkĕnê ʾāreṣ); Isa 26:9 (// lāʾāreṣ), 18 (// ʾereṣ); Lam 4:12 (// malkê ʾereṣ); Nah 1:5 (// hāʾāreṣ).

[65] Dahood claims that the *hiphil* participle mĕmîtām carries an imperative force here (*Psalms I: 1–50*, 98–99). But evidence for this use of the participle is not well established. Nevertheless, his overall understanding of the verse is surely on the mark. The optative seems to continue the imperative force of qûmâ and pallĕṭâ in v. 13. See G. Ravasi, *Il libro dei Salmi: Volume Iᵒ (1–50)* (Bologna: Edizione Dehoniane, 1985)

[66] Note the same idiom in Akkadian and Aramaic curses. (1) In Akkadian: *eliš ina balṭūti lissuḫšu*, "Above (i.e., in this world as opposed to the netherworld) may (Shamash) extirpate him from among the living" (Code of Hammurapi, xliii 36); (2) in Aramaic: *yshw šmk wšrk mn ḥyn*, "May they (these gods) extirpate your name and your place from among the living" (*KAI* #225 lines 9–10). Note that both texts use the same verb, *n-s-ḫ/ḥ*.

[67] Barthélemy (*Critique Textuelle de l'Ancien Testament* 2. 264) notes that the medieval Jewish exegetes Saadya and Yefet ben Eli had understood *ḥdl* to mean "world" and that Abraham ha-Babli believed that a change had occurred in the text affecting the last two consonants (i.e., a metathesis). He also mentions in this connection Abuwalid, Joseph Qara, Ibn Ezra, Radaq, and Isaiah of Trani.

"Seeing" in this context involves more than visual contact. Both *r-ɔ-y* and synonymous *n-b-ṭ* (*hiphil*) in v. 11d come close to the sense of Italian *vedersi* or German *sich sehen*, which imply the experience of social interaction with others. Because the idiom "to see God/Yhwh" most frequently means to commune with him in the temple precincts, some commentators posit a cultic meaning of the phrase even here.[68]

The double name *yāh yāh* is unique to this verse and has stimulated a fair amount of discussion. Only 1QIsa[a] and the Syriac do not reflect a double name here, reading *yh* and *lmry*ɔ respectively. Aquila and Theodotion have ια ια. Vg has *dominum dominum*. The LXX paraphrases with τὸ σωτήριον τοῦ θεοῦ; the first noun may be an attempt to guard against the statement that a human being could actually "see" God. The *Targum of Isaiah* achieves the same effect by translating the verb as if it were the Hebrew *niphal* (cf. Ps 84:8): "I shall not appear again before the Awesome One, Yhwh . . . ." One might be tempted to postulate a misreading of *waw* in the divine name as *yod* with a separation of the resultant *yhyh* into *yh yh*. But this is most unlikely in the case of the divine name which appears more frequently than any other in the MT. Most probably even in ancient times scribes were especially careful in copying the Tetragrammaton.

Then what is to be made of *yāh yāh*? W. G. E. Watson and others have suggested that v. 11a be scanned as an example of the "terrace pattern" in poetry.[69] The first *yāh* belongs to one colon, the second to the next, so that the translation would run something like:

> I shall never see Yah,
> Yah in the land of the living.

But although such a division of the verse is supported by the Masoretic punctuation, it clashes with the structure of the following matching bicolon, where no such pattern is possible ("Nevermore shall I behold [other] human beings (*ɔādām*) // with those who dwell . . .").

The *lectio difficilior yāh yāh* must be taken seriously, despite a general disinclination to do so. I shall present here several attempts at a solution.

---

[68] See, e.g., B. Duhm, *Das Buch Jesaja*, 280; Begrich, *Der Psalm des Hiskia*, 24.

[69] Watson, *Classical Hebrew Poetry*, 208.

First, *yāh yāh* might be a deliberate repetition of the name *yāh*. Such repetitions are attested elsewhere in MT, though only in a few places: Exod 34:6 (*yhwh yhwh*); Ps 22:2 (*ʾēlî ʾēlî*). But in these two passages the divine name is a vocative and comes at the beginning of the colon. In Ps 22:2 it is clearly a kind of emphatic address.[70] A more apposite parallel might be sought in 2 Sam 19:1, 5. When David weeps over his slain son Absalom he calls out, *běnî ʾabšālôm běnî běnî ʾabšālôm . . . ʾabšālôm běnî běnî* (19:1) and *běnî ʾabšālôm běnî ʾabšālôm běnî běnî* (19:5). The mourner's repeated calling of the name of the departed loved one, who can never answer, heightens the tone of sorrow and loss. One might be inclined to think that something similar lies behind *yāh yāh*. Because the poet is convinced he will never see Yhwh again, perhaps he lingers as it were over the name, conveying a sense of the poignancy of his separation from God. For the Israelite, it was this separation that constituted death's greatest sorrow.

Second, there are a few instances in the MT of the divine name *yāh* followed by the fuller form of the Tetragrammaton (as well as other divine epithets). In addition to Isa 38:11b, P. D. Miller lists as examples of this phenomenon Pss 68:19 (*yāh ʾělōhîm*)[71]; 130:3 (*yāh ʾǎdōnāy* [*yāh yhwh* in some manuscripts])[72]; Isa 12:2 (*yāh yhwh*; the parallel in Exod 15:2 has *yhwh*).[73] He finds a further example in one of the Khirbet Beit Lei inscriptions (Inscription B), though his interpretation of *yh* as a divine name in this text is less secure.[74] These biblical examples make

---

[70] The phenomenon of the double address is characteristic of Luke. Cf. "Martha, Martha" (Luke 10:41); "Simon, Simon" (22:31); "Saul, Saul" (Acts 9:4).

[71] Since this is within the Elohistic Psalter, one might posit an original *yāh yhwh*.

[72] But in this passage the *yh* could be the vocative particle, as *ʾǎdōnāy* is almost certainly vocative: "O Lord/Yhwh" (see n. 73 below).

[73] P. D. Miller, "Psalms and Inscriptions," 329. Miller inadvertently cites Isa 38:8 as the passage containing *yāh yāh*.

[74] Miller (ibid., 328) reads and translates Inscription B as follows:

> *pqd yh ʾl ḥnn*
> *nqh yh yhwh*
> Take care (of me), O Yah gracious God!
> Absolve (me), O Yah Yhwh!

Although this translation is plausible, because the element *yh* precedes a vocative in both cases one must reckon with the possibility that it is to be parsed not as the divine name *yāh* but as the vocative particle *yâ*, known from Phoenician, Ugaritic, Syriac, and Arabic. This is the interpretation of F. M. Cross in his discussion of this text ("The Cave Inscriptions from Khirbet Beit Lei," in *Near Eastern Archaeology in the Twentieth Cen-*

it difficult to deny the possibility that on occasion one could refer to God by a repeated form of the Tetragrammaton or part thereof. In PsHez *yāh yāh* is possibly a variant of this usage, consisting of a reduplication of the shortened form of the Tetragrammaton, *yāh*.[75]

For the MT's *bĕʾereṣ haḥayyîm* 1QIsa[a] reads *ḥayyîm* (without the article), which is probably the preferable reading given the fact that in poetry the article tends to occur less frequently than in prose. Elsewhere I have attempted to show that in a number of poetic passages the meaning of "the land of life/the living" came to denote the "'Land of Life'" par excellence, viz., the Jerusalem temple.[76] Should the expression here be translated "the land of the living" (i.e., the world of living human beings as opposed to the dead) or "the Land of Life" (i.e., Yhwh's temple)?

In the present context *bĕʾereṣ haḥayyîm* is surely meant to contrast with *bĕšaʿărê šĕʾôl* in IAa. Since Sheol is the land of death par excellence, one would be justified in translating the phrase in question "the land of the living" in this passage. This contrast is indicated not only by the opposite meanings of these phrases but by the fact that in the entire psalm only they contain the preposition *bĕ-* used in a locative sense.

But the other meaning is also possible, and does not necessarily exclude the first. Some years ago J. S. Kselman drew attention to the break-up of the parallel word-pair *šaʿar // bayit* between the beginning and end of PsHez (vv. 10c, 20c).[77] This suggests that the poet intended

---

tury: *Essays in Honor of Nelson Glueck* [ed. J. A. Sanders; Garden City, NY: Doubleday, 1970] 302 and 306 n. 17). See also J. Hoftijzer and K. Jongeling, *Dictionary of the North-West Semitic Inscriptions* (2 vols.; HdO 21; Leiden: Brill, 1995) 430. In his edition J. C. L. Gibson has a very different reading of the text, although he also reads *yh yhwh* and takes it as a divine name (*Textbook of Syrian Semitic Inscriptions: Volume I: Hebrew and Moabite Inscriptions* [Oxford: Clarendon Press, 1971] 58).

[75] For stylistic evidence for the double reading of the divine name, see Chapter 7, **Rhetorical-Critical Observations**.

[76] Barré, "*ʾrṣ (h)ḥyym*," 40–50.

[77] J. S. Kselman, "Design and Structure in Hebrew Poetry," in *SBL Seminar Papers 1980* (ed. P. J. Achtemeier; SBLSP 1980; 19: Chico, CA: Society of Biblical Literature, 1980) 2; L. R. Fisher, ed., *Ras Shamra Parallels: The Texts from Ugarit and the Hebrew Bible: Volume I* (AnOr 49; Rome: Pontifical Biblical Institute, 1972) 158 (§II 137). The pair is attested in Ugaritic (CTA 1007:5–6; 3 II:3–4) and Hebrew (Gen 28:17; Deut 6:9; 11:20). It probably derives from the break-up of the expression, "the gate(s) of the house of X" (2 Chr 24:8).

a contrast not only between * šaʿărê šĕʾôl* and *ʾereṣ (ha)ḥayyîm* but also between the former expression and *bêt yhwh*. Since the temple of Yhwh was the "land of life" par excellence, and the diametrical opposite of the netherworld, it would form an even starker contrast with Sheol than the "land of the living." Thus *ʾereṣ (ha)ḥayyîm* in this passage may have a Janus-like ambivalence: in view of the reference to Sheol a few lines earlier it denotes the sphere of human existence in this world as opposed to the netherworld; but in view of the end of the poem it alludes to the Jerusalem temple.[78] The fact that the poet uses the quasi-cultic terminology of "see[ing]" Yhwh in the *ʾereṣ (ha)ḥayyîm* gives some support to the latter interpretation.

Emended Text and Translation

IAa 10a   *ʾănî ʾāmartî*

     b   *bĕdōm yāmay ʾēlēkâ*

     c   *bĕšaʿărê šĕʾôl puqqadtî*

     d   *wĕmar šĕnôtāy*

IAb 11a   *ʾāmartî*

     b   *lōʾ ʾerʾeh yāh yāh*

     c   *bĕʾereṣ ḥayyîm*

     d   *lōʾ ʾabbîṭ ʾādām ʿôd*

     e   *ʿim yôšĕbê ḥāled*

A. Mournful Departure for the Netherworld

10a   (Once) I had thought:

   b   Mourning for my days, I must depart;

   c   to the gates of the netherworld I have been consigned,

   d   weeping bitterly for my years.

---

[78] On the issue of ambiguity in Hebrew poetry, see P. R. Raabe, "Deliberate Ambiguity in the Psalter," *JBL* 110 (1991) 213–27.

B. Separation from God and Humankind

11a	I had thought:
b	Never (again) shall I see Yah-Yah,
c	in the land of the living/of life;
d	Nevermore shall I behold (other) human beings among those who dwell in the world.

Rhetorical-Critical Observations

The two subsections of IA exhibit different stichometric arrangements. Prescinding from the monocola *ʾănî ʾāmartî* and *ʾāmartî*, IAa (v. 10) is a tricolon and IAb (v. 11) consists of two bicola. The only other tricolon in PsHez is the coda (v. 20), which therefore forms a structural inclusion with v. 10. Moreover, IAa (i.e., minus v. 10a) is capable of being scanned as a complex chiasmus:

bĕdōm yāmay	a	*bĕ-* + construct chain (sg. + pl.)
ʾēlēkâ	b	1st sg. verb
bĕšaʿărê šĕʾôl	c	*bĕ-* + construct chain (pl. + sg.)
puqqadtî	b	1st sg. verb
wĕmar šĕnôtāy	a	*wĕ-* + construct chain (sg. + pl.)

> In mourning for my days
> I must go away
> to the gates of Sheol
> I have been consigned
> (in) bitter weeping for my years.

IAb also contains a chiastic feature, involving the last two words in the bicola vv. 11bc and 11de. The construct phrase *bĕʾereṣ ḥayyîm* is a sg. noun followed by a masc. pl. The second construct phrase, *yôšĕbê ḥāled*, contains the same elements, but in reverse order: a masc. pl. followed by a sg. noun.

There are some noteworthy sonant patterns in IA. In IAa the most obvious is the alliterative *bĕšaʿărê šĕʾôl . . . šĕnôtāy* in v. 10cd. In IAb, note the /ʾ ʾ y y/ sound pattern in *ʾerʾeh yāh yāh*. This is echoed in v. 11de, with the addition of the sound /ʿ/ as /ʾ ʾ ʿ ʿ y/: *ʾabbîṭ ʾādām ʿôd ʿim yôšĕbê.*

Several features serve to connect subsections IAa and IAb. Both make use of anaphora. Each colon of the tricolon v. 10b–d begins with a labial /b, w/ and the first cola of the two bicola in v. 11 each begin with /l/. The second colon of the first bicolon in IAb (v. 11c) repeats the /b/ alliteration one final time (*bĕʾereṣ*), connecting IAa with IAb. Since *mr* (1QIsaᵃ) in v. 10d refers to "bitter weeping," this image (which ends IAa) forms a thematic lead-in to IAb. Weeping is followed by two references to another ocular function, seeing (vv. 11b, 11d).

IA also has some connections with Part II. The two occurrences of *ʾāmartî* at the beginning of IA form a link with the beginning of IIA, i.e., v. 15, where this verb occurs for the last time. A second link with IIA is effected by the vocable *mar* in the final colon of IAa, which reappears in the final colon of IIAa and of IIAb. The anaphoric *lōʾ . . . lōʾ* in v. 11b, d is reprised in IIB—specifically, IIBa (vv. 18a, c). Another connection with this subsection is the word *šĕʾôl* in vv. 10c and 18a.

The phrase *šʿry šʾwl* in v. 10c interplays with several other expressions in PsHez. With the preposition *bĕ-* it forms a foil to *bĕʾereṣ (ha)ḥayyîm*," the land of the living," in the next subsection (v. 11c) as well as to *ʿal-bêt yhwh* in the coda (v. 20c). On the one hand, these interplays give some support to the translation "the gates"—rather than "the gatekeepers"—of the netherworld." On the other hand, the chief concern of the next subsection, IAb, is the psalmist's eternal separation from all those beings whose relationship to him makes life worth living (expressed in the merism Yhwh/humankind), those with whom the poet will no longer be able to interact in this world. If *šʿry šʾwl* is rendered "the gatekeepers of the netherworld" it forms an effective contrast with "Yah Yah" and "(fellow) human beings" in v. 11: the psalmist has been deprived of interactions with those dear to him and forced to exist instead in the company of those shadowy beings whose function is to make sure he stays in the netherworld.

Finally, IA displays several literary links with the coda (v. 20). First, both IAa and the coda are tricola and both contain ten words, as I have mentioned.[79] Second, I have already alluded to the "distant parallelism" between *bĕšaʿărê šĕʾôl* and *ʿal-bêt yhwh* in v. 20. Another connection between IA and the coda is *yāh yāh*. Despite the controver-

---

[79] Note the apocryphal "Apostrophe to Zion" (11QPSᵃ 22:1–10), which likewise begins and ends with a tricolon. The remainder of the poem consists entirely of bicola.

sial nature of this term, it is undoubtedly some form of the Tetragrammaton, which occurs elsewhere in the poem only at the beginning and end of the coda.

A biblical parallel to IA may be found in Jer 22:10, where the concepts of going away, weeping and mourning, absence from the land, and not seeing (again) are all present:

> ʾal-tibkû lĕmēt
>   wĕʾal-tānūdû lô
> bĕkû bākû lahōlēk
>   kî lōʾ yāšûb ʿôd wĕrāʾâ
>   ʾet-ʾereṣ môladtô

> Do not *wee*p for one who is dead,
>   and do not *mourn* for him;
> Weep rather for him who is *gone away*;
>   for he will *not* return *again* and *see*
>   the land of his birth.[80]

General Comments

At the outset of PsHez we meet the psalmist in the act of lamentation. What is unique about this act in the pages of the Hebrew Scriptures is that it is not performed for a deceased relative or important national figure. Rather, the poet is proleptically conducting as it were a funeral lament for himself in anticipation of his imminent death. More specifically, he is mourning his "days" and "years" (= his lifetime) as if they were dear departed loved ones. His actions are reminiscent of stories about pious Jews during the Holocaust who recited the Kaddish for themselves just before their death, fearing that there would be no one to recite the prayer for the dead over them after they had gone.[81]

---

[80] If W. L. Holladay's interpretation is correct, the "one who is dead" is Josiah and "him who is gone away" refers to Jehoahaz, gone in exile to Egypt. Here too "going away" probably has overtones of death (*Jeremiah 1: A Commentary on the Book of the Prophet Jeremiah Chapters 1–25* [Hermeneia; Philadelphia: Fortress, 1986] 587).

[81] Another example of the psalmist's "proleptic" mourning for himself may be found in Psalm 22. I have argued that the correct reading of v. 18a is *spd kl ʿṣmwty* (MT:

IA is permeated by the imminence of death. The psalmist declares that he *has already been* consigned to the gates (or gatekeepers) of the netherworld. Death for him is not a possibility, nor even a probability, but a palpable certainty. From this moment on he will "no longer" have contact with his God or his fellow human beings. Next to the loss of his own life, the psalmist expresses the most profound regret not for the cessation of life's pleasures but for the end of communion with God and his people. For the Israelite these are the greatest losses that death can bring.

The text of PsHez gives no clues as to the reason for this certainty. In the larger context of Isaiah 38, of course, the source is evident. In 38:1b Isaiah informs Hezekiah in no uncertain terms that he is about to die: "You shall die, you shall not recover." The prophet's word is Yhwh's word; there is no room for doubt. In this context, following upon 38:1–8, vv. 10–11 may be read as a reflection of the state of the king's mind when he received this news, although there is no evidence that in its original, pre-Isaian context these verses had any reference to this narrative. Moreover, from the very outset of the poem it is clear that the poet sees Yhwh as the cause of his fate. Apart from the context of 38:1–8, it is likely that the passive form *puqqadtî* is a "divine passive"— i.e., expressing obliquely the poet's conviction that it is God who has decreed his untimely death. Not only has Yhwh shortened his life, not only has he apparently forsaken him, but he has gone so far as to hand him over to the ultimate enemy—the netherworld.

As often happens in laments and in the lament section of thanksgiving hymns, the netherworld, that most terrifying of images, figures prominently. Here it appears dead-center in the opening tricolon ("the gates of Sheol") in v. 10c. A neo-Assyrian parallel to the distressed speaker's description of himself at the gates of Sheol is found in the "Righteous Sufferer's Prayer to Nabu":

gamar napištua Šidduk[išarra] ayēše [lu]ulliki
aktalda ana abul mūti Nabû ammini tumašširanni

ʾspr kl ʿṣmwty), based on the Syriac: wʾyllw kwlhwn grmy, "and all my bones have mourned" or "have intoned my funeral lament." The *spd* is most likely an infinitive absolute used as a finite verb. Here too the psalmist is mourning for himself before his death by enemies, who are stripping him like one fallen on the battlefield (vv. 18b–19). See my article, "The Crux of Psalm 22:17c," 291–94, 303–4.

My life is over—
O Shidduk[isharra],[82] where can I go?
I have arrived at the gate of death—
O Nabu, why have you forsaken me?[83]

The expression "gates of Sheol" is a kind of metonymy, standing for the netherworld city as a whole. To represent the realm of the dead in this way draws attention to several aspects of Sheol. (1) The figure of Sheol the city emphasizes the fact that those who die are no longer citizens of earthly towns but of the great underworld. They belong to the land of the dead. (2) The "gates" of death/Sheol mark the threshold between life and death. Once one has crossed this ultimate bourne there is no returning to the land of the living. (3) The figure of the gates of the netherworld vividly expresses its eternity; for once these are shut behind the one who enters there is no exit, as in the case of someone trapped in a besieged city.[84] This thought is echoed movingly in the Song of Jonah (2:7):

> *yāradtî hāʾāreṣ*
> *běrīḥêhā baʿădî lěʿôlām*

> Down I went to the netherworld;
> its bars (locked) behind me forever!

"The gates of Sheol" in Isa 38:10c come close to being personified, as perhaps in Matt 16:18. The personification of Sheol is a phenomenon of some frequency in the OT. The poet speaks not simply of going to Sheol but of being handed over into the power of a malevolent and even demonic force. This is especially true if *šʿry* is read as "gatekeepers" rather than "gates." This detail adds a note of horror to the already traumatic shock of the realization that life is over.

Begrich observes that the opening words of the prayer in v. 10a (*ʾănî ʾāmartî*) mark the psalm form-critically as a *Danklied*. He points to the

---

[82] A name for the god Nabu.

[83] A. Livingstone, *Court Poetry and Literary Miscellanea* (State Archives of Assyria 3; Helsinki: Helsinki University Press, 1989) 32 lines 9–10.

[84] In his annals Sennacherib boasts with reference to Hezekiah, whom he trapped in besieged Jerusalem, "I made it impossible for him to go out of his city-gate" (cf. *CAD* A/I, 84).

same expression introducing a recital of the poet's distress in Pss 30:7, 10–11; 31:23; 66:18; 116:4b–6, 11; Jonah 2:5; Lam 3:54; Sir 51:10–11.[85] But perhaps more significant is what the beginning of the poem does not say. Commentators have noted something missing in this opening section of PsHez. One expects to find some address to Yhwh, as is common at the beginning of most psalms whether of lament or thanksgiving, but there is none. Not until the very end of Part I does the psalmist address direct speech to Yhwh. It may be no accident that in IA the first direct mention of God's is not one of his standard names or epithets but the anomalous, almost stammering *yāh yāh*. It almost seems as if the poet cannot bring himself to pronounce the name of the One who is at one and the same time the cause of his misery and the greatest source of joy for the Israelite.[86]

The direct reference to "mourning" and "bitterness" (i.e., bitter weeping) in the opening subsection signals the importance of the theme of mourning in the poem as a whole. This is picked up again at the end of Part I and is finally reversed in the coda. The poet does not view his situation dispassionately but is thrown into deep depression at the prospect that his life has virtually ended. The movement from that depression to rejoicing forms an important aspect of the drama of PsHez.

[85] Begrich, *Der Psalm des Hiskia*, 17.
[86] Cf. Amos 6:10.

CHAPTER 4

Similes of Woe

Part IB (vv. 12–14)

The Masoretic Text

IBa	12a	*dôrî nissaꜥ wĕniglâ minnî̂*
	b	*kĕʾōhel rōꜥî̂ᵃ*
	c	*qippadtî kĕʾōrēg ḥayyayᵗ*
	d	*middallâ yĕbaṣṣĕꜥēnî̂ᶻ*
	e	*miyyôm ꜥad-laylâ taślîmēnî̂ˢ*
	13a	*šiwwîtî ꜥad-bōqer b kāʾărî̂ᶻ*
IBb		*kēn yĕšabbēr c kol-ꜥaṣmōtāyᵃ*
	d	*miyyôm ꜥad-laylâ taślîmēnî̂ˢ*
	14a	*kĕsûs ꜥāgûr kēn ʾăṣapṣēpᶻ*
	b	*ʾehgeh kayyônâᵃ*
	c	*dallû ꜥênay lammārômᶻ*
	d	*ʾădōnāy ꜥāšĕqâ-lî ꜥorbēnî̂ˢ*

Textual Remarks

[12a] *dôrî nissaꜥ wĕniglâ minnî:*
1QIsaᵃ: *dwry nsꜥ yʾklh mny;* 1QIsaᵇ: [ ]ꜥ *wngl[ ]y;* LXX: τὸ λοιπὸν τῆς ζωῆς μου· ἐξῆλθε καὶ ἀπῆλθεν ἀπ᾽ ἐμοῦ;[1] Aquila: γενεά μου [ ]; Sym-

---

[1] A number of interpreters (e.g., Touzard, "De la conservation du texte hébreu," 88; Linder, "Canticum Ezechiae," 53; Begrich, *Der Psalm des Hiskia*, 26, n. 1; Barthélemy, *Critique Textuelle de l'Ancien Testament* 2. 265) assume that *dôrî* is rendered by the

machus: [ ]; Theodotion: ἡ γενεά μου [ ]; Vg: generatio mea ablata est et convoluta est a me; Syriac: *dry šql wᶜbr mny*; *Targum of Isaiah*: *mdwry psq mbny dry ᵓtnṭylw ywmy ᵓtqṣyṣw wglw mny*.

In Biblical Hebrew *dôr* essentially denotes a "generation." This term, both the Hebrew and the English, has two main areas of reference: the social, in which the reference is to one's family or contemporaries, and the temporal, in which the reference is to a period of time, namely the life span of a generation of human beings.[2] All of the ancient versions of this passage understand *dôr* within this semantic range. Most of them translate with "generation": Vg, Aquila, and Theodotion, and the Syriac. The LXX has a periphrastic rendering, "the rest of my life(time)." The *Targum of Isaiah* is conflate and periphrastic here and has two or three translations of the word.[3]

LXX as ἐκ τῆς συγγενείας μου. But this is incorrect. The LXX translates *lᵓ ᵓbyṭ ᵓdm ᶜwd ᶜm ywšby ḥdl dwry nsᶜ* with οὐκέτι μὴ ἴδω ἄνθρωπον ἐκ τῆς συγγενείας μου, κατέλιπον τὸ λοιπὸν τῆς ζωῆς μου· ἐξῆλθεν. . . . Since κατέλιπον = *ḥdl* and ἐξῆλθεν = *nsᶜ*, it stands to reason that the intervening τὸ λοιπὸν τῆς ζωῆς μου = *dôrî*. Unless one holds the unlikely view that *ᶜm ywšby* was completely missing in the *Vorlage*, ἐκ τῆς συγγενείας μου is to be explained as follows. It results from the fact that the LXX translator took *ḥdl* as a verb and thus could not parse *ywšby* as a construct form. First, he was forced to "read" *ywšby* as *yôšebay*, interpreting it to mean "those who dwell with me." Second, either his *Vorlage* had *m* (the preposition *min*) before *ywšby* instead of *ᶜm* or he misread it as such. He rendered this *mywšby* periphrastically as ἐκ τῆς συγγενείας μου, "from my family." (A participle can sometimes, especially in poetry, take a suffix instead of the preposition that usually appears after it: e.g., Isa 51:6: *yôšěbêhā*, "those who dwell in it [= the land]," for *yôšěbê bāh* [Ps 24:1]. Note how Vg renders *wěšōkěnêhem* [Job 26:5] as *et qui habitant cum eis,* "and those who dwell *with* them.") At least this was probably the translator's attempt to make sense of these words. The whole line of the LXX is to be translated, "I will never again see a member of my family (lit., "a human being from my family"). I have had to leave behind the rest of my life(time). It has departed . . . ." Thus Hebrew *dôrî* corresponds to τὸ λοιπὸν τῆς ζωῆς μου "(I have left behind) *the rest of my life(time),*" not to ἐκ τῆς συγγενείας μου.

[2] D. N. Freedman and J. Lundbom, דור *dôr*, *TDOT*, 3. 174.

[3] The *Targum of Isaiah* is both periphrastic and conflate here, and actually gives two or even three different translations of Hebrew *dôrî*. In the first *dôrî* is translated with the preceding term, in the second and third with the words that follow. The first translation is *mdwry psq*, "*my dwelling* has ceased," which renders Hebrew *ḥdl dwry*. The second is more complicated. In this case the targum renders Hebrew *dwry nsᶜ wglh mny* with *mbny dry ᵓtnṭylw ywmy ᵓtqṣyṣw wglw mny*, "from the men of *my generation* my days have been plucked up and cut off and exiled from me." Here *mbny dry* clearly

But the consensus among interpreters for quite some time has been to claim that neither the social nor the temporal meaning of *dôr* fits here. Rather, they appeal to Aramaic[4] as the key to its proper meaning in this passage, viz., a "dwelling(-place)."[5] So understood, the term would likely be an Aramaism, since *dôr* in this sense occurs in Aramaic but probably not in Biblical Hebrew.[6]

It is not difficult to see why interpreters adopt this position. First, the Hebrew meaning of the term "generation" in the more common, social sense certainly does not work here. Second, the term comes immediately before *n-s-ᶜ* (*niphal*), which is the technical term for the pulling up of tent-stakes and ropes, i.e., "to strike" a tent (its opposite is *ḥ-n-y* or *n-ṭ-y*). For this reason it seems intuitively to make sense, at least at first glance, to assign to *dôr* a meaning that "fits" with this verb.[7] Since "dwelling" seems to fit reasonably well with *n-s-ᶜ*—actually, it is appropriate not for any dwelling but only for a tent, which is secured by ropes or pegs—whereas "generation" and "lifetime" do not, the reasoning is that one should opt for "dwelling" rather than "lifetime."

But although superficially this reasoning seems sound, in reality it is wrong. In order to appreciate this we must look carefully at the nature

---

reflects Hebrew *dôrî*. Note that in this case it uses a standard meaning of the term, not an "Aramaic" meaning as in the first translation. But the *subject* of the verbs that follow, the first and third of which correspond to Hebrew *nsᶜ wnglh* and which are in the plural, is *ywmy*, "my days" = "my lifetime." In the Hebrew text *dôrî* is the subject of these verbs. Thus on one level at least the targum has a translation for Hebrew *dôrî* similar to that of the LXX, "the rest of my lifetime." See previous note.

[4] Cf. Syriac *d-w-r*, "to dwell" (Payne Smith, *A Compendious Syriac Dictionary*, 87), *dayyar*, "dwelling" (ibid., 91), Biblical Aramaic *mādôr*, "dwelling" (E. Vogt, *Lexicon Linguae Aramaicae Veteris Testamenti* [Rome: Pontifical Biblical Institute, 1971] 97).

[5] This interpretation goes back at least to Ibn Ezra and Kimchi (Linder, "Canticum Ezechiae," 54). Among later interpreters, see Linder, ibid., 54–55; Duhm, *Das Buch Jesaja*, 280; Touzard, "De la conservation du text hébreu," 88; Begrich, *Der Psalm des Hiskia*, 25; G. Fohrer, *Das Buch Jesaja* 2. 183; Wildberger, *Jesaja 28–39*, 1442–43; Kaiser, *Isaiah 13–39*, 398; B. S. Childs, *Isaiah* (OTL: Louisville: Westminster John Knox, 2001) 279; Blenkinsopp, *Isaiah 1–39*, 479; de Boer, "Isaiah xxxviii 9–20," 177; BDB, 190; HALAT, 209 (which classifies *dôr* in this passage as a derivation of *dôr* I—as distinct from *dôr* II, "generation").

[6] In my article on Isa 51:13–53:12 ("Textual and Rhetorical Considerations," 17) I implied that *dôr* in Isa 53:8b could mean "dwelling" and allowed the possibility of its having this meaning in Isa 38:12a. I obviously withdraw the latter suggestion, though the former is not impossible in that passage.

[7] So Wildberger, *Jesaja 28–39*, 1442–43.

of a simile.[8] Like a metaphor, a simile has a tenor and a vehicle. Now part of the genius of an artful metaphor or simile lies in the *tension* between the tenor and the vehicle. Aristotle's example of a metaphor in his *Rhetoric* is "Achilles is a lion." Whether this is phrased as a metaphor or as a simile ("Achilles is like a lion"), there must be a tension, a semantic *distance* between the tenor ("Achilles") and the vehicle ("lion"). In a discussion of P. Ricoeur's thought on this subject, in a section dealing with Aristotle's understanding of this concept, K. Simms underscores this fact:

> What this [the metaphor] comes down to is the idea of *substitution*—one word for another, and one thing for another . . . . But not just any substitution will do—the effect must be *allotrios*, alien, insofar as the transposition should be from ordinary, current, or usual terminology to unusual usage—otherwise there would be no point to the metaphor. Thus *metaphor says what is not proper*—Achilles is not a lion, he is a person. . . .[9]

Later on, in discussing Ricoeur's thought on metaphor, Simms accentuates the point that metaphor says "what is not proper." Speaking of Ricoeur's discussion of the three "tensions" that every metaphor must have, he notes that the most important for Ricoeur is the third, a tension which lies in "the relational function of the copula":

> . . . "Achilles is a lion." On this *is* hinges an interplay of sameness and difference: Achilles is at once the same as a lion, but not a lion. This third tension is the most important of them all for Ricoeur in producing, and defining, metaphorical truth. *A metaphor "preserves the 'is not' within the 'is'"* . . . .[10]

Therefore, ironically and counter-intuitively, to choose "dwelling" as the translation of the tenor *dôrî* because it fits better with the verb that

---

[8] I would like to express my thanks to my colleagues, R. F. Leavitt and G. H. Stevens, who directed me to the philosophical literature on metaphor cited below.

[9] K. Simms, *Paul Ricoeur* (Routledge Critical Thinkers: Essential Guides for Literary Studies; London/New York: Routledge, 2003) 63 (the emphasis in the last line is mine).

[10] Ibid., 75 (emphasis mine). The last line is a quotation from Ricoeur's *The Rule of Metaphor: Multi-Disciplinary Studies of the Creation of Meaning in Language* (Toronto/Buffalo: University of Toronto Press, 1975) 249.

properly goes with the vehicle *ʾōhel* is wrong *precisely because* it fits *better* with the vehicle and its predicate than does "lifetime." So translated the simile would say what *is* proper rather than what is not proper and would lack the requisite "is not" of a metaphor (or simile). By choosing the meaning "dwelling" the tension between tenor and vehicle evaporates, and what results is a poor excuse for a simile. This is precisely what we see in a translation of v. 12ab like G. Fohrer's, where the tenor is "mein *Zelt*lager" and the vehicle is "ein Hirten-*zelt*."[11] Essentially this sentence says: "My tent . . . is like a tent." Compare this to a proper example of a simile using the same verb, Job 19:10b: *wayyassaᶜ kāᶜēṣ tiqwātî*, "He has uprooted my hope like a tree." Here the tenor, "hope," is far distanced semantically from the vehicle, "tree." The latter is a proper object of this verb, the former is not. "Hope" therefore does not at all "fit" with *n-s-ᶜ*. It is *not* a "proper" object of this verb, the effect is truly ἀλλότριος and unusual, and precisely for this reason Job 19:10b is a masterful example of a simile. The same holds true for "lifetime" as the subject of *n-s-ᶜ* in Isa 38:12a.

For these reasons, notwithstanding the almost universal consensus favoring the translation "dwelling," *dôrî* in v. 12a is to be understood exclusively in the sense of "lifetime" (as the LXX understood it),[12] an attested Biblical Hebrew nuance of this word. Moreover, the temporal meaning of *dôrî* fits perfectly, as a few others have pointed out, with the tenor *ḥayyay*, "my life (span)," in the subsequent simile (v. 12cd).[13] In v. 12a *dôrî* has no reference whatsoever to a "dwelling," and thus the contention that it is an "Aramaism" here must be rejected once and for all.

---

[11] *Das Buch Jesaja*, 2. 183.

[12] The LXX's paraphrase is quite logical. Since the psalmist has already lived part of his "lifetime," one cannot really speak of his (whole) "lifetime" being taken away from him, only what remains of it—therefore, "the rest of my lifetime."

[13] Linder ("Canticum Ezechiae," 55) notes that *ḥayyay* in the subsequent bicolon is "the parallel expression" to *dôrî* but comes down in favor of the "dwelling" interpretation. One of the very few modern commentators that translates it here in the sense of "lifetime" is J. N. Oswalt, *The Book of Isaiah: Chapters 1–39* (NICOT; Grand Rapids: Eerdmans, 1986) 649: "my span of life." See also R. B. Y. Scott, "Isaiah: Text, Exegesis, and Exposition, Chapters 1–39." *IB* 5. 375: "Not **mine age** or **my dwelling** but 'my life span'."

The versions seem to disagree on the voice of the first verb, *nsᶜ* (MT: *nissaᶜ* [*niphal*]). The LXX translates,"he/it has gone away."[14] Quite possibly the LXX parses *nsᶜ* as *qal* here. The Syriac reads, "(he has) taken away," which is a possible translation of *n-s-ᶜ*, though more properly of the *hiphil*. For *dôrî nissaᶜ* the *Targum of Isaiah* has a conflate rendering, "From the sons of my generation my days are plucked up and cut off,"[15] where *ʾtnṭylw*, "lift up, pull up," renders *nissaᶜ*. Vg has "has been taken away." Hence the LXX and Syriac have active forms while the MT, Vg, and the *Targum of Isaiah* have passive forms. This evidence is best explained as different ways of reading *nsᶜ* (viz., as a *qal* or a *niphal*) rather than as an indication of a different form in their *Vorlagen*. In the final analysis the weight of the first two witnesses is not sufficient to overturn the MT's reading *nissaᶜ*. True, the use of the *niphal* of the root *n-s-ᶜ* is rare in Biblical Hebrew, occurring in only two other passages: Job 4:21; Isa 33:20b.[16] But significantly, both of these passages mention pulling up the tent-cord/tent-peg as a metaphor for death or cessation, as is implied in Isa 38:12a.[17]

A far more difficult problem is to decide on the best reading of the next verb, *wĕniglâ* in the MT. The earliest witness to this reading is 1QIsa[b], where *wngl*[ ] is visible on the photograph. It is difficult to tell whether the LXX's translation reflects a *qal* or a *niphal* verb in its *Vorlage*, though the only other passage where the LXX uses ἀπέρχομαι to translate *g-l-y* is Isa 24:11, where the MT and 1QIsa[a] have *glh* (*qal*). However, εἰσέρχομαι translates the *niphal* in Isa 49:9. The Syriac and the *Targum of Isaiah* also translate with active verbs: "has passed away/has departed (from me)." But this may not necessarily indicate a Hebrew *Vorlage* with something other than a *niphal* verb. These versions may simply have interpreted the rare *niphal* form as virtually identical to the *qal* in meaning.

Beyond the issue of which verbal conjugation to read here there is the question of the root of the verb. Several ancient witnesses attest to a root other than *g-l-y*. The most significant alternative is 1QIsa[a],

[14] ἐξέρχομαι renders *n-s-ᶜ* in only one other passage, Num 11:31, but there the verb is in the *qal*.

[15] Translation by Chilton, *The Isaiah Targum*, 75.

[16] On Job 4:21, see below.

[17] Several NT passages speak of taking down the tent as a death metaphor (2 Cor 5:1; 2 Pet 1:14), but in these later passages the imagery is somewhat different insofar as "tent" refers to the body.

which is probably to be read *yklh*, although *wlkh* may be possible.[18] Not only does this reading lack the initial *nun* but it reads a different root altogether—*k-l-y*, "to come to an end," rather than *g-l-y*. The roots *g-l-y* and *k-l-y* differ phonetically only with respect to the initial consonant, i.e., whether it is voiced or unvoiced. Thus we could be dealing here with a variant reading resulting from an auditory error. Begrich opts for the reading *wngl* from *g-l-l*, "to roll up,"[19] which is supported by Vg's *convoluta est*.[20] In this case the two verbs would describe pulling up the tent (i.e., its pegs and/or ropes) and subsequently rolling it up as the shepherd prepares to move on. But as Begrich admits, *g-l-l* is never used in Biblical Hebrew for rolling up a tent.[21] Furthermore, the presence of *minnî* creates another obstacle to reading *g-l-l* in this colon. The preposition *min* does occur with the root *g-l-l* in the *qal* in the sense of rolling a stone away from some *place*[22] but not rolling up something away from some*one*. Moreover, such an expression makes no sense. Begrich is aware of the problem and obviates it by the methodologically objectionable expedient of deleting *minnî*,[23] although this term is attested by all the ancient versions that contain this passage.

But is Begrich correct in claiming that *g-l-y* does not fit in this context? Now this verb has two basic meanings, "to reveal" and "to depart." One of the problems here is that there are very few if any other examples of *g-l-y* in the *niphal* with the latter sense, which it would presumably have if the MT's reading is correct. Two other possible examples of this usage are both in Isaiah, 23:1 and 49:9. The latter text reads:

---

[18] Goshen-Gottstein (*The Book of Isaiah*, 167) has a raised circle over the *yod*, indicating that in his view it could be read either a *yod* or a *waw*. The letter certainly appears to be the typical *yod* of this script and not the *waw* (in 1QIsa^a the two letters are distinct). Parry and Qimron read the letter in question as a *yod* (*The Great Isaiah Scroll*, 65). But even if *yod* is the correct reading, as is likely, it may well have resulted from a corruption of an original *w*.

[19] *Der Psalm des Hiskia*, 27.

[20] Followed by *HALAT*, 184; Wildberger, *Jesaja 28–39*, 1443; J. A. Soggin, "Il 'Salmo di Ezechia' in Isaia 38, 9–20," *BibOr* 16 (1974) 177.

[21] In post-biblical Hebrew, on the other hand, *g-l-l* (*hophal*) describes folding up the curtains of the Tent of Meeting. See Jastrow, *Dictionary of the Targumim*, 249.

[22] Gen 29:3, 8, 10.

[23] *Der Psalm des Hiskia*, 27. He is followed by Wildberger, *Jesaja 28–39*, 1440, 1443.

> . . . saying to the prisoners, "Come out" ($\underline{s}\bar{e}^{\flat}\hat{u}$),
> and to those in darkness, *higgālû*.

Does the *niphal* imperative properly belong to the semantic area "to reveal" or "to depart" in this passage? Only a few translators support a connection with the latter.[24] But that the verb belongs to the former semantic range is clear from the occurrences of the word-pair *y-ṣ-ʾ* and *g-l-y*.[25] Decisive for resolving this question is 1 Sam 14:11, where *g-l-y* (*niphal*) and *y-ṣ-ʾ* (*qal*) are used synonymously:

> So both of them *showed themselves* (*wayyiggālû*) to the garrison of the Philistines, and the Philistines said, "Look, Hebrews are *coming out* (*yōṣĕʾîm*) of the holes where they have hidden themselves" (*NRSV*).

This passage reflects a context almost identical to Isa 49:9: people who were in a dark place (prison or a cave) coming forth into the light and thereby showing themselves.

With the elimination of Isa 49:9, the only passage in the MT that may contain the same usage of *g-l-y* (*niphal*) as occurs in Isa 38:12 (MT) is Isa 23:1. Unfortunately, this is also a difficult passage:

> a *hêlîlû ʾŏniyyôt taršîš*
> b   *kî-šuddad mibbayit*
> c *mibbôʾ mēʾereṣ kittîm*
> d   *niglâ-lāmô*

The most accurate translation of this passage that has appeared thus far is, in my opinion, that of *REB*:

> Wail, you ships of Tarshish,
>   for the harbour is destroyed;
> The port of entry from Kittim
>   is swept away.[26]

---

[24] D. J. A. Clines, ed., *The Dictionary of Classical Hebrew: Volume II: ב–ו* (Sheffield: Sheffield Academic Press, 1995) 350: "depart." Possibly *NIV* supports this interpretation with its translation: "Be free!" (= "Go free"?).

[25] 1 Sam 14:11; Job 12:22.

[26] The translators of the *NEB* read *mābît* for the MT's *mibbayit* and *mābôʾ*, "port of entry," for *mibbôʾ*. See L. H. Brockington, *The Hebrew Text of the Old Testament: The Readings Adapted by the Translators of the New English Bible* (Oxford: Oxford University Press, 1973) 183.

Most translations render *niglâ lāmô* as "it was revealed to them" or the like.[27] But to whom does "them" refer, since the previous verb is 2d person and there are no 3d person antecedents? It is doubtful that this refers to *ʾŏniyyôt* (fem.), since *lāmô* can be substituted for *l-* plus the 3d masc. sg. or pl. but not the fem. pl. suffix and because the other pronominal reference to Tarshish ships in this poem is feminine—viz., *mĕʿuzzĕken* in the inclusion verse (v. 14). Most likely *lāmô* does not function as the indirect object here but as part of a periphrastic "impersonal passive" construction consisting of a 3d masc. passive verb followed by the preposition *l-* + suffix.[28] This can be seen, for example, in Isa 53:5, where *nirpāʾ lānû* means literally "'it' (dummy subject) is healed with regard to us" = "we are healed."[29] Hence if *niglâ* is interpreted within the semantic range of "depart" rather than "reveal," *lāmô* does not denote an indirect object but functions like the *dativus (in)commodi*. The person(s) to whom the preposition refers is the logical subject. In this verse this is *mbwʾ*, which should be pointed as the masculine noun[30] *mābôʾ*, "entrance > port of entry" (as in Ezek 27:3), not the infinitive construction *mibbôʾ* as in the MT.[31]

---

[27] *RSV*: "[From the land of Cyprus] it is revealed to them"; *NJPSV*: "[As they came from the land of Kittim] this was revealed to them"; *NAB*: "[From the land of the Kittim] the news reaches them"; *NJB*: "The news has reached them [from Kittim]"; *NIV*: "[From the land of Cyprus] word has come to them"; Blenkinsopp, *Isaiah 1–39*, 340: "When they came from Cyprus they found it out." But the last translation (see also *NJPSV*) cannot be a correct rendering of *mibbôʾ*. If the author had meant "*when* they came" the preposition would have been *b-* or *k-*, but not *min*. With the last-mentioned preposition one would have to translate "after they came. . . ."

[28] See P. Joüon and T. Muraoka, *A Grammar of Biblical Hebrew* (2 vols.; Subsidia Biblica 14; Rome: Pontifical Biblical Institute, 1991) 462 (§128ba); Waltke and O'Connor, *An Introduction to Biblical Hebrew Syntax*, 384–85 (§23.2.2e); D. R. Meyer, *Hebräische Grammatik* (4 vols.; Berlin: de Gruyter, 1972) 3. 83 (§109).

[29] Other examples of this construction are: Gen 2:23: *lĕzōʾt yiqqārēʾ ʾiššâ*, lit., "With regard to this (person), 'it' shall be called 'Woman'" = "This person shall be called 'Woman'"; 2 Sam 17:16: *pen yĕbullaʿ lammelek*, lit., "lest 'it' be swallowed up with regard to the king" = "lest the king be swallowed up"; Isa 53:8: *nuggaʿ* (1QIsaᵃ: *nwgʿ* [MT: *negaʿ*]) *lāmô*, lit., "'it' was stricken with regard to him" = "he was stricken"; and Lam 5:5: *lōʾ hûnaḥ lānû*, lit., "'it' has not been allowed to rest with regard to us" = "we have been given no rest."

[30] For the gender of *mābôʾ*, see Jer 38:14: *ʾel-mābôʾ haššĕlîšî ʾăšer bĕbêt yhwh*.

[31] See M. L. Barré, "'Tarshish Has Perished': The Crux of Isaiah 23,10," *Bib* 85 (2004) 118 n. 20.

Hence 23:1cd may be literally translated, "As for the port of entry (*casus pendens*), 'it' has been swept away from the land of Cyprus with regard to it" = "The port of entry has been swept away from the land of Cyprus."

If this interpretation of Isa 23:1 is correct, there is a second example of *g-l-y* (*niphal*) ("depart") + *min* in the Hebrew Bible. This fact supports the plausibility of the MT's reading of Isa 38:12a.

As for the reading of the root *k-l-y* in 1QIsaᵃ, it would fit with *dôrî* if here it means "lifetime." As I have indicated, however, the predicate of the simile should fit in a literal sense with the vehicle but not with the tenor. Also, *minnî* creates a problem. It does not make sense to speak of a period of time coming to an end "from" someone, and no other viable meaning of the preposition *min* seems to fit here.

[12b] *kĕʾōhel rōʿî:*

1QIsaᵃ: *kʾwhl rʿy*; 1QIsaᵇ: *kʾhl rʿy*[ ]; LXX: ὥσπερ ὁ καταλύων σκηνήν; Aquila: ὡς σκέπη ἑταίρων μου; Symmachus: ὡς σκηνὴ[ν] ποιμένων; Theodotion: ὡς σκηνὴ οἱ φίλοι μου; Vg: quasi tabernaculum pastorum; Syriac: *ʾyk mšknʾ drʿwtʾ*; *Targum of Isaiah*: *kmškn drʿy*.

The difficulty in this colon is the suffix on *rōʿî*. One would have expected *rōʿeh* or perhaps the plural, *rōʿîm*. The *Targum of Isaiah* and the consonantal text of 1QIsaᵃ agree with the MT. Unfortunately 1QIsaᵇ has a lacuna just after *rʿy*. Other ancient witnesses presuppose an absolute plural form: Vg, the Syriac, Aquila, Symmachus, and Theodotion. The LXX has a curious translation: "like one who takes/tears down a tent." Possibly the translator read *rʿy* as a form of the verb *r-ʿ-ʿ*, "to shatter, ruin."[32] It is most likely, however, that, immediately preceding a simile relating to the production of fabrics (v. 12cd), this image also has to do with some human occupation. Thus whatever form of the word is to be read, it should refer to shepherding. The solution most frequently proposed for this difficulty is to postulate that *rōʿî* is a corruption from an original plural, *rōʿîm*.[33] The chief objection to such a solution is that it is difficult to see what could have triggered the loss of final *mem* in this word.

---

[32] So Goshen-Gottstein, *The Book of Isaiah*, 168 n.

[33] Begrich, *Der Psalm des Hiskia*, 27; Castellino, "Lamentazioni individuali accadiche ed ebraiche," 153.

The most likely "solution" to this apparently problematic reading is to realize that it is not problematic after all. The word is correct as it stands in the MT, even as regards its vocalization. However, the morphological ending here is not the 1st sg. suffix. Rather, the term represents an archaic orthography of the participle of a *lamed-he* verb. The masc. sg. participle of such verbs would originally have had the form **bániyu* (which can be seen from Ugaritic and Akkadian).[34] With the loss of the case-ending this would become **bániy* > **bánī* > **bónī* > *bōnī* and finally *bōné(h)*,[35] the Standard Biblical Hebrew form. However, there are a number of examples both in the MT and in ancient Hebrew manuscripts in which the older *-î* morphological ending is preserved on participles and other verb forms. The most significant for our purpose are two examples of a *lamed-he* participle (which is what *rōʿeh*, "shepherd," is) from Dead Sea Psalms manuscripts: *ʿty* for the MT's *ʿōṭeh*, "the one who covers," in 4QPs[d] (Ps 104:2) and *ʿśy* for the MT's *ʿōśeh*, "the one who makes/creates," in 4QPs[d] and 4QPs[l] (Ps 104:4).[36] Thus in Isa 38:12b *rōʿî* is a "correct" form of the word "shepherd," or more accurately, a form correct for one stage of Hebrew orthography predating Standard Biblical Hebrew. Therefore it may belong to the penultimate stage in the development of the participle as outlined above.[37]

---

[34] See S. Segert, *A Basic Grammar of the Ugaritic Language* (Berkeley: University of California Press, 1984) 74. Segert cites an Akkadian transliteration of a III-*y* masc. participle which illustrates this: *la-i-ya = lāʾiya*, with *-a* being the accusative case-ending (ibid.).

[35] For the stages of this development, see H. Bauer and P. Leander, *Historische Grammatik der hebräischen Sprache des Alten Testaments: I* (Hildesheim: Georg Holms, 1965 [reprint of the 1922 edition]) 584 (§73b).

[36] See P. W. Flint, *The Dead Sea Psalms Scrolls and the Book of Psalms* (STDJ 17; Leiden: Brill, 1997) 97. Compare pausal *téšî*—read rather *téšśî*—from **tiššî*, the 2d masc. sg. *qal* (*yqtl*) of the verb *n-š-y* I, "to forget," in Deut 32:18 for Biblical Hebrew *tiššeh*. Note also in the Samaritan Pentateuch the forms *nbny* for the MT's *nibneh* (Gen 11:4), *ʾwdy* for the MT's *ʾôdeh* (Gen 29:35), and *yḥzy* for the MT's *yeḥĕzeh* (Num 24:4).

[37] Von Legelshurst (*Die Hiskiaerzählungen*, 39) observes that *rʿy* here might be a "Nebenform zu רֹעֶה"; so also Goshen-Gottstein (*The Book of Isaiah*, 168 n.). Could the *yod mater lectionis* here represent the *segol* + *he* (-*eh*) in *rōʿeh*? E. Qimron thinks this is unlikely in instances in which *yod* represents final *e*: "The *yod* would correspond to Tiberian *ṣere*, not *segol*" (*The Hebrew of the Dead Sea Scrolls* [HSS 29; Atlanta: Scholars Press, 1986] 20 [§100.33]).

[12cd] *qippadtî kā'ōrēg ḥayyay middallâ yĕbaṣṣĕ'ēnî*:

1QIsa[a]: *sprty k'wrg ḥyy mdlh ybṣ'ny*; 1QIsa[b]: [ ]; LXX: πήξας, τὸ πνεῦμά μου παρ᾿ ἐμοὶ ἐγένετο ὡς ἱστὸς ἐρίθου ἐγγιζούσης ἐκτεμεῖν; Aquila: συνέσπασα[ν] ὡς ὑφαίνων ζωήν μου ἀπὸ ἀντίου αὐτῆς ἐκτέμνει με; Symmachus: συνεσπάθη<ν> ὡς ὑφάντης τὴν ζωήν μου ἀπὸ καταρισμοῦ ἐξέτεμέν με; Theodotion: ἐστενώθη ὡς ὑφαίνων ἡ ζωή μου ἀπὸ συνεργῶν αὐτῆς ἐξέτεινεν; Vg: praecisa est velut a texente vita mea dum adhuc orirer succidit me; Syriac: *'tqpdw 'yk syrs ḥyy w'yk nwl' dqryb lmtgddw*; Targum of Isaiah: *'tqplw knḥl gydwdyn*[38] *ḥyy myqr mlkwty 'n' gly*.

This is one of the most difficult lines in PsHez, surpassed in opacity only by vv. 16a–17b. The precise meaning of some of the terms as well as of the simile itself is not easy to grasp with precision. Because the majority of problems in this verse occur in the first colon, the best procedure would be to deal with the less complicated second colon first. This approach also has the advantage of allowing the information gleaned from the second colon to shed light on the first.

It is clear that certain terms in this verse are related to the technology of weaving. The OT record has left us little in the way of such technical vocabulary,[39] which complicates the task of interpretation.[40] Apparently two types of looms were in use in Palestine in biblical times: the horizontal and the vertical loom, the latter being the more typical. In the case of the vertical loom, two vertical beams were erected and between them was placed a third, horizontal beam or shaft. The warp (vertical) threads were suspended from this, sometimes being weighted down with clay weights or (later) with a second horizontal beam.[41] Into the warp the woof or weft (horizontal) threads were woven, perhaps with the use of a shuttle. When the piece of cloth

---

[38] The reading here, *knḥl gydwdyn* (lit., "like a stream with high banks"), is quite likely a corruption from *knwl grd'yn*, "like the web/fabric of weavers" (see Begrich, *Der Psalm des Hiskia*, 29; Stenning, *The Targum of Isaiah*, xxi, 126), which would correspond to the LXX's ὡς ἱστὸς ἐρίθου, "like a weaver's web."

[39] A rare exception is Judg 16:13–14.

[40] Even in modern times and contemporary languages few speakers outside of a particular trade are conversant with its argot. How many native speakers of English, for example, would understand the technical terminology of weaving today—terms such as "heddle," "shed," "selvedge," "thrum," etc.?

[41] See recently E. Marcus and M. Artzy, "A Loom Weight from Tel Nami with a Scarab Seal Impression," *IEJ* 45 (1995) 136–49.

was finished, the weaver would cut the warp threads on top which hung down from the horizontal shaft.

The first word in the second colon, the *dis legomenon dallâ*, is a clear example of a *terminus technicus* from the weaving trade. It is best translated by English "thrum," a technical term referring to the left-over warp threads that hang down from the horizontal beam of the vertical loom (from the root *d-l-l*, "to hang down, dangle"). The only other occurrence of *dallâ* is in Cant 7:6, where it refers to the dangling locks of the beloved. The relation to the root sense "hanging down" is obvious in both texts. All the ancient versions misunderstood this technical term, though most of them perceived that it had some connection with weaving.[42]

The second word in the colon is also a technical term in this profession, namely, *b-ṣ-ʿ*, "to cut off, snip (threads)."[43] In rabbinic Hebrew it functions as a technical term in the weaving profession.[44] The root is also attested in an Old South Arabic cognate of *b-ṣ-ʿ*, namely *b-ḍ-ʿ*, where it has the meaning "to cut off (the head)."[45] D. Kellermann ascribes this sense to the Hebrew verb as well and specifically in Isa 38:12d.[46] The meaning of the term in the present context is chiefly literal, as it refers to severing something from the thrum.

---

[42] LXX: ἐρίθου, "weaver"; Aquila: ἀντίου αὐτῆς, "its/her loom"; Symmachus: καταρτισμοῦ ("restoration, furnishing" [*sic*]; perhaps an error for κατάρτιος, a part of the loom [LSJ, 910]); Theodotion: συνεργῶν αὐτῆς, "its/her fellow-workers"; Vg: dum adhuc ordirer, "while I was still laying the warp"; the Syriac: *nwlʾ*, "web" or "loom."

[43] D. Kellermann, "בצע *bṣʿ*," *TDOT*, 2. 205.

[44] Ibid., 207.

[45] Kellermann (ibid.) adds to this definition "or the lifecord," but I have not been able to corroborate the sense of "cutting the 'lifecord'" for this root. J. C. Biella (*Dictionary of Old South Arabic, Sabaean Dialect* [HSS 25; Chico, CA: Scholars Press, 1982] 52) gives the meanings "slay and strip (an enemy in battle)" and "attack"; in his glossary A. Jamme translates it "behead" (*Sabaean Inscriptions from Maḥram Bilqîs [Mârib]* [Baltimore: Johns Hopkins, 1962] 430); A. F. L. Beeston, et al. (*Sabaic Dictionary* [English-French-Arabic] [Louvain-la-Neuve: Éditions Peeters, 1982] 27) give the meanings "impose tribute *on*" and "fatally wound s[ome]o[ne] in battle."

[46] Ibid., 205–6. Some believe that this meaning of *b-ṣ-ʿ* may be found in Jer 51:13: *bāʾ qiṣṣēk // ʾammat biṣʿēk*. RSV translates, "Your end has come, the thread of your life is cut." *JPS* has, "Your time is come, the hour of your end," but notes concerning the last two words: "Meaning of Heb. uncertain." Cf. W. L. Holladay, *A Concise Hebrew and Aramaic Lexicon of the Old Testament* (Grand Rapids: Eerdmans, 1988) 45: "the cubit of your being cut off = of your end." Whether one takes *bṣʿk* here as a verb or a noun, it probably has to do with the ending of one's life. But the meaning of *ʾammat* in this

The MT almost certainly understands Yhwh to be the subject of this verb: "He cuts me off from the thrum." The verb in the LXX has no object. The Syriac and Theodotion also lack the object, though Vg, Aquila, and Symmachus have it.[47] The lack of the object could reflect a *Vorlage* with *ybṣᶜ* rather than *ybṣᶜny*.[48] This issue cannot be resolved here, since it depends on precisely what the vehicle of the simile is. But a point that should be made is that *mdlh ybṣᶜny* is a very odd expression. No one can literally sever the poet from the "thrum, warp threads." This would be a possible meaning only if one could establish a figurative or metaphorical significance for *dlh*. Not only has no one proposed this, but such an interpretation seems quite unlikely in this context. In other words, the MT's reading of this colon is problematic. But before giving a final judgment on this issue we must ascertain the meaning of *ᵓrg*, which is the vehicle of the simile.

The MT points this as the participle *ᵓōrēg*, "weaver."[49] Its reading is supported by 1QIsaᵃ and several of the versions: Vg, Aquila, Symmachus, and Theodotion. Begrich, however, has suggested that it refers rather to something woven,[50] which agrees with the LXX (ἱστός), the Syriac (*syrs*), and the *Targum of Isaiah* (emended: *nwl*).[51] One advantage of reading the word this way would be that it makes a better complement to the vehicle in the preceding bicolon, *ᵓōhel*, which is likewise something woven of cloth. Since he believes that *ᵓrg* is not attested in Biblical Hebrew with the meaning "web, that which is woven on the loom," Begrich appeals to *ᵓārîg*, which he calls "an Ara-

---

passage is unclear, and *RSV*'s translation "the thread of your life" seems to be something of a stretch.

[47] The lack of the suffix is also reflected in the Syriac, which agrees with the LXX: *wᵓyk nwlᵓ dqryb lmtgddw*, "and like a web that is close to being cut off." This is similar to the LXX: ὡς ἱστὸς ἐρίθου ἐγγιζούσης ἐκτεμεῖν, "like the web of a (female) weaver, who is about to cut (it) off." Cf. Theodotion.

[48] The fact that the LXX lacks the suffix is not necessarily evidence that it was also lacking in its *Vorlage*. See the caution by E. Tov, *The Text-Critical Use of the Septuagint in Biblical Research* (Jerusalem Biblical Studies 3; Jerusalem: Simor, 1981) 247.

[49] This interpretation of the word explains why the MT takes Yhwh as the subject of *ybṣᶜny*. If the vehicle of the simile is a person—or more specifically, the action of a person (human or divine)—the tenor might also be expected to be a person: thus according to this logic weaver = vehicle, Yhwh = tenor.

[50] *Der Psalm des Hiskia*, 29.

[51] The *Targum of Isaiah* reads *nḥl*, a corruption of *nwl*.

maic expression."[52] But whereas *ʾārîg* does occur in rabbinic Hebrew,[53] and thus *might* represent the correct vocalization of *ʾrg* here, there is no evidence that it occurs as a noun with this meaning in Aramaic. The standard Aramaic and Syriac lexica do not list a noun *ʾārîg.[54]

The versions mentioned above—and Begrich—are probably correct in taking *ʾrg* as denoting what is woven rather than the weaver, but he is likely wrong in assuming that *ʾrg* in the sense of "web, woven cloth" does not exist in Biblical Hebrew. In a number of ancient languages, terms for "loom" can also denote that which is woven on the loom— e.g., Syriac *nawlāʾ* and *qěwāyāʾ*, each with these two meanings,[55] Greek ἱστός, and Latin *tela*. Now Hebrew *ʾrg* with the meaning "loom" is attested in Judg 16:14. While Samson was asleep next to a loom—probably a horizontal loom—Delilah wove seven locks of his hair with the weft and made them tight with the pin. Then she shouted out, "The Philistines are upon you, Samson!" Immediately he "awoke from his sleep, and pulled away the pin, the loom [*ʾereg*], and the web" (RSV). According to the majority of interpreters *ʾereg* here refers to the loom. But *ʾereg* very possibly has the extended meaning of "that which is woven on the loom" in Job 7:6:

$$\textit{yāmay qallû minnî ʾāreg}$$
$$\textit{wayyiklû běʾepes tiqwâ}$$

In the first colon *ʾāreg* (the pausal form) is almost without exception translated as the "shuttle" of a loom, a part that moves back and forth in weaving the cloth—"My days are swifter than a weaver's shuttle" (RSV). Those who understand the colon in this way assume that the point of the comparison involving *q-l-l*, "to be quick," is the movement of some part of the loom in weaving the cloth. But the second colon makes this less certain: "They (= my days) end when (or: "as

---

[52] *Der Psalm des Hiskia*, 31.

[53] Ibid., 119; G. H. Dalman, *Aramäisch-Neuhebräisches Handwörterbuch zu Targum, Talmud und Midrasch* (Frankfurt am Main: Kaufmann, 1922) 40.

[54] It is significant that the *Comprehensive Aramaic Lexicon* (<http://cal1.cn.huc.edu>) lists no form *ʾryg* or the noun *ʾrg* in any of the Aramaic dialects.

[55] Payne Smith, *A Compendious Syriac Dictionary*, 332.

soon as") the thread runs out."[56] The reference to the thread running out or coming to an end (*k-l-y*) suggests that *q-l-l* does not refer to how rapidly any part of the loom moves (e.g., the shuttle) but rather to how quickly a woven product is *finished*. This is how most of the versions interpreted the simile, translating *ʾereg* as "web, woven cloth."[57] The translation of Ishodad of Merv, one of the Syrian Church fathers, is similar: *ʾyk nwlʾ dšlm zqwrh wmṭʾ lgddʾ*, "like a web which its weaver completes and it reaches the thrums . . . ."[58] In sum, there is no compelling evidence that *ʾereg* means "shuttle" here or elsewhere in Biblical Hebrew; "web, woven piece of cloth" is at least as plausible a translation in Job 7:6 as "shuttle." And if *ʾrg* can have this meaning here, it can in Isa 38:12 as well.

Having argued for "a weaving" or "piece of cloth" as the vehicle of the simile,[59] we are now in a position to deal with other issues in this verse. The question was raised earlier as to whether one should read *ybṣʿ* or *ybṣny* in v. 12d. Once it is determined that the vehicle is not a person (weaver) it becomes less likely that the subject of this verb is Yhwh. Rather, the colon is most probably to be parsed as an asyndetic relative clause. This interpretation has been recognized by de Boer, who translates, "like a weaver, who will cut me off from the thrum,"[60] and *NAB*: "like a weaver who severs the last thread." I believe these translations are correct as to their interpretation of the syntax, but not in their translation of *ʾrg*. As can be seen from this translation, how one understands the syntax of v. 12d affects how one reads the verb. The textual evidence does not appear to be strong enough to eliminate the suffix *-ny*. For one thing, if the verb originally lacked the *-ny* suffix, it is difficult to see what might have triggered the attachment of this

[56] N. Habel, *The Book of Job: A Commentary* (OTL; Philadelphia: Westminster, 1985) 151.

[57] The *Targum of Isaiah* has *ywmy qlw mn gdd qwyn*, "my days are swifter than a web" (on *gdd qwyn* = "web" see Payne Smith, *A Comprehensive Syriac Dictionary*, 60; but on p. 493 the entry after *qwyn* reads: "said to mean *a spider*"); Aquila, Symmachus, and Theodotion have ὕφασμα, "web, woven garment"; Vg has *tela*, "web." The LXX's rendering is quite different: "my life is more insignificant (or "faster"?) than chatter."

[58] Cited from H. M. Szpek, "The Peshitta on Job 7:6: 'My Days Are Swifter Than an אֶרֶג,'" *JBL* 113 (1994) 288.

[59] The MT's reading of *ʾrg* as *ʾōreg*, "weaver," may derive in part from the apparent parallel with *rōʿî*, "shepherd," in the previous simile. But the point of comparison in these similes is not these two professions themselves but *something made of cloth* that is germane to each (a tent, a piece of woven cloth).

[60] De Boer, "Isaiah xxxviii 9–20," 178.

suffix to the verb. Yet *-ny* cannot be correct. A less drastic emendation than eliminating the suffix altogether would be to read the *yod* in *-ny* as a *waw*: *yĕbaṣṣĕ'ennû*, the masc. suffix referring back to the noun *ʾereg*, which is presumably masc. also. The verb could be parsed as impersonal,[61] resulting in the translation: "(like a piece of woven cloth) which one severs from the thrum"[62] or even "when/after one severs it from the thrum." Later in the transmission of this text, when the relative function of this clause was misunderstood, it was taken as a line grammatically independent of the preceding. As a result, two things happened: Yhwh was assumed to be the subject of the verb and the psalmist was assumed to be its object, so that *-nw* became *-ny*.[63]

As a result of the foregoing considerations, the structure of the simile becomes clearer. Now in every simile there are actually two predicates, although usually only the one associated with the tenor is expressed. In similes of the type found in PsHez the vehicle has an unexpressed predicate—e.g., v. 13bc: "Like a lion (shatters bones), so he shatters all my bones." The meaning of the first verb (*qpdty*) has yet to be determined, but the basic form of the simile may be represented as follows:

I am/my life is[64] *q-p-d*-ed as a piece of cloth (is *q-p-d*-ed)
　　which one severs from the thrum
　　(or: when/after one severs it from the thrum)

This overview of the simile is important for another reason, for it shows that the second colon actually stands outside of the simile. The verb *b-ṣ-'* is not the predicate of the vehicle at all but is part of a circumstantial clause that modifies the first colon. Therefore the idea of "cutting off" is not part of the simile itself unless such a meaning can be argued for *q-p-d*. These data counsel caution as regards giving prominence to this colon in the interpretation of v. 12cd. Whether one translates the second colon as "which one severs from the thrum" or "when/after one severs it from the thrum" the simile itself is concerned

---

[61] See GKC, §144d.

[62] According to Linder ("Canticum Ezechiae," 57), this emendation was proposed by N. Schlögl, but Linder gives no reference.

[63] A similar case is 11QPsa^a xvi 15 (Ps 145:6), which reads *ʾspr* for the MT's suffixal form (*ʾsprnh*).

[64] On this "double subject" construction, see below.

with what happens to the woven cloth *after* it has been severed from the warp threads. If *b-ṣ-ᶜ* is part of a metaphor for the death of the psalmist, anything that is done to the cloth afterwards would be anti-climactic. Therefore, it is unlikely that this passage is an example of the topos of "cutting the thread of life"[65] as commonly believed.

This brings us to the last and most problematic term to be discussed in this verse, *qippadtî*. But before undertaking the involved task of ascertaining its meaning in this passage we must first deal with an issue of syntax. Whether one accepts *qippadtî* as the correct reading here or not, we are confronted with what appears to be two subjects of a single predicate: the "I" of the first verb and the noun *ḥayyay*. A number of commentators resolve this by emending the verb to a 2d[66] or 3d person sg. form,[67] with *ḥayyay* as its object or subject respectively: "You have . . . my life . . . " or "My life has been . . . ." But emendation here is unwarranted. This particular construction was noted in Gesenius-Kautsch-Cowley[68] and was more recently discussed by W. R. Garr, who terms it the "double subject construction" in Hebrew. "In this clause type, the verb agrees with the possessive suffix of a noun, not with the nominal itself."[69] As an example of this construction, he cites Ps 57:5:

napšî bĕtôk lĕbāᵓîm ᵓeškĕbâ
I lie down/my soul lies down in the midst of lions.

As another example, this time in the passive voice, Garr cites Ps 73:21:

---

[65] Biblical Hebrew attestations of this topos may be found in Jer 51:13; Ezek 37:11; Job 6:9; 27:8; Ps 88:5 (on the foregoing passages see D. Kellermann, "בצע *bṣᶜ*," *TDOT*, 2. 207). "The thread of life" also appears in Akkadian contexts as *qû napišti* (*CAD* Q, 287; N/1, 298). In Syriac one finds expressions such as *nwl ḥyᵓ*, "the web of life," which occurs as the object of *g-d-d*, "to cut off" and figurative uses such as *qrb nwlᵓ lgddᵓ* (Payne Smith, *A Compendious Syriac Dictionary*, 60).

[66] So Linder, "Canticum Ezechiae," 57; Begrich, *Der Psalm des Hiskia*, 29. Begrich mentions earlier commentators who also emended the verb to 2d person sg.—*qippadtā*: H. Gunkel, O. Eissfeldt, W. Staerk, and F. Bühl. In the twentieth century this translation has been followed by commentators such as Wildberger (*Jesaja 28–39*, 1440) and Kaiser (*Isaiah 13–39*, 398).

[67] So Duhm, *Das Buch Jesaja*, 280; von Legelshurst, *Die Hiskiaerzählungen*, 40; Fohrer, *Das Buch Jesaja*, 2. 183. Linder ("Canticum Ezechiae," 57) reads a 3d pl. form.

[68] GKC §144l–p.

[69] W. R. Garr, "The Grammar and Interpretation of Exodus 6:3," *JBL* 111 (1992) 389.

wĕkilyôtay ʾeštônān
And I was/my kidneys were pierced.[70]

Isa 38:12c is most likely another example of this construction. The form of the verb should be parsed as a *qal* passive: *quppadtî*.[71] As can be seen from the examples cited above, this usage is not easy to render in English—"I have been/my life has been . . . ." Since an acceptable translation into English demands a choice between "I" and "my life" as subject, it seems best to follow the ancient versions[72] and construe the latter as the grammatical subject in the translation: "My life has been . . . ."

The verb *qpdty* is a *hapax legomenon* in Biblical Hebrew,[73] a fact which makes it more difficult to discern its meaning here. Virtually all commentators and lexica give as its meaning in this passage one of two possibilities: "to roll/fold up" or "to cut off."[74] Let us first look at the uses of the root *q-p-d* elsewhere in the MT, to see if they give any support to either of these proposed translations. Two apparent derivatives of the root that occur in the MT are the *tris legomenon* *qippō/ôd* (Isa 14:23; 34:11; Zeph 2:14) and the *hapax legomenon* *qĕpādâ* (Ezek 7:25).

(1) The animal called *qippō/ôd* in Hebrew[75] is the "hedgehog" or,

---

[70] Ibid., 390.

[71] It is not easy to see why the Masoretes pointed this *hapax legomenon* as a *piel* rather than a *qal*. The Syriac cognate occurs only in the *peal* (= *qal*) and the *ethpeal* (= passive of the *peal*) (see R. Payne Smith, *Thesaurus Syriacus* [Oxford: Clarendon Press, 1879–1901] cols. 3687-88). I would therefore parse *qpdty* as a *qal* passive. (Note that the Syriac translates it as a passive [*ethpeal*] form: ʾtqpdw.) It may have been pronounced /qōpadtī/ in Biblical Hebrew (see Chapter 3 n. 45).

[72] I.e., Symmachus, Theodotion, Vg, the Syriac, the *Targum of Isaiah*.

[73] A form of this verb (the "*qal* passive" participle) occurs once in Hebrew of the Second Temple period: Sir 4:31. Here *qpwdh* occurs as a variant to *qpwṣh*. The correctness of the latter reading is assured by the contrast between an "open" (*ptwḥḥ*) and a "clenched" or "closed" (*qpwṣh*) fist. Deut 15:7–8 speaks of closing (*q-p-ṣ*) one's hand to a poor brother (i.e., refusing to give), the opposite of which is to give with an "open" (*p-t-ḥ*) hand, which appears several verses later (15:11). See Skehan and Di Lella, *The Wisdom of Ben Sira*, 177. Therefore *qpwdh* does not appear to be the original reading here but is a later variant.

[74] KB (2d ed.), 845; BDB, 891; *HALAT*, 1043; F. Zorrell, *Lexicon Hebraicum et Aramaicum Veteris Testamenti* (Rome: Pontifical Biblical Institute, 1968), 729; Holladay, *Concise Hebrew and Aramaic Lexicon*, 321.

[75] Modern lexicographers treat the occurrence in Zeph 2:14 (*qippôd*) as a special case, since the animal in question here is mentioned together with the *qāʾat* (some kind of unclean bird) and is described as lodging *bĕkaptōrêhā*, "on/among her (Nineveh's)

according to some, the "porcupine"[76] and is so translated in the versions.[77] BDB claims that the porcupine is so named in Semitic from its defensive strategy of "rolling itself together" into a ball.[78] But this is incorrect. This is the defensive behavior of the hedgehog but not of the porcupine, which rather defends itself by threatening attackers with its sharp quills. It does not roll itself up. On the one hand, if it is true that the Hebrew term can refer to both animals, they must have something in common other than the ability to curl up into a ball, since only one of the two animals is capable of this. On the other hand, what they most obviously do have in common is a bristly or spiny hide.

There are other reasons for questioning the validity of the etymology of *qippō/ôd*. First, it may not be derived from *q-p-d* but from a closely related root. The Arabic term for "hedgehog" is *qunfud̲* and the Ethiopic is *qʷenfez*,[79] suggesting a derivation from a root *q-p-d̲* rather than *q-p-d*. The Hebrew cognate should be *qpwz*.[80] This fact would counsel a degree of caution in drawing any solid semantic conclusions about the verb *q-p-d* from the noun *qippō/ôd*.[81] Second, if

---

capitals." Roberts observes, "Its presence on the capitals does not necessarily point to a bird, since in a ruined city many of the capitals would be lying on the ground" (*Nahum, Habakkuk, and Zephaniah*, 193). On the other hand, the problem here could be the confusion evident in the Hebrew text between *qippôd* and *qippôz*.

[76] Zorell (*Lexicon Hebraicum et Aramaicum Veteris Testamenti*, 730) notes that the animal in question could be either a hedgehog or a porcupine; *HALAT* (1043–44) gives only "Igel" (hedgehog) as a translation; BDB (891) gives only "porcupine."

[77] The LXX translates *qippōd* as ἐχῖνος ("hedgehog") in Zeph 2:14; Isa 14:23; 34:11, 15 (in Isa 34:15 the MT has *qippōz*, whereas 1QIsa^a has *qwpd* [an error for *qpwd*?]); Vg has *ericius* ("hedgehog"); the Syriac has *qwpd'* ("hedgehog, porcupine" [Payne Smith, *A Compendious Syriac Dictionary*, 497]).

[78] BDB, 891.

[79] In the Aramaic dialects, Syriac *quppĕdâ* (Payne Smith, *A Compendious Syriac Dictionary*, 497) and Mandaean *qunpud* (E. S. Drower and R. Machuch, *Mandaic Dictionary* [Oxford: Oxford University Press, 1963] 408). For the Arabic, see Lane, 2569; for the Ethiopic, see A. Dillmann, *Lexicon Linguae Aethiopicae* (Leipzig: Weigel, 1865) col. 450.

[80] This form does occur once (Isa 34:15), but apparently as the name of an egg-laying animal. Holladay's lexicon gives the possibilities "a type of small tree-snake" or "a kind of owl" (*Concise Hebrew and Aramaic Lexicon*, 321). Could *qpwz* in this case be an error for *qpwd*? Note Syriac *qûpdā'*, "owl" (Payne Smith, *A Compendious Syriac Dictionary*, 497). This would fit with the other unclean bird mentioned in this passage, the *dayyôt* (*dis legomenon*; cf. Deut 13:14).

[81] Moreoever, the Hebrew textual evidence with regard to the name of this animal shows some confusion. In Isa 14:23 MT has *qippōd* whereas 1QIsa^a reads *qpz*; in Isa 34:15 MT has *qippôz*, whereas 1QIsa^a has *qwpd*.

there is a connection with *q-p-d*, it is more likely that the bristly nature of the hedgehog's hide is the source of the name rather than its ability to curl up into a ball. The common name for the "sea urchin" in a number of Semitic languages is literally "hedgehog of the sea"—Syriac *quppĕdāʾ dĕyammāʾ*,[82] modern Arabic *qunfud al-baḥr*,[83] modern Hebrew *qippōd-yām*.[84] Now in the case of this animal it is clear that it did not receive this name from an ability to roll itself up, for the sea urchin is incapable of doing this, since it is already in the shape of a ball. The only notable feature that hedgehogs and sea urchins have in common is—again—their bristly or spiny exterior.[85]

(2) Ezekiel 7 is a long oracle of doom against the land, filled with vivid images of the horrors about to come upon the people. In this context the prophet foretells, *qĕpādâ bāʾ ûbiqšû šālôm wāʾên*, "*qĕpādâ* is coming, and they will seek *šālôm* but there shall be none" (7:25). The context here gives no support for a meaning of *qĕpādâ* connected with "roll up." If that were the case *qĕpādâ* would make no sense whatsoever in this verse. Nor could it derive from a root meaning "to cut off," the other commonly proposed meaning of *q-p-d* in Isa 38:12c. "Cutting off" would imply the annihilation of the people, which is hardly the case since they are described immediately afterwards as "seeking *šālôm*." The only nuance that works here is "to bristle (with fear)," which is the meaning of the Syriac root and underlies the identical cognate noun.[86] In the context of Ezekiel 7 the word refers to a situation opposite to well-being or security, namely terror and horror symptomized by the bristling or contraction of the skin (i.e., "goose bumps"). In any case, the usage of this noun in Ezek 7:25 would seem to give evidence that "to bristle" is the basic meaning of the Hebrew as well as the Aramaic root, not "roll/fold up" or "cut (off)."

In post-biblical Hebrew *q-p-d* is not attested in the *piel* but rather in the *hiphil* with the meaning "to be angry, insult; be particular about,

---

[82] Payne Smith, *A Compendious Syriac Dictionary*, 497.

[83] Wehr, *A Dictionary of Modern Written Arabic*, 793. The Greek word for "hedgehog," ἐχῖνος, also means "sea urchin." The LXX translates *qippōd* with this term in Zeph 2:14; Isa 14:23; 34:11, 15).

[84] R. Alcalay, *The Complete Hebrew-English Dictionary*: מילון עברי-אנגלי שלם (rev. ed.; Bridgeport, CT: Prayer Book Press, 1974) col. 2318.

[85] Greek uses the term ἐχῖνος for both the hedgehog and the sea urchin.

[86] Payne Smith, *Thesaurus Syriacus*, col. 3687; Payne Smith, *A Compendious Syriac Dictionary*, 512–13.

care for."[87] J. Levy may be correct in deriving this extended sense of the root from the more basic nuance, "to draw together"[88]—i.e., in reference to the skin contracting or bristling with anger (whereas in Syriac the contraction of the skin is connected with the emotion of fear). There is no indication that it has anything to do with rolling/folding up.

Thus far we have seen nothing in Biblical or post-biblical Hebrew to justify "roll/fold up" as a possible or legitimate translation of *q-p-d* in Isa 38:12c. To support this translation, lexicographers appeal to the cognate languages. A number of the standard Hebrew lexica and other studies adduce the Arabic cognate *q-f-ḏ* in support of the "rolling up" hypothesis, asserting that it has the meaning, "to wind a turban (on the head)."[89] But the appeal to the Arabic cognate in this case is a textbook example of the misuse of lexical evidence. The root basically refers to a type of ailment of horses or camels that leaves a *raised* bump on the surface of the leg or foot. It is this sense of "raising" that is essential to the root, which by itself has nothing whatsoever to do with winding or rolling up. As regards the turban, both E. W. Lane[90] and J. G. Hava[91] cite the Arabic expression, *iᶜtamma al-qafaḏa*, which they translate, "He wound the turban (on his head, etc.)." Here both give a rather free translation of the verb, which properly means, "He attired himself with the turban."[92] The verb *iᶜtamma* (the eighth form of the root) has to do with being *tall*, and thus in the expression given actually denotes wearing headgear that makes one look taller. Hence, "nothing in the word *qafaḏa* indicates rolling or wrapping, and when it refers to a turban it is its height, rather than the action of putting it

---

[87] Jastrow, *Dictionary of the Targumim*, 398; J. Levy, *Wörterbuch über die Talmudim und Midraschim* (4 vols.; 2d ed.; Berlin: Benjamin Harz, 1924) 4. 351. The verb has the same meaning in Jewish Aramaic (ibid.).

[88] Ibid.

[89] BDB, 891: "wind turban snugly"; *HALAT*, 1043: "(die Kopfbinde) fest zusammenbinden"; KB (2d ed.), 845: "(die Kopfbinde) fest zusammenrollen" Zorell, *Lexicon*, 729: "*(cidarim capiti) totam circumvolvit*"; Jenni, *Das hebräische Piᶜel*, 238: "(die Kopfbinde) fest zusammenrollen."

[90] E. W. Lane, *Arabic-English Lexicon* (8 vols.; London: Williams and Norgate, 1863–93 [reprint: 2 vols.; Cambridge: Islamic Texts Society, 1984]) 2148.

[91] J. G. Hava, *Arabic-English Lexicon* (Beirut: Catholic Press, 1951) 619.

[92] See M. Ibn Manẓūr, *Lisān al-ᶜArab* (20 vols.; Beirut: Dār Beirut lil-Tibāᶜa walNašr, 1955) 3. 364–65.

on, that is highlighted. . . . The Arabic root . . . by itself never carries the meaning 'to roll up.'"[93]

In the course of our discussion we have touched on Syriac *q-p-d*, which refers to contracting or something that happens the to skin—bristling, shrivelling, shrinking, etc. The only nominal derivative in Syriac is *qĕpādāʾ*, "shrunkenness; bristling, stiffening from terror."[94] How, then, can Brockelmann list "zusammenrollen" as one of the Syriac root's meanings?[95] Listings like this are misleading because they fail to distinguish widely attested usages in the language (e.g, "to bristle, shrink, wrinkle") from what appear to be unique *ad hoc* renderings—in this case, *translations of Isa 38:12c*. The Peshitta translates v. 12c with the cognate verb: *ʾtqpdw ʾyk syrs ḥyy*, "My life has been X-ed like threads/cords," where X is probably to be rendered "shrunk" or the like. In his *Lexicon Syriacum* K. Brockelmann gives the definition "convolutus est" ("rolled up") under the *ethpeal* of this root. But this is immediately followed by the notation "Js 38 12."[96] In other words, his translation represents his *ad hoc* interpretation of the Syriac root in this one text from the Peshitta. R. Payne Smith's translation is: "contracta est instar vittae contextae vita mea," "My life has been contracted/shortened like a woven fillet." Nowhere in his discussion of this entry does he mention "to roll up" as a possible meaning.[97] This understanding of the verb as "rolled up" *in this passage* goes back at least as far as Ephrem of Syria, who translated the Peshitta's *ʾtqpdw* by *ʾtkrkw*: *ʾtkrkw ʾyk syrs ḥyyʾ dyly wzʿrw*, which R. Payne Smith translates as, "convolvuntur dies meae sicut fila . . . et breves factae sunt," "My days are rolled up like a thread . . . and have become short(ened)."[98] Similarly, the *Targum of Isaiah's ʾtqplw knḥl gydwdyn ḥyy* is to be read *ʾtqplw knwl grdyn ḥyy*, "My life has been rolled up

---

[93] Private communication from J. Kaltner. I am most grateful to Prof. Kaltner for researching the background of this verb in classical Arabic for me. On this subject, see his recent work, *The Use of Arabic in Biblical Hebrew Lexicography* (CBQMS 28: Washington: Catholic Biblical Association of America, 1996).

[94] Payne Smith, *A Compendious Syriac Dictionary*, 513.

[95] E.g., KB (2d ed.), 845; *HALAT*, 1043.

[96] *Lexicon Syriacum*, 682.

[97] Payne Smith, *Thesaurus Syriacus*, col. 3687.

[98] Ibid. The fact that Ephrem adds a second verb, *wzʿrw*, "and (my lifetime) has been shortened," may be significant for understanding the sense of *q-p-d* intended here. See below, pp. 105.

like the web of weavers."[99] But apart from this exegetical tradition associated with this single passage there is apparently no evidence that the verb ever meant "to roll/fold up" in the Aramaic dialects.[100]

Begrich claims that *q-p-d* is "evidently a technical term from the weaving profession,"[101] a view shared by Kutscher.[102] There is really no evidence for this other than the fact that it occurs in a verse that contains a number of technical terms from the weaving profession. But given this context it is possible. Nevertheless, it is difficult to see how folding or rolling up the finished piece of cloth could be a *terminus technicus* of textile manufacturing. The weaving process is concluded when the warp threads (thrum) are severed, not when the finished cloth is rolled or folded up. The latter action is incidental to its production. Furthermore, almost none of those who support the "rolled up/folded up" interpretation offers any explanation of the precise significance of this image in this context.[103]

It is not surprising, then, to find some claims that *q-p-d* means "to cut (off)." Vg has, "My life has been cut off." The Syriac translates with *ʾtqpdw*, cognate to the Hebrew. J. Payne Smith lists as one meaning of the *ethpeal*, "to be shortened, cut off (as ropes)."[104] But though she does not supply source references with definitions in her dictionary, there can be little doubt that the text she has in mind is the Peshitta of Isa 38:12, where *ʾyk syrs* can be translated "like ropes" (or better in this context, "like cords, threads"). R. Payne Smith's comprehensive Syriac lexicon lists no such meaning.[105] Again, "cut off" is an *ad hoc* translation that ignores the wider lexical evidence in the attempt to find a meaning that seems to fit a particular context. In conclusion, the evidence is also wanting to justify "cut (off)" as a viable translation of Hebrew *q-p-d*.[106]

---

[99] See Begrich, *Der Psalm des Hiskia*, 29; Stenning, *The Targum of Isaiah*, xxi, 126.

[100] The online *Comprehensive Aramaic Lexicon* (<http//:cal1.cn.huc.edu>) lists "to roll up" as a meaning of the Syriac root, but associates this with Isa 38:12 only.

[101] *Der Psalm des Hiskia*, 28.

[102] *The Language and Linguistic Background of the Isaiah Scroll (1QIsaᵃ)*, 269.

[103] Barthélemy (*Critique textuelle de l'Ancien Testament* 2. 266) notes that the image is that of the weaver *rolling up* his finished work so that the loom might be free (for someone else to use)! This strikes me as an exceptionally anemic image, hardly the basis of a powerful simile of death like the others that occur in IBa.

[104] Payne Smith, *A Compendious Syriac Dictionary*, 513.

[105] Payne Smith, *Thesaurus Syriacus*, col. 3687.

[106] Symmachus, Aquila, and Theodotion show no awareness of "roll up" or "cut

The foregoing discussion demonstrates a total lack of evidence from Hebrew or its ancient cognate languages upon which to base the translation "to roll/fold up" or "cut off" for *qpdty* in Isa 38:12. Hence despite its many adherents, this line of interpretation should be abandoned.

A minority of interpreters, having given up on making any sense of *qpdty*, turn to an alternative reading offered by 1QIsa[a]—*sprty*, which likewise occurs in the *piel*. Whereas in Biblical Hebrew this verb form can only mean "to count, recount, tell," in post-biblical Hebrew it also has the meaning "to cut, shear." In the present passage it would have to have the latter sense, as the context supplies no suitable object for "count, tell," etc.[107] De Boer[108] and G. R. Driver[109] have argued that this word means "to cut" in Isa 38:12. But while de Boer characterizes this reading as "an explanation of the *hapax legomenon* of M[T],"[110] in Driver's view it "makes sense as good as, if not actually preferable to, that of the Massoretic text."[111] Driver stands virtually alone in

---

off" as translation options for *qippadtî*. Symmachus and Aquila translate with forms of the verb συσπάω, "to draw together, shrivel up, shrink," while Theodotion employs στενόω, "to contract, narrow." These translators thus place the Hebrew verb within the semantic range of Syriac *q-p-d*. The case of the LXX is somewhat more complicated, which uses the verb πήγνυμι. It renders the MT's *kĕʾōhel rōʿî qippadtî*, "like one who sets up (πήξας) a tent and then takes it down"—thus taking *qippadtî* with the preceding rather than the following words. It is not easy to follow the LXX here. In no Semitic language is the root *q-p-d* attested with the meaning "to set up (a tent)." But the LXX uses πήγνυμι to translate Hebrew *q-p-ʾ* in several passages (Exod 15:8; Job 10:10; Sir 43:19). Did it "read" *q-p-ʾ* in Isa 38:12c?

[107] R. Weiss put forth an ingenious theory to explain this variant reading ("Textual Notes," *Textus* 6 [ed. S. Talmon; Jerusalem: Magnes, 1968] 127–28). He notes that where earlier biblical books have the root *p-q-d* in the sense of "counting, numbering (the people)," later tradition tended to substitute the root *s-p-r* (*piel*) for this purpose. A prime example is 2 Sam 24:2 // 1 Chr 21:2. Weiss speculates that the Qumran scribe, seeing *qpdty* in the text he was copying, might have construed this difficult *hapax* as *pqdty*—especially in light of this form's earlier occurrence in v. 10c—and substituted the more "modern" term, *sprty*. But this hypothesis is unlikely because of the fact that "count" simply does not fit in this verse. Weiss wants to have "days" as the object of the verb, but both "days" and "years" in v. 10 are too far removed from the present verse for the poet to have taken them as objects of this verb. There is nothing for the poet to "count" here, and so Weiss's explanation of 1QIsa[a]'s reading is improbable.

[108] De Boer, "Isaiah xxxviii 9–20," 172.

[109] G. R. Driver, *The Judaean Scrolls: A Problem and a Solution* (Oxford: Blackwell, 1965) 444. Driver translates the word here "cut short."

[110] De Boer, "Isaiah xxxviii 9–20," 172.

[111] Driver, *The Judaean Scrolls*, 444.

accepting the 1QIsaᵃ reading, except for the *NEB* and *REB*, which adopt his reading.[112] Perhaps the main reason why so few have accepted it is that *s-p-r* (*piel*) in the sense of "cut" is not otherwise attested until Mishnaic Hebrew. There is no other evidence of it among the Dead Sea Scrolls. Thus it seems to be an example of the tendency in the textual tradition underlying this scroll to "update" outdated or no longer understood terms with current ones.

So it seems we are left with no alternative but to make some sense of *qpdty*. An important clue to a possible solution of the riddle of this verb lies in v. 12d, if the interpretation proposed above is correct. If so, the simile (v. 12c) refers to something that happens *after* the finished piece of woven cloth is severed from the loom. The material most commonly used in Mesopotamia and probably also in Israel for making cloth was wool.[113] Now once a piece of woolen cloth is woven and removed from the loom, it requires further processing before it can be made into clothing.[114] This fact is reflected in a passage from the fourteenth-century English poem *Piers Plowman*:

> Clooth that cometh fro the wevyng is noght comly to were
> Til it be fulled under foot or in fullyng stokkes,
> Wasshen wel with water and with taseles cracched,
> Ytouked and yteynded and under taillours hande (15:450–453).

Woollen cloth must be *fulled* before it is suitable for wearing. Fulling is the process whose purpose is to clean and shrink the fabric, tightening the weave, making it stronger, denser, and more compact. The fulling process can, under certain circumstances, result in dramatic shrinkage of the fabric. Cleaning the fabric is necessary to remove the natural grease that adheres to the fibers, which inhibits the dyeing process. Fulling involves scouring and beating the cloth. In ancient times the latter was done by treading on it, striking it with a fuller's mallet, and

---

[112] R. E. Clements (*Isaiah 1-39* [NCB; Grand Rapids: Eerdmans; London: Marshall, Morgan, & Scott: 1980] 292) also reads the verb as *s-p-r*, following 1QIsaᵃ, but opts for a 2d masc. rather than the 1st person form.

[113] P. J. King and L. E. Stager, *Life in Biblical Israel* (Library of Ancient Israel; Louisville: Westminster John Knox Press, 2001) 147–48.

[114] See G. H. Dalman, *Arbeit und Sitte in Palästina: Band 5: Webstoff, Spinnen, Weben, Kleidung* (7 vols; Beiträge zur Forderung christlicher Theologie, 2. Reihe: Sammlung wissenschaftlicher Monographien 36; Gütersloh: Bertelsmann, 1937) 5. 145–46.

later by mechanical means ("fullyng stokkes"). We possess even less information about the fulling of cloth in ancient Israel than we do about weaving, but there are several references to fullers in the MT. Three passages mention the "Fuller's Field" (*śĕdēh kôbēs*) near Jerusalem[115] and one is thought to refer to "fullers' lye" (*bōrît mĕkab-bĕsîm*).[116] E. Jenni believes that the *qal* participle properly refers to the action of the fuller in the processing of newly woven fabric[117] whereas the *piel* participle refers to the washing of already produced clothing goods.[118]

The shrinking, tightening, and condensing of the newly woven fabric is one of the main purposes of fulling. For this reason in several Semitic languages a term denoting "shrink, condense" is used as a *terminus technicus* for fulling. In rabbinic Hebrew,[119] Aramaic,[120] and Arabic[121] "fuller" is *qaṣṣār* from the root *q-ṣ-r*, "shorten, shrink, full."[122] Unlike Hebrew *k-b-s*, this term does not refer to a particular

---

[115] 2 Kgs 18:17; Isa 7:3; 36:2.

[116] Mal 3:2.

[117] It is likely that *kibbēs* is related to Akkadian *kabāsu*, "to tread, trample," and thus originally denoted washing *fabrics* clean by treading on them (although apparently the Akkadian does not use the verb with reference to fabrics). As noted earlier, trampling washed textiles taken from the loom was one of the ways of cleaning and processing the woven fabric. It is known, for example, that cloth was fulled this way in Roman times (see "Fullo," in *A Dictionary of Greek and Roman Antiquities* [ed. W. G. Smith; London: John Murray, 1875] 551-53). It is interesting to note that properly speaking *kibbēs* is used exclusively of washing *clothes* and never of washing the body (for which *r-ḥ-ṣ* is used). Exceptions to this rule are figurative uses, such as the psalmist asking God to "thoroughly wash" him like a piece of dirty clothing (Ps 51:2, 9; the reference to being "whiter than snow" [v. 9] is more appropriate on a literal level of clothing, not human skin) and Jeremiah's command to Jerusalem to "wash your heart clean of wickedness" (Jer 4:14). Although Jer 2:22 is often translated "though you wash *yourself* with lye . . . " (*RSV*), the image is actually metaphorical, referring to washing a soiled piece of clothing like Psalm 51 (cf. the mention of being "*stained* [*niktām*]" with guilt; i.e., you can wash it and wash it, but the stain will not come out).

[118] *Das hebräische Piʿel*, 163.

[119] Jastrow, *A Dictionary of the Targumim*, 1408.

[120] Jewish Palestinian Aramaic: M. Sokoloff, *A Dictionary of Jewish Palestinian Aramaic of the Byzantine Period* (Ramat-Gan: Bar Ilan University Press, 1990) 501; Syriac: Payne Smith, *A Comprehensive Syriac Dictionary*, 516.

[121] Lane, 2533.

[122] The Akkadian cognate of *q-ṣ-r* is, by Geer's law, *k-ṣ-r*. The verb is not used of fulling but does have the nuance "condense" (see *AHw*, 456).

step in the fulling process but rather to one of its principal desired results, the compacting of the cloth's fibers.

The sense "to shrink, contract" appears to be adequately attested for Syriac *q-p-d*. According to Brockelmann, the verb has the meaning "to draw together tightly" (*constringere*) also in Arabic and Tigre.[123] For the Biblical Hebrew root this sense is also supported by the translations of Isa 38:12c by Aquila, Symmachus, and Theodotion. All three render the verb as a 3d person passive sg. or active pl., the latter being a common way of expressing the passive, as in Aramaic. The clearest is Theodotion, who renders the Hebrew verb with ἐστενώθη from στενόω, "to contract." The reading of Aquila and Symmachus is more difficult to interpret—συνέπησαν and συνεπέσθη respectively. It is not clear what verb these forms derive from. Field notes that they could be derived from συμπαίω, "to dash (or) beat (something) against," but this etymology has its problems.[124] He suggests rather συσπάω, "to draw (or) squeeze together," noting that in Lam 5:20 the LXX has this verb (συνέσπασαν) where the Syr has ʾtqpdw. Alternatively, one might propose a derivation from συμπιέζω, which also means "to squeeze together." Hence certainly Theodotion and quite possibly Aquila and Symmachus too translate *qpdty* with verbs meaning "to contract" and "to squeeze together" respectively, both of which could refer to aspects of the fulling process.[125]

I suggest that it is precisely this kind of "shrinking" that this verb refers to, similar to *q-ṣ-r* in post-biblical Hebrew, Aramaic, and Arabic. Since *qpdty* is a *hapax legomenon* in Biblical Hebrew, we have no way of knowing its usages outside of this passage. But the use of synonymous *q-ṣ-r* is instructive. This verb and its cognates are used in Hebrew and Ugaritic in a figurative sense to denote the lessening of one's days (i.e., one's lifetime).[126] Two of the Biblical Hebrew passages

---

[123] *Lexicon Syriacum*, 682: "tg. קְפַד, h. קָפַד, ar. *qfd* constrinxit ["drew tightly together"]"; see also Levy. *Wörterbuch über die Talmudim und Midraschim*, 4. 350.

[124] *Origenis Hexaplorum Quae Supersunt* 2. 505 n. Even in the NT period αι was pronounced like ε, not η, so that one would expect συνέπεσαν for Aquila's translation. And for Symmachus one would expect συνεπέθη (for συνεπαίθη), not συνεπέσθη.

[125] "To squeeze together" suggests "wringing," which was done to the cloth after it had been sufficiently trodden upon and was ready to be dried (i.e., as in Roman times; see Smith, *A Dictionary of Greek and Roman Antiquities*, 551).

[126] Hebrew: Pss 89:46; 102:24; Prov 10:27; Ugaritic: *tqṣrn ymy bʿlhn*, "shortened shall be the days of their/his lord" (G. del Olmo Lete and J. Sanmartín, *A Dictionary of the*

in which this usage occurs are from the Psalter, both in a lament context:

> *hiqṣartā yĕmê ʿălûmāyw*
> *heʿĕṭîtā ʿālāyw bûšâ*

You have shortened the days of his (the king's) youth,
you have "crowned" him with disgrace (Ps 89:46)

> *ʿinnâ badderek kōḥô*
> *qiṣṣar yāmāyw* (MT: *yāmāy*)
> *ʾōmar ʾēlî ʾal-taʿălēnî baḥăṣî yāmāy*
> *bĕdōr dōrîm šĕnôtêkā*

He has broken my strength in midcourse(?),
    he has shortened my days;
I say: "O my God, do not take me away at the midpoint of my days;
    your years last forever!" (Ps 102:23–24)

Above I mentioned Ephrem of Syria's translation of Isa 38:12c: *ʾtkrkw ʾyk syrs ḥyyʾ dyly wzʿrw*, "My lifetime is rolled up like a thread *and has become short(ened)*." Why does Ephrem add the italicized words? Despite his translation of Hebrew *q-p-d* as "roll up" he perhaps realized that in this passage the verb had something to do with shortening the psalmist's lifetime. As we shall see, the subsequent simile (v. 12e–13a) is also concerned with the reduction of the psalmist's life span.

It is not clear why the poet uses the verb *q-p-d* here rather than, say, *q-ṣ-r*. One reason may be that there is no evidence that the latter verb in Biblical Hebrew had the connotation "to full." It is possible that *q-p-d* was commonly used for this process, but this is not clear because there are no more examples of it in this period. The most likely reason for the choice of *quppadtî*, I submit, is the poet's earlier use of its anagram, *puqqadtî*, in v. 10c. The latter occurs in the third colon of IA and the former in the third colon of IB.

Ugaritic Language in the Alphabetic Tradition [trans. W. G. E. Watson; HdO 67; Leiden: Brill, 2003] 716).

A final matter to be discussed with regard to v. 12cd involves the word-order of v. 12c. The LXX's *Vorlage* apparently had the sequence *qpdty ḥyy kᵓrg*:

LXX		MT
πήξας	=	*qpdty*
τὸ πνεῦμά μου παρ' ἐμοὶ	=	*ḥyy*
ἐγένετο ὡς ἱστὸς	=	*kᵓrg*
ἐρίθου	=	*mdlh*
ἐγγιζούσης ἐκτεμεῖν	=	*ybṣᶜ*

Pace Goshen-Gottstein,[127] LXX does not translate *mdlh* by ἱστός (this word translates ᵓrg) but rather by ἐρίθου, "weaver."[128] The LXX translator evidently parsed *mdlh* as a derivative from *d-l-l* II, "to weave," a root attested in Syriac and Jewish Babylonian Aramaic.[129] He took the *-h* termination as designating a female weaver (hence ἐγγιζούσης), and perhaps understood the *m-* as a participial preformative. Although one might argue that the translator was relatively free as regards the word-order of his translation, and hence that his rendering may not correspond exactly to the word-order of the *Vorlage*, the genitival phrase ὡς ἱστὸς ἐρίθου cannot reflect a Hebrew text with any word-order but *kᵓrg mdlh*. Since the translator construed these words as a construct phrase, the order of words was fixed and could not be varied. The text before the LXX translator of v. 12cd must have read *qpdty ḥyy kᵓrg mdlh ybṣᶜ(nw?)*. With *NEB*[130] I accept the LXX's reading here as more original than that of the MT, which reflects a scribal transposition of earlier *ḥyy kᵓrg*. Compare the transposition in 1QIsaᵇ (v. 19b) of *kmwny hywm* (MT, 1QIsaᵃ) to *hywm kmwny*.

The justification for this transposition is not simply the witness of the LXX but the fact that in the case of unmarked relative clauses, especially those involving the comparative particle, the noun preceded by *k-* is followed immediately by the clause.[131] The latter is usually

---

127 Goshen-Gottstein, *The Book of Isaiah*, 168 n.

128 Male or female—ἔριθος is anceps.

129 Brockelmann, *Lexicon Syriacum*, 164; M. Sokoloff, *A Dictionary of Jewish Babylonian Aramaic of the Talmudic and Geonic Periods* (Ramat-Gan: Bar Ilan University Press; Baltimore: The Johns Hopkins University Press, 2002) 340.

130 See Brockington, *The Hebrew Text of the Old Testament*, 189.

131 E.g., Deut 32:11; Isa 61:10b; 62:1; Jer 23:29; Hos 6:3; Pss 49:13, 21; 83:15; 125:1; Job 7:2; 9:26; 11:16.

introduced by the verb, but at times by something else, such as a prepositional phrase, as in the case of Isa 53:7: *kaśśeh laṭṭebaḥ yûbāl*, "like a sheep that is led to the slaughter." This is the case in our verse: *kĕ³ereg middallâ yĕbaṣṣĕ^cennû*. Hence *k³rg* should be the last word in its colon.

[12e] *miyyôm ^cad-lāylâ tašlîmēnî*:
1QIsaᵃ: *mywm ^cd lylh tšlymny*; 1QIsaᵇ: [ ]; LXX: ἐν τῇ ἡμέρᾳ ἐκείνῃ παρεδόθην; Aquila: ἀφ᾽ ἡμέρας ἕως νυκτὸς ἐπλήρωσέν με; Symmachus: *ditto*; Theodotion: *ditto*; Vg: de mane usque ad vesperam finies me; Syriac: *mn ³ymm³ w^cdm³ llly³ ³šlmtny*; *Targum of Isaiah*: *ymmy wlylw-wty šlymw*.

Because the correlative terms "day" and "night" are frequently associated with the language of personal lament in both biblical and extrabiblical literature,[132] commentators usually interpret this bicolon as describing the poet's suffering or, more precisely, its extended continuation—hence *NAB*'s "day and night you give me over to torment." But if this were the case, the Hebrew would more likely be *yômām wālaylâ*. Rather, in this passage the words can only refer to a period "*from* day(break) *to* night(fall)."[133] *NRSV*'s translation is on the mark: "From day to night you make an end of me." The time references therefore do not denote duration (e.g., how long the poet is tormented) but mark off a definite span of time, from the beginning of day to the onset of night, within which he is or will be the object of the verb *š-l-m*.

This information helps to interpret *tašlîmēnî*. The correct understanding of the two verbs is the main exegetical problem in this bicolon. It is clear that *tašlîmēnî* must denote something negative, continuing the theme of v. 12a–d.

One line of interpretation takes the position that the standard meanings of the common Semitic root *š-l-m*, whose basic sense is "to come to an end, be finished," do not fit here and posits another root behind

---

[132] See Jer 9:1; 14:17; Pss 22:2; 32:4; 42:3; 88:1; Job 7:4; 30:16-17; Lam 2:18. The same image appears in Akkadian laments; see, for example, *Ludlul bēl nēmeqi* I 107, II 102–3, III 7–8; *CAD* M/2, 294.

[133] So *NJPSV*; cf. *NJB* (where *yôm* is rendered "dawn"). This understanding of the phrase was earlier noted by Linder ("Canticum Ezechiae," 58, 71: "binnen Tagesfrist") and Fohrer (*Das Buch Jesaja*, 2. 189: "vom Morgen bis zum Beginn der Dunkelheit").

this word. De Boer has suggested a *šaphel* form of a root *l-m-y*, cognate with Akkadian *lamû* (from earlier *lawû*), "to surround, besiege."[134] But this proposal is hardly convincing. Not only is such a verb unattested in all periods of Hebrew, but positing an unattested Hebrew verb in the extremely rare *šaphel* conjugation makes the suggestion doubly dubious. G. R. Driver appeals to an Arabic root *ṯ-l-m*, which he claims has the meaning "to afflict, torment."[135] But J. Kaltner has recently demonstrated that such a sense does not belong to the Arabic root's semantic field.[136]

A second line of interpretation is represented by Begrich's position. He derives the term in question from *š-l-m* but concludes it is necessary to look beyond Biblical Hebrew for a suitable meaning. He and others have appealed to a nuance attested in the Aramaic cognate, viz., "to hand over" (also in Akkadian), an interpretation which has found a number of adherents, especially among German scholars.[137] Since the Hebrew verb is not attested with this meaning, Begrich adds this occurrence to his list of alleged "Aramaisms" in PsHez.[138] This translation of the verb finds support in the LXX, which has παρεδόθην, "I have been handed over." The chief weakness of this interpretation is that the text contains no reference to the person/thing to whom the poet is allegedly "handed over."

The *hiphil* of *š-l-m* can mean "to finish, bring to an end."[139] Yet in the MT it is never otherwise attested with the sense of "finishing off" a person. But there is a single passage in which this root is used with a time designation, Isa 60:20: *wĕšālĕmû yĕmê ʾeblēk*, "And the days of your mourning shall come to an end." The use of the verb with time references is found only in this passage from Trito-Isaiah and appears as well in the Dead Sea Scrolls. There it is used in the *hiphil* with *yāmîm* or *qēṣ* (in the sense of a specific period of time).[140] The mean-

---

134 De Boer, "Isaiah xxxviii 9–20," 181.
135 "Isaiah i–xxxix," 56.
136 Kaltner, *The Use of Arabic in Biblical Hebrew Lexicography*, 80–81.
137 *Der Psalm des Hiskia*, 32-33. See also Wildberger, *Jesaja 28–39*, 1440, 1443; Fohrer, *Das Buch Jesaja 2.* 185, 189; Seybold, *Das Gebet des Kranken im Alten Testament*, 151 n. 32; G. Gerlemann, "שלם *šlm* genug haben," *THAT*, 2. 920; M. Wagner, *Die lexikalischen und grammatikalischen Aramaismen im alttestamentlichen Hebräisch* (BZAW 96: Berlin: Töpelmann, 1966) #310; *HALAT*, 1421.
138 *Der Psalm des Hiskia*, 33.
139 See, for example, BDB, 1022.
140 CD 4:8,10; 10:10; 4Q215 4:3.

ing in this case would be "to complete a certain period of time, bring it to an end," etc.

This is the meaning of *taslîmēnî* in v. 12e.[141] At first sight this seems unlikely, since the object of the verb is "me" (i.e., the poet) rather than a time reference. But when the poet says that God brings him to an end he means that he brings him to the end of his life[142] or, phrased in a slightly different way, he brings his *lifetime* to an end. The interchangeability of "my life, vitality" (cf. *napšî* = "my*self*") with "my life *span*" is reflected in the usages of Hebrew *ḥayyîm*, which can denote either my life principle (which thus comes close to "myself") or my life span. That the latter is the case in the present subsection is indicated by the fact that the focus of IBa is precisely the life(time) of the sufferer (*dôrî* in v. 12a and *ḥayyay* in v. 12c). This is further indicated by the use of "I" and "my life" in the "double subject construction" in v. 12c discussed above.

Support for this interpretation comes from Job 4:20, the only other passage in MT containing a correlative expression equivalent to *miyyôm . . . ᶜad-laylâ*, namely *mibbōqer lāᶜereb yukkattû*, "(In the time) from morning to evening they are shattered to pieces." J. Rimbach is no doubt correct in his paraphrase of the first colon as, "In the space of one day they are cut off."[143] M. Pope has recognized the parallel between Job 4:20–21 and Isa 38:12 and translates the latter, "Finished in a single day."[144] The idea of the wicked perishing in the space of a day—or part of a day—finds expression in a curse formula which occurs with some frequency in Babylonian entitlement *narûs*[145] with reference to anyone who removes the monument: *ūma išten lā balāssu*

---

[141] This meaning of the verb in this passage was accepted by Linder, "Canticum Ezechiae," 57, who notes that this interpretation was held by A. Knobel, F. Delitzsch, H. Grimme, J. Knabenbauer, E. Laur, and N. Schlögl (no references given). Note similarly the translation of Soggin ("Il 'Salmo di Ezechia' in Isaia 38,9–20," 4): "nel termine di un giorno mi ha finito!" (Soggin reads a 3d person verb here).

[142] See Zorrell (*Lexicon Hebraicum et Aramaicum Veteris Testamenti*, 853), who catches the correct nuance of this verb: "al[i]q[ue]m ad vitae *finem perduxit*," "to bring someone to the end of [his/her] life."

[143] J. Rimbach, "'Crushed Before the Moth' (Job 4:19)," *JBL* 100 (1981) 245.

[144] M. Pope, *Job* (AB 15; 2d ed.; Garden City, NY: Doubleday, 1973) 38.

[145] These documents are generally known by the name *kudurru*, which recent studies have shown to be a misnomer—they are not actually "boundary stones." See K. E. Slanski, "Classification, Historiography, and Monumental Authority: The Babylonian Entitlement *narûs* (*kudurrus*)," *JCS* 52 (2000) 98.

liqbû, "May (the gods named on this monument) decree that he live not even a single day (longer)."[146] The point of Isa 38:12e therefore is *how quickly* God is bringing the psalmist's life to an end. The lifetime of the protagonist, mentioned several times earlier in Part I,[147] is now reduced to less than a day, a theme very close in meaning to that of shrinking the poet's life in v. 12cd. All of this would suggest a translation like, "(In the time) from day(break) to night(fall)"[148]—or, "(Between) day(break) and night(fall)"—"you make an end of m(y) lif)e."

But Driver has raised an objection to translating the line this way. He notes that bringing someone's life to an end is something that happens in an instant and not over a period of time.[149] The *yqtl* would seem to point to a continuous or incomplete action. In light of this, I suggest that the verb be translated as a future. It is clear from what the poet has said thus far that he expects his life to end very soon. Virtually every line in the poem up to this point manifests this conviction. He sees himself on the verge of death and believes that Yhwh will not let him live out one more day. A translation of the verb in the future tense would fit this context: "(Between) day(break) and night(fall) you will finish me off."

The interpretation of *taślîmēnî* as "you will finish me off" fits perfectly with the theme of the preceding two bicola in IBa (vv. 12a–d), which might be entitled "Life Has Come to an End," and actually forms a climax to this subsection. A translation like "bring to an end, finish off" conforms well to the two similes in this section, which also allude to death through the images of the lifetime being taken away or drastically shortened. On the other hand, the translation given by Begrich ("You hand me over") not only does not fit with this theme but assumes—wrongly—that the poet begins to speak of his sufferings at this point, although he claims that the *Klagelied* ends with v. 14.

A final issue with regard to *taślîmēnî* is whether the MT's reading preserves the correct person of the verb. The MT is supported by 1QIsa[a] and 1QIsa[b], which have the same reading, as well as the Syriac

---

[146] L. W. King, *Babylonian Boundary-Stones and Memorial-Tablets in the British Museum* (London: British Museum, 1912) IV col. 4 line 7 (p. 23). Cf. *CAD* B, 51.

[147] I.e., *yāmay* and *šĕnôtāy* in v. 10a,d, *dôrî* in v. 12a.

[148] I.e., in the space of half a day, of (approximately) a twelve-hour period.

[149] "Isaiah i–xxxix," 56.

(*ʾšlmtny*) and Vg (*finies me*).[150] But on the basis of the translations of Symmachus, Aquila, and Theodotion ("from day to night he has filled me") a number of interpreters read a 3d sg. form here rather than the 2d sg.[151] Touzard's objection to the 2d person reading probably reflects the thinking of most of those who take this option: "c'est plus tard seulement que l'auteur s'addresse directement à Dieu."[152] Since in the psalmist's only other reference to Yhwh's actions toward him in Part I, i.e., in the next bicolon (v. 13bc), he speaks of God in the 3d person (*yĕšabbēr*), the 2d person is unexpected here and seems out of place. But there is evidence that the poet deliberately included *two* direct addresses to God in IBb, as did the psalmist in Ps 22:13–22. This is a case where evidence from the poetic structure should take precedence over one's sensibilities about what the poet "should" have written. (See **Rhetorical-Critical Observations** below.)

[13a] *šiwwîtî ʿad bōqer:*

1QIsaᵃ: *š/śpwty ʿd bwqr*; 1QIsaᵇ: [ ]; LXX: [ ] ἕως πρωΐ; Aquila: [ ]; Symmachus: [ ]; Theodotion: ἐτέθην ἕως πρωΐ; Vg: sperabam usque ad mane; Syriac: [ ];[153] *Targum of Isaiah*: *nhymyt ʿd ṣprʾ*.

The verb in this final colon presents even greater difficulties for the interpreter than the one in the preceding colon. No known meaning of the root *š-w-y* fits in this context. Most nineteenth- and twentieth-century commentators follow C. F. Houbigant[154] and emend to *šiwwaʿtî*, "I cry out (for help)."[155] This verb expresses some plaintive sound associated with suffering. In several poetic passages it is associated

---

[150] The *Targum of Isaiah* is alone in reading a 3d masc. pl. here: *šlymw*: "(my days and nights) have come to an end."

[151] Touzard, "De la conservation du texte hébreu," 92; Fohrer, *Das Buch Jesaja 2*. 185; Castellino, "Lamentazioni individuali accadiche ed ebraiche," 153. On the other hand, Duhm (*Das Buch Jesaja*, 280) emends the verb to a 1st sg. form based on the LXX's παρεδόθην.

[152] "De la conservation du texte hébreu," 92.

[153] Here the Syriac shows a haplography due to homoeoteleuton. The copyist's eye skipped from the first *mywm ʿd lylh tšlmny* to the second, omitting v. 13 entirely.

[154] Begrich (*Der Psalm des Hiskia*, 33) mentions Houbigant as the source of this suggestion, but he provides no bibliographical reference.

[155] Ibid., 52; Wildberger, *Jesaja 28–39*, 1443.

with the correlatives "day . . . night"[156] or "dawn,"[157] since this is the time when Yhwh is expected to bring his saving help.[158]

Such an interpretation encounters an objection similar to that of Driver's with regard to *taslîmēnî*: if the verb in this colon denotes some action that takes place over a period of time (i.e., "until dawn"), one would expect a *yqtl* form. Moreover, an interpretation that emphasizes the suffering of the poet does not fit the theme of IBb, viz., "Life Has Come to an End."

1QIsaᵃ has a very different reading for this word—*š/śpwty*. This might appear at first glance to derive from post-biblical *š-p-p* or *š-p-y*, "to crush."[159] Yet an intransitive sense is needed here. Driver reads the word in question as *śpwty*, not *špwty*, and analyzes it as *śappôtî*, cognate with Arabic *šaffa*, "to be worn out with pain."[160] Yet this reading too presumes a verb denoting continuous action, despite the *qtl* form. There is a more plausible explanation of the form in 1QIsaᵃ. Driver is on the right track in recognizing that the first letter is a *śin* rather than a *šin*. In his important work on the Hebrew of the Dead Sea Scrolls, E. Qimron points to a number of instances in which an original *samek* is replaced by a *śin* in the scrolls:[161] e.g., Isa 3:18 (1QIsaᵃ: *hšbyśym*; MT: *hšbysym*), 37:30 (1QIsaᵃ: *śpyḥ*; MT: *spyḥ*), 57:5 (1QIsaᵃ: *śᶜpy*; MT: *sᶜpy*). In addition, he gives examples from Sirach and other literature from the late OT period which indicate that the auditory confusion of *samek* and *śin* was not confined to 1QIsaᵃ but reflects the widespread loss of distinction between these two phonemes in this period.[162] *śpwty* therefore could theoretically be explained either as a confusion of the two phonemes or a hypercorrect spelling of *spwty*. Such a form would presumably be from a root *s-p-p*, but no such derivation works in this context.[163] I suggest that the MT and 1QIsaᵃ are each partly correct—i.e., each correctly preserves one or more of the radicals of the

---

[156] Job 16:20; Ps 88:1.

[157] Pss 88:14; 119:147.

[158] 1 Sam 11:9; Pss 5:4; 46:5; 90:14; 143:8.

[159] Cf. the related Biblical Hebrew root *š-w-p*, "to crush," probably attested in Gen 3:15 (see *HALAT*, 1342).

[160] Driver, "Isaiah i–xxxix," 56.

[161] E. Qimron, *The Hebrew of the Dead Sea Scrolls*, 28–30.

[162] Note also *śukkô* in Lam 2:6, a hypercorrect spelling for *sukkô*, "his tent-shrine."

[163] A root *s-p-p* is attested once in Biblical Hebrew, in the *hithpolel* (Ps 84:11), and apparently means "to lie at the threshold (*sap*)."

root this term derives from, but neither preserves all of them, though 1QIsaᵃ preserves two of the radicals. The root in question would be *s-p-y*, which in the *qal* means (1) "to sweep away (transitive)" and (2) "to vanish, pass away (intransitive)."[164] The latter occurs in Deut 29:18 and probably in Jer 12:4. In Jewish Aramaic[165] it can bear the meaning "to perish, die" ("umkommen"), and may have had such a nuance in earlier Hebrew. Thus I posit as the original reading *spyty*—a *qal* form, either *sāpîtî*, "I shall have vanished, perished," or possibly the *qal* passive, **suppêtî*,[166] "I shall have been swept away." Both forms would be identical in the consonantal text. Thus in the MT's *šiwwîtî* the *š* represents a misunderstanding of an earlier *ś*, which in turn is a hypercorrection of original *s*; we can never know, of course, whether the scribe who produced 1QIsaᵃ intended שׁפותי to be read *špwty* or *śpwty*, but this too would have derived from a word with initial *samek*. As regards the second root letter of this verb, 1QIsaᵃ is no doubt correct on reading *p* rather than *w*—the latter reflects an auditory error: /v/ for /f/ (i.e., spirantized *p*).[167] But the MT's reading of *y* as the third letter is to be preferred over against *w* in 1QIsaᵃ. The reading *spyty* (*qal*), "to perish, vanish/be swept away," forms a suitable complement to *š-l-m* (*hiphil*), "to finish off," in the preceding colon.

But if the verb behind 1QIsaᵃ's *š/śpwty* is actually *sāpîtî*, how is ʿad bōqer to be understood? As noted earlier, the *qtl* form speaks against an interpretation suggesting duration. Are we left, then, with "I have perished/vanished until morning"? This makes no sense, of course. The key to the correct interpretation of this colon is catching the precise nuance of the preposition ʿad in this colon. In v. 13a it cannot be translated as "until" as in v. 12e. Rather, here it has the specific nuance "by,"[168] as in the English idiom, "by the time X happens."[169] The

---

[164] *HALAT*, 721; cf. BDB, 705.

[165] According to *HALAT*, 721.

[166] For this form, see Williams, "The Passive *Qal* Theme in Hebrew," 47. The only example Williams cites of the first-person singular *qal* in the *qtl* of a *lamed-he* verbal stem is *ʿuśśêtî* in Ps 139:15.

[167] Sokoloff (*A Dictionary of Jewish Palestinian Aramaic of the Byzantine Period*, 563) gives *šw(w)y* (with medial /v/) as an alternative spelling of *špy* (with medial /f/), "peaceful, pleasant" (from *š-p-y*). Note also Hebrew *kôkāb* ("star") < **kawkab* < **kabkab(u)*.

[168] See R. J. Williams, *Hebrew Syntax: An Outline* (2d ed.; Toronto/Buffalo: University of Toronto Press, 1976) §311.

[169] Note the same usage of ʿad in fifth-century Aramaic, in an economic text:

preposition has this meaning in at least four OT passages, and interestingly in all of these it governs the object *bōqer* (or a construct phrase with *bōqer*) as in Isa 38:13a:

Judg 6:31:
ʾăšer yārîb lô yûmat ʿad-habbōqer
Whoever contends for him (i.e., Baal) shall be put to death
by morning.

1 Sam 25:22:
kōh-yaʿăśeh ʾĕlōhîm lĕʾōyĕbê dāwīd wĕkōh yōsîp ʾim-ʾašʾîr mikkol-
ʾăšer-lô ʿad-habbōqer maštîn bĕqîr
Thus may God do to David's enemies and more besides if *by morning* I leave remaining a (single) male from among all his adherents.

1 Sam 25:34:
kî lûlê mihart wattābōʾty[170] *liqrāʾtî kî ʾim nôtar lĕnābāl ʿad-ʾôr*
bōqer maštîn bĕqîr
... unless you had made haste and come to meet me, truly *by morning* light there would not have been left to Nabal so much as a (single) male.

2 Sam 17:22:
wayyāqom dāwīd wĕkol-hāʿām ʾăšer ʾittô wayyaʿabrû ʾet-
hayyardēn ʿad-ʾôr habbōqer ʿad-ʾaḥad lôʾ neʿdār ʾăšer lôʾ-ʿābar
ʾet-hayyardēn
And David and all the people who were with him arose and crossed the Jordan; *by morning* light not so much as one was left who had not crossed[171] the Jordan.

---

wʾšlmnk lky ʿd 30 lprmty, "I will pay you in full by the 30th of Pharmuthi" (A. Cowley, *Aramaic Papyri of the Fifth Century B.C.* [Osnabrück: Zeller, 1967 (reprint of the 1923 edition)] #35:5–6 [p. 130]) and in Jewish Babylonian Aramaic (Sokoloff, *A Dictionary of Jewish Babylonian Aramaic of the Talmudic and Geonic Periods*, 843–44).

[170] This is the reading of the Kethib. The Qere omits the -y.
[171] The use of the *qtl* form (*ʿābar*) here denotes completed action with respect to "by morning light," as in the case of *sāpîtî*.

It is noteworthy that three of these four texts occur in a context of the threat of imminent death, as in the case of Isa 38:12e–13a.

Finally, let us return to the Joban parallel cited above, 4:20. As the first colon (v. 20a) is virtually identical in meaning to Isa 38:12e, the second cola (i.e., Job 4:20b and Isa 38:13a) are also very close in meaning. In Job 4:20b the verb is *yōʾbēdû*, "they perish." There is, of course, no difference in meaning between "to perish (forever)" in Job 4:20b and "to vanish" in Isa 38:13a. Thus Job 4:20b provides some confirmation to the interpretation of Isa 38:13a proposed here. The phrase *sāpîtî ʿad-bōqer*, therefore, is to be translated as a future perfect, denoting an action that will have taken place by the following morning: "By morning I shall have perished/vanished."[172] This fits with the future tense in the preceding colon, "you will finish me off."

[13b] *kāʾărî kēn yĕšabbēr kol-ʿaṣmôtāy*:

1QIsa[a]: *kʾry kn yšbwr kwl ʿṣmwty*; 1QIsa[b]: [ ]; LXX: ὡς λέοντι· οὕτως τὰ ὀστᾶ μου συνέτριψεν; Aquila: [ ]; Symmachus: [ ]; Theodotion: ὡς λέων οὕτως συνέτριψεν πάντα τὰ ὀστᾶ μου; Vg: quasi leo sic contrivit omnia ossa mea; Syriac: [ ]; *Targum of Isaiah: kʾryʾ dnhym wtbr kl grmy ḥywtʾ*.

The MT has the *zakef* over *kāʾărî*, separating it from the following material. The LXX also appears to separate ὡς λέοντι from what follows. But that *kāʾărî* goes with the rest of v. 13b is hardly in doubt, considering the correlative force of *kĕ-* . . . *kēn*, "as . . . so." Note the same construction involving these correlative terms in v. 14a.

The lion, native to parts of the Near East in antiquity, was the most feared predator in the region. Over the centuries the population of this leonine subspecies has been reduced to a few in India today. Throughout the literature of the ancient Near East this animal was a symbol of ferocity.

In the MT *š-b-r ʿăṣāmôt*, with God as subject, appears only here and in Lam 3:4:

> *billâ bĕśārî wĕʿōrî*
> *šibbar ʿaṣmōtāy*

---

[172] A close semantic parallel to this construction is provided by Isa 17:14: *bĕṭerem bōqer ʾênennû*, "By morning, it [the terror] is no more" (*NJPSV*).

> He has made my flesh and my skin waste away,
> he has shattered my bones.

In this passage the expression is not part of a simile. What it and Isa 38:13b have in common is that in both *š-b-r* is in the *piel* (according to the MT) and Yhwh is the subject of the verb, the bones being those of the poet.

1QIsaᵃ has a variant reading—*yšbwr* (*qal*). But the MT is no doubt correct in pointing the verb as *piel*.[173] E. Jenni observes that only things that would ordinarily be considered "breakable" (such as wooden objects, pottery, etc.) are objects of this verb in the *qal*, whereas in the *piel* it governs much harder objects, e.g., things made of stone and even metal, which a person cannot break by his own strength.[174] This fact in itself shows that there is a more "intensive" aspect to the *piel* vis-à-vis the *qal* of *š-b-r*. One may go further and state that when the *piel* governs the object "bones" it has overtones of predation. In such cases the verb does not simply mean to cause bones to fracture but to shatter or crush them.[175] The underlying image in this instance is that of a wild beast crushing with powerful jaws. The more accurate translation would therefore be "shatter" or "crush" rather than "break."

There are two other OT texts where lions and Yhwh respectively do violence to the bones of human beings: Dan 6:25 (English 24) and Ps 51:10. The verbs employed in these passages also properly denote "shattering" or "crushing" of bones.

The first passage runs in part:

Before they (Daniel's accusers) reached the bottom of the den the lions overpowered them and *haddīqû* their bones.

---

[173] It is possible that in post-biblical usage the *qal* came to replace the *piel* in the topos of lions breaking the bones of human beings, and this is why we find the *qal* in 1QIsaᵃ. Note the *qal* participle in *ʾrywt šwbry ʿṣm ʾdyrym*, "lions that break the bones of the strong," in 1QH 5:7.

[174] Jenni, *Das hebräische Piʿel*, 181.

[175] Instructive here is the difference in meaning between the Akkadian verb *šatāqu* in the G-stem (= *qal*) and in the D-stem (= *piel*). In the G-stem it means "to split" (intransitive); in the D-stem, "to fissure, split into many parts" (intransitive). See *CAD* Š/2, 193–94.

It is clear from the way this verb, *d-q-q* (*haphel*), is used elsewhere in Daniel that it denotes (1) a violent and hostile action and (2) an action that does not merely fracture but shatters the object into pieces.[176] Dan 2:45 speaks of the stone hewn by God that shatters (*haddeqqet*) the statue of iron, bronze, clay, silver, and gold; 7:7, 19 describes the fourth, terrible beast that "devoured and broke in pieces" (*ʾākĕlâ [û]maddĕqâ*) and trampled on the remains with its feet.

Ps 51:10 is the only biblical passage aside from Isa 38:13 and Lam 3:4 where the poet speaks of Yhwh doing violence to his bones:

> *tašmîꜥēnî śāśôn wĕśimḥâ*
> *tāgēlnâ ꜥăṣāmôt dikkîtā*

> Let me hear[177] rejoicing and gladness;
> let the bones you have crushed rejoice!

Although a number of translations have "broken" rather than "crushed," the verb *d-k-y* (*piel*) does not mean simply to break bones. Cf. the related roots *d-k-ʾ* ("to beat to pieces, crush"), *d-w-k* ("to crush in a mortar"),[178] (Aramaic) *d-k-k* ("to crush"), and *d-q-q* ("to crush, pulverize").[179] Here too one might understand Ps 51:10 as alluding to the action of a predatory beast that crushes the bones of its victims with its terrible bite.[180]

These data support the MT reading of *š-b-r piel* rather than the *qal* in Isa 38:13b. Yhwh is likened to a raging lion who does not merely break but shatters/crushes the bones of its victim. The use of the *yqtl* in

---

[176] See Vogt, *Lexicon Linguae Aramaicae Veteris Testamenti*, 45: "contudit, comminuit."

[177] Possibly, one should read *taśbîꜥēnî* here ("sate me" = the Syriac [*ʾsbꜥyny*]). See M. L. Barré, "Mesopotamian Light on the Idiom *nāśāʾ nepeš*," *CBQ* 52 (1990) 50 n. 19.

[178] As a verb the root occurs only in Num 11:8, with reference to crushing manna in a mortar. Note the nominal derivative *mĕdôkâ*, "mortar," in the same passage.

[179] For a discussion of these related roots, see H. F. Fuhs, "רכא *dākhāʾ*," *TDOT*, 3. 195–208. Note "The Semantic Field 'To Crush, Pulverize'" (p. 195).

[180] On the other hand, the position espoused by some early twentieth-century commentators, namely that the reference is to some disease or physical infirmity of the poet, does not commend itself. See E. R. Dalglish, *Psalm Fifty-One in Light of Ancient Near Eastern Patternism* (Leiden: Brill, 1962) 141–42: "The expression 'bones which thou hast crushed' . . . does not suggest that the psalmist was physically ill."

this context suggests life-threatening trauma to the victim and possibly repeated attacks by the lion.

This interpretation finds some confirmation in *kol ʿaṣmôtay*. Only here in the MT is Yhwh said to crush *all* of someone's bones. An attack by a lion may leave a person with several bones crushed (e.g., in the arms and legs). But "all my bones" implies a predator's assault which has left no bone unshattered.

[13d] {*miyyôm ʿad-laylâ tašlîmēnî*}:

1QIsaᵃ: *mywm ʿd lylh tšlymny*; 1QIsaᵇ: [ ]*ẏlh tšlymny*; LXX: ἀπὸ γὰρ τῆς ἡμέρας ἕως τῆς νυκτὸς παρεδόθην; Aquila: [ ]; Symmachus: [ ]; Theodotion: [ ]; Vg: de mane usque ad vesperam finies me; Syriac: [ ]; *Targum of Isaiah*: *ymmy wlylwwty šlymw*.

As noted earlier, this colon is repeated from v. 12e and hence is secondary,[181] although it is difficult to identify precisely what in the text "triggered" its addition at this point. Sweeney calls it a "refrain,"[182] but this is unlikely. The fact that in its first occurrence (v. 12e) it forms an integral part of the bicolon vv. 12e–13a, whereas in v. 13d it does not, argues that it is not a refrain.

The secondary character of this colon is apparent from several considerations. First, as we have seen, v. 12e, with the time references to "day" and night," is properly continued in the next colon by *ʿad-bōqer*, "by morning." The expressions "From day(break) . . . to night(fall) . . . by morning" form a continuous time sequence.[183] Verse 13d is disconnected from this sequence and is thus a misplaced, truncated fragment of this cohesive image. Second, prescinding from v. 13d, IBa and IBb are structurally identical. Each contains three bicola, the

---

[181] The secondary character of this colon, i.e., that it is an erroneous repetition from v. 12e, is maintained by a number of commentators. Touzard ("De la conservation du texte hébreu," 94) calls it "douteuse" and also doubts that it was present in the earliest recensions of the LXX. He further notes that it was considered secondary by T. K. Cheyne. This view is shared by Duhm, *Das Buch Jesaja*, 280–81; Linder, "Canticum Ezechiae," 58; Begrich, *Der Psalm des Hiskia*, 33; Wildberger, *Jesaja 28–39*, 1443; Kaiser, *Isaiah 13–39*, 398; Fohrer, *Das Buch Jesaja*, 2. 185; and Blenkinsopp, *Isaiah 1–39*, 481.

[182] M. A. Sweeney, *Isaiah 1–39* (FOTL 16; Grand Rapids: Eerdmans, 1996) 489.

[183] Another reason for maintaining that vv. 12e and 13a are a unit is the alphabetic run beginning in the former and continuing in the latter. See below under **Rhetorical-Critical Observations**.

first two of which contain similes (see below under **Rhetorical-Critical Observations**). Verse 13d is a secondary colon that disrupts this pattern. Third, vv. 12e–13a make up the last in a series of the three bicola that constitute IBa. All three have as their subject the ending of life, which is not the topic of IBb, where v. 13d occurs. Finally, as noted earlier, there is only one instance in PsHez of the last member of a bicolon or tricolon containing more than three words, namely v. 14d. As the last member of a tricolon, v. 13d with four words would be unusually long.

[14a] *kĕsûs ʿāgûr kēn ʾăṣapṣēp*:

1QIsaᵃ: *ksws ʿwgr kn ʾṣpṣp*; 1QIsaᵇ: *ksyʾs ʿgwr k̊n̊[ ]*; LXX: ὡς χελιδών, οὕτως φρωνήσω; Aquila: [ ] *equus agor*[184] [ ]; [ ] αγουρ ορνίσω; Symmachus: *sicut hirundo inclusa sic cantabo*; [ ] ἐγκεκλεισμένη τρίβω; Theodotion: *sis agor*;[185] [ ] αγουρ στρουθίσω; Vg: *sicut pullus hirundinis sic clamabo*; Syriac: *ʾyk snwnyʾ dmnṣrʾ nṣrt*; *Targum of Isaiah*: *kswsyʾ dʾḥyd wmnṣyp kyn nṣypyt*.

In v. 14ab the psalmist likens the plaintive sounds he had uttered during his suffering to those produced by certain birds. The name of the bird(s) in this simile consists of two nouns, both of which are *dis legomena* in the MT, found elsewhere only in Jer 8:7. The problem of identification is complicated by the fact that in the Jeremiah passage the two nouns are joined by the copula *wĕ-* and by the variant reading *sîs* (Qere) for *sûs* (Kethib) in both passages.[186]

One frequently encounters that claim that *ʿāgûr* is a gloss. But the mere fact that the second noun is connected with *sîs/sûs* in Jer 8:7 as well makes this quite unlikely. Moreover, recent epigraphic evidence has rendered this claim untenable.

A singularly important piece of evidence for the identification of the *sû/îs ʿāgûr* came to light with the publication of the Deir ʿAllā texts.

---

[184] Jerome is the source of this reference for Aquila's translation, and also for that of Symmachus and Theodotion. Obviously by *equus* here Jerome indicates that Aquila had read *sws* as the Hebrew word for "horse" (= Greek ἵππος). See Field, *Origenis Hexaplorum Quae Supersunt* 2. 506–07 n. 39.

[185] See previous note.

[186] Both passages show *sws* in the consonantal MT. But whereas in Isa 38:14 the *waw* is pointed as *shureq* (*sûs*), in Jer 8:7 it is pointed with the *hireq* (*sîs*).

The so-called "First Combination" contains this bird-name (lines 7–8):

ky.ss^cgr.ḥrpt.nšr[187]
For the *ss^cgr* reproaches the griffon-vulture. . . .[188]

Although a fair amount of controversy still complicates the interpretation of this section of the inscription, P. K. McCarter, Jr., and J. A. Hackett are no doubt correct in maintaining a translation like the one given above. First, the name of this bird is written without the word-divider and governs what is to all appearances a singular verb.[189] Second, the basic thrust of the section in which this line occurs is part of a common ancient Near Eastern topos describing the "perversion" of the cosmos, signaled by a reversal of roles or of the characteristic behavior of people and animals. The reference to the *ss^cgr* "reproach[ing]" the large, intimidating griffon-vulture is part of this topos. The writer evidently sees something "unnatural" about this bird's squawking at such a formidable fowl. Hence if the griffon-vulture is large and formidable, the *ss^cgr* must be the opposite—small and normally timid. Several conclusions follow from this. (1) *sw/ys ^cgwr* in Isa 38:14a, without the copula, is the correct form rather than the form in Jer 8:7. The two words should be written as one, or perhaps parsed as a noun construct chain or a noun modified by an adjective. In any case, the two words together make up the name of a single species of bird.[190] (2) *sw/ys ^cgwr* is a small bird of some kind.

G. A. Rendsburg has proposed that Deir ʿAllā *ss^cgr*/Hebrew *sû/îs-ʿāgûr* finds its etymon in a bird-name mentioned in a third-millennium Eblaite list: *sa-su-ga-lum*.[191] Since L-signs in Eblaite regularly corre-

---

[187] In discussing the Deir ʿAllā texts I use the transliteration of J. A. Hackett, *The Balaam Text from Deir ʿAllā* (HSM 31; Chico, CA: Scholars Press, 1980). The text cited here appears on p. 25.

[188] Although *nšr* can on occasion denote the eagle, more frequently it designates the griffon-vulture. See G. R. Driver, "Birds in the Old Testament: I: Birds in Law," *PEQ* 87 (1955) 8–9.

[189] P. K. McCarter, Jr., "The Balaam Texts from Deir ʿAllā: The First Combination," *BASOR* 239 (1980) 49–60; Hackett, *The Balaam Text*, 25, 27.

[190] Hackett, *The Balaam Text*, 47; McCarter, "The Balaam Texts from Deir ʿAllā," 54. The LXX, Vg, the Syriac, and the *Targum of Isaiah* corroborate that the name designates a single species of bird.

[191] G. A. Rendsburg, "Eblaite *sa-su-ga-lum* = Hebrew *ss^cgr*," in *Eblaitica: Essays on the Ebla Archives and Eblaite Language: Volume 3* (ed. C. H. Gordon and G. A. Rendsburg; Winona Lake, IN: Eisenbrauns, 1992) 151–53.

spond to /r/ in other Semitic languages, the *lum* (/rum/) poses no major problem for his theory. Minus the Eblaite nominative case-ending *-u* and the mimation (*-m*), the word in question could have been realized phonetically as /sasugar/ or more precisely—given the evidence from Deir ʿAllā, Isaiah, and Jeremiah—/sasʿugar/. But three problems with Rendsburg's identification come to mind. (1) As he admits, in the Eblaite syllabary the sound /s/ is usually expressed by Z-signs. However, he does provide a handful of examples in which the sound is represented by S-signs. (2) Although the vocalization of Deir ʿAllā *ssʿgr* is unknown, the second element is *ʿāgûr* in the two examples in the MT. This fact does not fit well with Rendsburg's hypothesis, since the order of the vowels (/a-u/)is reversed in the Eblaite word (/u-a/). However, in 1QIsaᵃ this second element is written *ʿwgr*, which points to a vocalization /ʿūgār/ (or /ʿōgār/)—unless this is a scribal error. (3) Finally, it is difficult to see how an original /sas/ could have become /sūs/ or /sīs/. On the other hand, there is no assurance that the vowel letter in the first syllable in the Hebrew occurrences is original and not a scribal alteration.[192]

At present the consensus of opinion is that the species in question is some kind of swallow or swift. Rendsburg, on the other hand, identifies it as the golden oriole.[193] But on this point he is certainly not correct, as we shall see.

Important data on the identity of this bird are also provided by the ancient versions. In both Isa 38:14a and Jer 8:7a the LXX has χελιδών, "swallow." Vg has *pullus hirundinis*, "the young of a swallow," in Isa 38:14a and simply *hirundo*, "swallow," in Jer 8:7. The *Targum of Isaiah* has *swsyʾ*, "swallow" or "swift," in Isa 38:14a and two words, *kwrkyʾ wsnwnytʾ*, "and a crane (or "swallow" or "swift"?)[194] and a swallow,"

---

[192] W. G. Lambert's explanation on this point seems reasonable: "The *w*'s in the Masoretic text need not go back to the author, but can have been inserted later . . ." (review of C. H. Gordon and G. A. Rendsburg, *Eblaitica: Essays on the Ebla Archives and Eblaite Language: Volume 3* [Winona Lake, IN; Eisenbrauns, 1992], in *Bulletin of the School of Oriental and African Studies* 58 [1995] 349).

[193] Rendsburg, "Eblaite *sa-su-ga-lum* = Hebrew *ssʿgr*," 153.

[194] Payne Smith (*A Compendious Syriac Dictionary*, 211) defines *kwrkyʾ* as "a crane," but follows the definition with "perh[aps] a swift or a swallow." Brockelmann (*Lexicon Syriacum*, 346) also defines it as a crane (*grus*). The matter is complicated by the fact that the word is thought to derive from Akkadian *kurkû*, whose meaning is not certain (*CAD* K, 561-63 defines it as a "goose"; *AHw*, 510 is more vague: "eine Haushuhnart").

in Jer 8:7. The Syriac has *snwnyt² dmnṣr²*, "a twittering swallow," in Isa 38:14a and *kwrky² wsnwnyt²* (= the *Targum of Isaiah*) in Jer 8:7.

Some evidence is provided by other ancient Near Eastern languages. J. A. Hackett translates the Deir ʿAllā bird-name as "swift," noting Jewish Aramaic *sûsyā²*.[195] But M. Jastrow gives "swallow" as the meaning of this term.[196] McCarter's translation agrees with Hackett's, but he allows "swallow" as a possibility.[197]

What help does the Eblaite bird-list cited by Rendsberg provide toward identifying the species in question? In the list *sa-su-ga-lum* is equated with Sumerian nam-dar-mušen. But what bird does the Sumerian refer to? The matter appears to have been settled in a review of the book in which Rendsburg's article appeared. The judgment of one of the foremost contemporary Sumerologists/Assyriologists, W. G. Lambert, is that "[Rendsburg's] conclusion is completely sound."[198] Here he is referring to the identification of the Eblaite *sa-su-ga-lum* with the Sumerian bird-name. However, Lambert maintains that Rendsburg's identification of the bird in question as a golden oriole is incorrect. "The Sumerian in the list is not to be read nam-dar, but sim-dar, since nam is not the name of a bird while sim is. It equates with the Akkadian *sinntu*, customarily rendered 'swallow'."[199]

In summary, the available evidence leads to the conclusion that the *sû/îs ʿāgûr* denotes a single species of bird, namely the swallow or some subspecies thereof. Two points should be made here with respect to vocalization. (1) The reading of 1QIsa\ᵃ, *sws ʿwgr*, better fits the vocalization given in the Eblaite list (/sasʿugar/) than *sws ʿgwr* (MT) and is therefore to be preferred. (2) It is apparent from the division of the name by scribes that the term was completely unintelligible to them. Thus the vocalization of the first syllable as /sūs/ ("horse"?) or /sīs/ has

[195] *The Balaam Text from Deir ʿAllā*, 132.

[196] *A Dictionary of the Targumim*, 967.

[197] "The Balaam Texts from Deir ʿAllā," 54.

[198] *Bulletin of the School of Oriental and African Studies* 58 (1995) 349–50. I am indebted to N. Veldhuis of the University of California at Berkeley for bringing this review to my attention.

[199] Ibid., 349. As noted above, the Syriac translates *sws ʿgwr* in Isa 38:14a with *snwnyt²*, which is cognate to Akkadian *sinntu* mentioned by Lambert, which is likewise translated "swallow" (see Payne Smith, *A Compendious Syriac Dictionary*, 382; Jastrow, *A Dictionary of the Targumim*, 1005).

no claim to antiquity and is no doubt sheer conjecture. Lambert comments: "The only reliable vowels attested for this bird name are those of the Ebla list."[200] As for the spelling of the name, although the Deir ʿAllā text spells it as a single word, it is possible that Judahite scribal tradition interpreted it as two separate words, as may be seen from Isa 38:14a (MT and 1QIsaᵃ) and Jer 8:7. In other words, it is possible that the name of the bird was spelled as two separate words in the original text of PsHez. Thus I compromise and spell it with the *maqqep*: *sas-ʿûgār*.

As regards the characteristic sound this bird makes, the onomatopoetic *ṣipṣēp* denotes a high-pitched chirping or cheeping sound.[201] The same verb in Jewish Palestinian Aramaic is used to represent the sound associated with mice, which is usually described as "squeaking."[202] Thus we would expect the *sas-ʿûgār* to be a small bird whose call is a high-pitched chirping sound, which fits the swallow. Ancient Israelites apparently associated this sound with the high-pitched whining sound humans sometimes make when weeping or lamenting.

[14b] *ʾehgeh kayyônâ*:

1QIsaᵃ: *ʾhgh kywnʾ*; 1QIsaᵇ: [ ]; LXX: καὶ ὡς περιστερά, οὕτως μελετήσω; Aquila: [ ]; Symmachus: [ ]; Theodotion: [ ]; Vg: meditabor ut columba; Syriac: *wʾyk ywnʾ nhmt*; *Targum of Isaiah*: *wnhymyt kywnh*.

The likening of a sufferer's groans to the moaning of a dove is a commonplace in ancient Near Eastern literature. The idiom occurs also in Isa 59:11[203] and is a topos often encountered in Akkadian lament

[200] *Bulletin of the School of Oriental and African Studies*, 349.

[201] On this point, see G. R. Driver, "Birds in the Old Testament: II: Birds in Life," *PEQ* 87 (1955) 132.

[202] Sokoloff, *A Dictionary of Jewish Palestinian Aramaic*, 469: "squeak, chirp."

[203] Also probably in Ezek 7:16, where one should read *kĕyōnîm hōgîyôt*, "like mourning doves," for MT *kĕyōnê haggēʾāyôt*, "like the doves of the valleys" (cf. Gʰ, Theodotion, and Vg; see W. Zimmerli, *Ezekiel 1: A Commentary on the Book of the Prophet Ezekiel, Chapters 1–24* [Hermeneia; Philadelphia: Fortress, 1979] 198–99); and in Nah 2:8 (English 7), where one should read *wʾmhtyh mnhgwt <hgwt> kqwl ywnym*, "Her maidservants are led away // 'Moaning' like the sound of doves" (cf. Vg and the *Targum of Isaiah*; see Roberts, *Nahum, Habakkuk, and Zephaniah*, 60–61).

literature—e.g., [*kīm*]*a summe adammuma gimir ūmēya*, "I moan [lik]e a dove all my days."[204] Unlike the simile in the preceding colon, there is no doubt about the species of bird intended in v. 14b. The ancients likened the cooing sound of the dove to low-pitched sounds humans often make when moaning or mourning. That the sound is low-pitched is clear from the use of this verb to denote sounds like the growling of a lion (Isa 31:4) and the rumbling of God's voice (Job 37:2). Within its total semantic range *h-g-y* and its derivatives denote sighing, mourning, lamenting (Isa 16:7; Jer 48:31; Ezek 2:10; Ps 90:9) in addition to moaning.[205] Thus the verb has a range quite similar to that of Akkadian *damāmu*, which also means "moan, mourn."[206]

[14c] *dallû ʿênay lammārôm*:

1QIsa[a]: *dlw ʿyny lmrwm*; 1QIsa[b]: [ ]; LXX: ἐξέλιπον γάρ μου οἱ ὀφθαλμοὶ τοῦ βλέπειν εἰς τὸ ὕψος τοῦ οὐρανοῦ; Aquila: ἠραιώθησαν [οἱ] ὀφθαλμοί μου εἰς ὕψος; Symmachus: [ ] βεβίασμαι ἀναδέξαι [ ]; Theodotion: [ ] σέσωκας [ ]; Vg: adtenuati sunt oculi mei suspicientes in excelsum; Syriac: *ʾrymt ʿyny lmrwmʾ*; *Targum of Isaiah*: *zqpyt ʿyny dyyty ly rwḥ mn qdm dškyntyh bšmy mrwmʾ*.

The present reading of the MT does not yield good sense. The basic meaning of *d-l-l* I seems to be "to be thin, scarce" (as in Syriac[207]), with the derived sense "to be poor, oppressed" (Akkadian[208] and Hebrew[209]), "to be low, humble(d)" (Modern Arabic[210] and Old South Arabic[211]). There is no evidence that it connotes physical weakness. Furthermore, this root never occurs with "eyes" anywhere else in the MT.

---

[204] *CAD* S, 380.
[205] Clines, *The Dictionary of Classical Hebrew: Volume II:* ב–ו, 487–88.
[206] *CAD* D, 59–61; compare its Hebrew cognate *d-m-m*, "drone, moan, mourn" (see especially Levine, "Silence, Sound," 90–106). See also A. Negoita, "הגה *hāghāh*," *TDOT*, 3. 321–22.
[207] See Payne Smith, *A Compendious Syriac Dictionary*, 92.
[208] See *AHw*, 153; *CAD* D, 178.
[209] *HALAT*, 214.
[210] Wehr, *A Dictionary of Modern Written Arabic*, 311.
[211] Biella, *Dictionary of Old South Arabic: Sabaean Dialect*, 95. See also H.-J. Fabry, "דל *dal*," *TDOT*, 3. 209–10.

In his monograph Begrich suggests the emendation *kālû*, a suggestion made by earlier commentators.[212] A number of factors support this reading, which has been widely accepted. First, in a number of passages the root *k-l-y* is associated with *ʿênayim*, with which it forms a fixed expression.[213] Second, the LXX points to *kālû* with its rendering ἐξέλιπον, "they have ceased," one of the meanings of *k-l-y*. Rather than indicating a *Vorlage* with *ḥdlw*, as Begrich seems to think,[214] it is far more likely that its Hebrew text read *klw*. The reason for this assertion is first of all the fact that in the majority of passages containing the idiom *kālû ʿênayim*[215] the LXX translates with ἐκλείπειν. Hence, *pace* Begrich and those who follow him on this point,[216] the LXX corroborates the emendation of the MT's *dlw* to *klw*. Second, during certain periods *dalet* and *kap* were quite similar in appearance.[217] Third, the fuller form of the idiom, *klw ʿynym l-/ʾl-X*, occurs also in Deut 28:32; Pss 69:4; 119:82, 123; Lam 4:17; 1QH 9:5.[218] The presence of *lammārôm* in Isa 38:14c indicates that we are dealing with this fuller form of the expression (with *l-/ʾl*), which again indicates that *dlw* is erroneous. Finally, striking confirmation of the presence of this expression in v. 14c is found in Ps 119:122–23:

> *ʿărōb ʿabdĕkā lĕṭôb*
> *ʾal-yaʿašqūnî zêdîm*
> *ʿênay kālû lîšûʿātekā*
> *ûlĕʾimrat ṣidqekā*

---

[212] *Der Psalm des Hiskia*, 37–38. Touzard ("De la conservation du text hébreu," 96) also read *klw*, as did Linder ("Canticum Ezechiae," 59), who notes that N. Schlögl (no reference given) had read *klw*.

[213] Lev 26:16; 1 Sam 2:33; Job 11:20; 17:5; 31:16; Pss 69:4; 119:82, 123; Jer 14:6; Lam 2:11; 4:17.

[214] *Der Psalm des Hiskia*, 24 n. 3.

[215] I.e., Deut 28:65; 1 Sam 2:33; Jer 14:6; Pss 69:4; 119:82, 123; Lam 2:11; 4:17.

[216] E.g., Wildberger, *Jesaja 28–39*, 1444.

[217] E.g., in the script of 1QIsaᵃ the top halves of these two letters are virtually identical. See further F. M. Cross, "The Development of the Jewish Scripts," in *The Bible and the Ancient Near East: Essays in Honor of William Foxwell Albright* (ed. G. E. Wright; Garden City, NY: Doubleday, 1961) 148–49.

[218] The expression without *l-/ʾl* is found in Lev 26:16; Deut 28:65; 1 Sam 2:33; Jer 14:6; Job 11:20; 17:5; 31:26; Lam 2:11.

> *Stand surety* for your servant,
> do not let the proud *oppress* me!
> *My eyes have . . .-ed*[219] for your saving help,
> and for your saving word.

These two successive bicola contain the same series of terms that appear in Isa 38:14b, but in reverse order: (1) the rare use of ʿ-r-b in the sense of delivering someone from distress, with the poet as object; (2) the verb ʿ-š-q, again with the poet as object; and (3) the idiom *kālû ʿênayim lĕ-*. This passage thus provides overwhelming support for the emendation of MT *dallû* to *kālû* in our passage.

How is this expression to be translated? The standard interpretation is that the psalmist's eyes have worn out or failed from the strain of continuously looking (to God) for deliverance. In the majority of attestations of *klw ʿynym l-/ʾl* the object of the preposition represents some aspect of God's saving help. Thus, according to this view, in Ps 69:4 the eyes give out "waiting for my God" (*mĕyaḥēl lēʾlōhāy*); in Ps 119:82, they fail (from looking) "for your word" (*lĕʾimratekā*); in v. 123, (from looking) "for your salvation (*lîšûʿātekā*) and your saving word (*ûlĕʾimrat ṣidqekā*)"; in Lam 4:17, (from looking) "for help for us" (*ʾel-ʿezrātēnû*); and in 1QH 9:5, (from looking) "for respite (from suffering)" (*lmnwḥ*).

M. I. Gruber has proposed a different understanding of the expression *klw ʿynym*. On the basis of Hebrew, Ugaritic, and Akkadian evidence he makes a convincing case for the position that the idiom is really a shortened form of *kālû dimʿôt ʿênayim*, something like "to exhaust the eyes' tears"—in idiomatic English, "to cry one's eyes out."[220] In other words, the idiom does not mean that the eyes have *worn* out but that its tears have *run* out. By way of corroborating evidence he cites a Ugaritic text (*KTU* 1.16 I 25–27 = CTA 16.1.25–27) where the same verb appears:

[219] I defer the translation of the expression here, as it will become apparent only after the discussion to follow.

[220] M. I. Gruber, *Aspects of Nonverbal Communication in the Ancient Near East* (2 vols.; Studia Pohl 12; Rome: Pontifical Biblical Institute, 1980) 1. 390–400. Gruber's view has been endorsed by N. M. Waldman, "The Imagery of Clothing, Covering, and Overpowering," *JANES* 19 (1989) 170.

bn al tbkn al tdm ly
  al tkl bn qr ʿnk

My son, do not weep, do not mourn for me;
  do not *exhaust*, my son, *the fountain of your eyes.*

The same topos is known in Akkadian. Gruber cites the following text in evidence:

nangul libba[šu] uṣarripka dimāšu iqtâ[221]
He became depressed; he cried bitterly to you, his tears were all used up.

Although overlooked by Gruber, further evidence that the Hebrew idiom denotes profuse weeping, not eyestrain, may be found in its sole occurrence published thus far from the Dead Sea scrolls (1QH 9:5):

. . . *wdmʿty knhly mym*
  klw lmnwḥ ʿyny [. . .]

. . . and my tears (flow) like rivers of water,
  My eyes have become exhausted (of their tears), seeking rest.[222]

The first colon clearly depicts profuse weeping, and stands in parallelism with the idiom under consideration in the second colon. The latter might be rendered more idiomatically, "I have cried my eyes out (praying) for respite (from my sufferings)."

In a number of instances the expression is followed by the preposition *lĕ-/ʾel.* Influenced by the Ugaritic parallel, Gruber translates this word "over" in several occurrences.[223] But in the biblical examples the function of the preposition should rather be taken as denoting directedness toward something or someone.[224] The examples of *kālû*

---

[221] Gruber, *Aspects of Nonverbal Communication* 1. 370.
[222] Note the collocation of *mānôaḥ* and *kilyôn ʿênayim* ("the weeping out of the eyes") in Deut 28:65.
[223] Deut 28:32; Lam 4:17; Ps 119:123.
[224] Among the biblical instances of the idiom only in Deut 28:32 could it possibly be translated as weeping profusely "over" (*lĕ/ʾel*) someone as in the Ugaritic passage cited by Gruber. This text speaks of parents weeping their eyes out *ʾĕlêhem*, i.e., their chil-

ʿênayim followed by *lĕ-/ʾel* break down into two groups: (1) with an impersonal object, denoting divine help/relief that is awaited,[225] and (2) with a personal object—viz., Yhwh. Two biblical examples of the second use of the idiom are Ps 69:4b and Lam 4:17. The first reads: *kālû ʿênay mĕyaḥēl lēʾlōhîm*, "I have cried my eyes out waiting for my God." Here the preposition probably goes both with the participle *mĕyaḥēl* as well as with *kālû ʿênay*. Lam 4:17 reads:

> *ʿwdynh*[226] *tiklênâ ʿênênû*
> *ʾel-ʿezrātēnû hābel*
> *bĕṣippiyyātēnû ṣippînû*
> *ʾel-gôy lōʾ yôšîaʿ*
>
> . . . We cried our eyes out
>   to "our Help," to no avail;[227]
> In our watchtower we kept looking
>   for a nation that could not save (us).

Isa 38:14 is an example of the second usage, where *lammārôm* should be construed as a divine epithet, "the Most High."[228] The standard translation "to heaven" is unlikely because, prescinding from this passage, in no occurrence of the idiom does *l-* ever refer to a place. Hence v. 14c is to be translated, "I have cried my eyes out to the Most High."

---

dren who have been forcibly taken away from them. But even here the translation "for them" is far more likely.

[225] The examples are: *lĕʾimrātekā*, "for your promise" (Ps 119:82); *lĕʾimrat ṣidqekā*, "for your promised salvation" (Ps 119:123); *lĕmānôaḥ*, "for rest/respite" (1QH 9:5).

[226] The interpretation of this term is difficult. The consonantal Kethib points to a reading *ʿôdēnâ*, but the last vowel is *qibbuṣ*, agreeing with the Qere *ʿwdynw = ʿôdênû*.

[227] The passage is usually interpreted as an expression of how none of Judah's allies (*ʿezrâ*) came to her aid in the time of national crisis. As both *ʿezrâ* and *gôy* are objects of the preposition *ʾel*, it would seem to stand to reason that both denote human allies. But the suffix on *ʿezrātēnû* sounds overspecific if the term means no more than "help" or "an ally." If that were the case one would expect simply *ʾel-ʿezrâ*. In this bicolon the parallelism may not be "synonymous"—i.e., referring to the human ally under two different terms. Here it is better taken as "meristic"—i.e., referring to divine aid in the first colon and human aid in the second, stating as emphatically as possible that *no one in heaven or on earth* came to Judah's aid. If this is the case, *ʿezrātēnû* is an epithet of Yhwh, allowing the translation of v. 17a given here. This translation is bolstered by instances of this noun with the 1st sg. suffix in which it unambiguously functions as a divine epithet: Pss 22:20; 40:18.

In the present context *kālû ʿênay* functions virtually as a *verbum dicendi*, as is often the case in Semitic languages with terms that denote weeping. In other words, such words or expressions indicate not only the physical act of shedding tears and attendant plaintive sounds but the act of verbal supplication that accompanies them as well.[229] The next bicolon (v. 14d) gives the words that the psalmist tearfully utters. That the idiom functions in this way here is clear from numerous parallels, biblical and extrabiblical, of which I cite here only two. First, Ps 119:82:

> *kālû ʿênay lĕʾimrātekā lēʾmôr*[230]
> *mātay tĕnaḥămēnî*

> I have cried my eyes out for your promise, *saying*:
> "How long will (it be before) you console me?"

Second, compare the following line from the eighth-century treaty between Ashur-nirari V and Matiʾilu of Arpad (rev V 14):

> *limrur bik[īssunu m]ā aḫla mā ina adê ša aššur-nērārī šar [mat aššur] niḫtiṭi*[231]

> May [they] wee[p] bitterly, [*say*]*ing*: "Woe (to us, for) we have sinned against the treaty of Ashur-nerari, King of [Assyria]!"[232]

[14d] *ʾădōnāy ʿāšĕqâ-lî ʿorbēnî*:
1QIsa[a]: *ʾdwny ʿwšqh ly wʿrbny*; 1QIsa[b]: [ ]*wh ḥšqb l*[ ] *ʿrbny*; LXX: πρὸς τὸν κύριον, ὃς ἐξείλατό με; Aquila: κύριε [κύριε] συκοφαντία ἐμοὶ *ἐγγύσαι με; Symmachus: [ ]; Theodotion: [ ]; Vg: domine vim patior sponde pro me; Syriac: *mryʾ pṣny wbsmyny*; *Targum of Isaiah*: *yhwh qbyl ṣlwty ʿbd bʿwty*.

---

[228] Dahood (*Psalms I: 1–50*, xxxvii) takes *mārôm* as a divine epithet in Isa 38:14. See further ibid., 44–45, 63, 177; Zorell, *Lexicon Hebraicum et Aramaicum Veteris Testamenti*, 472–73; H.-P. Stähli, "רום *rûm*, hoch sein," *THAT*, 2. 758.

[229] Gruber, *Aspects of Non-Verbal Communication*, 384.

[230] Some take *lʾmr* as an erroneous dittography, based on the preceding *lʾmrtk*. This reading is attested as early as 11QPs[a] (10:1).

[231] S. Parpola and K. Watanabe, *Neo-Assyrian Treaties and Loyalty Oaths* (State Archives of Assyria 2; Helsinki: Helsinki University Press, 1988) 12, V lines 14–15.

[232] Compare also Akkadian *šumma amēlu ibtanakki u ana ili amaḫḫarka*, "If a man keeps weeping and (says) to (his) god, 'I beseech you . . .'" (*CAD* B, 37).

1QIsa[b] reads "[Yh]wh" for MT's "Lord." But in light of the latter divine name in v. 16a, there is no compelling reason to prefer *yhwh* over *ʾădōnāy*. It is interesting that although the divine name *yhwh* appears in PsHez several times (vv. 20a, 20c; *yh yh* in v. 11b), whenever God is invoked in the psalm the form of address is *ʾădōnāy* (i.e., here [MT] and v. 16a).

The MT reads a *qtl* fem. verb in this colon followed by the preposition *l-* with the 1st person suffix—*ʿāšĕqâ-lî*. Here again 1QIsa[b] has a reading at variance with the MT, reading the same verb that it and the MT have in v. 17d. But it is difficult to see how "to love, desire" is appropriate here. The majority of commentators emend the MT to a nominal form, *ʿošqâ*. This feminine by-form of the noun *ʿōšeq* is unattested in Biblical Hebrew[233] but is thought to find support in 1QIsa[a]'s *ʿwšqh*.[234] However, the 1QIsa[a] reading can be explained otherwise. The form *ʿwšqh* could be an impersonal passive construction,[235] a 3d fem. sg. form, either *qal* passive or *pual* (the two forms are indistinguishable)[236]—*ʿuššĕqâ lî*.[237] Although such passive constructions are usually thought to contain only masc. 3d person verbs,[238] the form here could represent a confusion or conflation of the impersonal passive with other impersonal constructions that do not involve the passive, yet which attest both masc. and fem. verb forms.[239] In such constructions the grammatical subject of the verb is a "dummy" subject ("it") and the logical subject is governed by the preposition *lĕ-*:

[233] Or later Hebrew.

[234] 1QIsa[b] reads *ḥšqh* instead of *ʿšqh*—i.e., from *ḥ-š-q*, the same root that occurs in v. 16c. 1QIsa[a]'s reading (*ʿwšqh*) is to be preferred here.

[235] For other examples of this construction, see n. 29 above.

[236] On the *qal* passive, see Waltke and O'Connor, *An Introduction to Biblical Hebrew Syntax*, 373–76 (§22.6).

[237] In only one case does the MT point an occurrence of this root as a *pual*—*hamʿuššāqâ*, "oppressed one," an epithet modifying personified Sidon (Isa 23:12). But from the context it is more likely that the form is *piel*—in other words, that it is Sidon who is doing the oppressing. This is reflected in the LXX's translation in the active voice: ἀδικεῖν. It is perhaps best to leave the consonantal MT as it is but to repoint as a *piel* participle, describing Sidon as the "oppressor" of the nations by her reckless pursuit of wealth. If *ʿsqh* in Isa 38:14d is in fact a *qal* passive rather than a *pual*, it would probably have been pronounced /ʿōšĕqā/ in Biblical Hebrew (see Chapter 3 n. 45).

[238] GKC, §121a.

[239] See Waltke and O'Connor, *An Introduction to Biblical Hebrew Syntax*, 376 (§22.7a; example 2 = Ps 68:15) and n. 45.

"'it' is oppressed with regard to me" = "I am oppressed."[240] This analysis of ʿwšqh has the advantage of proposing a reading that is compatible both with the MT and 1QIsaᵃ as well as of not creating a noun that has no clear attestation in any period of the language. This construction expresses the fact that the subject is experiencing or feeling oppression without explicitly stating its source. This is no doubt deliberate on the part of the poet. Whereas earlier in the poem he had bluntly identified Yhwh as the cause of his suffering (vv. 12e, 13b), he appears to be less bold when addressing the deity directly.

Emended Text and Translation

IBa	12a	*dôrî nissaʿ wĕniglâ minnî*
	b	*kĕʾōhel rōʿî*
	c	*quppadtî ḥayyay kĕʾereg*
	d	*middallâ yĕbaṣṣĕʿennû*
	e	*miyyôm ʿad laylâ tašlîmēnî*
	13a	*sāpîtî ʿad bōqer*
IBb	13b	*kāʾărî kēn yĕšabbēr*
	c	*kol ʿaṣmôtāy*
	d	{*miyyôm ʿad laylâ tašlîmēnî*}
	14a	*kassas-ʿûgār kēn ʾăṣapṣēp*
	b	*ʾehgeh kayyônâ*
	c	*kālû ʿênay lammārôm*
	d	*ʾădōnāy ʿuššĕqâ lî ʿorbēnî*

A. Life Has Come to an End

My lifetime has been pulled up and taken away from me
    like a shepherd's tent;
I have/My life has been shrunk like a piece of cloth
    after it has been cut from the thrum.
Between day(break) and night(fall) you will finish me off,
    by morning I shall have vanished.

---

[240] See n. 29 above.

B. Suffering and Outcry

Like a lion he crushes
    all my bones.
Like a swallow I chirp (plaintively),
    I moan like a dove.
I have cried my eyes out to the Most High (saying):
    "O Lord, I am oppressed! Be my surety!"

Rhetorical-Critical Observations

The subsections IBa and IBb share several general similarities, as to the number of cola and words, and specifically as to the number of verbs in each. First, each subsection consists of three bicola and each contains eighteen words.

	Verse			Words
IBa	12ab	4+2	=	6
	12cd	3+2	=	5
	12e-13a	4+3	=	7
	TOTAL			18
IBb	13bc	3+2	=	5
	14ab	4+2	=	6
	14cd	3+4	=	7
	TOTAL			18

Moreover, IBa and IBb show a reversal in terms of the number of words in the lead colon of each bicolon—i.e., where IBa has four words in this colon, IBb has three, and vice-versa:

IBa	Words	IBb	Words
12a	4	13b	3
b	2	c	2
c	3	14a	4
d	2	b	2
e	4	c	3
13a	3	d	4

Second, there is a discernible pattern in this section of the number of verbs in each and the person of these verbs. As each subsection of IB contains three bicola or six lines, each also has six verbs. Further, each has the same number of verbs in each person: three 3d person verbs, two 1st person verbs, and one 2d person verb:

	IBa	IBb
3d person:	*nsᶜ*	*yšbr*
	wnglh (1QIsaᵃ: *yklh*)	*klw* (MT: *dlw*)
	ybṣᶜnw (MT: *ybṣᶜny*)	*ᶜšqh*
1st person:	*qpdty*	*ᵓṣpṣp*
	spyty (MT: *šwyty*)	*ᵓhgh*
2d person:	*tšlymny*	*ᶜrbny*

One also notes an almost identical sequence of the person of the verbs: IBa: 3d (2x), 1st, 3d, 2d, 1st; IBb: 3d, 1st (2x), 3d (2x), 2d.

Assonance is quite evident in this section of PsHez. The first two verbs in IB are connected by alliteration (*n-* . . . *n-*) as are the last two (*ᶜ-* . . . *ᶜ-*). In IBa the sound /mi/ at the beginning of a word (i.e., the preposition *min*) occurs three times in IBa (vv, 12–13a), once in each bicolon. IBb is dominated by the alliteration of initial /k/ sounds, eight times in this subsection: *kāᵓārî, kēn, kol, kĕᵓōhel, kĕsas-ᶜûgār, kēn, kayyônâ, kālû*. In v. 12a the assonance based on the syllable /ni/ in the two verbs *nissaᶜ wĕniglâ* has been noted before.[241] But the assonance is more extensive. The colon in question contains three examples of this syllable in close proximity, each separated from the next by two syllables: *nissaᶜ wĕniglâ minnî*. The first and last words of the bicolon v. 12ab contain the same sounds but one, a kind of sonic inclusion: *dôrî* . . . *rōᶜî*. Striking too is the nearly identical sound of *puqqadtî* (earlier *pōqadtî*) in v. 10c and *quppadtî* (earlier *qōpadtî*) in v. 12c, each occurring in the third colon of their respective subsections (IAa and IBa).

Clearly the most characteristic feature of IB is its use of similes, which appear in the poem only here (with the exception of *kāmônî* in v. 19b). They are distributed between the two subsections so as to occur only in the first two of the three bicola in each subsection (viz., in vv.

[241] Van der Westhuizen, "Isaiah 38:10–20," 201.

12ab, 12cd, 13bc, and 14ab). In the last bicolon of each there is no comparative particle, but there is a 2d sg. verb, a form ending in -*ēnî*, a feature which occurs only here in Part I. Comparative *kĕ*- occurs twice in IBa (v. 12bc), whereas the fuller form of the simile (*kĕ*- . . . *kēn*) appears in IBb (vv. 13b, 14a), making a total of seven comparative particles in this section. What is more, the similes follow a definite sequence. In the first two (v. 12ad) the vehicle is connected with human occupations: shepherding, weaving-fulling. The next (v. 13b) uses the image of a lion, and the last two refer to different species of birds (v. 14ab).

12ab	simile (human)	*kĕ*-
cd	simile (human)	*kĕ*-
12e-13a	no simile	2d sg. verb + -*ēnî*
13bc	simile (lion)	*kĕ*- . . . *kēn*
14a	simile (swallow)	*kĕ*- . . . *kēn*
b	simile (dove)	*kĕ*-
cd	no simile	2d sg. verb + -*ēnî*

The sequence of humans, lion, birds also appears in Amos 3:3–5.

This section exhibits some interesting similarities to the central stanza of Psalm 22 (vv. 13–22). Both passages divide into two subsections, are of the lament genre, and contain references to three animals (one of which is a lion). Particularly significant is the fact that both subsections conclude with a sudden shift to the *2d person*, addressing Yhwh. In both the first address is a complaint about how Yhwh is killing the psalmist, while the second is a plea to God for deliverance from suffering.[242] The switch to the 2d person in both psalms is sudden and deliberate. This stylistic arrangement provides an argument against the frequent proposal to emend *tašlîmēnî* in v. 12e to a 1st or 3d person form.

There is a second, more subtle inclusory device in IBa which is rare—and perhaps unique—in Biblical Hebrew: the presence of two alphabetic runs, one at the beginning and the other at the end of this subsection. Verse 12a ends with the consonantal sounds (i.e., not

---

[242] See Barré, "The Crux of Psalm 22:17c," 297–99.

counting vowels or *matres lectionis*) /l m n/ (*wngl mn*).[243] A longer sequence appears in vv. 12e–13a: /l m n s p/ (*tšlmn spt*). In the OT period there was a variant alphabetic sequence in which the position of the letters ʿ*ayin* and *pe* were reversed, attested in several acrostic poems in the MT.[244] The odds against five letters occurring in exact alphabetic sequence by sheer coincidence are astronomical. Both runs begin with the second half of the alphabet (*lamed* to *taw*) and are incomplete. The fact that the longer of the two runs ends in the word *sāpîtî*, "I shall have vanished," is probably no coincidence. The cutting short of the alphabetic run before its conclusion, in the midst of a word that means "to disappear/vanish," may allude literarily to the fact that the poet's life has likewise been cut short—the principal theme of IBa.

IBb is further marked off by an inclusion, which is thematic in nature. It begins with what amounts to an accusation of Yhwh as the one who has caused the psalmist's suffering, under the figure of a lion crushing its victim's bones (v. 13bc). It concludes with a second accusation, namely the psalmist's characterizing his suffering as "oppression," implying that Yhwh is the oppressor. (See further below in **General Comments**.) The accusation in v. 13bc also picks up the tone on which IBa had ended, where the psalmist accuses Yhwh of bringing his life to an end (v. 12e).

Finally, there is a major two-part inclusion encompassing Part I: v. 14bc forms an inclusion with vv. 10b,d, which is itself an inclusion. The two bird similes referring to plaintive, mournful sounds reprise the poet's action in v. 10b, where he mourns (*dm*) for his days.[245] The profuse weeping expressed by *kālû* ʿ*ênay* finds its semantic equivalent in *mr* in v. 10d referring to "bitter (i.e., profuse) weeping" for his years.

---

[243] The length of the first run depends on whether one reads *w(n)glh* (MT) or *yklh/wklh* (so 1QIsaᵃ) in v. 12a. If one reads the latter, the run could consist of four or even five consonants: /(y) k l m n/.

[244] Acrostics containing this sequence include Psalms 9–10; Lamentations 2–4. But evidence from some ancient versions suggests that the *pe*-ʿ*ayin* sequence was original to several other poems as well. In Lamentations 1 4QLamᵃ has the order *p*, ʿ, as do the other acrostic chapters in Lamentations. As a number of commentators have noted, Psalm 34 reads more smoothly if the sequence of the ʿ*ayin* and *pe* lines is reversed. Finally, the ʿ*ayin* and *pe* lines are reversed in the LXX translation of Prov. 31:10-31.

[245] In Akkadian literature, the idiom "to moan/mourn like a dove" is expressed most frequently with the verb *damāmu*.

Mourning		Profuse Weeping	
10b	(*dōm*) "for my days"	10d	(*mar*) "for my years"
14a	swallow-like sounds	14c	crying one's eyes out
14b	dove-like sounds		

The topos of mourning like a bird (sometimes two birds) coupled with profuse weeping appears in Akkadian lament poetry. I cite here two examples:

> *adammum kīma summatum mūši u urra*
> *nangulākuma abakki ṣarpiš*[246]

> I mourn/moan like a dove night and day,
> I am depressed, I weep bitterly.[247]

> *adammum kīma summati mūša u urra*
> *ina d[ī]mti bullulāku*[248]

> I mourn/moan like a dove night and day,
> I wallow in (my) [t]ears.

This topos appears with some frequency in Babylonian lament literature.[249] This consideration, together with the fact that these two motifs appear together nowhere else in Biblical Hebrew literature, is evidence that the topos in Isa 38:14a–c is borrowed from Akkadian.

---

[246] Ebeling, *Die akkadische Gebetserie "Handerhebung"*, 132 lines 64–65.

[247] Note the collocation here of the verb *damāmu* = Hebrew *d-m-m* (as in v. 10b), "like a dove" (as in v. 14b), and "*bitter* weeping" (Akkadian *ṣarpiš* = Hebrew *mar* [v. 10d]).

[248] Mayer, *Untersuchungen zur Formensprache der babylonischen "Gebetsbeschwörungen"*, 83 (cited by Mayer from an unpublished text).

[249] See, for example, Lambert, "Dingir.šà.dib.ba Incantations," 275 lines 12–14; M.-J. Seux, *Hymnes et prières aux dieux de Babylonie et d'Assyrie* (LAPO 8; Paris: Editions du Cerf, 1976) 164. Two other examples of this topos contain the reference to the poet mourning "like a *lallāru*," where the ambivalent term probably designates the mournful sounding bird rather than the professional mourner (see *CAD* L, 48): *Ludlul* I 107–09 (see W. G. E. Lambert, *Babylonian Wisdom Literature* [Oxford: Clarendon Press, 1960] 36; but read [*kīma lall*]*āru* [see critical apparatus]); and idem, "Three Literary Prayers of the Babylonians," 58, lines 131–33.

The verbs ṣ-p-p (*pilpel*) and h-g-y in v. 14ab refer to sounds which were thought to resemble sounds of lamentation—the former a high-pitched whimpering or whining and the latter a kind of low-pitched moaning. The reference to these bird-sounds is perhaps a kind of merismus, indicating that in his grief the psalmist covers the entire range of culturally typical mournful sounds, from high to low, expressing the totality of his dejection.

IBb shows a number of connections to IA. PsHez begins with references to the poet's thinking—lit., "*saying* (to himself)"—(*[ʾănî] ʾāmartî* in vv. 10a, 11a) and to his not *seeing* (*lōʾ ʾerʾeh* in v. 11b, *lōʾ ʾabbîṭ* in v. 11d). These themes reappear at the end of Part I in v. 14cd, in reverse order (thematic chiasmus). Just as the poet "shall no longer see" Yhwh in v. 11a, so in v. 14c he has "cried his eyes out" to God (as *mārôm*, "the Most High") in v. 14c. Both actions involve the eyes. Second, v. 14d is the first example in the poem of direct speech, which is often if not usually introduced by the verb *ʾāmar* (vv. 10a, 11a).

The theme of IBa may be summed up in the phrase "Life Has Come to an End." Each of the first two bicola present an image of the end of life: pulling up the tent rope (v. 12ab), shrinking the life span. The focus of IBb is rather on the poet's suffering. The final bicolon contains two verbs whose specific meaning is "to end, (cause to) perish"—š-l-m (*hiphil*) and s-p-y, emphasizing that the life of the psalmist is soon to end.

General Comments

IA had ended with the poet's painful realization that all too soon he would no longer be "among those who dwell in the world," since his dwelling would be in Sheol (v. 10c). IBa picks up on this theme and develops it further.

The psalmist's life is virtually at an end; he no longer has a dwelling-place in the world of the living. These two sides of the same reality are captured in the ephemeral image of the shepherd's tent in v. 12a. It reflects the fact that the life span (*dôrî*) is non-permanent and even fragile like the simple tent of the shepherd, which is easily and quickly dismantled. The verb n-s-ᶜ used here, lit., "to pull up," is the key to the main image in this bicolon, namely, terminating the tent as a human dwelling-place by pulling up the tent-cord or tent-peg. But in other contexts the verb can connote journeying, moving on to the next grazing land. The image comes to mind of Abraham with his flocks, pulling up tent ropes (or stakes) and moving on to his next temporary residence.[250] This aspect of the verb has a poignant sense for the poet, since unlike Abraham his "tent" will not be set up again. He has moved on to his final dwelling-place, Sheol.

The next bicolon makes use of a similar image symbolizing life's end. It is similar to the preceding image insofar as the vehicle in both similes is a product made from cloth and is characteristic of a particular trade. Perhaps on some level these two common occupations stand for everyday life in the world of human beings, of which the psalmist must now take his leave. Verse 12d alludes to the weaving of a piece of cloth, which is completed when the weaver severs the thrum. But this is not the end of the process. Immediately after this it is taken by the fuller to undergo shrinking and compacting. The poet's life is shrunken—i.e., shortened—like the cloth itself (v. 12c). The "length of days" that every Israelite hopes for as a life span has thereby been suddenly reduced, so that he finds himself virtually at the end of that period of time. The subsequent bicolon makes clear how much it has been diminished: he is now living his last day in this world and tomorrow's rising sun will find him gone (vv. 12e–13a).

With IBb a new set of images begins. Throughout this subunit the poet engages in lamentation. He calls attention to his great suffering, expressed in formulaic language, and ends by crying out to Yhwh in his distress. The vehicles in the similes that appear in this section are not connected with human occupations, as in the foregoing section, but with animals.

At the beginning of IBb (v. 13bc) the poet makes a specific reference for the second time to Yhwh's hostility against him (the first in v. 12e). In the first bicolon he likens God's behavior toward him to the attacks of a bone-crushing lion. The latter statement should probably be construed as the diametric opposite of Psalm 23's portrayal of Yhwh as the good shepherd. Far from being one who protects and cares for the sheep, the typical understanding of the shepherd's role, Yhwh has become the lion, the predator most feared by shepherds and their flocks in the ancient Near East. It may be no coincidence that the only

---

[250] E.g., Gen 12:9; 20:1.

other occurrence of the phrase *š-b-r ʿăṣāmôt* ("to crush bones") associated with Yhwh in the MT, Lam 3:4, where again the bones in question are those of the speaker, occurs in a section in which Yhwh is also depicted as the opposite of the good shepherd. D. R. Hillers describes this section: "Through vs. 9, the dominant theme of Lam 3 might be called a reversal of the Twenty-third Psalm: the Lord is a shepherd who misleads, a ruler who oppresses and imprisons."[251]

The last set of similes in IB have two species of birds as their vehicles. Here the psalmist emits sounds that resemble those of these birds. Begrich has interpreted this in light of Isa 29:4, where *ṣ-p-p* (*pilpel*) describes sounds made by the dead.[252] The verse he cites makes reference to sounds made by a "ghost" (*ʾôb*). But the following bicolon (38:14cd), which speaks of crying one's eyes out, as well as the inclusive connection to the same topos in v. 10, mourning (*dōm*) and bitter weeping (*mar*), indicate that the real concern here is the extreme depression of the psalmist. The examples of the topos in Akkadian lament literature refer to the suffering of the poet because of his affliction, never to sounds made by the dead. Hence the main concern of Isa 38:14ab is the psalmist's depression. It is possible, however, that on a secondary level this verse alludes to the ghost imagery, especially in light of the fact that in v. 10c he speaks of himself as already being in the netherworld.

The second part of the mourning-and-weeping topos focuses on profuse weeping. The terms "mourning" and "weeping" occur together with some frequency in biblical and extra-biblical lament literature. The way that "mourning" is carried out in particular cultures varies throughout the world—i.e, the specific behaviors that the mourner acts out to express grief. The physical act of "weeping," on the other hand, is less susceptible to variation. What is emphasized here by means of the idiom "to cry one's eyes out" is the intensity of

---

[251] D. R. Hillers, *Lamentations* (AB 7A; 2d ed; New York: Doubleday, 1992) 124. See also J. S. Kselman and M. L. Barré, "New Exodus, Covenant, and Restoration in Psalm 23," in *The Word of the Lord Shall Go Forth: Essays in Honor of David Noel Freedman in Celebration of His Sixtieth Birthday* (ed. C. L. Meyers and M. O'Connor; ASOR Special Volume Series 1; Winona Lake, IN: Eisenbrauns, 1983) 100–101.

[252] *Der Psalm des Hiskia*, 37. See also Coetzee, "The 'Song of Hezekiah'," 16. In Isa 8:19, both *ṣ-p-p* (*pilpel*) and *h-g-y*, the verbs used in Isa 38:14ab, are used to describe the sounds made by mediums and wizards.

the weeping. The poet has exhausted the eye's source of tears, and can shed no more. This expression implies that he has reached the end of his ability to express his grief and also an end to his tearful appeals to God for help, which have gone unanswered.

Closely connected to this profuse weeping topos are the words the poet utters in the final colon of Part I. Although it is the first time he actually speaks aloud in the poem, it does not represent some kind of spiritual breakthrough, as one might expect. Conventional lament behavior in Israel usually included an oral constituent, namely calling upon God through one's tears for release from distress. The short prayer—almost an ejaculation—uttered here has all the components of a prayer for deliverance: (1) an address to God ("O Lord"), (2) a petition requesting deliverance ("Be my surety!"), and (3) a statement of the motivation underlying the petition ("[For] I am oppressed").

The poet's choice of words in this short prayer is significant, in particular the two verbs *ʿ-š-q*, "to oppress," and *ʿ-r-b*, "to stand surety (for someone)." Wildberger observes that these are a matched set in Hebrew legal terminology. The former is a technical term denoting ruinous financial oppression by a creditor. The latter is its specific remedy, whereby one party elects to take upon himself the indebtedness of another by "standing surety" for the one thus oppressed.[253] In the present context, of course, the language is not literally economic but figurative, as elsewhere in the MT.[254] The second verb is somewhat harder to translate, but it would entail undoing the wrong effected by *ʿ-š-q*.[255] In the only other biblical text where these two verbs appear together (Ps 119:122–23), the oppression comes from "the proud." But here it is Yhwh who is the source of both oppression and its reversal. The use of *ʿ-š-q* points the finger at God as the oppressor, whom the poet has already blamed for his sufferings (vv. 12e, 13bc) and whom a few verses later he identifies as the cause of his problems in general (v. 15b).[256] But here he does not do so directly. Instead, he makes use of an

---

253 *Jesaja 28–39*, 1463. Wildberger cites as examples Amos 4:1; Jer 6:6; 22:17. See also E. Lipiński, "ערב I *ʿārab*," *TDOT*, II. 328.

254 E.g., Gen 43:9; 44:32.

255 In these verses the imperative *ʿărōb ʿabdĕkā*, "Stand surety for your servant (= for me)," is equivalent to the prohibitive, *ʾal-yaʿašqūnî*, "Do not let (the proud) oppress me."

256 Wildberger, *Jesaja 28–39*, 1463.

impersonal construction (ʿšqh ly) which gives prominence to his experience or feeling rather than to the cause or source of the oppression: "I feel oppressed/I am experiencing oppression." The psalmist then appeals to Yhwh to become the undoer of the oppression Yhwh has brought upon him. If we set aside the economic connotations of this language, it becomes evident that this amounts to asking God to redress the wrongs he has endured—and which Yhwh has caused— i.e., to deliver him from his sufferings.

The bold manner in which the poet speaks of God's hostility toward him, as in v. 13bc, is in some ways reminiscent of the discourse of Job. Yet there are major differences. Lacking in PsHez is any conviction on the part of the psalmist of his innocence or sinlessness before God. Such a conviction is never mentioned in Part I, and v. 17ef dispels any idea that he held such a view about himself. Indeed, as in the case of most OT laments, the protagonist gives no evidence of knowing why Yhwh has decided to act as he has, any more than Hezekiah does in Isa 38:1–2, when the prophet announces to him that his life will shortly end. Nor does the author of the poem communicate this information to the reader.

The first half of PsHez is virtually a lament, devoid of hope or thanksgiving. The entire section is cast in extremely somber tones, overshadowed by the imminence of death and the abandonment by a deity who has become the psalmist's tormentor. It is no wonder that some commentators have found it difficult to classify this psalm as a thanksgiving hymn. But Part I is not the whole story. In fact, the poet has given us a clue to this effect by the opening words "I *had* thought." These words introduce not only IAa or even IAa + IAb, but all of Part I. This section reflects his thinking during the darkness of his depression and suffering, when death seemed inevitable. In Part II this negativity will be undone.

CHAPTER 5

Deliberation, Prayer, Deliverance

Part IIA (vv. 15–17)

The Masoretic Text

IIAa   15a   *mâ-ʾădabbēr wĕʾāmar-lî*[t]
         b   *wĕhûʾ ʿāśâ*[a]
         c   *ʾeddaddeh kol-šĕnôtay*[t]
         d   *ʿal-mar napšî*[s]

IIAb   16a   *ʾădōnāy ʿălêhem yiḥyû*[a]
         b   *ûlĕkol- b bāhen ḥayyê rûḥî*[z]
         c   *wĕtaḥălîmēnî wĕhaḥăyēnî*[s]
         17a   *hinnēh lĕšālôm b mar-lî mār*[a]

IIAc   c   *wĕʾattâ ḥāšaqtā napšî*[p]
         d   *miššaḥat bĕlî*[z]
         e   *kî hišlaktā ʾaḥărê gēwkâ*[t]
         f   *kol-ḥăṭāʾāy*[s]

Textual Remarks

[15a] *mâ-ʾădabbēr wĕʾāmar-lî*:

1QIsa[a]: *mh ʾdbr wʾwmr lwʾ*; 1QIsa[b]: *mh ʾdbr wʾm*[̇   ]; LXX: [ ];
Aquila: *τί λαλήσω καὶ εἶπέν μοι; Symmachus: [ ]; Theodotion: [ ]
*αὐτῷ; Vg: Quid dicam aut quid respondebit mihi; Syriac: *wmnʾ ʾmll
ʾmr ly*; *Targum of Isaiah*: *mʾ ʾmlyl tšbḥʾ wʾymr qdmwhy*.

The two textual issues to be considered in this line are : (1) Is the MT's reading, *wĕʾāmar* (3d person), preferable here or rather *wāʾōmar* (1st person), as attested in 1QIsaᵃ? (2) Is the preposition + suffix *lî*, as in the MT, or *lô(?)* as in 1QIsaᵃ?[1]

The Syriac follows the MT as does Vg. But the *Targum of Isaiah*'s paraphrastic translation is, "What praise shall *I* utter and *declare before him?*" This indicates a *Vorlage* in which the second verb was 1st sg. and a preposition with a 3d masc. suffix, which corresponds in both details to 1QIsaᵃ's reading. Theodotion's αὐτῷ also corresponds to *lô*,[2] "to him."

The MT's reading of the second verb as 3d person appears questionable on several grounds. First, it would be more natural to read these synonymous verbs as a hendiadys.[3] A switch of persons in the middle of the colon does not seem too likely. Second, the MT's 3d person form is suspicious because it looks like an accommodation to the narrative context of PsHez. "He (Yhwh) has said to me" reads easily as an allusion to Yhwh's word to Hezekiah (through Isaiah) announcing his imminent death (Isa 38:1). For if *wʾmr* is parsed as a 3d person form, it would be most naturally followed by *lî* rather than *lô*.

There are also structural considerations that argue for taking *wʾmr* as 1st person. As noted earlier, this verb occurs elsewhere within PsHez only in v. 10, at the beginning of Part I. The repetition of a word or phrase from the beginning of one section of a poem to the beginning of the following section is one means of indicating stanza divisions. *ʾāmartî* introduces Part I, which concentrates on the poet's realization of his imminent death and on the rehearsal of his various afflictions. *mh . . . ʾmr* introduces Part II and with it a shift in subject matter as well as mood (indicative to interrogative). At this point the speaker has essentially finished bewailing his maladies and considers using speech for a different purpose—to extricate himself from his suffering by requesting divine aid. The introductory function of *ʾ-m-r* in both parts

---

[1] The *waw* has a very short tail and thus could be confused with the *yod*. But because the letter in question has a head that is characteristic of the *waw* in 1QIsaᵃ, and distinct from the upside-down V shape of the *yod*, it is almost certainly the former.

[2] Field, *Origenis Hexaplorum Quae Supersunt* 2. 507.

[3] Note the two terms in virtual parallelism in Ps 116:10–11; Job 10:1–2 (with the same speaker).

of PsHez, where there is no doubt that *ʾāmartî* in v. 10 is 1st person, suggests that *wᵉmr* in v. 15a is 1st person also.

A more difficult issue in this colon is the suffix on the preposition following this verb. Coming just after a brief prayer to Yhwh (v. 14b) and just before a second prayer (vv. 16a–17b), the prepositional suffix -*ô* would be the more "natural" reading. On the other hand, given the frequent *waw/yod* confusion in the MT, either reading would be plausible from a paleographic point of view.

There is no doubt as to the syntactic viability of the reading *lô*— "What can I say *to him* (viz., Yhwh)?" The question is whether *lî* is a realistic option in this passage. *d-b-r* (*piel*) + *lě-* has the sense "to speak on behalf of" in 2 Kgs 4:13.[4] By extension, *lě-ʾel* can be translated "(to speak) in defense of" in a juridical context, as in Job 13:7:

halěʾēl tědabběrû ʿawlâ
wělô tědabběrû rěmiyyâ

Are you going to speak falsely on God's behalf?
Will you speak deceitfully in his defense?[5]

But the juridical atmosphere so pervasive in the speeches of Job is entirely lacking in PsHez.

Several biblical passages containing parallels to PsHez in general or v. 15 in particular also give some support to the reading *lô*. The first is the beginning of Job's speech in Job 10:1–22, which contains a striking number of parallels to PsHez (vv. 1–2): *ʾădabběrâ běmar napšî // ʾōmar ʾel-ʾelōah*, "I *will speak* out in the bitterness of my soul, I *will say to* God...."[6] The second is 2 Sam 7:20:

[4] BDB, 515.

[5] Cf. *REB*: "on God's behalf ... in his defence."

[6] The other parallels between this response of Job and PsHez are given below. In the right column I give my restoration of the Hebrew text, which differs from the vocalized—but not consonantal—MT in vv. 14d and 15a.

Verse	Job 10:1–21	Verse	Isa 38:10–17
1-2	*ʾădabběrâ // ʾōmar ʾel-ʾelōah*	15a	*ʾădabbēr wěʾōmar lô*
1	*běmar napšî*	15d	*ʿal-mar napšî*
2ff	Entreaty to God	16a–17b	Entreaty to God
3	*taʿăšōq ... yēgîaʿ kappêkā*	14d	*ʿuššěqâ-lî*
5	*yāmêkā ... šěnôtêkā*	10bd	*yāmay ... šěnôtāy*
16	*kaššaḥal*	13b	*kāʾărî*
21	*ʾēlēk* (= "to die")	10b	*ʾēlēkâ* ("to die").

ûmah-yyôsîp dāwīd ʿôd lĕdabbēr ʾēlêkā wěʾattâ yādaʿtî ʾet-ʿabdĕkā
ʾădōnāy yhwh

And *what* more *can* David *say to you, since* you know your
servant, O Lord Yhwh?

Both passages contain the verb *d-b-r* (*piel*) followed by *l-* / *ʾel* governing a 2d or 3d person referent, viz., Yhwh. Although the verb in 2 Sam
7:20 is 3d person, David here is speaking of himself in the 3d person,
and so sense-wise this is equivalent to a 1st person form. Moreover, this
construction is followed immediately in the 2 Samuel passage by a use
of the copula *w-* identical to that in Isa 38:15b, where the subject is likewise Yhwh. The context of this passage is also similar in some respects
to the passage under consideration. David is saying here that there
would be no reason for him to go on speaking to Yhwh, since the latter
already knows everything anyway. Similarly, the psalmist in PsHez is
saying here that there would be no reason for him to go on speaking to
Yhwh, but for a different reason—not because Yhwh is omniscient but
because Yhwh has already decided on a course of action.

Hence the preponderance of versional evidence, structuring devices
in the poem, biblical parallels, and context all support the reading
ʾōmar lô, "shall I say to him," rather than the MT's ʾāmar lî, "he has
said to me."[7]

[15b] *wěhûʾ ʿāśâ*:

1QIsaᵃ: *ʷhyʾh ʿśh lyʾ*; 1QIsaᵇ: [ ]; LXX: [ ]; Aquila: *αὐτὸς δὲ ἐποίησεν; Symmachus: [ ]; Theodotion: *καὶ αὐτὸς ἐποίησεν; Vg: cum ipse
fecerit; Syriac: *whw ʿbr*;[8] Targum of Isaiah: *whwʾ ʾsgy ṭbwwn lmʿbd
ʿmy*.

---

[7] This is the position of Touzard, "De la conservation du text hébreu," 98; Linder,
"Canticum Ezechiae," 70; Begrich, *Der Psalm des Hiskia*, 41; Duhm, *Das Buch Jesaja*,
281; von Legelshurst, *Die Hiskiaerzählungen*, 41; Wildberger, *Jesaja 28–39*, 1440, 1444;
Kaiser, *Isaiah 13–39*, 398; Fohrer, *Das Buch Jesaja 2*. 185; Clements, *Isaiah 1–39*, 292;
Oswalt, *The Book of Isaiah: Chapters 1–39*, 680; Nyberg, "Hiskias Danklied," 88; and
Castellino, "Lamentazioni individuali accadiche ed ebraische," 152. Obviously I no
longer support the reading or translation of this colon that I argued for in my earlier
publication on this passage, namely, "What can I say on my behalf [*lî*]?" ("Restoring
the 'Lost Prayer'," 399).

[8] The verb *ʿbr* most likely reflects a scribal confusion of the Syriac letters *dalat* and
resh, which are identical except for the position of the diacritical dot—hence read *whw*

The ancient Hebrew manuscripts of Isaiah that preserve this line and the versions agree with the MT. 1QIsaᵃ has, "and/since he has done this *to me.*" Vg has "since he himself has done (it) to/for me." The *Targum of Isaiah* paraphrases with, "since he has shown me so much goodness."[9]

If one reads the MT without regard for the poetic form of the passage, it seems possible at first glance to connect these words with *ʾāmar lî* (MT) and translate, "He has promised me and he has done it."[10] This interpretation could appeal to other OT passages where the two verbs occur in this sequence with the clear meaning "promise . . . do," especially Num 23:19a: *hahûʾ ʾāmar wĕlōʾ yaʿăśeh,* "Has he promised, and he will not do it?" (*NRSV*). In the context of Isa 38:1–8 this might seem to refer to Yhwh's promise through Isaiah to add fifteen years to Hezekiah's lifetime (v. 5),[11] especially since immediately after this the prophet says, "This is the sign to you from Yhwh, that Yhwh will do (*yaʿăśeh*) this thing that he has promised (*dibbēr*)" (v. 7).

But such an interpretation is untenable for a number of reasons. First, one would expect the *hûʾ* to accompany the first verb, not the second if this is the correct understanding (cf. Num 23:19a). Second, this interpretation would demand a very unlikely scansion of the bicolon, with the caesura after *ʾădabbēr.* This would create a bicolon with the word pattern 2 + 4, which is completely at odds with the colometry of PsHez. Third, as noted above, it is obviously based on the narrative context, whereas, as we have seen, PsHez is a poem composed independently of this context and introduced into the narrative later by the Isaian editors. Fourth, it is clear that the psalmist's plaintive plea in v. 14d has not been answered, since he must appeal to God again at greater length in vv. 16a–17b, and only after this is he delivered. For these reasons it is most unlikely that v. 15 contains a positive note as this interpretation would assume. In any case, the strong case for

---

ʿbd, "and he has done (it)." The latter appears as a variant in some manuscripts (Brock, *The Old Testament in Syriac,* 68).

[9] The translation is that of Stenning, *The Targum of Isaiah,* 126.

[10] Linder ("Canticum Ezechiae," 61) notes that the early nineteenth-century exegete E. F. C. Rosenmüller had read the text this way, translating "Promisit ille mihi, et ipse praestitit" (*Scholia in Veteris Testamenti Libros* [Leipzig: J. A. Barth, 1821–] 2. 546).

[11] The connection of v. 15ab with v. 5 was made by Ibn Ezra. See M. Friedländer, *The Commentary of Ibn Ezra on Isaiah* (2 vols.; New York: Feldheim, 1873) 1. 166.

reading ʾōmar lô, "(What) can I say to him?" makes this reading of the verse impossible.

Most commentators and translations assume that ʿāśâ has an implied object, namely the various afflictions the poet mentions in Part I—in other words, the things that God has "done" to him. Therefore one frequently finds the word "it" supplied as the object of ʿāśâ in translation. Such a translation could well be correct. However, it is more likely that here as elsewhere in the MT[12] the verb is used absolutely to denote a divine action. Most of these absolute uses of ʿ-ś-y denote salvific actions for Israel or the just individual, which are accordingly viewed in a positive light. Occasionally, however, this absolute use of the verb can denote an adverse action.[13] Accordingly it is probably best to translate v. 15b "since[14] he has acted," i.e., "since he has acted/taken action (to destroy me)." In any case, it is extremely unlikely in this context that this verb denotes a positive action of Yhwh vis-à-vis the psalmist.[15]

The speaker in PsHez hesitates to address Yhwh further because apparently he is convinced that the deity has already made a decision and entered upon a certain course of action—namely, to bring his life to an end (cf. v. 12e). Yhwh is not a god who is easily deterred from his purpose. He does not alter his decisions lightly: "God is not . . . a

---

[12] 1 Kgs 8:32, 39; Jer 14:7; Ezek 20:9, 14, 22; Pss 22:32; 37:5; 52:11; Dan 9:19.

[13] E.g., as in Ps 39:10:

neʾĕlamtî lōʾ-ʾeptaḥ pî
  kî ʾattâ ʿāśâ

I am silent, I do not open my mouth,
  for you have acted.

As is evident from v. 11 Yhwh's "action" in this case is some kind of punishment—"your stroke . . . the blows of your hand"—as in PsHez.

[14] In this colon the copula wĕ- has an infrequently attested nuance, "since, for," as in 2 Sam 7:20, cited above.

[15] Several interpreters of Isa 38:15b seem to think that the expression "[Yhwh] has acted" refers to the divine act of salvation on behalf of the psalmist (e.g., see P. D. Miller, *They Cried to the Lord: The Form and Theology of Biblical Prayer* [Minneapolis: Fortress, 1994] 190–91; Oswalt, *The Book of Isaiah: Chapters 1–39*, 686). But this understanding cannot be correct. Nothing in the poem up to this point suggests any salvific activity on the part of Yhwh vis-à-vis the psalmist. On the contrary, up to this point all the deity's actions alluded to are hostile to the psalmist (from his vantage point). The divine deliverance of the poet is mentioned for the first time in v. 17c–f and not earlier.

mortal, that he should change his mind."[16] This fact alone would give one pause about requesting a change in the divine plan of action. Nor is there any reason to suppose that the poet's mind set is that of Job, who is fully convinced of his personal innocence and challenges God to prove him in the wrong. The fact that he later relates that Yhwh had taken away "all my sins" (v. 17f) implies an awareness and acceptance of his own sinfulness, which would also contribute to his reluctance to entreat God. One must also bear in mind that the psalmist has already prayed to God for deliverance. Verse 14cd states explicitly that he has entreated Yhwh through bitter tears to relent, but has received no answer. This fact too bears significantly on his hesitancy to address Yhwh again at this point.

[15c] *ʾeddaddeh kol-šĕnôtay*:

1QIsaᵃ: *ʾdwdh kwl šnwty*; 1QIsaᵇ [ ]; LXX: [ ]; Aquila: *προβιβάσω πάντα [ ]; Symmachus: ἀναλογίσομαι πάντα τὰ ἔτη μου; Theodotion: *καθοδήγησιν πάντας τοὺς ἐνιαυτούς μου; Vg: recogitabo omnes annos meos; Syriac: *wʾnd klh šnty*; *Targum of Isaiah*: *mʾ ʾplḥ wʾšlym qdmwhy kl šnyʾ dʾwsyp ʿl ḥyy*.

As regards *ʾddh*, 1QIsaᵃ is similar to the consonantal text of the MT, but derives the verb from a different root than indicated in the MT. Aquila's translation appears to reflect the MT. It might be best to discuss first Begrich's emendation of this term to *ʾdkh* (*ʾôdĕkâ*), which he translates, "danken will ich dir."[17] Such an emendation is hypothetically possible. As for the emendation of *d* to *k*, we have already seen that the MT's *dlw* in v. 14c should be read as *klw*. But this emendation assumes that the deliverance that the psalmist sought in v. 14d has been granted. Yet nothing in vv. 14 or 15ab indicates this. If anything, the latter argues against it, as we have seen. Despite the textual difficulty of vv. 16a–17a, the psalmist has not obtained the longed-for deliverance at this point in the poem, as is clear at the very least from the imperative *wĕheḥăyēnî* in v. 16c, "let me recover!"

C. Westermann has pointed out two important factors with regard to *y-d-y* (*hiphil*) and its use in the OT. (1) The verb is sometimes used in

---

[16] Num 23:19 (NRSV); see also 1 Sam 15:29.
[17] *Der Psalm des Hiskia*, 17, 53.

the sense "to confess, acknowledge," etc. Thus it is in some sense a *verbum dicendi*, insofar as the speaker says or proclaims something. That "something" in Hebrew poetry is most frequently what Yhwh *has done* for the psalmist, i.e., the deliverance from suffering the psalmist has requested.[18] (2) He also notes that this verb describes a response to an action.[19] Thus in lament psalms, aside from (a) laments which contain a sudden report that the psalmist's prayer has been answered[20] or (b) in the "vow of praise" section of such psalms, where the psalmist gives voice to his vow or determination to praise Yhwh in the future (i.e., *after his prayer has been answered*), this verb is used only to denote the psalmist's praise for an already experienced act of deliverance. Hence it is premature to claim that the psalmist is rendering thankful praise to God in v. 15c.

The Masoretic pointing of *ʾddh* indicates a derivation from the root *d-d-y*, a *hithpael* with assimilated *t*.[21] The meaning usually given is "to walk slowly, solemnly, deliberately."[22] But the matter is more complicated. The root *d-d-y* is a *dis legomenon* in the MT, supposedly occurring here and in Ps 42:5b. But it is highly unlikely that it is present in either passage.[23] In post-biblical Hebrew and Jewish Aramaic the *(h)ithpael* describes the hopping motion of birds[24]—not slow or solemn movement—which hardly fits the context of Isa 38:15. *HALAT* renders it "to wander" in this text.[25]

But the root in question could also be *n-d-d*. Although it more commonly means "to flee"[26] or "stray,[27] "to wander" is preferable in a few passages. The only ancient version that reflects this root in its translation is the Syriac: "and he has driven away all my sleep"—literally,

---

[18] C. Westermann, "ידה *jdh* hi. preisen," *THAT*, 1. col. 676.

[19] Ibid., col. 675.

[20] E.g., Pss 6:9; 22:23; 28:6.

[21] GKC, §55g.

[22] Zorell, *Lexicon Hebraicum et Aramaicum Veteris Testamenti*, 167; BDB, 186.

[23] For detailed evidence supporting this assertion, see M. L. Barré, "'Wandering About' as a Topos of Depression in Ancient Near Eastern Literature and in the Bible," *JNES* 60 (2001) 185–87.

[24] Jastrow, *Dictionary of the Targumim*, 280–81; Levy, *Wörterbuch über die Talmudim und Midraschim*, 1. 378.

[25] *HALAT*, 205.

[26] Isa 10:31; 21:15; 22:3; 33:3; Pss 55:8; 68:13; Nah 3:7.

[27] Hos 7:13.

"caused all my sleep to flee away." The verb here is *ʾnd* (*aphel*) from *n-d-d*. In the OT this root appears with *šēnâ* ("sleep") in Gen 31:40; Esth 6:1 and frequently in post-biblical Aramaic texts.[28] Barthélemy notes that this interpretation was shared by a number of medieval Jewish commentators: Saadya, Yefet ben Eli, Judah ibn Balaam, Joseph Qara, and Eliezer of Beaugency.[29] It has also been supported by a few modern interpreters, including A. B. Ehrlich[30] and R. B. Y. Scott,[31] and the following modern English translations: *NJPSV, RSV, NRSV,* and *TEV.*

This line of interpretation is ruled out, however, by one of the most prominent poetic features of PsHez. The major stylistic device unifying the entire poem, from its first subsection (IAa) to the coda, is the parallel word-pair *yôm* // *šānâ*, where the terms are in the plural with the 1st person pronominal suffix: "my days" // "my years." The integrity of this dominant structural feature demands the reading *šnwty.* Here *šnty,* "my sleep," is out of the question. Moreover, none of the ancient witnesses except the Syriac reads a 3d person form here, which also argues against this reading of the verse.

The other attested meaning of *n-d-d* is "to wander." Duhm proposed reading a *qal* form from the root *n-d-d* in this passage, *ʾeddědâ.*[32] G. R. Driver also derived the term in question from this root and with this meaning.[33] Their insight is corroborated by 1QIsa[a], which reads *ʾdwdh,* i.e., *ʾeddôdâ,* the 1st sg. cohortative of *n-d-d* (in the "pausal" form common at Qumran[34]). This reading requires no emendation of the consonantal text. Although its more common meaning is "to flee," *n-d-d* has the meaning "to wander about" in Hos 9:17 and Job 15:23,[35] where the "wandering" is the result of divine punish-

---

[28] See Barré, "'Wandering About'," 186 n. 48.

[29] *Critique Textuelle de l'Ancien Testament* 2. 273.

[30] A. B. Ehrlich, *Randglossen zur hebräischen Bibel* (7 vols.; Leipzig: Hinrichs, 1908–14) 4. 140.

[31] Scott, "Isaiah: Text, Exegesis, and Exposition, Chapters 1–39," *IB* 5. 376.

[32] Duhm, *Das Buch Jesaja,* 281.

[33] "Isaiah i–xxxix," 56: "I wander to and fro." This translation has been adopted by *NEB/REB.*

[34] Qimron mentions "clear pausal forms appearing out of pause in the DSS" (*The Hebrew of the Dead Sea Scrolls,* 51 [§311.13d]).

[35] *HALAT,* 635 ("umherirren").

ment.[36] In Isa 38:15c this behavior on the part of the poet is likewise perceived as the result of divine disfavor or punishment. Compare the punishment of Cain to be a "wanderer" (*nād*) on the earth in Gen 4:12.[37] The expression "to wander about" is frequently found in ancient Near Eastern and biblical literature as a topos denoting grief or depression.[38]

The form of this verb, to be read *ʾeddĕdâ*, is cohortative, corresponding to *ʾēlēkâ* in v. 10b, the only other cohortative in PsHez. In the context, *ʾeddĕdâ* seems to convey a nuance of necessity, as does the first cohortative. Furthermore, in light of v. 15ab, which is interrogative, this bicolon should probably also be understood as a question following upon the interrogative v. 15ab: "Must I wander about (depressed) all my years . . . ?"

The objection might be raised at this point that the poet's reference to his wandering "all the years of [his] life" (i.e., for the rest of his life) contradicts the interpretation proposed above for v. 12e, according to which the the poet laments that God is bringing his life to an end in the space of a single day.[39] But vv. 12e and 15cd simply represent two different hyperbolic ways of stating one's misery in temporal terms. The "contradiction" would hardly have bothered an ancient Near Eastern poet, especially in the context of lament, which is more interested in piling up descriptions of suffering than in rigorous logic. That this is the case here also may be seen from the Babylonian parallel to v. 12e cited above, viz., "May (the gods named on this stone) decree that he live not even a single day (longer)." Only two lines further the same text goes on to wish that the person live in misery for *a long time*: "Days of drought, years of famine may they (i.e., these gods) assign as his lot."[40]

---

[36] In Job 15:23a Eliphaz is describing the fate of the wicked man: *nōdēd hûʾ lĕlehem ʾayyâ* [MT: *lallehem ʾayyēh*], "He wanders as food for the vulture" (in support of the reading *ʾayyâ* see LXX γυψίν, "for vultures"). This reading is followed by Pope, *Job*, 113, 117; and Habel, *The Book of Job*, 247.

[37] Here the root is *n-w-d*, "wander," a by-form of *n-d-d*.

[38] For an extensive discussion of the evidence for this assertion, see Barré, "'Wandering About'," 177–87.

[39] This objection is raised by Linder, "Canticum Ezechiae," 62.

[40] The translation of King, *Babylonian Boundary-Stones*, IV col. 4, line 7 (p. 23).

[15d] *ʿal-mar napšî:*

1QIsa[a]: *ʿl mwr npšy*ᵓ; 1QIsa[b]:[ ]*n̊pšy*; LXX: καὶ ἀφείλατό μου τὴν ὀδύ-
νην τῆς ψυχῆς; Aquila: [ ]; Symmachus: ἐπὶ τῇ πιρκίᾳ τῆς ψυχῆς μου;
Theodotion: ἐπὶ τὴν πιρκίαν ψυχῆς μου; Vg: in amaritudine animae
meae; Syriac: *ʿl mrrᵓ dnpšy*; *Targum of Isaiah: wšyzyb mmrr npšy.*

The phrase *mar nepeš* occurs ten times in the MT. In six of these
occurrences *mar* functions as an adjective[41] and in four as a noun.[42] A
generic translation that covers all of these would be "(the quality of
being) unhappy, upset." Like other expressions formed with *nepeš,
rûaḥ,* or *lēb(āb), mar nepeš* refers to an emotional state, here a negative one. In certain narrative occurrences it expresses a sense of feeling
discontented or resentful for various unspecified reasons.[43] But in
others it is associated with terminology that clearly alludes to sorrow
or depression. Such is the case, for example, in 1 Sam 1:10, where
Hannah is described as *mārat nepeš* in a passage whose predicate is
bākōh tibkeh ("she weeps profusely"). It is evident from the context
that she is depressed because she is barren. In such a passage the idiom
could legitimately be translated "despondent, depressed." This is also
true of Ezek 27:31, where *mar nepeš* appears in the midst of numerous
culturally appropriate behaviors denoting sorrow/depression (wailing
aloud, crying out bitterly, casting dust on the head, wallowing in ashes
[v. 30]; shaving the head, donning sackcloth, weeping, and lamentation
[v. 31]) over the fall of the prince of Tyre. Finally, in Job 7:11 *bĕmar
napšî* is parallel to *bĕṣar rûḥî,* "in the distress of my spirit."

In the context of PsHez the primary significance of *mar nepeš* is the
negative physical and psychological state of the psalmist, occasioned
by the threat of imminent death and by his afflictions. The expression
may also reflect some feeling of depression or resentment occasioned
by Yhwh's "oppression" of him (v. 14d).[44]

In this colon *ʿal* is to be translated "because of," one of its more frequent connotations. Note the formal and semantic similarity of the
bicolon v. 15cd to Ps 42:10b, where *bĕ-* (in *bĕlaḥaṣ ᵓôyēb*) is functionally

---

[41] Judg 18:25; 1 Sam 1:10; 22:2; 2 Sam 17:8; Job 3:20; Prov 31:6.
[42] Isa 38:15; Ezek 27:31; Job 7:11; 10:1.
[43] Judg 18:25; 1 Sam 22:2; 2 Sam 17:8.
[44] See the discussion of *ʿšqh-ly* (v. 14d) above.

equivalent to *ᶜal* in Isa 38:15d as is *(qōdēr) ᵓēlēk*, "I walk about (depressed)," to *ᵓeddĕdâ*.[45]

Verse 15cd should most probably be interpreted as a continuation of the deliberative process begun in v. 15a and therefore translated as a question. The psalmist is asking himself whether, despite his fear that further entreaty of Yhwh would be pointless or even work to his disadvantage, he should resign himself to continuing for the rest of his existence in the miserable state in which he presently finds himself or should make a final attempt to persuade God to change his fate.

[16ab] *ᵓădōnāy ᶜălêhem yiḥyû ûlĕkol-bāhen ḥayyê rûḥî:*[46]
1QIsaᵃ: *ᵓdwny ᶜlyhmh wḥyw*[47] *wlkwl bhmh ḥyw rwḥw*[48]; 1QIsaᵇ: *ᵓdny ᶜl* [ ]*hm yḥ̊yw wlkl bhn*[ ]; LXX: κύριε, περὶ αὐτῆς γὰρ ἀνηγγέλη σοι, καὶ ἐξήγειράς μου τὴν πνοήν; Aquila: κύριε, ἐπ᾽ αὐτοῖς ζήσονται καὶ εἰς πάντα [τὰ] ἐν αὐτοῖς ζωὴ πνεύματός μου; Symmachus: [ ]; Theodotion: [ ]; Vg: Domine sic vivitur et in talibus vita spiritus mei; Syriac: *mryᵓ ᶜlyhwn nḥwn mṭl hlyn ḥyᵓ drwḥy*; *Targum of Isaiah: yhwh ᶜl kl mytyᵓ ᵓmrt lᵓḥᵓh wqdm kwlhwn ᵓḥyyᵗᵓ rwḥy.*

The poet answers his own question by abruptly ending his deliberation and addressing a prayer to Yhwh without introduction. The first part of this prayer is without doubt the most difficult line in PsHez, and one of the most troublesome verses in the entire MT. Concerning this text the eighteenth-century scholar C. F. Houbigant is reputed to have said, "Felix qui potest haec verba ut sunt interpretari," "Fortunate is the one who can interpret these words as they are."[49] H. Wild-

---

[45] See Barré, "'Wandering About'," 182–83.

[46] I published an extensive study of this line in "Restoring the 'Lost' Prayer of Hezekiah (Isaiah 38:16–17b)," *JBL* 114 (1995) 385–99. The present study is in agreement with the findings of that article. Various points made there are here expanded upon, and others are added to that earlier treatment.

[47] Burrows (*The Dead Sea Scrolls of St. Mark's Monastery*, xxxii) reads *yḥyw*. But in the Great Isaiah scroll *waw* and *yod* are quite distinct. A careful examination of the photograph shows the first letter to be the typical *waw* of this scribe, not the *yod*. This reading has been confirmed by Goshen-Gottstein, *The Book of Isaiah*, 169; and Parry and Qimron, *The Great Isaiah Scroll*, 65.

[48] The text presents several important variant readings to the MT: *wḥyw* for MT *yḥyw*, *bhmh* for MT *bhn*, *ḥyw* for MT *ḥyy*, and *rwḥw* for MT *rwḥy*

[49] Cited (without reference) by Touzard, "De la conservation du texte hébreu," 99.

berger has aptly dubbed it "an exegete's nightmare."[50] Thus far no arrangement or redivision of the consonantal MT has yielded good sense, despite many attempts. Three pieces of information that we have gleaned thus far about PsHez are significant for the task of restoration. (1) The fact that Parts I and II of the poem contain exactly sixty words each indicates a concern for balance on the part of the author. We should therefore not expect that the corruption in these lines involves any significant loss or addition of words. (2) With the exception of the opening and conclusion of PsHez, which are tricola (vv. 10b–d, 20a–c), and the monocola (*ʾănî*) *ʾāmartî* in vv. 10a, 11a, the poem consists entirely of bicola. The presumption would be that this corrupted section is also a bicolon. (3) As we noted earlier (see Chapter 1), the last colon of each bi- or tricolon in PsHez is, with the exception of v. 14d, quite short, consisting of two or three words at most. In the case of three-word cola one of the words is a proclitic (vv. 11e, 13a, 15d, 20c). Thus we expect the restored bicolon to consist of a comparatively long colon followed by a short one of no more than three words.

Contrary to the view of a number of interpreters, some of 1QIsaᵃ's variant readings vis-à-vis the MT in PsHez prove to be superior to those of the MT, i.e., closer to the original text of the poem, a fact that E. Ulrich has already established.[51] After a thorough investigation of this passage, I maintain that this holds true for v. 16ab. Here we still have a text that has suffered corruption, but the extent of corruption is less advanced than in the MT.[52]

Converting the reading of v. 16ab in 1QIsaᵃ to standard Biblical Hebrew orthography and morpholology, we arrive at the following text:

ʾdny ʿlyḥm wḥyw wlkl bḥm ḥyw rwḥw

One noteworthy deviation from the MT is the reading *bḥmh* (for standard Biblical Hebrew *bḥm*) over against MT's *bḥn*. The latter is a difficult reading. There are no plural antecedents to which this feminine form could refer. Does 1QIsaᵃ represent an attempt to improve the

[50] Wildberger, *Jesaja 28–39*, 1444.

[51] See above, p. 7.

[52] What is preserved of this line in 1QIsaᵇ is identical to the MT.

text here or does it present a text closer to the original? This question cannot be answered with certainty on the basis of the textual evidence, but at least one cannot dismiss the reading of 1QIsaᵃ *a priori* as inferior. The MT's *bhn* is admittedly ancient, attested as early as 1QIsaᵇ, where the top of the final *nun* is just visible on the photograph. Yet the *nun* could be explained by the fact that "Hebrew and Aramaic sources from the Second Temple period onward . . . reflect the loss of the phonological distinction between *m* and *n* in final position"—i.e., both were pronounced /n/.[53] It is significant in this connection that Aquila's absurdly literal translation[54] (ca. 130 A.D.) reflects the reading of the term as it appears in 1QIsaᵃ. It agrees with the MT in every respect except for ἐν αὐτοῖς (masc.) rather than ἐν αὐταῖς (fem.) for the MT's *bhn*. The fact that Aquila read a masculine pronoun here argues for *bhm* in his *Vorlage*.[55] Being the slavishly literal translator that he was, he would surely have translated with ἐν αὐταῖς if the text before him had read *bhn*.

One is immediately struck by the disproportionately high concentration of *waw*s functioning as copula or terminal morpheme (the 3d masc. pl. verbal ending and the 3d masc. sg. pronominal suffix) in the last five words of v. 16ab in 1QIsaᵃ—*whyw wlkwl bhmh ḥyw rwḥw* (followed by *wtḥlymny whḥyny* in v. 16c). Such a high concentration of prefixal and suffixal *waw*s in such a short span of words raises the suspicion that some are secondary. Several of these could be explained as the result of dittography. The *waw* in *wlkwl* could have resulted from attraction to the plural ending on preceding *whyw*. Similarly, the final *waw* in *rwḥw* could have resulted from attraction to the conjunctive *waw* on *wtḥlymny*. If these are deleted, the resulting text is:

ʾdny ʿlyhm whyw lkl bhm ḥyw rwḥ

Some of the versions also give evidence of a *Vorlage* with alternative readings in this passage, readings that are significant for its reconstruction. The most important witness here is the LXX, whose *Vorlage* may be reconstructed provisionally as:

---

[53] Qimron, *The Hebrew of the Dead Sea Scrolls*, 27.

[54] On the nature of Aquila's translation, see Würthwein, *The Text of the Old Testament*, 55.

[55] Kennicott also lists 10 manuscripts that read *bhm*.

ʾdny ʿlyh mḥwḥ lk wmḥyh/wtḥyh rwḥ(y?)[56]

As the term behind ἀνηγγέλη one could posit either a finite form, *ḥwḥ*, or a participle, *mḥwḥ*.[57] The latter is more likely, since it adheres more closely to the lettering of 1QIsaᵃ (minus allomorphic accretions): *ʾdny ʿlyh mḥw-* and *ʾdny ʿlyhm wḥy-* respectively. Note that the LXX's περὶ αὐτῆς γὰρ ἀνηγγέλη reflects the *Vorlage ʿlyh mḥwḥ*, which contains no *waw* after the *mem*, whereas 1QIsaᵃ has *ʿlyhm wḥyw* (minus the allomorphic *-h* ending on the first word). As regards the second verb, which the LXX renders as καὶ ἐξήγειράς, this could be plausibly reconstructed as *wtḥyh*[58] or as a second participial form, *wmḥyh*. For if the LXX translator could render one participle (viz., *mḥwḥ < mḥyḥ*) with a finite verb (ἀνηγγέλη), he could have done the same with a second participle (*wmḥyh*) as well. If one does reconstruct the second verb as *wmḥyh*, it makes sense for the translator to render it as a 2d person (ἐξήγειράς), since it comes immediately after the *Vorlage*'s reading of *lkl* as *lk* (i.e., *lēkā* = σοι). Finally, the last word in the reconstruction above could have been either *rwḥy* or simply *rwḥ*. The latter is a plausible restoration since the LXX translator is known to have added pronouns (here "my" = μου) *ad sensum* that were not represented in his *Vorlage*.[59]

What information can be gleaned from this translation? First, the LXX supports the deletion of *waw* before *lk(l)*, as suggested above, with its translation σοι rather than καὶ σοί, reflecting a *Vorlage* which had *lk(l)* rather than *wlk(l)*. The fact that it also has no καὶ before ἀνηγγέλη supports the deletion of (initial) *waw* on the first verb in

---

[56] This provisional retroversion is identical to that of Nyberg ("Hiskias Danklied," 87) except that he has *wḥyyt* instead of *wtḥyh* as the second verb. Touzard's restoration of the second verb is the first option I have proposed here—*tḥyy* or *tḥyh* ("De la conservation du text hébreu," 101). For my final view on the retroversion, see n. 74 below,

[57] The LXX translates participles as finite verbs in certain cases. See, for example, 1 Sam 2:6–7, where it translates the participial epithets (referring to Yhwh), viz., *mēmît ... mēḥayyeh ... môrîd ... môrîš ... maʿăśîr ... mašpîl ... mērômēm ... mēqîm*, as θανατοῖ ... ζωογονεῖ ... κατάγει ... πτωχίζει ... πλουτίζει ... ταπεινοῖ ... ἀνυψοῖ ... ἀνιστᾷ.

[58] Cf. Touzard, "De la conservation du text hébreu," 100; The rendering of Hebrew *ḥ-y-y* by (ἐξ)εγείρω is unique in the LXX. But compare the likewise unique translation of this root by virtually synonymous ἀνίστημι in the superscription of PsHez (v. 9).

[59] See Tov, *The Text-Critical Use of the Septuagint*, 224–25.

1QIsa[a] as well (*whyw*). Second, and most significantly, the LXX's *Vorlage* obviously read a *2d person sg.* verb form in v. 16b (ἐξήγειράς), not a 3d person pl. as in the case of the MT and 1QIsa[a]. It reflects a Hebrew text with a participle *mhwh* (from *h-w-y*, "to report") as the first verb and possibly the participle *mhyh* (*piel* or *hiphil*, from *h-y-y*, "to live") or *thyh* as the second.[60] The translator chose to render both of these as finite aorist verbs. The aorist passive ἀνηγγέλη would most likely reflect a passive form in the Hebrew, most probably a *pual* (*měhuwweh*), although the *pual* of this verb is not attested in Biblical Hebrew.

The *Targum of Isaiah* also contains several significant renderings that differ markedly from the MT. The first appears in ʿl kl myty[ʾ] ʾmrt l[ʾ]h[ʾ]h, "With regard to all the dead you (Yhwh) have promised to give life (to them)." Here ʾmrt l[ʾ]h[ʾ]h is paraphrastic, but clearly reflects a 2d masc. sg. verb in contradistinction to the 3d masc. pl. forms in 1QIsa[a] and the MT (*whyw* and *yhyw* respectively). The second variant is the targum's rendering of the last two words in v. 16ab, which is not a paraphrase: ʾh[yy]t[ʾ] rwh[y], "You (Yhwh) have given life to my spirit," where the MT has *hyy rwhy* (1QIsa[a]: *hyw rwhw*). Not only does the targum agree with 1QIsa[a] and the LXX in reading a verb rather than a noun here, but it reads *both* verbs in v. 16ab as *2d person sg.* instead of 3d pl. forms. Noteworthy too is the fact that the targum reads the first verb as a derivative of *h-y-y*, "to live," not *h-w-y*, "to announce" (as in the LXX's *Vorlage*), in agreement with the MT, 1QIsa[a], 1QIsa[b], and Aquila.

Taking this evidence into account, I postulate the following as an earlier stage of v. 16ab:

ʾdny ʿlyhm hyh lkl bhm hyh rwh

A striking feature of this hypothetical stage of the text of v. 16ab is a repeated sequence of five letters: *hm hyh . . . hm hyh*. These are to be combined and read as *hmhyh*, which would be the *piel* or *hiphil* participle of *h-y-y* preceded by the article: *hammĕhayyeh* or **hammahăyeh* respectively. Emending left-over *lkl* to *kll* and redividing several words, I postulate that the original reading of v. 16ab was:

---

[60] The Syriac also reflects the root *h-w-y* in its reading *nhwn*.

ʾdny ʿly hmḥyh kl lb
hmḥyh rwḥ

O Lord Most High, you who give life to every heart,
  who give life to (every)[61] spirit . . . .

A significant parallel to the restored text given above appears in a later chapter of Isaiah—namely, 57:15, which contains the same word-pair[62] with the same verb, *ḥ-y-y* (*hiphil*), repeated in each colon:

mārôm wĕqādôš ʾeškôn
wĕʾet-dakkāʾ ûšĕpal-rûaḥ
lĕhaḥăyôt rûaḥ šĕpālîm
lĕhaḥăyôt lēb nidkāʾîm

I dwell in a high and holy place,
  and with the crushed and lowly of spirit;
to *give life to/revive the heart* of the lowly,
  to *give life to/revive the spirit* of the crushed.

This is the only other passage in the MT which contains the word-pair *lēb // rûaḥ* as the object of *ḥ-y-y* in the *hiphil*. It is significant too that the *Targum of Isaiah* translates the two Hebrew verbs with *aphel* (= Hebrew *hiphil*) forms: (*ʾmrt*) *Pḥʾh* and *ʾḥyyṭʾ*. On the basis of the Isaiah 57 parallel and the targum I parse restored *hmḥyh* in Isa 38:16ab as the *hiphil* rather than the *piel* participle.

The structure of the reconstructed unit precisely fits the expected colometric pattern in PsHez. The first colon is long, containing five words (ten syllables or four accents). The second (final) colon is very short, consisting of two words (four syllables or two accents).

Perhaps the most unexpected term in this restoration is the archaic divine title *ʿēlî*, possibly to be vocalized *ʿālî*, with a by-form *ʿāl*. Its existence as an ancient Israelite divine name was first argued by H. S.

---

[61] On the omission of *kol* in Hebrew poetry, note the following passages in which it is present in the first but not the second colon: Pss 18:23; 20:4; 70:5; 77:13; 90:9; 143:5; Isa 18:3; 41:11; 49:11; 63:7; Jer 22:22 (see H. Ringgren, "The Omitting of *kol* in Hebrew Parallelism," *VT* 32 [1982] 99–103).

[62] See Avishur, *Word-Pairs*, 477.

Nyberg in 1935.[63] Though still somewhat controverted,[64] there appears to be too much evidence in its favor at this point to reject it as a genuine, early Israelite divine epithet. In particular, its occurrence as the divine element in a personal name in one of the ninth-eighth century ostraca from Samaria is hardly in doubt: *yhwᶜly*, "May *ᶜēlî* keep alive."[65] Interestingly, here *ᶜly* governs the same verb as in our passage. The scribal tradition generally confused this name with forms of the preposition *ᶜal*, as in Isa 38:16a. Thus strictly speaking the word does not have to be "restored" here. The only emendation necessary is to separate the MT's *ᶜlyhm* into *ᶜly hm-*, the latter being the beginning of the *hiphil* participle *hammaḥăyeh*.

What disturbance to the text led to the chain of events that resulted in this degree of corruption? In my earlier article on this passage I identified the "chief culprit" as the rare divine epithet *ᶜēlî*.[66] But after further research, I would assign only a secondary causality to this term. The origin of the problem is to be found, rather, in the innocent-looking combination of letters *hm*.

Remarkable as it may sound, we may literally speak of a backward "migration" of these letters from the beginning of *hmḥyh* to the end of *ᶜly*. This phenomenon, documented from readings of the MT and 1QIsaᵃ in other biblical passages, also explains other aspects of the textual corruption, such as the change of the verb "to live" from singular (as witnessed by the LXX and the *Targum of Isaiah*) to plural (as in the MT, 1QIsaᵃ, 1QIsaᵇ).

---

[63] H. S. Nyberg, *Studien zum Hoseabuche: Zugleich ein Beitrag zur Klärung der alttestamentlichen Textkritik* (UUÅ 6; Uppsala: Almqvist & Wiksells, 1935) 57–60, 74, 89, 120. On *ᶜēlî* see also M. Dahood, "The Divine Name *ᶜēlî* in the Psalms," *TS* 14 (1953) 452–57; D. N. Freedman, "Divine Names and Titles in Early Hebrew Poetry," in *Pottery, Poetry, and Prophecy: Studies in Early Hebrew Poetry* (Winona Lake, IN: Eisenbrauns, 1980) 113; A. Cooper, "Divine Names and Epithets in the Ugaritic Texts," in *Ras Shamra Parallels: The Texts from Ugarit and the Hebrew Bible: Vol. III* (ed. S. Rummel; AnOr 51; Rome: Pontifical Biblical Institute, 1981) 451–58; P. K. McCarter, *1 Samuel* (AB 8; Garden City, NY: Doubleday, 1980) 70–71, 73; and M. H. Pope, "A Resurvey of Some Ugaritic-Hebrew Connections," *Maarav* 7 (1991) 201–2.

[64] The presence of this divine epithet in the MT is denied by B. Schmidt, "AL," *DDD* (rev. ed.) 14–17.

[65] See Dahood, "The Divine Name *ᶜēlî* in the Psalms," 452–53; Gibson, *Hebrew and Moabite Inscriptions*, 10, lv line 2 and p. 13. On the date of the ostraca, see ibid., 5–6.

[66] "Restoring the 'Lost' Prayer," 392.

The first stage: עלי המחיה.[67] It is clear from Isa 57:15 that ḥ-y-y (*hiphil*) + *lēb* // *rûaḥ* is a viable Biblical Hebrew idiom. Hence *hmḥyh kl lb ... hmḥyh rwḥ* is a plausible restoration from that point of view. It is also plausible because of the fact that it follows the lettering of 1QIsa[a] and the LXX *Vorlage* very closely,[68] especially in comparison with earlier proposed emendations.

The second stage: עלי הם חיה. What is interesting to note as regards this *hiphil* participle is that it is one of several examples in ancient Hebrew of the הם having become *detached* from initial position. This could happen because monosyllabic forms like *hm* were, at one stage in the orthography, written not with final but with *initial-medial mem*, a phenomenon also witnessed in the Severus Scroll.[69] Thus, depending on the spacing of the letters, a scribe could take a form like המפרצים either as הַמְפֹּורָצִים (Neh 2:13: Kethib) or הֵם פְּרוּצִים[70] (Qere). The same phenomenon is attested in Isa 8:19 according to the reading of 1QIsa[a], הם צפפים והם הגים, where the MT has המצפצפים והמהגים. Note also Isa 9:6, where the MT has לסרבה, with final *mem* in medial position (Codex Leningradensis [Kethib][71]); 1QIsa[a] reads לם רבה. Hence the "migration" of *hm* in Isa 38:16 began with the splitting off of הם from המציה, yielding עלי הם חיה.

Once this had happened, הם could only be parsed as the independent masc. pl. pronoun. At first the left-over *ḥyh* was understood as a 3d sg. *qal* verb, as witnessed indirectly by the LXX's περὶ αὐτῆς (γὰρ) ἀν-ηγγέλλη = ʿlyh mḥwh < ʿlyh mḥyh < ʿly hmḥyh and the *Targum of Isaiah*'s singular verbs. But preceded now by stand-alone הם, this 3d sg. verb was "corrected" to a 3d pl., *ḥyw*. *This is the reason why the MT reads a plural verb here (yḥyw)*. Later, as 1QIsa[a] shows, the first verb was supplied with the copula in a misguided attempt to improve an already confused text: *wḥyw*. The MT's *yḥyw* represents a yet further

[67] Because a significant aspect of the discussion of *hm* is related to whether the *mem* is initial-medial (מ) or final (ם), in the discussion of this term I will depart from the use of transliteration of the Hebrew and present the relevant words in Hebrew script.

[68] See n. 74 below.

[69] J. P. Siegel, *The Severus Scroll and 1QIsa*[a] (SBLMasS 2; Missoula, MT: Scholars Press: 1975) 8–14.

[70] Siegel (ibid., 12) notes: "Some older texts of Neh. 2:13 still read הם פרוצים (with initial-medial M); this was changed to (or understood as) הם פרוצים."

[71] The Qere is למרבה. The Aleppo Codex reads לם רבה according to Goshen-Gottstein's edition of the text (*The Book of Isaiah*, 35).

change, abetted by the confusion of *yod* and *waw* in later paleography.

The third stage: עליהם חיו. At some point the הם—which by this point may have been regularized to הם[72]—came under the influence of ʿly, which is indistinguishable consonantally from the suffixal form of the preposition. The rarity of this divine name contributed to this (con)fusion.

The three-stage process outlined here is not mere hypothesis. We can actually see evidence of it elsewhere in Isaiah, viz., 30:7. Here the MT reads רהב הם שבת (second stage) and 1QIsaᵃ רהבהם שבת (third stage), whereas a number of scholars posit as the original reading רהב המשבת (first stage).[73]

It is significant that in Isa 8:19 1QIsaᵃ shows the detachment of הם from *two successive participles*. Most likely the same thing happened in our passage, namely that the same process occurred, probably at the same time, in the case of the second המחיה: כל לב הם חיה > כל לב המחיה > כלל בהם חיו > כל לב הם חיו >. The readings *ḥyw* and *bhm* in this hypothetical history of the text are both attested by 1QIsaᵃ and the second (indirectly) by Aquila. The leftover *kll* was at some point changed to the more intelligible *lkl* (*lĕkōl*) and *bhm* became *bhn* in the MT, probably through auditory error.

How does one account for the fact that the LXX preserved the *singular* form of both verbs in v. 16ab? In the history of the textual tradition underlying the LXX, part of the first original *hmḥyh* was dislocated and attracted to ʿly, as happened in the pre-masoretic tradition. But in the case of the LXX *only the* h *was attracted*, so that the *m* remained with the following letters, which still spelled the masc. sg. participle, *mḥyh* (which later became *mḥwh*). In the textual tradition behind the MT it was the dislocation of the first *two* letters (*hm*) in "the second stage," when these became an independent 3d masc. pl. pronoun (ʿly hm ḥyh), that caused the word in question to be changed to a plural finite verb form—*ḥyw*. In the case of the LXX *Vorlage*, the *h* of the second *mḥyh* was lost through syncope at some point in the

[72] It is possible that the initial-medial form of the *mem* was retained—at first—even in the third stage, when הם was attached to עלי. 11QPsᵃ 5:8 has an unusual form, [א]לוהיכם, "your God," with the initial-medial *mem* as the final letter of a polysyllabic word.

[73] E.g., Wildberger, *Jesaja 28–39*, 1158; Childs, *Isaiah*, 225–26; J. Blenkinsopp, *Isaiah 1–39* (AB 19; New York: Doubleday, 2000) 413; Duhm's view is similar (*Das Buch Jesaja*, 218), except that he reads the penultimate letter *bet* as a *mem*: רהב המשמת.

transmission of the Hebrew text but the rest of the word was preserved—*mḥyh*.[74]

What does it mean to "cause the heart/spirit to live" in Isa 38:16 and
57:15? It is not impossible that this refers to God's role as the author of
all life, insofar as heartbeat and breath are signs of life, but the reference is more likely to reviving those who are "dead" in a figurative
sense. The word *lēb(āb)* occurs only two other times in the MT in con-
junction with *ḥ-y-y*—in Pss 22:27 and 69:33. Here *lēb* is the subject of
the verb in the *qal*. From the context of these two passages it is clear

---

[74] Having presented what I judge to be the *Urtext* of v. 16ab, on the basis of this I
can now make some adjustments to my provisional reconstruction of the LXX *Vorlage*
given above. The second predicate is definitely *mḥyh*, whereas above I presented this
verbal form only as a possibility. Hence the LXX's *Vorlage* of v. 16ab read: *ʾdny ʿlyh
mḥwh* [< *mḥyh*] *lk wmḥyh rwḥ(y?)*. If this restoration is correct, one should be able,
beginning from this *Urtext*, to show how the LXX *Vorlage* assumed the form I posit
above. In particular, one should be able to account for the missing letters *l*, *b*, and *h*
immediately following *lk*. Below I give the hypothetical textual history of that part of
the *Vorlage* which I reconstruct as *mḥwh lk wmḥyh* (= ἀνηγγέλη σοι καὶ ἐξήγειράς):

Urtext:	*hmḥyh*	*kl lb*	*hmḥyh*
	mḥyh	*kl lb*	*hmḥyh*	Attachment of first *h-* to preceding ʿly
	mḥyh	*kl b*	*hmḥyh*	Loss of second *l* through haplography
	mḥyh	*kl*	*bhmḥyh*	Attachment of *b* to following *hmḥyh*
	mḥyh	*kl*	*bmḥyh*	Syncope of article *h* after "preposition" *b*
	mḥwh	*kl*	*bmḥyh*	Common *waw/yod* confusion
	mḥwh	*lk*	*bmḥyh*	Metathesis of *kl* under influence of *mḥwh*
Vorlage:	*mḥwh*	*lk*	*wmḥyh*	Auditory confusion of *w* and post-vocalic *b*

The first scribal error was a haplography, *kl b* for *kl lb*. Only if the two *lamed*s occur
together in the text, as in the reconstruction given above, is this haplography possible.
This left an "orphaned" *b*, which was naturally taken with the following word (if it had
been attached to the preceding word, *klb* would mean "like the heart" or "dog"—both
implausible). Now *bhmḥyh* looks like a participle preceded by the preposition *b-* and
the article *h*. The latter was then elided as a result of syncope—*běhammaḥăyeh* >
bammaḥăyeh—which is what usually happens in Biblical Hebrew. Another error
occurred in the first *hmḥyh*. Sometime after the article had been moved to the end of
ʿly, resulting in ʿlyh (LXX: περὶ αὐτῆς), *mḥyh* became *mḥwh*, probably the result of the
common *waw/yod* confusion. This triggered the next error, namely reading *lk* for *kl* via
metathesis, providing an indirect object for this *verbum dicendi*. Finally, coming after
lěkā the *b* in *bmḥyh* was spirantized and hence capable of being confused with *w*, to
which it was changed (auditory error). The change of original *kl* to *lk* (*lěkā*), "to you,"
made it possible for the LXX translator to render the participle *wmḥyh* as a 2d sg. verb:
καὶ ἐξήγειράς.

that this idiom refers primarily to a happy mood.[75] (The Akkadian equivalent, *libbu balāṭu*, has the same meaning.[76]) Its opposite is *lēb m-w-t* (1 Sam 25:37), which connotes extreme depression.[77] Since Isa 57:15 makes explicit reference to depression (cf. *šĕpal-rûaḥ*), "causing the heart to live" must denote primarily lifting the spirits of the individuals in question. The prayer in Isa 38:16-17b is preceded by *mar napšî*, which is also a designation of depression or despondency,[78] and ends with *mar-lî . . .* , which likewise bespeaks a dejected mood. Therefore when the poet addresses Yhwh as "the one who causes every heart . . . (every) spirit to live" and then calls upon God to "cause me to live," he is praying for divine deliverance from the deep depression in which he finds himself, brought on by his illness and the realization of his shortened life span.[79] Of course, he could not be delivered from this depression unless he were first delivered from what caused it. One must also bear in mind that the ancient Israelites did not make a sharp distinction between physical and psychological suffering.

[16c-17b] *wĕtaḥălîmēnî wĕhaḥăyēnî hinnēh lĕšālôm mar-lî mār:*
1QIsa^a: *wtḥlymny whḥyny hn lšlwm mr ly mʾwdh*; 1QIsa^b: [ ]*lymny whḥyny hnh*[ ]*ly mr*; LXX: καὶ παρακληθεὶς ἔζησα [ ]; Aquila: καὶ σωφρονίσεις με καὶ ζωώσεις με ἰδοὺ περὶ τῆς εἰρήνης μου πικρὸν ἐμοὶ

---

[75] This is particularly evident in Ps 69:33, where the idiom *lēb ḥ-y-y* stands in synonymous parallelism to *ś-m-ḥ*, "to rejoice."

[76] In an Old Babylonian letter, a despondent subject, who styles himself "the son of a ghost," says to his queen: *šulum bēltīya matīma ul illikamma libbī ul ibluṭ*, "No greeting from my lady has ever reached me, with the result that my heart has not lived/revived' (i.e., I have not been able to shake off my depression)" (see B. R. Foster, "Letters and Literature: A Ghost's Entreaty," in *The Tablet and the Scroll: Near Eastern Studies in Honor of William W. Hallo* [ed. M. E. Cohen et al.; Bethesda, MD: CLD Press, 1993] 101–2).

[77] 1 Sam 25:36–38 narrates the end of Nabal. There can be little doubt that *wĕlēb nābāl ṭôb ʿālāyw* ("And Nabal's heart was merry within him") in v. 36 is meant to contrast sharply with *wayyāmāt libbô bĕqirbô* (lit., "His heart died within him") in v. 37. In this context the latter expression can only betoken a sudden, complete reversal of mood—from cheerfulness to the most profound depression.

[78] See 1 Sam 30:6; Job 3:20; 7:11; 21:25; Prov 14:10; Ezek 27:31.

[79] See Jenni, *Das hebräische Piʿel*, 62. Jenni claims that although *ḥ-y-y* in both the *piel* and *hiphil* can mean "to restore (someone) to life," the *piel* is always used in a life-threatening context, which is not the case with the *hiphil*.

πικρόν; Symmachus: καὶ ἀνέθαλάς με καὶ ζωώσεις με ἰδοὺ περὶ τῆς εἰρήνης μου πικρὸν ἐμοὶ πικρόν; Theodotion: *ditto*; Vg: corripies me et vivificabis me, ecce in pace amaritudo mea amarissima; Syriac: *ʾḥlmny wʾḥny hʾ lšlmʾ mr ly mrrʾ*; *Targum of Isaiah: wʾḥyytny wqyymtny hʾ lᶜbdy ʾwrytʾ sgy šlmʾ qdmk wʾt myty mrrʾ lršyᶜyʾ bkyn kd ydᶜyt ywm mwty špkyt dmᶜty bṣlw qdmk mr ly sgy.*

The first verb is not from *ḥ-l-m* I, "to dream,"[80] but a homophonous root meaning "to become strong, hale," rare in Biblical Hebrew.[81] It occurs elsewhere in the MT only in Job 39:4[82] but also in Sir 15:20; 49:10 and in 4Q222 fr. 1.2; 4Q470 fr. 2.4. It is common in Aramaic and Syriac as part of the vocabulary of healing.[83] Although earlier commentators changed the *taw* to a *he*, changing the verb to an imperative, this is not necessary.[84] In Biblical Hebrew poetry the *yqtl* (prefixed) form of the verb at times approximates an imperative in meaning.[85] The copula,

[80] M. Weinfeld has recently proposed taking the two verbs to mean "make me dream and restore me to health," based on the fact that many Mesopotamian parallels to PsHez contain a dream sequence in which the sufferer is told that he will be delivered from his affliction ("Job and Its Mesopotamian Parallels—A Typological Analysis," in *Text and Context: Old Testament and Semitic Studies for F. C. Fensham* [ed. W. Claassen; JSOTSup 48; Sheffield: JSOT/Sheffield Academic Press, 1988] 219). The main problem with such a hypothesis is that dream sequences presaging healing and restoration are otherwise unknown in OT literature. Thus the claim that there is an allusion to one here—based on a single word—is difficult to accept. De Boer also takes the verb in this sense, yielding the odd translation: "Thou makest me dream, make me live too!" ("Isaiah xxxviii 9–20," 178).

[81] On the probability that two separate roots underlie *ḥ-l-m*, see M. Ottosson, "חלם *chālam*," *TDOT*, 4. 427.

[82] Begrich has argued for its appearance in another Isaian passage, 53:10, reading *heḥĕlîm ʾet-śām* for MT *heḥĕlî ʾim-tāśîm* (*Studien zu Deuterojesaja* [ed. W. Zimmerli; TBü 20; Munich: Kaiser, 1963] 64), but this is most unlikely. See Barré, "Textual and Rhetorical-critical Observations on the Last Servant Song," 22.

[83] See Payne Smith, *A Compendious Syriac Dictionary*, 144. In the *aphel* it means "to heal, cure, restore (to health)." In my earlier publication on this section I had mentioned the occurrence of this verb in the Aramaic Prayer of Nabonidus from Qumran Cave IV, where it appears to be mentioned in the context of the king's recovery from the *šĕḥîn* disease (4QPrNab 4:1) ("Restoring the 'Lost Prayer'," 393). But it is now believed that the fragment containing this verb belongs to a different column from the one on which the prayer appears and thus is not part of this prayer (see P. Grelot, "La prière de Nabonide (4 Q Or Nab)," *RevQ* 9 [1978] 493).

[84] E.g., Linder, "Canticum Ezechiae," 65.

[85] Waltke and O'Connor, *Biblical Hebrew Syntax*, 509 (§31.5ab).

used sparingly in poetry, was probably added later, as often happened; it is not reflected in Vg or the Syriac.

The second verb is another occurrence of *ḥ-y-y* (*hiphil*). Having styled Yhwh as the one who enlivens or revivifies all creatures in the preceding bicolon (*hammaḥăyeh*), the poet in effect asks God to be true to this epithet and be a life-giver for him (*haḥăyēnî*) once again— i.e., to restore him to health (physical and psychological).[86]

The most troublesome section of this poetic line follows immediately after the two verbs just discussed: *hinnēh lĕšālôm mar-lî mār*. Because the last three words provide the key for understanding the rest of the line, I shall discuss them first.

There is a difference of opinion as to whether the last of these words is from *m-w-r*, "to change," or from *m-r-r*, "to be bitter."[87] The former interpretation is more common, yielding translations like, "Behold, my bitterness has changed into peace."[88] This interpretation is doubtful, however, as the verb *m-w-r* is not attested in the *qal*. If it is derived from *m-r-r* the expression makes even less sense with the preceding words: "Behold, it was for (my) peace (that) my bitterness was bitter" or the like.[89] Moreover, no other example of a X *l-* X construction can be documented from the MT,[90] which makes it difficult to accept Kutscher's strained defense of this reading as "a pun in Hebrew."[91] The plain fact is that as far as one can determine *mar-lî mār* simply does not make good sense in Biblical Hebrew and therefore is probably wrong.

1QIsa[a] contains an important variant reading for these three words: *mr ly² m²wdh*, the last word being an allomorph of *mĕ²ōd*. This reading

---

[86] Something similar is found in an Akkadian lament prayer where the poet likewise gives a particular epithet to the deity (the N-stem participle *muppalsu* with the stative termination) and then, using the same root, asks the god to act this way toward him (using the N-stem imperative). The text reads: *muppalsāta kīniš naplisanni*, "You are one who looks (on people) with favor, (so) look with steadfast favor on me!" (Lambert, "Dingir.šà.dib.ba Incantations," 278, 280, lines 101, 103, 105, 107).

[87] Nyberg, "Hiskias Danklied," 89; Wildberger, *Jesaja 28–39*, 1440 (eliminating *mār* and translating "Sieh, zum Heil dient mir die Bitternis").

[88] Cf. *NAB*; Nyberg, "Hiskias Danklied," 89.

[89] So de Boer, "Isaiah xxxviii 9–20," 178; Soggin, "Il 'Salmo di Ezechia'," 177; Castellino, "Lamentazioni individuali accadiche ed ebraiche," 152; Kaiser, *Isaiah 13–39*, 399.

[90] E.g., one never finds *ṣar-lî ṣar/ṣār* in the MT.

[91] Kutscher, *Language and Linguistic Background*, 251.

is corroborated by the *Targum of Isaiah*: *mr ly sgy*, "It is very bitter for me." Despite the testimony of these ancient witnesses, and although *mar lî mĕʾōd* is attested in Biblical Hebrew[92] whereas *mar-lî mār/mar* never is, all but a few commentators have continued to opt for the MT's reading.[93] But the second *mr* could be a corruption from an earlier *md* (= /mōd/), the end-result of a process involving the quiescence of the *ʾalep* and the common confusion of *dalet* and *resh*: *mʾd* > *md* > *mr*. In the Dead Sea Scrolls *mʾd* was written either *mʾwd(h)* or *mwʾd(h)*, clearly showing that the *ʾalep* had quiesced and that the word was pronounced /mōdā/.[94] This is also indicated by the variant *mwdh* (/mōdā/) for *mʾwdh* in 1QS10:16; 1QH11:3. The Severus Scroll (*terminus ad quem*: 70 A.D.) has *ṭwb mwt* for MT's *ṭwb mʾd* in Gen 1:31, also indicating a monosyllabic pronunciation of this word (*mwt* being an auditory error for *mwd* = /mōd/). In Origen's Secunda the word is transliterated as a monosyllable: μωδ.[95]

The disinclination on the part of scholars to accept the reading of v. 17b in 1QIsaᵃ is no doubt due largely to *hinnēh lĕšālôm* in v. 17a. As read in the MT, the end of v. 17 demands that the final word, *mr*, be parsed as a verb, otherwise the sentence lacks a predicate. But if the reading witnessed by 1QIsaᵃ and the *Targum of Isaiah* is correct, the three words following *hinnēh lĕšālôm* have no syntactic connection with the preceding. Thus either *mar lî mĕʾōd* is correct and *hinnēh lĕšālôm* is wrong or vice-versa.

There is substantial evidence that semantically *šālôm* belongs with the *Wortfeld* of "strength" and "life," which immediately precede it, rather than with subsequent *mar-lî mĕʾōd*. First, in Hebrew, Aramaic, Akkadian, and Egyptian literature "life" and "health" (Semitic *š-l-m*) are frequently associated.[96] "Strength" and "health" are often con-

---

[92] In Ruth 1:13; the causative form, *hēmar lî . . . mĕʾōd*—"(God) has made things very bitter for me"—appears in 1:20.

[93] Exceptions are Goshen-Gottstein (*The Book of Isaiah*, 169 n.), who accepts *mr ly m(ʾ)d* as the probable reading of the text; and H.-J. Fabry, מרר *mrr*, *TDOT*, 9. 17.

[94] Kutscher, *Language and Linguistic Background*, 167, 499.

[95] See E. Brønno, *Studien über hebräische Morphologie und Vokalismus auf Grundlage der mercatischen Fragmente der zweiten Kolumne der Hexapla des Origenes* (Abhandlungen für die Kunde des Morgenlandes 28; Leipzig: Brockhaus, 1943) 362.

[96] In Biblical Hebrew: *(h)ḥyym w(h)šlwm* (Mal 2:5; Prov 3:2); in Aramaic: *ḥyyn wšlm* (see J. C. Greenfield, "Scripture and Inscription: The Literary and Rhetorical Element in Some Early Phoenician Inscriptions," in *Near Eastern Studies in Honor of*

joined in Hebrew, Ugaritic, Egyptian, and Old South Arabic.[97] Note the blessing of "life," "health," and "strength/vigor" invoked upon the king in the bilingual Karatepe inscription (*KAI* #26 A III:2-7).[98] Second, Isaiah 57—a close parallel to Isa 38:16 as we have seen—associates "healing" (vv. 18, 19) and the bestowing of *šālôm* (vv. 19, 21) just after the section which speaks of "giving life" to the "heart" and "spirit." Third, there is a clear sonant connection of *taḥălîmēnî* (conjoined with *šālôm*) with *wĕtašlîmēnî* in v. 12e. On the semantic level *taḥălîmēnî* reverses the baneful actions mentioned in that verse.

There is no ancient Hebrew or versional evidence against the MT's *hinnēh lĕšālôm*. But as it stands it has no syntactic relation either to *taḥălîmēnî wĕhaḥăyēnî* or to *mar-lî mĕʾōd*. It is precisely the phrase *hinnēh lĕšālôm* that lies at the heart of the corruption that has caused so much trouble for interpreters of vv. 16c–17b, though few if any have recognized this fact. The problem may be corrected by reading *hnḥl šlwm*[99] (*ḥet* misread as *he*), parsing *hnḥl* (*hanḥēl*) as the *hiphil* imperative from *n-ḥ-l*—lit., "cause to inherit" > "grant."[100] In a number of poetic occurrences in Biblical Hebrew as well as in later Hebrew the aspect of "inheriting" loses much of its force and the verb comes to mean simply "to grant as a permanent possession."[101] In the context of terms referring to healing, life, etc., *šālôm* is best understood as "health" rather than "peace," although the latter is not impossible in this context.

William Foxwell Albright [ed. H. Goedicke; Baltimore: The Johns Hopkins University Press, 1971] 265–66); in Akkadian: *šulmu u balāṭu* (see *CAD* B, 46–50); in Egyptian: *ʿnḫ wsnb* (see A. Erman and H. Grapow, *Wörterbuch der aegyptischen Sprache* [5 vols.; Berlin: Akademie Verlag, 1961] 1. 197 ["Leben und Gesundheit"]).

[97] In Biblical Hebrew: Ps 29:11; in Ugaritic: *UT* 1019:3-4; in Egyptian: *ʿ3* is frequently paired with *wḏḫ* with the meaning "wohlbehalten und heil" (see Erman and Grapow, *Wörterbuch*, 1. 237; in Old South Arabic: *wfym wʿztm* (see Biella, *Dictionary of Old South Arabic, Sabaean Dialect*, 360).

[98] Apparently in imitation of older Anatolian formulae; see M. L. Barré, "An Analysis of the Royal Blessing in the Karatepe Inscription," *Maarav* 3 (1982) 188–89.

[99] Or perhaps *hnḥl <ly> šlwm*.

[100] Alternatively, but less likely in my view, one might posit an original *tn(h) ly šlwm* ("give me health/well-being!") resulting from a confusion of *he* and *taw* and an erroneous writing of the preposition *lĕ*- instead of *lî*.

[101] 1 Sam 2:8 (object: *kissēʾ kābôd*); Job 7:3 (object: *yarḥê šāwʾ*); Prov 3:35 (object: *kābôd*); 1QH 17:15 (object: *rwb ymym*).

In summary, the emended bicolon vv. 16a–17b looks like this:

	Words	Syllables	Accents
ʾǎdōnāy ʿēlî hammaḥǎyeh kol lēb	5	10	4
hammaḥǎyeh rûaḥ[102]	2	4	2
taḥǎlîmēnî wĕhaḥǎyēnî hanḥēl šālôm	4	12	4
mar lî mĕʾōd	3	4	2[103]

[17cd] wĕʾattâ ḥāšaqtā napšî miššaḥat bĕlî:

1QIsaᵃ: wʾth ḥšqth npšy mšḥt klw; 1QIsaᵇ: wʾth ḥšqt npšy[ ]; LXX: εἵλου γάρ μου τὴν ψυχήν, ἵνα μὴ ἀπόληται; Aquila [ ]; Symmachus: σὺ δὲ εὐδόκησας τὴν ψυχήν μου μὴ διαφθεῖραι; Theodotion: [ ]; Vg: tu autem eruisti animam meam ut non periret; Syriac: wʾnt ṣbyt bnpšy dlʾ tklʾ bḥblʾ; Targum of Isaiah: wʾt ʾtrʿytʾ bḥyy bdyl dlʾ lḥblʾ npšy.

The MT could be translated something like, "But you loved my soul from the pit of annihilation." It is evident that the verb "loved" (or "clung to") does not make good sense here. But this reading is supported by 1QIsaᵃ and 1QIsaᵇ as well as by Symmachus, the Syriac, and the *Targum of Isaiah*.

For the MT's unlikely ḥāšaqtā read ḥāśaktā ("hold back, spare") with Begrich and others.[104] This reading is corroborated by the LXX (εἵλου), Vg (*eruisti*), and a number of parallel passages.[105] Note especially Sir 51:2:

> ky pdyt mmwt npšy
> ḥśkt bśry mšḥt
> wmyd šʾwl ḥṣlt rgly

---

[102] In this transcription I have included the *ḥatef*s and the *pataḥ furtivum*, although they would almost certainly not have been present in the earliest form of the text.

[103] The emendations proposed for these lines result in word-count identical to that of the MT. After these emendations Part II still contains sixty words.

[104] *Der Psalm des Hiskia*, 48. So also Duhm, *Das Buch Jesaja*, 282; Touzard, "De la conservation du text hébreu," 103; Linder, "Canticum Ezechiae," 70; Castellino, "Lamentazioni individuali accadiche ed hebraiche,"154. Barthélemy (*Critique Textuelle de l'Ancien Testament* 2. 275) notes that Houbigant had adopted this reading because of the fact that ḥ-š-q always takes a preposition but ḥ-ś-k does not (no reference given).

[105] See Job 33:18; Ps 78:50.

For you have redeemed *my life* from Death,
You have spared/held back my flesh *from the Pit,*
You have delivered my feet from the clutches of Sheol.

The root meaning of the verb *ḥ-ś-k* appears to be "to hold back, restrain." In a somewhat extended sense it can denote "to spare" (from disaster). But there are contexts where neither meaning really fits. The English phrase to "hold (something) back" usually implies that the object in question has not yet been released from one's grasp or has not been set in motion. But in some passages it is clear that the verb refers to pulling back that which has *already* been let go. This is the case, for example, in 2 Sam 18:16, when Joab sounds the trumpet and "pulls back" the forces that were already pursuing the enemy. This is different from saying that Joab "held back" the troops in the sense of not deploying them in the field. They were already engaged in action and he had to interrupt and reverse that action. In Isa 14:6 the verb occurs again in a context of pulling back pursuing forces. In his wrath (*ʾap*) the merciless king did not "hold/pull back" his troops from pursuit of his victims. These parallels are noteworthy insofar as they bring out an important observation with regard to Isa 38:17cd. In the passage under consideration, Yhwh does not simply "spare" the psalmist's life. Rather, he *pulls back* or *brings back* that life, which, because of God's prior decision to "act" against the psalmist (v. 15b), was *already on its way to destruction*—or rather, which had already found itself at the very gates of the netherworld (v. 10c). For this reason *ḥ-ś-k* is a very appropriate verb in this context and implies more than the translation "spare" would suggest. The same nuance is present in Job 33:18a: *yaḥśôk napšô minnî-šaḥat* ("He [God] *holds back* his life from the Pit") and 33:30a: *lĕhāšîb napšô min saḥat* ("to *bring back* his life from the Pit"), which are to be understood in the context of 33:22a: *wattiqrab laššaḥat napšô*, "His life *draws near* the Pit."

For MT *bĕlî* 1QIsaᵃ has *klw* (or, less likely, *kly*). If one opts for a derivation from the root *k-l-y*, the possibilities attested in Hebrew are *kālâ*, *killāyôn* (both in Biblical Hebrew) and *kĕlāyâ*, "destruction, extinction" (rabbinic Hebrew).[106] Theoretically a form like **kĕlî* would also be possible (a homonym of *kĕlî*, "vessel") but such a word

---

[106] Jastrow, *Dictionary of the Targumim,* 642.

is nowhere attested in Hebrew. The noun *kālû* occurs in Jewish Aramaic with the meaning "finishing, venting full wrath" according to Jastrow.[107] Thus one might regard the reading of 1QIsaᵃ as an Aramaism.[108] As a substantive *bĕlî* occurs only a few times in Biblical Hebrew,[109] so that the 1QIsaᵃ reading may be an example of "updating" rare of obsolescent (or poetic) biblical vocabulary.

There is no other example in Biblical Hebrew of a *nomen rectum* qualifying *šaḥat*. But 1QH3:19 has something similar:

> *ky pdyth npšy mšḥt*
> *wmšᵓwl ᵓbdwn*

> For you have redeemed my life from the Pit,
> and from the Sheol of annihilation.

The fact that the terms *šĕᵓôl* and *ᵓăbaddôn* occur together several times in the MT[110] accounts for their juxtaposition in this poem. But the phrase *šᵓwl ᵓbdwn* is unusual, since here what it usually considered a proper noun (Sheol) is in construct with second noun, which is also a name for the netherworld. "Abaddon" derives from the root *ᵓ-b-d*, "to perish, cease to be." Thus one could translate "the Sheol of Abaddon," "Sheol of annihilation," or "the netherworld of annihilation." The last option would be close to *šaḥat bĕlî*, "the pit/Pit of annihilation." This qualification characterizes the "Pit" as the place where the individual's life is annihilated, extinguished, ceases to be.

[17ef] *kî hišlaktā ᵓaḥărê gēwkā kol-ḥăṭāᵓāy*:
1QIsaᵃ: *kyᵓ hšlkth ᵓḥry gwkh kwl ḥṭᵓy*; 1QIsaᵇ: *ky hšlkt ᵓḥry gwk kl ḥṭᵓy*; LXX: καὶ ἀπέρριψας ὀπίσω μου πάσας τὰς ἁμαρτίας μου; Aquila: [ ]; Symmachus: [ ]; Theodotion: [ ]; Vg: proiecisti post tergum tuum omnia peccata mea; Syriac: *mṭl dšdyt bstr gwšmk klhwn ḥthy*; *Targum of Isaiah*: *ᵓry ᵓrḥyqtᵓ mn qdmk kl ḥṭᵓy*.

---

[107] Ibid., 640.
[108] In an earlier publication I had opted for this reading, but would now consider it unlikely. See "Restoring the 'Lost' Prayer," 399 and n. 58.
[109] Viz., Ps 72:7; Mal 3:10 (see *HALAT*, 127).
[110] Job 26:6; Prov 15:11; 27:20.

The expression "to cast X behind one('s back)" is found six times in ancient Hebrew literature.[111] In every occurrence but this one the object is either Yhwh or his law.[112] Thus the particular form of the expression in v. 17ef is unique in the MT.[113] Basically the idiom means "to forget" or, more precisely, "to put out of mind." To cast something behind one's back is the opposite of having it in front of oneself—i.e., where a person can see it—as in the adage, "Out of sight, out of mind." Just as to have Yhwh's ordinances "before" one means to be mindful of them, implying observance, so when one casts them behind one's back they are no longer visible and thus in effect forgotten, disregarded. The connection is made explicit in the *Targum of Isaiah's* translation, "Then you 'distanced' all my sins *from in front of you*." In Ezek 23:35 "forget me" precedes "cast me behind your back." Compare "I will not forget you (Jerusalem)" with "Your walls are ever before me" in Isa 49:15–16. Therefore for Yhwh to cast the psalmist's sins behind his back is tantamount to forgetting them entirely, consigning them to oblivion. "Forgetting" or "not remembering" sins, in turn, means both blotting them out and cancelling the punishment the perpetrator deserves for having committed them. The connection between "blot out your transgressions" and "not remember your sins" is found in Isa 64:5, and between "remember their iniquity" and "punish their sins" in Jer 14:10; Hos 8:13; 9:9. The full import of Isa 38:17ef is that Yhwh has decided to abort his "action" against the psalmist (cf. v. 15b), to forget all his sins (= forgive them and cancel their punishment), and therefore to pull him back from the pit of destruction which he was nearing.

How is *kî* to be translated in this passage? It is evident that the act of forgiving the psalmist's sins is functionally equivalent to his healing/deliverance from death. Sin and death were commonly associated as cause and effect in the ancient Near East and in Israel.[114] For this reason *kî* here should probably not be translated "for," which

---

[111] 1 Kgs 14:9; Neh 9:26; Ps 50:17; Ezek 23:35. Note also 4QpHos^b 2:4: *mṣwwtyw hšlykw ʾḥry gwm*, "They cast his commandments behind their back."

[112] Object = "me" (= Yhwh): 1 Kgs 14:9; Ezek 23:35; object = Yhwh's law: Neh 9:26 ("your law"); Ps 50:17 ("my words"); 4QpHos^b 2:4 ("his commandments").

[113] But compare 1QH 17:15: *wlhšlyk kwl ʿ[wnwtyh]m*, "and to cast away all [the]ir in[iquities]."

[114] See, for example, Pss 38:4; 39:12; 40:13; 51:6; 90:8–9.

would imply a subordination to, and to some extent a differentiation from, deliverance. A preferable translation of the particle in this case would bring out its emphatic sense: "indeed, surely, yes," etc.

Emended Text and Translation

IIAa	15a	*mâ ʾădabbēr wĕʾōmar lô*
	b	*wĕhûʾ ʿāśâ*
	c	*ʾeddĕdâ kol šĕnôtay*
	d	*ʿal mar napšî*
IIAb	16a	*ʾădōnāy ʿēlî hammaḥăyeh kol lēb*
	b	*hammaḥăyeh rûaḥ*
	c	*taḥălîmēnî wĕhaḥăyēnî* 17a *hanḥēl šālôm*
	b	*mar lî mĕʾōd*
IIAc	c	*wĕʾattâ ḥāśaktā napšî*
	d	*miššaḥat bĕlî*
	e	*kî hišlaktā ʾaḥărê gēwkā*
	f	*kol ḥăṭāʾāy*

A. Deliberation

IIAa	15a	What (words) can I speak, what can I say to him,
	b	since he has (already) acted?
	c	Must I wander about (depressed) all my years
	d	because of my despondency?

B. Prayer

IIAb	16a	"O Lord Most High, you who give life to every heart,
	b	who give life to every spirit—
	c	Restore my strength, let me recover, 17a grant me health/peace,
	d	(for) bitter indeed is my anguish!"

C. Deliverance

IIAc   c   And then you pulled back my life
       d   from the Pit of annihilation;
       e   Yes, you cast behind your back
       f   all my sins!

Rhetorical-Critical Observations

In IAa the verb *ʾ-m-r* (1st person) is followed by a verb of motion, in the cohortative form, *ʾlkh* (v. 10ab). This is matched at the beginning of the second half of the poem with another occurrence of 1st sg. *ʾ-m-r*, followed by another verb of motion, *n-d-d* (v. 15a, c)—the only other cohortative in the poem.

The syllable /mar/ in PsHez has structural significance. It marks off the beginning and end of the first subsection of each major part of PsHez—viz., *ʾ-m-r . . . mar* in IAa and *ʾ-m-r . . . mar* in IIAa. Further, it forms an inclusion in Part I (vv. 10a and 14c). In this case structure and content work together: there are no more occurrences of the syllable after v. 17b, which signals the turning point in the poem—the deliverance recounted in IIAc (v. 17c–f) . There are seven occurrences of the syllable in PsHez, each of which occurs at a juncture within the poem:

Syllable	Word	Verse	Position	Referent
mar	*ʾāmartî*	10a	Beginning of IAa	Poet
mar	*mar*	10d	End of IAa	Poet
mar	*ʾāmartî*	11a	Beginning of IAb	Poet
mār	*mārôm*	14c	End of IIBb	Yhwh
mar	*ʾōmar*	15a	Beginning of IIAa	Poet
mar	*mar*	15d	End of IIAa	Poet
mar	*mar*	17b	End of IIAb	Poet

In three instances the source of the syllable is the noun *mar* itself, "bitterness," which is clearly a major theme within the poem. In three others, its source is the verb *ʾāmar*, which itself plays a major structural role by introducing the two halves of PsHez. That the poet intended some relationship between *mar* and this syllable in the three occurrences of *ʾāmar* is also suggested by vv. 15a and 16b, where two occurrences of /mar/ are followed by the preposition *l-*.

One notes that the central appearance of /mar/ differs from the others in several respects. First, the syllable is long, not short, as in the other cases. Second, the word in which it appears is neither from the root *ʾ-m-r* nor *m-r-r*. Rather, it is part of a divine epithet, *mārôm*, "the Most High." There is evidence that points to a connection between *mar*, "bitterness," and this word. One inclusive device in Part I is the repetition of the two-part motif "mourning" and "copious weeping." "Mourning" appears at the beginning of Part I in the term *dōm* in v. 10b, and again at the end in the topos "I moan/mourn (*ʾehgeh*) like a dove" in v. 14b. "Copious weeping," as I have argued, is how one should translate *mar* in v. 10d (lit., "bitter weeping"), and this corresponds to the idiom *k-l-y ʿênayim* in v. 14c, which immediately precedes *mārôm*.

A notable phonic feature in IIA is a striking sonant chiasmus linking the beginning of IIAa and the end of IIAb, and which provides a further argument for reading *měʾōd* here rather than the MT's *mār*:

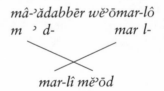

This chiasmus envelops the first two subsections of IIA, which focus on the poet's actions (i.e., deliberation in the former, petition in the latter), separating them from those of Yhwh in IIAc (i.e., the deliverance).

Moreover, the phrase *mar lî měʾōd*, is anticipated by an almost identical sequence of consonants in the last bicolon of Part I. The third and fourth words of v. 14b are *lmrwm ʾdny*. Prescinding from the vowel-letter *waw* here, the first six consonants are *l m r m ʾ d*. Both sequences of consonants occur at a juncture within the poem.

Further examples of assonance in IIAb are *maḥ . . . maḥ* in v. 16ab combined with *taḥ . . . ḥaḥ* in v. 16c. This sound combination is continued in IIAc with *śak . . . šaḥ . . . šlak* and *ʾaḥ* in v. 17c–e, where the related sounds /ś/ and /š/ preface this syllable except for the last example. Note too the build-up of /k/ and /ḥ/ in IIAc: *kî hišlaktā ʾaḥărê gēwkā kol ḥǎṭāʾāy*. Each word contains one of these related sounds in the sequence /k k ḥ k k ḥ/. Finally, the syllable /kol/ occurs once in each subsection of IIA, tying them together: v. 15c (IIAa), v.16a (IIAb), and v. 17f (IIAc).

An impressive extrabiblical poetic parallel to *wĕtaḥlîmēnî wĕhaḥǎyēnî* in v. 16c and *miššaḥat bĕlî* in v. 17d is found in the Akkadian poem *Ludlul bēl nēmeqi* (IV 3–6):

> *[bēl]ī upatt[in]anni // [bēl]ī uballiṭanni*
> *[ina ḫašt]i ekimanni // [ina kara]šê eṭ[ṭer]anni*[115]

> My lord (i.e., Marduk) *strengthened* me,[116]
> My lord *brought* me *back to life/health*;
> He rescued me from *the pit*,
> He saved me from *destruction*.[117]

In this passage *ḫaštu* and *karašû* are exact equivalents of *šaḥat* and *bĕlî* respectively.[118] They follow references to the poet's having been "strengthened" and "given life," which correspond precisely to his request in v. 16c: *taḥǎlîmēnî wĕhaḥǎyēnî*, "Restore my strength, give me life."

The act of deliverance alluded to in v. 17c–f constitutes a reversal of v. 10c, where the poet had been "consigned" or "handed over to the netherworld." This is especially clear from Ps 78:50, which is formally one of the closest parallels to Isa 38:17cd:

> *yĕpallēs nātîb lĕʾappô*
> *lōʾ-ḥāśak mimmāwet napšām*
> *wĕḥayyātām lĕdeber hisgîr*

---

[115] For the reading *eṭṭeranni*, see M. Held, "Pits and Pitfalls in Akkadian and Biblical Hebrew," *JANES* 5 (1973) 175 n. 20 (cf. *Šurpu* 4:43–44). Lambert, on the other hand, reads *id-[kan]ᵃⁿ-ni*, "He summoned me [from] destruction" (*Babylonian Wisdom Literature*, 58).

[116] For this translation, see *AHw*, 847; Black, *A Concise Dictionary of Akkadian*, 270. Lambert (*Babylonian Wisdom Literature*, 59) translates, "[My Lord] set me on my feet."

[117] Translation mine.

[118] The two parallel terms occur in the same sequence in *Šurpu* 4:43–44. A "commentary" on *Šurpu* 4:44 translates *karašû* as *qubūru*, "the grave" (*CAD* Q, 293).

He cleared a path for his anger,
he did not *hold back* their soul(s) from Death,
but *handed over* their lives to Pestilence.

Such a passage establishes a connection between not holding back one's life from Death, the personified netherworld, and handing that life over to Pestilence. *p-q-d bĕ-* (Isa 38:10c) is equivalent to *s-g-r* (*hiphil*) *lĕ-*, and in both passages God is the agent.

The psalmist's prayer in vv. 16a–17b follows the same basic structure as the shorter "ejaculatory" prayer in v. 14d: *ʾădōnāy ʿuššĕqâ-lî ʿorbēnî.* Each contains the three basic elements of a prayer for deliverance: (1) an address to God, (2) a request for deliverance, and (3) a statement of the motivation underlying the request.[119] The two prayers differ in three respects: (1) the vocabulary is different, except that both begin with *ʾădōnāy*; (2) the order of the elements in v. 14d is address, motivation, and request, whereas in vv. 16a–17b it is address, request, motivation; (3) each of the three elements has been expanded in the longer prayer. The following schema highlights the similarity:

Element	Short Prayer (14d)	Longer Prayer (16a–17b)
Address	*ʾădōnāy*	*ʾădōnāy ʿēlî hammaḥăyeh kol lēb hammaḥăyeh rûaḥ*
Petition	*ʿorbēnî*	*taḥălîmēnî wĕhaḥăyēnî hanḥēl šālôm*
Motivation	*ʿuššĕqâ lî*	*mar lî mĕʾōd.*

General Comments

Part II marks a decided shift in the emphasis of the poem. Whereas Part I was concerned almost exclusively with the author's suffering— facing its reality (IA) or describing what that suffering is like (IB)—in Part II there are only two brief allusions to personal suffering (vv. 15d, 17b). The focus of PsHez shifts from affliction to deliverance and beyond. The transition from illness to health takes place in IIA. Thus it is a crucial section of the poem.

---

[119] On this pattern in biblical prayers (address, petition, motivation) see M. Greenberg, *Biblical Prose Prayer as a Window to the Popular Religion of Ancient Israel* (Berkeley: University of California Press, 1983) 11.

Unfortunately, precisely at this crucial juncture the text becomes garbled—particularly in v. 16. Yet the situation is not as desperate for the exegete as it might first seem. Careful attention to structure and content makes it possible to discern with some degree of confidence what the poet is saying. We note first that in v. 15 he begins with the question "What can I say . . . ?" which seems to suggest a deliberation with himself. Verse 17c–f is rather straightforward and presents few problems of interpretation. These lines describe in stereotypical language the deliverance from his affliction. Verses 16a–17b are the most difficult in this subsection. Yet this much seems clear: the poet addresses God (*ʾădōnāy*) and cries to him for deliverance (*wĕtaḥă-lîmēnî wĕhaḥăyēnî*). These data support the division of IIA into three subsections rather equal in size (each containing two bicola):

IIAa	15a–d	The Poet's Deliberation
IIAb	16a–17b	Petition to Yhwh
IIAc	17c–f	Divine Deliverance

The first two of of these end with an allusion to the poet's suffering, by means of the term *mar*: *ʿal-mar napšî* (v. 15d), *mar-lî mĕʾōd* (v. 17b).

As the curtain rises on the Scene II (i.e., Part II) of PsHez it is evident that nothing has changed from the end of Part I. We are given to understand that despite the psalmist's profuse weeping (v. 14c) and his petition to Yhwh for relief (v. 14d) at the end of Part I his fate remains the same. There is no reprieve, no deliverance. In fact, the only reference to the divine action is an allusion to God as the cause of this suffering (v. 15b).

If the poem is not to end here it is up to the psalmist to advance the action by some move on his part. But what move? It is not clear what course of action should be taken at this point. Thus the subsection IIAa could appropriately be entitled "What Do I Do Now?" What alternatives are left to the poet now that the usual expedients for moving the deity to pity—i.e., lamentation and petition—have failed? In the face of the divine silence it is reasonable to assume that the sufferer must try again to address God. Whether one reads the last word of v. 15a as *lî* (MT) or *lô*, the sense of v. 15ab is that the poet is painfully aware that there is nothing he could say that could realistically be expected to change God's mind. "He has acted" and that is that. And so in v. 15a he deliberates with himself as to whether he should even try again to speak to him. On the one hand, it appears to be the logical move to make; on the other, there is little reason for thinking that it will make any difference.

But the poet's deliberation takes a second step. Granted that further petition might prove pointless, the alternative is not a pleasant one. That alternative would be to linger in his present unbearable state indefinitely. For even though he seems certain that his life is about to end, what if it should be the divine will that he continue in his suffering for many years to come? Should he resign himself to wandering about in a state of profound depression for the rest of his life, which might drag on for many years?

Perhaps it was this horrifying prospect that moved the poet, despite his hesitations, to address Yhwh again in prayer. Despite the formal similarities of this second prayer (vv. 16a–17b) to the one uttered at the end of Part I (v. 14d), it is important to notice the difference in tone. Most significant is what the longer prayer does *not* contain. Unlike v. 14d, there is in it nothing of the sense of *accusing* God of "oppressing" the poet. And there is a more explicit acknowledgment of Yhwh's sovereignty over all life—"You who give life to every heart, who give life to every spirit." In its most fundamental sense the divine act of "giving life" is not something one can demand. All peoples of the ancient Near East were aware that "life" was a prerogative of the gods given to mortals only temporarily and only as a gift.

> When the gods created humankind
> They allotted death as the fate of humankind
> And retained life in their own hands.[120]

In the prayer of vv. 16a–17b the poet clearly speaks out of this mind-set, no longer accusing Yhwh because of what had happened to him but humbly asking that the God who for no merit of his own gave him life at birth now give him life once again (i.e., restore him to health and happiness). Of course, there may also be some subtle persuasion going on here—viz., by reminding Yhwh that it is his nature to give life and omitting to mention anything about his prerogative to take it away (contrast 1 Sam 2:6).

---

[120] *Gilgamesh* X iii 3–5 (Old Babylonian recension).

The last colon of the prayer, "(for) bitter indeed is my anguish" (v. 17b), is the last reference in PsHez to the psalmist's suffering. As in many biblical and extra-biblical laments it expresses the attempt of the one praying to stir the deity to pity at his miserable condition so that God would relent and act to deliver him from his distress. Significantly, this also marks the last appearance of *mar*, "bitter(ness)," which had made its first appearance in the poem in the opening subsection IAa (v. 10d), marking this whole part of the poem with the motif of bitter suffering.

The poem does not dwell on the circumstances of the deliverance, but simply states it succinctly as a fact. This may be somewhat surprising, given that the poem as a whole has built up to this moment. But this is precisely what we find, for example, in the Prayer of Jonah. With startling abruptness, after describing himself locked in the great underworld city forever with apparently no hope of release, the poet speaks of his deliverance (Jonah 2:6b):

> But (then) you brought up my life from the Pit,
> O Yhwh my God!

The fact that the deliverance in PsHez occurs immediately after the psalmist's prayer, just as in the case of Jonah's prayer,[121] indicates that we are to understand a cause-and-effect relationship between the two events.

As I noted in Chapter 2, Seitz does not want to read v. 17c–f as a reference to an actual healing but draws a line "between thanksgiving for a death sentence being removed and actual healing," claiming that "it is not clear that actual healing has occurred by the psalm's end." He further states, "The psalm contains no explicit reference to healing, and in fact includes [an] ardent request for the same (38:16)."[122] Seitz's rigid distinction between death sentence removed and healing is artificial and forced. As for his appeal to the psalmist's "ardent request" for healing in 38:16, this gives no support to his argument as it clearly comes *immediately before* the notation of divine healing. As I see it,

---

[121] Note that in the Prayer of Jonah this causal connection is explicitly stated. When his life was about to wink out forever, "my prayer came to you // in your holy temple" (2:7).

[122] *Zion's Final Destiny*, 168.

there can be no doubt whatsoever that the two images in Part IIAc (v. 17c–f) are images of deliverance and healing. In other words, it is precisely in these lines that the healing of the psalmist is clearly reported. (1) To be "pulled back" from the Pit of destruction (= Sheol) is to reverse the process of descending into the netherworld (expressed most frequently by the participle: *yôrēd/yôrĕdê šĕʾôl*) or of being handed over to Sheol (see the discussion of Ps 78:50 above). Hence the divine action in v. 17cd is *precisely the reversal of v. 10c*, where the psalmist is "handed over to the gate(keeper?)s of Sheol" (apparently by divine decree), except that in the latter verse the idiom is the Akkadian calque *p-q-d* (*piel*) *b-*. (2) Similarly, "to cast all (of one's) sins behind (God's) back," i.e., to forgive all of someone's sins, is also an idiom of healing. One must remember that healing and forgiveness went hand and hand in the minds of people of the ancient Near East.[123] Without forgiveness of sin there is no healing. (3) Beyond this, the fact that the psalmist can say "as I (give thanks) today" in v. 19b would be impossible if he were not already healed. One does not give thanks/praise for divine deliverance (*y-d-y* [*hiphil*]) until that deliverance is granted. Compare the second half of the refrain of Psalm 42–43 (42:6a–7aα, 12b; 43:5b): *hôḥîlî lēʾlōhîm kî ʿôd ʾôdennû*, "Hope in God, for I shall *yet* praise him. . . ." Whether one translates *ʿôd* here as "yet" (which I would consider preferable) or "again," the meaning is the same: the psalmist is confident that he *will* one day be thanking God, i.e., *once his prayer for deliverance has been answered.*

---

[123] On the connection between healing and the forgiveness of sin, see Pss 38:3; 41:4; 2 Chr 7:14.

CHAPTER 6

Who Can Praise Yhwh?

Part IIB (vv. 18–19)

The Masoretic Text

IIBa	18a	*kî lōʾ šěʾôl tôdekkā*ᵗ
	b	*māwet yĕhallĕlekkā*ᵃ
	c	*lōʾ-yĕśabbĕrû yôrĕdê-bôr*ᵗ
	d	*ʾel-ʾămittekā*ˢ
IIBb	19a	*ḥay ḥay hûʾ yôdekā*ᵗ
	b	*kāmônî hayyôm*ᵃ
	c	*ʾāb lĕbānîm yôdîa*ᶜᵗ
	d	*ʾel-ʾămittekkā*ˢ

Textual Remarks

[18a] *kî lōʾ šěʾôl tôdekkā*:

1QIsaᵃ: *kyʾ lwʾ šʾwl twdkh*; 1QIsaᵇ: *ky[ ]wl twḏk*; LXX: οὐ γὰρ οἱ ἐν ᾅδου αἰνέσουσί σε; Aquila: [ ]; Symmachus: [ ]; Theodotion: [ ]; Vg: quia infernus non confitebitur tibi; Syriac: *mṭl dlʾ šywl twdh lk*; *Targum of Isaiah*: *ʾry lʾ dbšʾwl mwdn qdmk*.

Although in v. 17e *kî* is probably to be translated as an asseverative (e.g., "surely"), here it most likely has its most common meaning, "for." In this case IIB is to be read as Yhwh's motivation for delivering

181

the psalmist, i.e., so that the latter might go on praising him.[1] Even though this may be God's motivation, this fact does not deter the psalmist from driving home the point to God throughout this section that dead persons cannot praise the deity, but rather only living ones.

The negative particle is placed before the subject, not the predicate: "It is not Sheol that gives you thanks." This leads the reader to expect somewhere in this section a statement of precisely *who can/does give thanks to Yhwh*—the burden of IIBb.[2]

[18b] *māwet yĕhallĕlekkā*:

1QIsa[a]: *wlw⁾ mwt yhllkh*; 1QIsa[b]: *mwt yhllk*; LXX: οὐδὲ οἱ ἀπο-θανόντες εὐλογήσουσί σε; Aquila: [ ]; Symmachus: [ ]; Theodotion: [ ]; Vg: neque mors laudabit te; Syriac: *⁾p l⁾ mwt⁾ nšbḥk*; *Targum of Isaiah*: *myty⁾ l⁾ mšbḥyn lk*.

The *lō⁾* in the preceding colon governs the subject (*māwet*, "Death") here as well. The omission of the negative at the beginning of this colon caused problems for the ancient versions. 1QIsa[a] as well as all the versions have a second negative, perhaps to preclude the erroneous interpretation that death (i.e., the realm of the dead) does praise Yhwh.[3] In this context *māwet* does not refer to the abstract concept of death but has a concrete meaning: either the realm of the dead or the dead themselves—as in the translation of the LXX and the *Targum of Isaiah*—though the two need not be distinguished in poetry.[4] The same is true of *šĕ⁾ôl* ("the Netherworld") in this passage.

---

[1] So explicitly Begrich, *Der Psalm des Hiskia*, 49; J. W. Watts, *Psalm and Story: Inset Hymns in Hebrew Narrative* (JSOTSup 139; Sheffield: JSOT Press, 1992) 119; Coetzee, "The 'Song of Hezekiah'," 18. Virtually all commentators accept this understanding of *kî* in this verse.

[2] For the motif that Sheol/the dead cannot praise Yhwh, see Pss 6:6; 30:10; 88:11–13; 115:17.

[3] For the formulaic pair *šĕ⁾ôl // māwet* (and vice-versa), see Avishur, *Word-Pairs*, 257.

[4] Cf. the LXX's translation of *māwet*, οἱ ἀποθανόντες, and the *Targum of Isaiah*'s *dbšywl*, "those in Sheol." Most probably in this verse the abstract nouns *māwet* and *šĕ⁾ôl*, in parallelism with the concrete *yôrĕdê bôr*, are to be taken in a concrete sense. For this "abstract // concrete" poetic construction see Watson, *Classical Hebrew Poetry*, 314–16 (§11.10).

[18cd] *lōʾ-yĕśabbĕrû yôrĕdê-bôr ʾel-ʾămittekā:*

1QIsa^a: *wlwʾ yśbrw ywrdy bwr ʾl ʾmtkh*; 1QIsa^b: *lʾ yśbrẇ ywrdy bwr ʾl ʾmtk*; LXX: οὐδὲ ἐλπιοῦσιν οἱ ἐν ᾅδου τὴν ἐλεημοσύνην σου; Aquila: οὐ προσδοκήσουσιν [οἱ] καταβαίνοντες [εἰς] λάκκον [ ]; Symmachus: [ ] οἱ καταβαίνοντες εἰς λάκκον τὴν ἀλήθειάν σου; Theodotion: [ ]; Vg: non expectabunt qui descendunt in lacum veritatem tuam; Syriac: *wlʾ nsbrwn lqwštk ʾylyn dnḥtyn lgwbʾ*; Targum of Isaiah: *lʾ msbryn nḥty gwb byt ʾbdnʾ lprqnk.*

Here one might have expected *lōʾ* to negate the subject, as in the preceding bicolon. The change—negation of predicate rather than subject—may be a stylistic variation signaling the end of the subunit. Other stylistic changes that achieve this purpose are the switch from singular abstract nouns (*šĕʾôl* and *māwet*) to the concrete plural *yôrĕdê bôr* and the change of direct object from the suffix *-kā* (twice) on the verbs to the same suffix on an abstract noun (*ʾămittekkā*).[5]

At first glance everything seems to be in order with this bicolon. *yôrĕdê bôr* is a standard expression for the dead (or mortally ill) and is occasionally parallel to *šĕʾôl* in the MT.[6] The verb *ś-b-r* (*piel*) usually takes the preposition *ʾel* or *lĕ-* before its object.[7] The idea that the dead can no longer "wait for" or "hope for" Yhwh's faithfulness and all that that implies is an attested trope.[8] There is no versional evidence pointing to a verb other than *ś-b-r*. Nevertheless, upon closer inspection this verb raises suspicions. First, given the synonymity of the three subjects in these interrelated bicola (*šĕʾôl*, *māwet*, and *yôrĕdê bôr*) and the synonymity of the first two verbs (*y-d-y* [*hiphil*] and *h-l-l* [*piel*]), one would expect the third verb in the series to be synonymous with the first two. But that verb, *ś-b-r* (*piel*), never occurs with these others and moreover is not a *verbum dicendi* as they are. Second, there appears to be some relationship between the verb in v. 18c and that in v. 19c, *y-d-ʿ* (*hiphil*), also a *verbum dicendi*. In the MT both govern the

---

[5] Note the same phenomenon, for example, in Ps 30:10b: *hăyôdĕkā ʿāpār // hăyāgîd ʾămittekā*, "Can Dust (= the Netherworld) praise *you* // can it tell of *your faithfulness?*" Cf. also Ps 88:11–13, cited below.

[6] Ezek 31:16; Ps 30:4; Prov 1:12.

[7] Pss 104:27; 119:166; 145:15.

[8] E.g., Gen 49:18; Isa 59:9, 11.

object *ʾămittekkā* or the like.[9] But *ś-b-r* never appears with this verb either.

These factors raise doubt as to whether *yśbrw* is the original reading.[10] A verb that would fit much better in this context is *s-p-r* (*piel*), "to recount, proclaim." The nineteenth-century exegetes A. Klostermann and C. J. Bredenkamp proposed this reading for the same reason.[11] The confusion of the two verbs is easy to explain as a confusion on the auditory level. With the assimilation of *śin* to *samek* in the later period, *sippēr* and *śibbēr* would have been distinguished only by a slight difference in the pronunciation of the middle radical, i.e., whether it was voiced or unvoiced. We have already seen an example of the *śin-samek* interchange in the case of *śwyty* (< *śpyty*) for *sāpîtî* in v. 13a. Unlike *ś-b-r*, *s-p-r* (*piel*) does appear in parallelism with both *y-d-y* (*hiphil*)[12] and *h-l-l* (*piel*).[13] It also stands in parallelism to *y-d-ʿ* in a number of passages.[14] Of these Ps 88:11–13 is particularly significant:

> *hălammētîm taʿăśeh-peleʾ*
> *ʾim-rĕpāʾîm yāqûmû yôdûkā*
> *hayĕsuppar baqqeber ḥasdekā*
> *ʾĕmûnātĕkā bāʾăbaddôn*
> *hăyiwwādaʿ baḥōšek pilʾekā*
> *wĕṣidqātĕkā bĕʾereṣ nĕšiyyâ*

Do you work wonders for the dead,
   do the shades rise up and *give* you *thanks*?

---

[9] See below, pp. 189–90.

[10] Theoretically one might argue that this third verb—i.e., coming after *y-d-y* (*hiphil*) and *h-l-l* (*piel*)—marks the end of a sequence insofar as its semantic range differs from that of the other two. Above I mentioned the switch from singular abstract nouns (*šĕʾôl* and *māwet*) to the concrete plural *yôrĕdê bôr* as having this function. But in the latter case *yôrĕdê bôr* is synonymous with the antecedent terms, which is not the case with *ś-b-r* vis-à-vis *y-d-y* and *h-l-l*.

[11] A. Klostermann, "Lautverschiebung im Texte des Hiskia-Psalms (Jes. 38, 9–20)," *Theologische Studien und Kritiken* 57 (1884) 163 (I am indebted to J. S. Kselman for obtaining a copy of this article for me); C. J. Bredenkamp, *Der Prophet Jesaia* (Erlangen: Deichert, 1887) 215.

[12] Pss 9:2; 75:2; 79:2; 88:11–12; cf. 1QH 1:29–30; 11QPs[a] 19:1.

[13] Ps 22:23; 1QH 3:23; 11:24–25.

[14] Job 39:3; Pss 78:3, 5–6; 88:12–13; 1QS 1:29–30; 11QPs[a] 19:2.

Is your steadfast love *proclaimed* in the grave,
　　your faithfulness in Abaddon?
Is your wonder *made known* in the darkness,
　　your righteousness in the land of oblivion?

This passage presents a series of three questions containing the sequence *y-d-y* (*hiphil*), *s-p-r* (*pual*), and *y-d-ᶜ* (*niphal*)—compare the sequence *y-d-y* (*hiphil*), *ś-b-r* (*piel*), and *y-d-ᶜ* (*hiphil*) in Isa 38:18–19. Note that the subjects of *s-p-r* are *ḥesed* and *ᵓĕmûnâ*, the latter being a cognate and synonym of *ᵓĕmet*, which appears as objects of *ś-b-r* (*piel*) and *y-d-ᶜ* (*hiphil*) in Isa 38:18d and 19d respectively. The context of the two passages is the same, viz., the conviction that the dead cannot praise God.

Although there is no versional evidence to support *s-p-r*, this reading finds corroboration in an ancient Hebrew manuscript—the so-called "Plea for Deliverance" in 11QPsᵃ 19:1–18. The first part of this poem is missing, but the first preserved lines read as follows:[15]

1　*ky lwᵓ rmh twdh lkh*
　　　wlwᵓ tspr ḥsdkh twlᶜh
2　*ḥy ḥy* (vacat) *ywdh lkh*[16]
　　　ywdw lkh kwl mwṭṭy rgl

For/surely it is not the maggot that can *give* you *thanks*,
　　nor can the (grave-)worm *proclaim* your steadfast love;
It is each living person that gives you thanks,
　　all those who totter on legs (can) give you thanks.[17]

---

[15] For the stichometry, see J. A. Sanders, *The Dead Sea Psalms Scroll* (Ithaca: Cornell University Press, 1967) 120.

[16] J. van der Ploeg ("Fragments d'un manuscrit de psaumes de Qumran (11QPsᵇ)," *RB* 74 [1967] 410) notes that the scribe had first written *ḥy ḥy hwᵓ ywdh lkh* and then erased the *hwᵓ*. A second, fragmentary copy of this poem (11QPsᵇ) contains the pleonasm *ḥy ḥy ywdkh lkh*. Both of these factors point to a conscious adaptation of PsHez.

[17] In the MT *m-w-ṭ* occurs a number of times with *rgl* (Deut 32:35; Pss 38:17; 66:9; 94:18). In these passages *rgl* is the subject of the verb. The 11QPsᵃ passage appears to use a by-form of this verb (i.e., **m-ṭ-ṭ*), but here *rgl* is not the subject. I would suggest that the expression be translated "those who totter on legs" as a reference to bipedal humankind, or perhaps more precisely to human beings who are on their "last legs"—

There can be no doubt that these lines are a paraphrase of Isa 38:18–19a. Nowhere else in the MT does the expression *kî lō> X tôdekkā/tôdeh lĕkā* occur, and nowhere else does one find *hay hay (hû>) yôdekā/yôdeh lĕkā*. The most obvious difference is that the author of the later poem has substituted for the parallel pair *šĕ>ôl // māwet* another word-pair that refers to death, *rimmâ // tôlēʿâ*, "maggot" // "(grave-)worm."[18] Moreover, in both cola the verbal suffix *-k* after *hwdh* has been replaced by the preposition *l*- plus the pronominal suffix—*lkh*. Finally, the two bicola of v. 18 have been changed into a single bicolon. But for our purposes what is most significant is the phrase *wlw> tspr hsdkh twlʿh*. This paraphrase provides evidence that the original verb in Isa 38:18c was *s-p-r* rather than *ś-b-r*.

Isa 38:18cd	11QPsᵃ 19:1
ky l> š>wl twdk	*ky lw> rmh twdh lkh*
mwt yhllk	
l> yśbrw ywrdy-bwr	*wlw> tspr hsdkh twʿlh*
>l >mtk	

If *s-p-r* is the correct verb, what does one make of the preposition *>el*? It is hardly likely that this marks the direct object of the verb. The two other instances in the MT where the verb's direct object is preceded by *>el* are suspect.[19] Rather, here *>l* must be the divine name *>ēl*, in

---

i.e., the sick or persons of extreme old age who are just barely able to walk. The bicolon would then mean that only the living can praise God, a category which includes even those who are so infirm they can barely be classified among the "living."

[18] Isa 14:11; Job 25:6.

[19] The only other passage in the MT where this might be possible is Ps 2:7a: *>ăsappĕrâ >el hôq yhwh >āmar >ēlay*, which is usually translated: "I will proclaim Yhwh's decree: He said to me. . . ." Virtually all the commentaries gloss over the syntactical problem raised by this unique occurrence of *s-p-r* + *>el*. I see two possible solutions. (1) The MT's *>l hq* represents a metathesis. Originally the text read *hq >l*—viz., *hoq >ēl*. Cf. the LXX: διαγγέλων τὸ πρόσταγμα κυρίου· Κύριος εἶπεν πρός με . . . , where the Greek τὸ πρόσταγμα κυρίου is a straightforward translation of *hoq >ēl*. The translation would be:

> I will proclaim El's decree,
> (that which) Yhwh said to me. . . .

The second colon I parse as an unmarked relative clause, "(that which) Yhwh said to me," forming a good parallel with "El's decree." The resulting bicolon is a chiasmus:

this case a vocative.[20] (See the discussion of *ʾel* in v. 19d below.)

Finally, a number of commentators have expressed doubts about the reading *ʾămittekā*.[21] On the one hand, it is irregular and unexpected that the last colon of the contiguous subsections IIBa and IIBb end with exactly the same colon. On the other, it is not totally out of the question. 1QIsa^a, 1QIsa^b, and all the versions support this reading except for the LXX and the *Targum of Isaiah*. The former reads τὴν ἐλεημοσύνην σου, and the latter *lprqnk*, "your salvation," neither of which presupposes a *Vorlage* with *ʾămittekā*. The LXX here may well reflect a *Vorlage* with *ḥasdekā*.[22] The fact that *ḥsdkh* appears in the "Plea for Deliverance" as the object of *s-p-r*—and also that this term is the subject of of *s-p-r* in Ps 88:12, a passage with strong parallels to Isa 38:18–19—supports the view that this was the original reading in Isa 38:18d rather than *ʾămittekā*.[23]

A	*ʾăsappĕrâ* (1st sg. form)	C'	*yhwh* (divine name)
B	*ḥoq* (decree)	B'	*ʾāmar* (pronounce[ment])
C	*ʾēl* (divine name)	A'	*ʾēlay* (1st sg. form).

(2) A solution that requires no rearrangement of the consonantal MT would be to read *ʾel ḥōq* as *ʾēl ḥaq* and to interpret this and *yhwh ʾāmar* both as unmarked relative clauses functioning as the objects of *ʾăsappĕrâ*:

I will proclaim what El has decreed,
    what Yhwh has said to me. . . .

According to the MT Ps 69:27 is another example of *s-p-r* + *ʾel*. But here the reading *yĕsappĕrû* in the final colon (// *rādāpû*) is suspect (cf. the LXX and the Syriac; see *HALAT,* 723).

[20] Ps 66:16 is another passage where the object of *s-p-r* (*piel*) is separated from its verb by a vocative:

lĕkû-šimʿû waʾăsappĕrâ
    kol-yirʾê yhwh
    ʾăšer ʿāśâ lĕnapšî

Come, listen, and I will relate (to you),
    O all (you) who fear Yhwh,
    what he has done for me.

[21] So Wildberger (*Jesaja 28–39*, 1445), who notes that B. Duhm, T. K. Cheyne, and F. Feldmann (among other earlier commentators) held this position, but gives no references.

[22] The LXX translates *ḥesed* by ἐλεημοσύνη 8x, mainly in Proverbs: Gen 47:29; Prov 3:3; 14:22; 15:27; 19:22; 20:28; 21:21; 31:27. However, it never translates *ʾĕmet* with this term. See T. Muraoka, *Hebrew/Aramaic Index to the Septuagint: Keyed to the Hatch-Redpath Concordance* (Grand Rapids: Baker Books, 1998) 19.

[23] Among those who accept the reading *ḥsdk* here are Duhm, *Das Buch Jesaia*, 283; Begrich, *Der Psalm des Hiskia*, 49; Wildberger, *Jesaia 28–39*, 1445 (possibly); von

[19ab] *ḥay ḥay hûʾ yôdekā kāmônî ḥayyôm:*
ıQIsaᵃ: (1)²⁴ *ḥy ḥy hwʾ ywdkh kmwny ḥywm;* (2) *ḥy ḥy ywdk kmwny ḥywm;* ıQIsaᵇ: *ḥy ḥy hwʾ ywdk ḥywm kmwny;* LXX: οἱ ζῶντες εὐλογήσουσίν σε ὃν τρόπον κἀγώ. ἀπὸ γὰρ τῆς σήμερον; Aquila: [ ]; Symmachus: [ ] σήμερον [ ]; Theodotion: [ ]; Vg: vivens vivens ipse confitebitur tibi sicut et ego hodie; Syriac: *ʾlʾ nwdwn lk ḥyʾ dʾkwty ywmnʾ;* *Targum of Isaiah:* *dḥy ḥy hwʾ ywdy qdmk kwty ywmʾ.*

The repeated *ḥy* is not to be translated "the living" (which would be simply [*h*]*ḥyym*) or—worse yet—by the unidiomatic "the living, the living," but rather "each living person." Although the form could be emphatic,²⁵ here it is probably distributive²⁶ and emphasizes the fact that it is not simply the living in general but each individual living person who gives praise to Yhwh. In other words, the psalmist is at pains to point out to God that it is in the divine interest to keep alive each and every individual who praises him. Some corroboration of this interpretation of *ḥay ḥay* is afforded by ııQPsᵃ 19:2. The colon immediately following a close paraphrase of Isa 38:19a reads *ywdw lkh kwl mwṭṭy rgl,* "(It is) *all* those who totter on legs who give you thanks." The presence of *kwl* in this paraphrase suggests a distributive (rather than emphatic) interpretation of *ḥy ḥy* in the preceding colon.

[19c] *ʾāb lĕbānîm yôdîaʿ:*
ıQIsaᵃ: (1) *ʾb lbnym ywdyʿ;* (2) *ʾb lbnym yhwdyʿ;* ıQIsaᵇ: *ʾb lbnym ywdʿ;* LXX: παιδία ποιήσω, ἃ ἀναγγελοῦσι; Aquila: [ ]; Symmachus: πατὴρ υἱοῖς γνωρίσει; Theodotion: [ ]; Vg: pater filiis notam faciet; Syriac: *wʾbʾ lbnyʾ nḥwʾ;* *Targum of Isaiah:* *dyn ʾbhn lbnyhwn yḥwwn.*

After the sequence of laudatory verbs used thus far in IIB—*y-d-y* (*hiphil*), *h-l-l* (*piel*), and *s-p-r* (*piel*)—the poet employs a related term,

---

Legelshurst, *Die Hiskiaerzählungen,* 44; Goshen-Gottstein, *The Book of Isaiah,* 170; van der Westhuizen, "Isaiah 38:10–20," 209.

²⁴ At this point in its text ıQIsaᵃ has a doublet, two versions of the words from *ḥy* to *lhwšyʿny.* Here and after subsequent lemmata "(1)" marks the first of these and "(2)" the second. See S. Talmon, "Aspects of the Textual Transmission of the Bible in Light of Qumran Manuscripts," in *Qumran and the History of the Biblical Text* (ed. F. M. Cross and S. Talmon; Cambridge, MA: Harvard University Press, 1975) 240–41.

²⁵ Waltke and O'Connor, *Biblical Hebrew Syntax,* 116 (§7.2.3c).

²⁶ Ibid., §7.2.3b.

y-d-ᶜ (*hiphil*), "to make known" God's saving deeds. Above we noted the appearance of *s-p-r* and *y-d-ᶜ* with *y-d-y* (*hiphil*) in Ps 88:11–13. The last mentioned is very close in meaning to *s-p-r* (*piel*), "to proclaim, recount (God's saving deeds)."

The verbs *s-p-r* and *y-d-ᶜ* occur together again in Ps 78:5b–6, which is another significant parallel to Isa 38:19, insofar as it gives expression to the theme of fathers making known to sons/children what God has done for Israel. Both verbs in this passage have the same indirect object, *libnêhem* (cf. Isa 38:18c and 19c):

> *ᵃ͗šer ṣiwwâ ͗et-ᵃ͗bôtênû*
> *lĕhôdîᶜām libnêhem*
> *lĕmaᶜan yēdĕᶜû dôr ͗aḥărôn*
> *bānîm yiwwālēdû*
> *yāqūmû wîsappĕrû libnêhem*
> *wĕyāśîmû bē͗lōhîm kislām*

> . . . (the ᶜēdût) which he commanded our *fathers*
> to *make known to their sons,*
> So that the future generation might know,
> the sons (yet) to be born,
> That they might arise and *recount* it *to their sons,*
> so that they could place their hope in God.

[19d] *͗el-ᵃ͗mittekkā:*

1QIsaᵃ: (1): *͗l ͗mtkh*; (2): *͗lwh ͗mtk*; 1QIsaᵇ: *͗lh ͗mtk*; LXX: τὴν δικαιοσύνην σου; Aquila: [ ]; Symmachus: περὶ τῆς ἀληθείας σου; Theodotion: [ ]; Vg: veritatem tuam; Syriac: *hymnwtk*; Targum of Isaiah: *gbwrtk wyydwn lmymr dkl ͗lyn qšwṭ*.

As in v. 18cd, the ancient witnesses listed above all support the MT's *ᵃ͗mittekkā* as the object of the verb in v. 19c with the possible exception of the LXX. Only in a very few instances does it render Hebrew *ᵉ͗met* by δικαιοσύνη, another of which occurs in Isaiah.[27] In the overwhelming majority of cases this word translates *ṣedeq* or *ṣĕdāqâ*.

If it is doubtful that the verb *s-p-r* (*piel*), restored in v. 18c above, takes the preposition *͗el* before a direct object, it is even less likely that *y-d-ᶜ* (*hiphil*) does. Nowhere in the MT does it take *͗el* or *lĕ-* before its

---

[27] Gen 24:49; Josh 24:11; Isa 39:8; Dan 8:12; 9:13.

object. Rather, here again *ʾl* is to be read as the divine name *ʾēl*, as in v. 18d. There is more support for this interpretation than in the case of v. 18d. The two major manuscripts of Isaiah from Qumran also support this reading. 1QIsa[b], a text that is consistently very close to the MT, reads *ʾlh* here. In theory this could be the plural demonstrative pronoun *ʾēlleh*,[28] but such a reading hardly fits the context. It is rather to be interpreted as the divine name *ʾĕlōah*, "God." Confirmation of this is found in 1QIsa[a], which presents a doublet of vv. 19a–20a, evidently from two different textual traditions.[29] Although the first member of the doublet reads the ambivalent *ʾl*, the second has *ʾlwh*, which can only be *ʾĕlōah*. The conclusion is that in this colon, as in v. 18d above, *ʾl* is to be read *ʾēl*, although *ʾĕlōah* is also a possibility.[30]

The divine name can only be parsed as a vocative in this passage: ". . . O God, your faithfulness." We have already seen one instance in Biblical Hebrew poetry in which the 2d masc. sg. suffix is paralleled by an abstract noun with the same suffix—Ps 30:10b.[31] Another example, quite instructive for the phrase under consideration, is Ps 71:22:

> *gam-ʾănî ʾôdĕkā biklî-nebel*
> *ʾămittĕkā ʾĕlōhāy*

> I too will praise you with the lyre,
> (I will praise) *your faithfulness, O my God.*[32]

In this case the same abstract noun + suffix (*ʾămittĕkā*) is accompanied by a divine name in the vocative.

Emended Text and Translation

IIBa	18a	*kî lōʾ šĕʾôl tôdekkā*
	b	*māwet yĕhallĕlekkā*
	c	*lōʾ yĕsappĕrû yôrĕdê bôr*
	d	*ʾēl ḥasdekā*

---

[28] A possibility raised by Talmon, "Aspects of the Textual Transmission," 241–42.
[29] Ibid.
[30] So also Nyberg, "Hiskias Danklied," 96.
[31] See n. 5 above.
[32] The LXX, Symmachus, and the Syriac read *ʾlhym* here instead of *ʾlhy*.

IIBb	19a	*ḥay ḥay hûʾ yôdekā*
	b	*kāmônî ḥayyôm*
	c	*ʾāb lĕbānîm yôdîaʿ*
	d	*ʾēl ʾămittekkā*

A. The Silence of the Dead

For it is not the Netherworld that gives you thankful praise,
    nor Death that extols you;
Neither can those who go down into the Pit proclaim,
    O God, your steadfast love.

B. The Praise of the Living

It is each living person that gives you thankful praise
    as I do this day;
It is the father that makes known to (his) children,
    O God, your faithfulness.

Rhetorical-Critical Observations

The two subsections of this stanza divide along thematic lines. IIBa is concerned with what or who can*not* praise God (viz., the dead), while IIBb focuses on who *can* praise him (viz., each living individual). The final cola of the two subsections are connected insofar as each begins and ends the same way—with *ʾēl* followed by two abstract nouns (*ḥesed* and *ʾĕmet*) which constitute a common word-pair,[33] both ending with the suffix *-kā*. The initial cola of the two subsections are connected by the fact that each ends with the verb *y-d-y* (*hiphil*), again with the suffix *-kā*. These verbs differ only in their initial consonant (*t-* and *y-* respectively). The verbs in IIBb occur at the end of the first colon of each of the two bicola. Each of these begins with /yōd-/, although they are from different roots.

This /yō/ sound functions as an alliterative thread linking the two subsections and the four bicola: *yôrĕdê* (v. 18c), *yôdekā* (v. 19a), *ḥayyôm* (v. 19b), *yôdîaʿ* (v. 19c). Another example of assonance is the

---

[33] See Avishur, *Word-Pairs*, 130, 274.

ending *-ek(k)ā* at the end of vv. 18a, 18b, 18d, 19a, and 19d. *tôdekkā* at the end of v. 18a forms a rhyme with *yôdekā* at the end of v. 19a.

IIB, the last secondary subsection in the body of the poem, shows a number of connections with the first subsection, IA. Only in these two subsections does the term *šĕᵓôl* appear. The repetition of this fearful name in v. 18a occurs in a context which makes it clear that its power over the psalmist has been broken by the divine deliverance. The first and third cola begin with *lōᵓ* in IIBa (preceded by *kî* in v. 18a), just as in vv. 11a and 11c. The negative particle occurs nowhere else in the poem. The expression "land of the living" in v. 11c is echoed by the only other appearance of the substantive "(the) living"—i.e., *ḥay ḥay*.[34]

Finally, there are some points of connection with IBa. Verse 19b (*kāmônî ḥayyôm*) repeats two elements from this subsection: the comparative particle *kĕ-* (only in vv. 12–14) and the word *yôm* (in the singular). But whereas all the similes in IB are negative, referring to the end of the psalmist's life or to his suffering, here the simile is positive, referring to the happy circumstance of giving thanks God for the experience of his salvation. Likewise *yôm*, which in v. 12e formed part of a formula that described his obliteration at God's hand, is now used to described the "today" of divine deliverance and the joyful response thereto.

General Comments

In one sense, the subsection under consideration forms a response to the act of deliverance narrated in vv. 17c–f. Yet the main purpose of this section is not to express the poet's gratitude to God for his saving act—this, as we shall see, is the subject of the coda. Its chief purpose, rather, is to remind God that only the living can praise him, in the hope that this reminder will prolong the life of the psalmist. This motif appears with some frequency in the psalms of lament and thanksgiving in the OT and in Akkadian prayers as well. A common ending of Akkadian laments of the sub-genre ŠU.ÍL.LÁ is *lubluṭ lušlimma dalīlīka ludlul*, "May I live/recover (and) get well, so that I may (go on) prais(ing)

---

[34] As *ḥay ḥay* refers back to *(ha)ḥayyîm* in v. 11c, could the poet also have intended a reference to the previous colon: *yāh yāh* (v. 11b)? *ḥay ḥay* is almost a sonant reversal of this only other doubled term in the poem. This was earlier noted by Castellino, "Lamentazioni individuali accadiche ed ebraiche," 153.

you."[35] Only the living can praise Yhwh. The chorus of praise that arises to him from the earth is comprised of individual living worshipers. The clear implication is that it is in Yhwh's best interest to keep this individual (viz., the poet) alive, so that he and others like him might go on praising his God. Otherwise, the chorus of praise would diminish to the point of disappearing altogether, leaving Yhwh in the undesirable position of having no one in the land of the living to sing his praises.

By associating himself with the other living who praise Yhwh (cf. "as I do this day," v. 19b), the poet establishes a synchronic connection between himself and all other believers existing at the present time who offer praise to the God of Israel. This is complemented in the next line by the diachronic dimension, with the reference to the father teaching his children about God's faithfulness, so that the chorus of praise might continue throughout Israel's generations. So that this chorus of praise might not die with the present generation, it is necessary that the tradition about God's salvific ways be handed on to the next generation (the *bānîm* in v. 19c). But this can only happen if their fathers are alive and well. There can be little doubt that the psalmist includes himself in the category of *ʾāb* ("father"), one who fulfills this role vis-à-vis his own children, especially his sons. Verse 19cd may therefore have a twofold aim, namely to encourage Yhwh to keep the psalmist alive so that he can pass on this teaching to the next generation, and perhaps also to encourage the Creator to provide the psalmist with (more?) offspring to perpetuate the earthly chorus of divine praise.[36]

In the first half of the poem the psalmist did not address God in prayer until the very end (v. 14d). Before this he had spoken of him as one who was swiftly bringing his life to an end (v. 12e) and who was crushing his bones like a lion (v. 13b). In that section the few references to Yhwh depicted him in Joban fashion as the poet's tormentor and destroyer. In IIB, however, he speaks as one who has experienced the

---

[35] See Mayer, *Untersuchungen zur Formensprache der babylonischen "Gebetbeschwörungen"*, 312.

[36] This section might also have in mind the two kinds of "life" the individual possessed in the thought of ancient Israel: the individual's personal life (i.e., the life of his *nepeš*) and an extended life through progeny. By mentioning "each living person" and "(the) father," the psalmist alludes to both.

divine *ḥesed* and *ʾĕmet* through God's act of deliverance (vv. 17c–f). The two halves of this subsection, and the body of the poem, conclude beautifully with the juxtaposition of God's name and his character as a loving, faithful savior: ". . . O God, your steadfast love . . . O God, your faithfulness."

Yhwh Has Saved Me!

The Coda (v. 20)

The Masoretic Text

20a *yhwh lĕhôšîʿēnî*[a]
  b *ûnĕgînôtay nĕnaggēn kol-yĕmê ḥayyênû*[t]
  c *ʿal-bêt yhwh*[s]

Textual Remarks

[20a] *yhwh lĕhôšîʿēnî:*
1QIsa[a]: (1) *yhwh lhwšyʿny;* (2) *yhwh lhwšyʿny;* 1QIsa[b]: *yhwh lhšyʿny;*
LXX: κύριε τῆς σωτηρίας μου; Aquila: [ ]; Symmachus: κύριε σῶσόν
με; Theodotion: [ ]; Vg: domine salvum me fac; Syriac: *mryʾ nprqn;*
Targum of Isaiah: yhwh lmprqnʾ ʾmr.

The *sillûq* after *ʾămittekkā* at the end of v. 19d shows that the MT
reads these two words as belonging with the following rather than the
preceding material (although it indicates something of a disjuncture
with the *ʾatnāḥ* after *lĕhôšîʿēnî*). In this respect the MT differs from a
number of the ancient witnesses. The doublet *ḥy ḥy . . . yhwh lhwšyʿny*
in 1QIsa[a] clearly shows that it understood the latter words as belonging with the preceding material. The LXX also links them with v. 19d:
". . . , O Lord of my salvation." The fact that the 1st sg. suffix appears
here, whereas the rest of v. 20b has only 1st pl. suffixes, probably

explains why these witnesses did not connect this phrase with what follows.[1] Virtually all modern commentators and translators, however, correctly take *yhwh lĕhôšîʿēnî* as the beginning of a separate section, distinct from IIBb. As we have seen from Chapter 1, v. 20 marks a major juncture within the poem, and the inclusive function of the double *yhwh* also marks this verse off as an independent unit.

The form *lĕhôšîʿēnî* is problematic. To all appearances it is the preposition *lĕ-* followed by the *hiphil* infinitive of the root *y-š-ʿ* with the 1st sg. suffix. This is probably how the Masoretes and certainly the *Targum of Isaiah* understood it, the latter translating, "Yhwh has promised to save us." But if the MT parses it as an infinitive, where is the governing verb? Begrich suggests restoring *ḥûšâ*, *qûmâ*, or *rĕṣēh*.[2]

In recent years hebraists have come to recognize the existence of an emphatic or asseverative particle *l-* (vocalization uncertain), formally identical to the preposition. In their recent work on Hebrew syntax, for example, B. K. Waltke and M. O'Connor parse *l-* in v. 20a as this emphatic particle and *hôšîʿēnî* as the imperative, translating: "YHWH, *do* save me!"[3] Methodologically, this is preferable to the analysis mentioned above, according to which the word is to be parsed as an infinitive, since it does not require supplying a governing verb for which there is no textual evidence in the Hebrew witnesses or the versions.

J. Huehnergard, however, in a thorough study of this Semitic morpheme, allows its occurrence in Hebrew with all finite verb forms *except the imperative*, since there is no evidence of its use with the

---

[1] So S. Talmon, "Aspects of the Textual Transmission of the Bible," 240.

[2] *Der Psalm des Hiskia*, 50. The closest parallel to *yhwh lĕhôšîʿēnî* is Ps 70:2:

　ʾĕlōhîm lĕhaṣṣîlēnî

　　yhwh lĕʿezrātî ḥûšâ

At first glance the verbal form here also seems capable of being parsed as the emphatic particle plus the imperative—"O God, deliver me . . . !" But the parallel version of Psalm 70, namely Ps 40:14–18, has *rĕṣēh ʾĕlōhîm lĕhaṣṣîlēnî*—"Be pleased, O God, to deliver me!" (v. 14). The oral or scribal tradition behind Psalm 40 supplied each colon with its own verb by adding *rĕṣēh* to the first colon. In Ps 70:2, however, the verb *ḥûšâ* at the end of the second colon does double-duty for both cola: "O God, (hasten) to deliver me, // O Yhwh, hasten to my aid!" (Another example of *ḥûš* governing an infinitive occurs in Ps 119:60.) This is a variation of what Watson calls "delayed identification" (*Classic Hebrew Poetry*, 336–38). The effect of this delay places great stress on the imperative "Hasten!" Cf. *NJPSV*: "Hasten, O God, to save me; O Lord, to aid me!"

[3] Waltke and O'Connor, *Biblical Hebrew Syntax*, 212 (§11.2.10i).

imperative in any other Semitic language.[4] The same point has been expressed by T. Muraoka.[5] In sum, *hwšyʿny* in this verse is not an imperative and not likely an infinitive. The resolution of the problem, I suggest, is to parse it as the 3d masc. sg. *qtl* form, *hôšîʿānî*.[6] This reading requires the alteration of a single vowel but no change to the consonantal text of the MT (or 1QIsaᵃ).

Besides Huehnergard's disallowance of asseverative *l-* with the imperative, there are several reasons for parsing the term in question as a 3d masc. sg. *qtl*. First, the poet's deliverance has already been explicitly mentioned in vv. 17c–f. Fortunately, the text is reasonably well preserved at this point so that there can be no doubt as to the import of this subsection (IIAc). Second, the section immediately following upon this, IIB, makes reference to praising and giving thanks to Yhwh, which clearly indicates that the saving action for which the thanks/praise is given *has already occurred*. This fact argues that translations like "Yhwh, save me!" cannot be correct.[7] Why would the poet pray for deliverance at the conclusion of the poem if that deliverance had already been granted? Third, v. 20bc is concerned with making music in the temple area, which in the context of this poem is another indication of a *response to the divine deliverance*. This implies that the line immediately preceding—i.e., v. 20a—is a statement of, not a petition for, deliverance and is the immediate motivation for the music-making. This is possible only if *lhwšyʿny* describes a salvific action that

---

[4] J. Huehnergard, "Asseverative **la* and Hypothetical **lu/law* in Semitic," *JAOS* 103 (1983) 591: "[Proposed examples of asseverative *la-* plus imperative in Hebrew] . . . must be rejected, however, for nowhere else in Semitic do we find asseverative **la-* with an imperative, and it is improbable that this restriction would uniquely not obtain in Hebrew."

[5] T. Muraoka, *Emphatic Words and Structures in Biblical Hebrew* (Jerusalem: Magnes; Leiden: Brill, 1985) 116. Muraoka tends in the direction of Huehnergard in his views on the particle (see second paragraph). But see n. 7 below.

[6] Another example of the asseverative *lamed* with the *qal* perfect in the Book of Isaiah may be present in Isa 44:17: *lkrt-lô ʾărāzîm*. The MT points the first words as an infinitive: *likrôt*. I. Eitan ("La particule emphatique 'la' dans la Bible," *REJ* 74 [1922] 11) recognized this passage as an example of the emphatic *lamed* with the *qal* perfect: *lĕkārat-lô ʾăzārîm*, "Indeed, he cut down cedars (for himself)." Huehnergard also lists Isa 44:17 as an example of the emphatic *l-* with the perfect ("Asseverative **la* and Hypothetical **lu/law* in Semitic," 591.

[7] Thus I do not agree with Muraoka, who refers to the translation "Jahvé est pret à me sauver" as "a happy rendering" of the two words (*Emphatic Words and Structures*, 116).

has already taken place. Hence v. 20a must be understood as a climactic, emphatic restatement of the central theme of PsHez, namely that Yhwh has indeed acted to save the psalmist. The emphatic nuance of the verb in this colon may be indicated in translation by an adverb such as "indeed," "truly," etc., or simply by an exclamation point: "Yhwh has saved me!"[8]

[20b] *ûnĕgînôtay nĕnaggēn kol-yĕmê ḥayyênû:*
1QIsa[a]: *wngnwty nngn kwl ymy ḥyynw;* 1QIsa[b]: *wngnwty nngn kl ymy ḥyynw;* LXX: καὶ οὐ παύσομαι εὐλογῶν σε μετὰ ψαλτηρίου πάσας τὰς ἡμέρας τῆς ζωῆς μου; Aquila: [ ]; Symmachus: καὶ ψαλμοὺς ἡμῶν ψαλ[λ]οῦμεν [ ]; Theodotion: [ ]; Vg: et psalmos nostros cantabimus cunctis diebus vitae nostrae; Syriac: *wtšbḥth nšbḥ klhwn ywmtʾ dḥyyn;* *Targum of Isaiah*: *wnygwn twšbḥtyh nngyn kl ywmy ḥyynʾ.*

Although the change from 1st sg. to pl. is not unknown in Hebrew poetry, there is reason to question the MT's reading of this line. PsHez is an intensely personal psalm, with at most a vague reference to other worshippers of Yhwh in the expression *ḥay ḥay* (v. 19). Thus the switch from "I, my" to "we, our" at the very end is unexpected in the writer's conclusion to his psalm. No doubt the 1st pl. forms represent a "democratization" of the poem, a phenomenon attested in the conclusion to a number of OT psalms.[9] But was this the original reading?

In most cases democratization amounts to adding a line or subsection containing terms that expand the focus of the poem beyond the 1st person sg. But here there is reason to believe that in v. 20 original 1st person sg. forms have been altered to 1st pl. One main reason for maintaining this view is the bizarre juxtaposition of 1st sg. and pl. forms in *ûnĕgînôtay nĕnaggēn*—lit., "and *we* will play (on) *my* stringed instru-

---

[8] This translation of v. 20a is almost identical to that given in L. Segond's translation of the Bible into French (*La Sainte Bible: Traduite d'après originaux hébreu et grec* [rev. ed.; Paris: Alliance Biblique Universelle, 1998] 715): "L'Éternel m'a sauvé!"

[9] I have in mind those psalms of the individual that end by broadening the focus of their concern beyond the psalmist to the community. The following psalms contain 1st person references throughout and then abruptly refer to or address to Israel or God's faithful, et al., at the end: Psalms 3 (v. 9b: "your people"); 25 (v. 22: "Israel"); 28 (vv. 8–9: "your people"); 51 (vv. 20–21: "Zion . . . Jerusalem"); 69 (vv. 33–37: "you lowly ones . . . the poor"); 131 (v. 3: "Israel").

ments." No satisfactory explanation of this incongruity has been proposed.[10]

The most important evidence for the secondary character of the 1st pl. forms in v. 20b is the LXX: "And *I* shall not cease praising you with the harp all the days of *my* life." This periphrastic translation differs significantly from the MT insofar as not only is the pronominal suffix on "days" in the 1st person sg. but so is the predicate as well (παύσομαι). This is particularly striking, given the fact that the tendency of all the other versions (Symmachus, Vg, the Syriac, the *Targum of Isaiah*) is to *multiply* the number of 1st *pl.* forms in v. 20 beyond what the Hebrew witnesses have.[11]

What *Vorlage* stands behind the LXX's translation? Oddly, there have been few attempts to answer this question. M. Touzard expressed the opinion that the LXX had read *wngynwty ʾngn kl ymy ḥyy*.[12] But I would explain this translation by postulating that the LXX translator did not read the noun *wngnwty* in his *Vorlage* at all. Rather, he read a word with one less vowel letter, *wngnty*,[13] which he parsed as a verb. Specifically, he parsed it as the 1st sg. *piel waw*-inversive (i.e., the *wĕqataltî* form): *wĕniggantî*. This explains his translating it in the future tense. In Isa 38:20b the nuance of duration implicit in "I shall not cease to praise" is undoubtedly influenced by the subsequent "all the days of my life," which denotes an indefinite extension of time into the future.

Scribal confusion between the nominal form of *n-g-n* and the finite verb is not limited to Isa 38:20. Another example occurs in Ps 69:13: *yāśîḥû bî yôšĕbê šāʿar // ûnĕgînôt šôtê šēqār*: lit., "Those who sit in the gate gossip about me, // and songs those who drink strong drink."

---

[10] It has been noticed that the same form appears in Hab 3:19, in a "subscription" to the psalm: *lamnaṣṣēaḥ binĕgînôtāy*. No one has satisfactorily explained the reason for the 1st pl. suffix here, but it could well be a scribal error for *lamnaṣṣēaḥ binĕgînô/ōt*, which occurs in the superscription to Psalms 4, 6, 54, 55, 67, and 76. The LXX and the Syriac have a 3d sg. suffix: ἐν τῇ ᾠδῇ αὐτοῦ and *btšbḥth* (= *bngyntw/bngynwtw*).

[11] Symmachus translates v. 20: "And *we* will play/sing *our* psalms [　]." Cf. Vg: "And *we* will sing *our* psalms all the days of *our* life . . ."; Syriac: "The Lord will save *us*; and *we* will sing his praises all the days of *our* life . . ."; *Targum of Isaiah*: "Yhwh has promised to save *us*; and *we* will play the music of his praise all the days of *our* life. . . ."

[12] M. Touzard, "De la conservation du text hébreu," 105.

[13] Goshen-Gottstein lists one Hebrew manuscript that has *wngnty* for the MT's *wngnwty* (*The Book of Isaiah*, 170).

Obviously there is something wrong in the second colon, which makes no sense. It has long been suspected that the noun *wngynwt* here is not right and that the correct reading is the 3d masc. pl. *piel* verb, *wĕniggĕnû*; the LXX, Symmachus, and the Syriac attest to a 3d pl. verb.[14] The verbal form is now confirmed by the oldest of the Psalms scrolls from Qumran, 4QPs[a], with the reading *wngnw*,[15] which yields a much more balanced bicolon: "... and those who drink strong drink *make up songs* (about me)."

In sum, the LXX translator evidently read *wngnty* rather than the MT's *wngnwty* and interpreted this as a verb, a *wĕqataltí* form. While I do not completely agree with his understanding of the grammar, I submit that his reading of this term as a 1st person verb rather than as a noun was correct.

If *wngnty* was originally the predicate in this verse, how did the LXX translator read *nngn*, the predicate as the sentence now reads in the MT? Instead of *nngn* I suggest the *Vorlage* of the LXX had *ngn*— i.e., *naggēn*, the *piel* infinitive absolute of *n-g-n*. The change to the later reading *nngn* can be plausibly explained as follows. Once *wngnty* was misinterpreted as a noun (cf. Ps 69:13) with a 1st sg. suffix—and later spelled *wngnwty*[16]—the sentence in v. 20b would have lost its predicate. When this happened scribes probably still correctly parsed *ngn* as an infinitive absolute, but interpreted it as a case of this grammatical form used as a finite verb. There is evidence that scribes sometimes "updated" these non-finite verbal forms, changing them to finite verbs. B. K. Waltke notes, for example:

> Scribes sometimes modernized archaic features of a verse. In Num 15:35 the S[amaritan] P[entateuch] replaces the old infinitive absolute construction of the MT (*rāgôm*) . . . [with] the imperative, *rigmû*, "stone."[17]

---

[14] The LXX and Symmachus translate with ἔψαλλον; the Syriac has *rnw*.

[15] See P. W. Flint and A. E. Alvarez, "The Oldest of All the Psalms Scrolls: The Text and Translation of 4QPs[a]," in *The Scrolls and the Scriptures: Qumran Fifty Years After* (ed. S. E. Porter and C. A. Evans; JSPSup 26; Sheffield: Sheffield University Press, 1997) 168.

[16] And still later *wngynwty* in some manuscripts. But this is an inferior reading. Neither of the earliest Hebrew manuscripts of Isaiah (1QIsa[a] and 1QIsa[b]) have the *yod*, nor does the Aleppo Codex (the text used in Goshen-Gottstein's *The Book of Isaiah* [see p. 170]) or the Leningrad Codex.

[17] Waltke, "How We Got the Hebrew Bible," 45. In another place Waltke observes: "Qumran biblical manuscripts often shift the infinitive absolute forms to finite forms" (Waltke and O'Connor, *Biblical Hebrew Syntax*, 595 n. 57).

Thus at some point in the scribal tradition the infinitive absolute *naggēn*, the original reading here, was updated by being changed to what certain scribes assumed from the context to be its appropriate finite equivalent, *nĕnaggēn*.[18]

The fact that the LXX translation does not reflect a literal rendering of the infinitive absolute construction *wĕnigganti naggēn* should occasion no surprise. This was often the case, especially in the Book of Isaiah.[19] In our passage the translator simply decided to use a broad paraphrase to capture the meaning of this construction.

In the cognate infinitive absolute construction, the infinitive may precede or follow its verb, though when combined with a *wqtl* form it can only be postpositive, as it is here. There is a growing consensus among hebraists that there is little if any difference in the meaning of the infinitive absolute whether it precedes or follows.[20] In both cases it gives some kind of emphasis, though further specification of this emphasis is difficult. Interestingly, if the infinitive absolute construction posited here is the correct reading in v. 20b (*wĕnigganti naggēn*), there is a correspondence between the emphatic construction in v. 20a (the asseverative *l-*) and that in v. 20b (the cognate infinitive absolute). Thus, as Yhwh has *indeed* saved the psalmist, the latter vows correspondingly that he will *surely* praise him with music as long as he lives.

I mentioned above that I do not agree with the LXX's interpretation of the form *wĕnigganti* in v. 20b as a *waw*-conversive construction. Rather, I take it as an example of what B. Waltke and M. O'Connor call the "perfective of resolve," which is translated into English as a future tense.[21] In response to Yhwh's saving action (v. 20a) the poet

---

[18] It is also possible—but less likely, in my view—that through dittography the first *nun* in *ngn* was read as two *nuns*, resulting in the MT's 1st pl. verb.

[19] See E. Tov, "Renderings of Combinations of the Infinitive Absolute and Finite Verbs in the LXX—Their Nature and Distribution," in *Studien zur Septuaginta: Robert Hanhart zu ehren: aus Anlass seines 65. Geburtstages* (ed. D. Fraenkel et al.; Abhandlungen der Akademie der Wissenschaften in Göttingen; Philologisch-historische Klasse, dritte Folge 190; Mitteilungen des Septuaginta-Unternehmens 20; Göttingen: Vandenhoeck & Ruprecht, 1990) 68: "Combinations of *qatol qatalty* are often rendered by a Greek verb only, as if the translator gave up an attempt to find a suitable equivalent for the two words of the Hebrew. . . . In most cases different translation techniques must be presumed. *The relatively large number of such renderings in Is[aiah]* . . . probably points in this direction" (emphasis mine).

[20] Waltke and O'Connor, *Biblical Hebrew Syntax*, 584–88 (§35.3.1).

[21] Ibid., 488 (§30.5.1d).

resolves to continue praising and thanking his God on the harp (or similar stringed instrument) for the rest of his life.

A number of factors corroborate *wěniggantî naggēn kol yěmê ḥayyay* as the earlier or original reading of v. 20b. First, as noted above, a 1st sg. verb fits better in a tricolon introduced by "Yhwh has truly saved *me*" than a 1st pl. form. Second, as we have seen, a prominent structural feature of PsHez, tying the whole poem together, is the word-pair *yāmîm // šānôt*. In Part I the pair occurs at the beginning of the poem, in vv. 10a and 10b (*yāmay // šěnôtāy*), creating an inclusion that rounds off the tricolon in the first subsection (IAa). It then appears at the beginning of Part II (v. 15b) and in v. 20b, with several differences. (1) The order of words is reversed (chiasmus). (2) The two words are prefixed by *kol*: *kol šěnôtay* and *kol yěmê ḥayy-*. In the MT the suffix on all these plural words is the 1st c. sg. (*-ay*) except for the occurrence in v. 20b, but the LXX's τῆς ζωῆς μου reflects *ḥayyay*. (3) Whereas we would expect the last member of the word-pair to be *yāmay*, as in Part I, in the coda it has been expanded by the synonymous *ḥayyîm* resulting in *kol yěmê ḥayyay*. These three words form a "triplet" in Biblical Hebrew.[22] The variation of an established pattern, such as the expansion of a word-pair by a third term in this instance, serves to indicate a conclusion, in this case the conclusion of the chiasmus (and of the poem as a whole). In any case one expects in this last member of the chiasmus the 1st sg. suffix (as in v. 15c), not the 1st pl. suffix. Third, there is a significant structural link between vv. 20bc and 15cd, which contains the other member of the word-pair *yāmîm // šānôt* in the second half of the poem, a link that has heretofore gone unnoticed. Here two non-contiguous bicola share an identical structure, a feature that appears only once in PsHez. (1) Both begin with a 1st sg. verb. In Part II only two cola begin with 1st sg. verbs, namely v. 15c and—if the reading proposed here is correct—v. 20b. (2) In both passages this verb is followed by the phrase *kol . . . -ay*, which again occurs only in these two verses. The two members of the word-pair are contained in this phrase. (3) The second colon of each consists of a prepositional phrase beginning with *ʿal* followed by two words forming a construct phrase. The preposition *ʿal* occurs nowhere else in PsHez.

---

[22] Gen 25:7; 47:8, 9, 28; 2 Sam 19:35; Prov 3:2; 9:11. For the term "triplet" (i.e., three synonymous terms used in parallelism or paratactically), see Avishur, *Word-Pairs*, 626.

Verse	1st sg. verb	*kol . . . -ay* phrase, word-pair	*ʿal* phrase
15c	*ʾeddĕdâ*	*kol šĕnôtay*	// *ʿal mar napšî*
20b	*wĕniggantî (naggēn)*	*kol yĕmê ḥayyay* //	*ʿal bêt yhwh*

[20c] *ʿal-bêt yhwh:*
1QIsa^a: *ʿl byt yhwh*; 1QIsa^b: *ʿl byt yhwh*; LXX: κατέναντι τοῦ οἴκου τοῦ θεοῦ; Aquila: [ ]; Symmachus: ἐν τῷ οἴκῳ [ ]; Theodotion: [ ]; Vg: in domo domini; Syriac: *bbyt dmry*; *Targum of Isaiah*: *ʿl byt mqdš dyhwh*.

At first glance the preposition *ʿal* is somewhat curious. One might have expected *bĕbêt yhwh*, "*in* the house of Yhwh,"[23] as in Symmachus, Vg, and the Syriac. But as we have seen, there is no question that *ʿal* is the correct preposition here, given the structural parallel with v. 15cd as well as the witness of the ancient Hebrew manuscripts, the LXX, and the *Targum of Isaiah*. In this context the preposition designates the area "in front of"—viz, the courtyard of—the temple.

The area that the poet has in mind is arguably the same as that denoted by the phrase *lipnê bêt-yhwh* in 1 Kgs 8:64 (// 2 Chr 7:7). This passage records that at one point in the dedication ceremony of the newly completed temple Solomon consecrated the "middle of the court that was before the house of Yhwh (*lipnê bêt-yhwh*)." The passage goes on to say that he offered burnt offerings, cereal offerings, and peace-offerings on the altar there. The area where these activities took place is most likely the courtyard in front of the *ʾûlām* or "vestibule," certainly not some area within the temple itself, where only the priests were allowed.[24] "The house of Yhwh" in 1 Kgs 8:64 //

[23] Cf. *šabtî bĕbêt-yhwh* // *kol-yĕmê ḥayyay* in Ps 27:4: "May I dwell in the house of Yhwh // all the days of my life." For *šabtî* = "May I dwell," see Kselman and Barré, "New Exodus, Covenant, and Restoration in Psalm 23," 299. The same cola occur in Ps 23:6 except that they are reversed and belong to different bicola.

[24] "The normal placement of sacrificial altars in the Hebrew Bible was in the courtyard in front of the temple. . . . There is no evidence of the use of sacrificial altars in the interior of the tabernacle or temple [i.e., the *hêkāl*]" (R. D. Haak, "Altar," *ABD*, 1. 164; see also N. H. Gadegaard, "On the So-Called Burnt Offering Altar in the Old Testament," *PEQ* 110 [1978] 35–45). Gadegaard argues plausibly that this altar was a kind of *bāmâ* within the temple precincts, since for a variety of reasons only this kind of structure could accommodate the sacrifices described in 1 Kgs 8:62–64. If he is correct, the

2 Chr 7:7 therefore denotes the *hêkāl* or main area of the temple complex and "before the house of Yhwh" probably refers to the courtyard in front of the vestibule.

Emended Text and Translation

20a	*yhwh lĕhôšîʿānî*
b	*wĕniggantî naggēn kol yĕmê ḥayyay*
c	*ʿal bêt yhwh*

Yhwh has saved me!
And (so) I will play music (to him) all the days of my life
before the house of Yhwh.

Rhetorical-Critical Observations

"Coda" is a musical term which is sometimes used in a literary context. In music it has the following characteristics. (1) It comes at the end of a movement or piece of music. (2) On the one hand, it is more or less independent of the foregoing movement, but on the other it is often bound to it in such a way that it cannot be easily dispensed with. (3) It rounds off the piece as a whole, often by restating themes and motifs of movements in the foregoing section(s). All of these characteristics fit v. 20. It is the last verse in PsHez. Strictly speaking it is not a continuation of IIB (vv. 18–19). The fact that the two main parts of PsHez have the same word-count (sixty words each) is a further indication that v. 20 is separate from the main body of the poem. Yet it is linked to the body insofar as it harks back to the theme of deliverance enunciated in vv. 17c–f and contains the last member of the chiastic word-pair *yāmîm // šānôt*. Finally, it recapitulates the end of IIA (i.e., v. 17c–f) and IIB, which deal with deliverance (cf. v. 20a) and thanksgiving (cf. v. 20bc) respectively.[25]

---

fact that these were always open-air structures (ibid., 40) provides a further argument that the ceremonies described in 1 Kgs 8:62–64 and 2 Chr 7:4–7 took place in the open courtyard "in front of" the temple proper. See also K. Galling, who likewise locates the altar of burnt offerings "in front of the temple" ("Altar," *IDB* 1. 97).

[25] In her analysis of *Hodayoth* 7:6–25, B. P. Kittel labels the last line as a coda and notes that it "draws together two images from the poem—the light image of Stanza E

Verse 20 begins and ends with the sacred tetragrammaton. This is the only time the full form of the sacred name appears in the poem. These occurrences form a link with the unusual *yāh yāh* in IA (v. 11b), which is formally a reduplication of the shorter form of the name. A number of studies have shown that Israelite poets showed some care in the use of divine titles and epithets in their poems.[26] In the Psalter, for example, one frequently notes the name forming an inclusion within the poem as a whole or within certain sections of the poem. Sometimes each section of the poem contains a divine name or epithet. The distribution of divine names in PsHez also gives evidence of a deliberate arrangement. *Each of the five major sections contains two divine names.* In the first three sections these are juxtaposed. In the last two they occur at specific junctures within the poem: at the end of IIBa and IIBb and at the beginning and end of the coda. In IA, IIB, and the coda the divine name is repeated:

Section	Verse	Divine Name	Translation	Syllables	
IA	11b	*yāh yāh*	Yah -Yah	1	1
IB	14cd	*mārôm ʾădōnāy*	Most High, Lord	2	3
IIA	16a	*ʾădōnāy ʿēlî*	Lord Most High	3	2
IIB	19b, d	*ʾēl . . . ʾēl*	God . . . God	1	1
Coda	20a, c	*yhwh . . . yhwh*	Yhwh . . . Yhwh	2	2

The unusual *yh yh* is formally a double name, though it is a variant of *yhwh*. IB and IIA contain the name *ʾădōnāy*, the only name the poet uses to address God. In IB this is immediately *preceded* by *mārôm* from the root *r-w-m*, "to be high," approximating "Most High" in English. In the next major section, IIA, *ʾădōnāy* appears again, this time immediately *followed* by a divine name synonymous with *mārôm*—namely *ʿēlî*, from the root *ʿ-l-y*, with the related meaning "to go up, ascend."[27] In IIB and the coda there is a repetition of a standard

---

and the earlier reference to the author's footsteps (from Stanza B)" (*The Hymns of Qumran: Translation and Commentary* [SBLDS 50; Chico, CA: Scholars Press, 1981] 133–34).

[26] See recently, for example, R. Youngblood, "Divine Names in the Book of Psalms: Literary Structures and Number Patterns," *JANES* 19 (1995) 171–81.

[27] These two roots appear in parallelism in the MT, but only in Isaiah: 14:13; 40:9.

divine name. Unlike the case of IA, IB, and IIA, the divine names in these final sections are separated from each other.

Within the body of the poem (i.e., prescinding from the coda), the number of syllables in the divine names forms a kind of chiasmus. The first and last pair are monosyllabic and the second two consist of *ʾădōnāy* plus a bisyllabic word. In v. 14cd this precedes *ʾădōnāy* and in 16a it follows it. The syllable count is: 1 1 2 3 : 3 2 1 1.

Finally, several inclusions find their resolution in the coda, all of which create a sharp contrast between the two members. One is a thematic inclusion bracketing the whole poem and consisting of the explicit contrast between mourning (*dōm* in v. 10b) and the playing of musical instruments (*wĕnigganî naggēn* in v. 20b). In the culture of the ancient Near East the sound of musical instruments, stringed instruments in particular, was synonymous with merrymaking and represented the exact opposite of mourning.[28] Note this contrast in the Sefîre inscription (I A 29–30):

> *wʾl ytšmᶜ ql knr [b]ʾrpd wbᶜmh . . . yllh*
> Let the sound of the lyre be heard no more in Arpad; (but rather) among its people (let there be) . . . wailing.[29]

Moreover, it is clear from other OT passages that playing stringed instruments such as the lyre was a common way of rendering thanksgiving or praise to Yhwh, especially in response to his saving actions.[30] Especially significant in this respect is Ps 71:22, which contains echoes of the vocabulary of IIB:

> I too will praise you (*ʾôdĕkā*) *with the lyre*,
>   (I will praise) your faithfulness (*ʾămittekā*), O my God.

The next verse indicates that the psalmist utters this thanksgiving to Yhwh for having "redeemed" (*p-d-y*) his life.

Above I alluded to another inclusion enveloping the entire poem formed by the word-pair *šaᶜar // bayit* in vv. 10c and 20c and to the

---

[28] Gen 31:27; 2 Sam 6:5; Isa 24:7–8; Neh 12:27; 1 Chr 13:8; 15:16; Job 21:12; Ps 98:5–6.

[29] J. A. Fitzmyer, *The Aramaic Inscriptions of Sefîre* (BibOr 19; Rome: Pontifical Biblical Institute, 1967) 12, 15.

[30] Pss 33:2; 43:4; 92:3; 147:7; 1 Chr 25:3.

word-pair *yāmîm // šānôt*, which forms an inclusion around Part II, the first member appearing in v. 15cd and the second in v. 20b. In v. 10c *šaʿar* refers to the netherworld, whereas *bayit* in v. 20c refers to its diametrical opposite, Yhwh's temple. The two constitute the nadir and the zenith of the cosmos respectively. In v. 15cd *kol-šěnôtay* occurs in a negative context, where the poet envisions the possibility of spending "all [his] years" = "the rest of [his] life" in unrelieved misery (i.e., if Yhwh does nothing to relieve his present affliction). This contrasts sharply with the use of the corresponding member in the very last line of the poem, where the expanded *kol-yěmê ḥayyay* also refers to the rest of the psalmist's life, but now spent in the joyful and life-giving activity of praising Yhwh forever in the forecourt of his temple.

General Comments

A number of the nineteenth-century commentators, and a few in the twentieth century as well, maintained that v. 20 is an addition to PsHez.[31] Begrich and most subsequent commentators have upheld its unity with the rest of the psalm.[32] The rhetorical-critical observations above provide the main evidence for refuting the former view. The coda is closely connected to the body of the poem by means of (1) the chiastic word-pair *yāmîm // šānôt*, (2) the striking formal similarity of vv. 15c and 20b, (3) the "distant" parallelism of *šaʿar* in v. 10c and *bayit* in v. 20c, (4) the inclusion formed by the polar opposites *šěʾôl* (v. 10c) and *bêt yhwh* (v. 20c), and (5) the inclusion of the divine name *yhwh* in its shortened, form *yāh yāh* (doubled) in v. 11b and the full form (twice) *yhwh . . . yhwh* in v. 20.

This last poetic unit of PsHez recapitulates the last part of the body of the poem—viz., IIAc + IIB, which allude to the poet's deliverance and his giving thanks to Yhwh. The restored form *wěniggantî* ("And I will play music [to him]"), following upon *lěhôšîʿānî* ("[Yhwh] has saved me!"), establishes a clear syntactic connection between God's saving act and the poet's response in the playing of musical instru-

---

[31] Among those of "die neuere Forschung" who considered v. 20 as an addition Begrich (*Der Psalm des Hiskia*, 3) mentions B. Duhm, T. K. Cheyne, K. Marti, and E. Kautzsch.

[32] Ibid. See also Seybold, *Das Gebet des Kranken*, 147 n. 4: "Es besteht kein Grund, in V 20 eine spätere Ergänzung zu sehen."

ments.[33] Whereas the poet's thanksgiving was only alluded to in IIB (v. 19b), here it is explicit.

The vow or resolution to praise Yhwh "all the days of [one's] life" should be seen against the background of vows to offer thanks (or a thank-offering—*tôdâ*) that appear in some lament psalms. In such cases the afflicted psalmist offers *tôdâ* to God when his prayer for deliverance has been answered.[34] By this offering the person is said to "fulfill" (*š-l-m* [*piel*]) this vow.[35] But in Isa 38:20 the vow or promise that the psalmist makes is not merely to praise God by offering a *tôdâ*. Theoretically, fulfilling the vow required the performance of some public act of thanksgiving, but there is no clear evidence of an expectation that such an act be performed repeatedly. In PsHez, by contrast, the poet vows to return thanks (to Yhwh) with musical accompaniment "all the days of [his] life." Such is his gratitude that apparently for him a once-and-for-all act of thanksgiving is not enough to express this adequately. Only one other psalm states explicitly the resolve to praise Yhwh forever in response to his deliverance.[36]

The use of the verb *n-g-n* here[37] might at first seem somewhat unexpected. One might have thought the poet would use *z-m-r* instead, a

---

[33] An interesting parallel to the theme of v. 20b, praising God with music as a form of thanksgiving for recovery from illness, may be seen in 1QH 11:22–24:

wᵉnhh bknwr qynh
lkwl ᵓbl yg[wn] wmspd mrwrym
ᶜd klwt ᶜwlh wᵓ[wn?]
wᵓyn ngᶜ lhhlwt
wᵓz ᵓzmrh bknwr yšwᶜwt
wnbl śm[hh wngynt? gy]lh
whlyl thlh lᵓyn hšbt

And I will groan to the accompaniment of the harp of lament
in all grief-stricken mourning and bitter wailing
until iniquity and wi[ckedess] have come to an end
and there is no more plague to cause *sickness*.
Then *will I sing upon the harp* of deliverance
and upon the lyre of jo[y and the lute of glad]ness
and upon the flute of praise *without ceasing*.

[34] See Jonah 2:10; Pss 56:13; 69:31; 116:17.

[35] Jonah 2:10; Pss 50:14; 56:13.

[36] Ps 30:13: *lᵉᶜôlām ᵓôdekkā*.

[37] The verb occurs in 1 Sam 16:16(2x), 17, 18, 23; 18:10; 19:9; 2 Kgs 13:15(3x); Isa 23:16; 38:20; Ezek 33:32; Pss 33:3; 68:26.

root that appears with some frequency in Hebrew poetry to signify thankful praise rendered to God.[38] In Biblical Hebrew verbs of praise and thanksgiving usually have reference—explicit or implicit—to articulated praise, i.e., uttered by the human voice.[39] But whereas *z-m-r* refers to both *singing* and the accompanying instrumentation, *n-g-n* seems to denote only the latter in some cases. Ps 68:26 is an unusual reference to the position of certain cultic personnel involved with music in a liturgical procession. The preceding verse mentions "processions . . . into the temple-area" (*hălîkôt . . . baqqōdeš*) and then goes on to mention the order of these personnel: "the singers in front, the musicians last (*'aḥar nōgĕnîm*), between them girls playing tambourines" (*NRSV*). From this context it appears that the role of the *nōgĕnîm* is limited to the playing of stringed instruments, whereas it is the singers (*šārîm*) who use their voices. This impression is contradicted by one passage where this verb is used, and two others where the nominal form (*nĕgînâ*) appears, to denote the "taunt-song(s)" of the poet's revilers. The first is the passage referred to earlier in this chapter, namely Ps 69:13, where the verb *wngnw* (restored—see above) must describe persons sitting at the city gate and strumming lyres as accompaniment to mocking *songs* which they improvise about the psalmist. The other two are Job 30:9 and Lam 5:14, where the nominal form has this meaning. The issue here is whether the poet's vow refers to praising God with instrumental music alone or with songs accompanied by such music. If the latter is the case, then the vow essentially differs little from a vow containing *z-m-r* or even *y-d-y* (*hiphil*). But if the former is the case, it is possible that the psalmist is referring to his role as a temple musician. In either case, the context and the sense of the passage dictate that the playing of stringed instruments is directly related to praising Yhwh. In other words, the poet does not resolve at this point to play music for the rest of his life simply in order to amuse himself or forget his past miseries. Rather, his resolution to play "before the house of Yhwh" makes it clear that the purpose of this activity is to render thanks to God. The LXX translation catches this nicely by adding σε ("you") *ad sensum* after εὐλογῶν ("praising").

---

[38] The verb is parallel to *y-d-y* (*hiphil*), for example, in Pss 7:18; 18:50; 57:10; 71:22; 103:14; 138:1.

[39] C. Barth, "זמר *zmr*," *TDOT*, 4. 92.

Does the picture presented in v. 20bc describe an ordinary Judahite playing music in thanksgiving for deliverance, or does the language suggest someone with a particular liturgical role? It is interesting that 2 Chr 5:12 relates that *the levitical singers and musicians* "stood east of the altar with a hundred and twenty priests who were trumpeters." It is likely that the same locale is to be assumed in the preceding verses, 1 Kgs 8:62–63, where Solomon and the people offered twenty-two thousand oxen and a hundred and twenty thousand sheep as "peace" offerings.

Now in his record of these events (i.e., the sacrifices reported in 1 Kgs 8:62–63) the Chronicler adds a detail about the presence of the priests with trumpets and levitical musicians with their instruments on this occasion. The two groups stood opposite each other.[40] Although the text is not entirely clear as to the physical arrangement of the various participants, it is reasonable to assume that both groups were standing, like Solomon, in the area "in front of the house of Yhwh."[41] Did temple musicians perform their functions here as a rule or only during this ceremony? It is difficult to answer this question, but the fact that the text notes the priests "were standing at their posts" or, perhaps better, "standing according to their offices"[42] (*ʿal-mišměrôtām ʿōmědîm*) seems to imply that the priests were in their *usual* place(s) for the ceremony. What is relevant to the present discussion is that the levitical musicians are also the subject of this participle—i.e., they too were standing in their accustomed places. The passage suggests that this "accustomed place" was near the altar of burnt offerings *in front of* the *hêkāl*. These passages give some basis, then, for locating temple musicians in an area in front of the main temple building as the place where they customarily performed their liturgical music.

Despite the unexpectedness of the 1st pl. forms on one level, it is not difficult to see why the coda assumed the "democratized" form it has in the MT. The democratization may have been implicit in the text itself. On the one hand, if we are to envisage the poet playing his music to Yhwh as one of a company of temple musicians, his act of thanks-

---

[40] 2 Chr 7:6.

[41] It is possible that this reference to musicians reflects an accurate historical memory (see J. M. Myers, *II Chronicles* [AB 13; Garden City, NY; Doubleday, 1965] 41).

[42] BDB, 1088.

giving must be seen as part of a larger chorus of praise that involves the worshipping community of Israel. On the other hand, whether or not the psalmist is implying that he was a temple musician, in the context of the Book of Isaiah as it now stands the actions in v. 20 are to be understood as those of King Hezekiah. In the ancient Near East the entrance of the king into the temple area to pray or give thanks to God was never regarded as merely a private act of piety. Because he was believed to be the representative of the people before God and the connection between the human and divine worlds, the entrance of the king—now healed of his illness—into the temple, the well-spring of life,[43] implicitly involved the whole nation. In some way it was also *their* entrance into the sphere of life and divine protection.[44] The addition of 1st person *plural* forms to the original text of the coda, however this came about, served to underscore this fact, though it was implicit from the beginning in the 1st person *singular* (in reference to the king).

[43] Cf. Ps 36:10.

[44] See similarly H. G. M. Williamson, "Hezekiah and the Temple," in *Texts, Temples, and Traditions: A Tribute to Menahem Haran* (ed. M. V. Fox et al.; Winona Lake, IN: Eisenbrauns, 1996) 47–52.

Form, Date, Authorship

Form

In the history of its interpretation PsHez has been assigned to various form-critical categories, usually to those of the individual lament or thanksgiving song of the individual. Other classifications include, for example, that of de Boer, who characterized it as a confession of trust;[1] K. Seybold, who classified it as a hymn of praise, along with most other psalms of sickness;[2] C. Westermann, who termed it "a lament that has been turned to praise."[3]

In his monograph on PsHez Begrich considered the establishment of the form of PsHez a priority and devoted a large part of his introduction to this subject.[4] He reasoned that the choice was between an individual lament and an individual thanksgiving song[5] and ended up opting in favor of the latter. For him one decisive piece of evidence was the presence of the introductory formula *ʾănî ʾāmartî* in v. 10a (and *ʾāmartî* in v. 11a). He noted that in a number of thanksgiving songs the

---

[1] "Isaiah xxxviii 9–20," 185: "The power of death will recede as long as the believer puts his faith in Yhwh's saving power, as long as he can give expression to his *trust in God* by reciting a *confession* such as 'Hezekiah's writing'" (emphasis mine).

[2] Seybold, *Das Gebet des Kranken im Alten Testament*, 147–53.

[3] Westermann, *Praise and Lament in the Psalms* (Atlanta: John Knox, 1981) 80.

[4] Begrich, *Der Psalm des Hiskia*, 4.

[5] Ibid., 6.

reference to the woes the psalmist experienced prior to his deliverance is prefaced by such a formula and cites in evidence Pss 30:7,10–11; 31:23; 66:18; 116:4b–6,11; Jonah 2:5; Lam 3:54; Sir 51:10–11.[6] As B. S. Childs observes, however, Begrich's "prior decision" that PsHez is a thanksgiving song influenced his reading of the text at least to some extent[7]— notably his reading of ʾ*ddh* in v. 15c as ʾ*dkh* = ʾ*ōdekkâ*, "I will give you thanks."[8] I have argued in Chapter 5 that this emendation is unwarranted.

There are in my view four pieces of evidence from the text itself which, in the last analysis, argue for a classification of this psalm as a thanksgiving hymn. I shall present these in inverse order of importance.

First, it is difficult to deny that the superscription (v. 9) supports the classification of PsHez as a thanksgiving psalm with the words, "when/after he had been sick *and had recovered from his sickness.*" One must keep in mind, of course, the limited value of psalm superscriptions for determining a psalm's form-critical classification. Nevertheless, whatever ancient editor composed this superscription undoubtedly understood PsHez—and intended that subsequent generations understand it—as a poem uttered or sung by Hezekiah *after* he had recovered from his affliction. There is simply no other way to interpret these words. If then it was uttered after his recovery, it could hardly be a lament but rather a grateful response to Yhwh's deliverance. This anonymous editor's view has value insofar as it is the earliest "commentary" that has come down to us on the nature of the psalm, a commentary that predates the earliest Hebrew manuscripts and ancient versions.[9]

Second, an important argument for classifying PsHez as a thanksgiving song has to do with its position in its present context. Watts

---

[6] Ibid., 17 (see also p. 11). Watts (*Psalm and Story*, 121 n. 3) erroneously references p. 54 of Begrich's work on this point. Sweeney (*Isaiah 1–39*, 495) repeats Watts' error.

[7] Childs, *Isaiah*, 284.

[8] Begrich, *Der Psalm des Hiskia*, 52.

[9] As I noted above (pp. 49–50), Seitz argues that "it is incorrect to translate the superscription as though it sets the entire action of the psalm *after* healing has taken place" (*Zion's Final Destiny*, 170). One reason he makes this claim is that he denies that the psalm actually speaks of the psalmist's healing (ibid., 168), a statement impossible to justify in light of IIAc. See my comments in Chapter 5 on v. 17c–f.

notes that "it is positioned similarly to other individual thanksgiving psalms in narrative contexts (Jon. 2, Dan. 2:20–30; cf. the hymn in Add. Dan. 28–68), which appear at points in stories where deliverance is expected [from the preceding narrative] but not yet accomplished."[10] Unlike the parallel narrative in 2 Kings, Isa 38:1–8 does not explicitly mention the healing of Hezekiah from his physical affliction.[11] The announcement of the deliverance is delayed until the crucial verse of PsHez, v. 17c–f.

Third, particularly crucial to the classification of PsHez is how one translates v. 20a. If *lhwšyʿny* is an imperative—the present consensus—then the psalm ends on a note of petition, which is most unusual at the conclusion of a thanksgiving song and which in any case marks an abrupt and illogical shift in the emphasis of the poem away from *thankful praise* for deliverance (vv. 18–19) back to *petition* for deliverance—although deliverance has already been granted! Since the petition for deliverance from affliction is one of the form-critical hallmarks of the lament psalm, a petition at this point in the poem would lead one to think that in the last analysis PsHez is a lament. But as we have seen, the verb in question is to be parsed not as an imperative but as a declarative *qtl* form with emphatic *lamed*, restating in the coda the central theme of deliverance from v. 17c–f.[12] Further, the action of playing stringed music in front of the temple is an unambiguous expression of thanksgiving in response to what Yhwh has *already* done for the poet.

Fourth, and most significant in my view, is the time sequence of past-perfect suffering (vv. 10–14 [vv. 10a, 11a: "I *had* thought"]) > past

[10] Watts, *Psalm and Story*, 127.

[11] The standard translation of 2 Kgs 20:7 is: "And Isaiah said, 'Bring a cake of figs. And let them take and lay it on the boil, *that he may recover*'" (*RSV*). But more than likely the concluding verse of this unit about Hezekiah's illness (vv. 1–7) originally narrated his cure. One should therefore translate with M. Cogan and H. Tadmor, "Then Isaiah said, 'Fetch a fig cake.' *They brought* one *and placed* it [*wayyiqḥû wayyāśîmû*] upon the boil *and he recovered* [*wayyeḥî*]" (*II Kings*, 253, 255 [emphasis mine]). Verses 1–7 were probably a self-contained tradition.

[12] Although he does not give a translation of *lhwšyʿny*, Sweeney (*Isaiah 1–39*, 490, 493) designates v. 20a as a "concluding affirmation of YHWH's deliverance," which is "formulated in objective language like v. 17a."

[13] E.g., the refrain, *kî-ʿôd ʾôdennû*, "for I shall *yet* praise him," in Psalm 42–43 (42:6, 12; 43:5).

deliverance (v. 17c–f [v. 17b: "Then you *pulled back* my life"]) > present thanksgiving (v. 19b: "As I *do this day*") > future praise (v. 20: "I *shall make music* . . . all the days of my life"). Most important within this framework is the psalmist's use of the verb *y-d-y* (*hiphil*) in v. 19ab: *ḥay ḥay hûʾ yôdekkā // kāmônî hayyôm*, "It is each living person that gives you thankful praise, *as I (give you thanks) this day*." Whereas the *yqtl* form of Hebrew verbs can be ambivalent as to tense (i.e., often capable of being rendered as future or present—and even past at times), here the implied verb in the 1st person sg. is unambiguously in the *present* tense because of *hayyôm*. The psalmist is rendering thankful praise to Yhwh *now*. In laments one sometimes finds the psalmist expressing the desire or hope to praise God in the future,[13] but never in such compositions is praise cast in the present tense. In a lament it is rather his complaints that are cast in the present tense, whereas the *qtl* verbs in the complaint section (vv. 10–14) describe his misery as a *past* experience.[14] Moreover, Westermann has pointed out two important factors with regard to the use of *y-d-y* (*hiphil*) in the OT. (1) The verb sometimes means "to confess, acknowledge," etc. Thus it is in some sense a *verbum dicendi*, insofar as the speaker says or proclaims something. That "something" in Hebrew poetry is most frequently *what Yhwh has done for the psalmist*, i.e., the deliverance from suffering the psalmist has requested.[15] (2) He also notes that this verb describes "a response to an action or a behavior."[16] Thus in lament psalms, aside from laments which contain a sudden report that the psalmist's prayer has been answered[17] or in the "vow of praise" section of such psalms, where the psalmist gives voice to his vow or determination to praise Yhwh in the future (i.e., after his prayer has been answered), this verb is used only to denote the psalmist's praise for an already experienced act of deliverance. The presence of this verb in the present tense (with the psalmist as subject—*kāmônî*) *after* the verses describing the poet's

---

[14] *ʾāmartî* (vv. 10a, 11a); *puqqadtî* (v. 10c); *nissaʿ wĕniglâ* (v. 12a); *quppadtî* (v. 12c); and *kālû* (v. 14c). Watts (*Psalm and Story*, 121) claims that Begrich argues in the same vein—i.e., that "the use of *ʾny ʾmrty* . . . at the beginning of the psalm sets the entire subsequent account of sickness in the past tense." It is clear from Watts' comment that he finds the issue of tense decisive.

[15] Westermann, "ידה *jdh* hi. preisen," *THAT*, 1. col. 676.

[16] Ibid., col. 675.

[17] E.g., Pss 6:9; 22:23; 28:6.

deliverance definitely classifies this composition as a thanksgiving song.

The difficulty interpreters have had in classifying PsHez no doubt stems to a great extent from the proportion of the lament element in the poem. Not only does the entire first half (vv. 10-14) consist of complaint, but this is even echoed in ʿal mar napšî (v. 15d) and mar lî mĕʾōd (v. 17b) in Part II. But despite the fact that the psalmist lingers to such an extent over his past sufferings, whereas the reference to deliverance appears in only two passages (vv. 17c-f, 20a), this *twofold* mention of deliverance is in itself quite significant. Notable too is the fact that the final sections of PsHez consist of references to deliverance alternating with references to thanksgiving—vv. 17c-f (deliverance), 18-19 (thanksgiving), 20a (deliverance), 20bc (thanksgiving).

The present consensus strongly supports Begrich's classification of PsHez as a thanksgiving song, although one in which the complaint or lament element is especially prominent.[18] In the last analysis there is hardly room for lingering doubts that Begrich was right on this point. When all is said and done, PsHez must be classified as a thanksgiving song. At the very least one must insist that the poem's emphasis focuses on the act of deliverance and consequent thanksgiving for this act rather than on the elements that led up to it (i.e., suffering, petition, deliberation).

Date

A. A Historical Reference

The dating of individual Hebrew "psalms"—whether within or outside of the Psalter—is notoriously difficult. The task is made somewhat easier if the composition under investigation can be shown to contain some historical referent that would situate it in a particular time-frame or exclude particular time-frames. The last line of PsHez, v. 20c, contains a phrase that has relevance for the question of date—ʿal-bêt yhwh, "before the house of Yhwh." In gratitude for deliverance from life-threatening illness the psalmist expresses his intention or vow

---

[18] See most recently Watts, *Psalm and Story*, 120 n. 4 and the literature cited there. To this list may now be added Sweeney, *Isaiah 1–39*, 494–96; Blenkinsopp, *Isaiah 1–39*, 484.

to praise God on stringed instruments for the rest of his life in the fore-court of the temple. Such an intention presumes that the Jerusalem temple was still standing at the time this composition was written and moreover that it was accessible to the psalmist as a place of worship where he could give thanks to his God.[19] It is difficult to believe that the climax and conclusion of this psalm, with its reference to giving thanks to Yhwh in the temple precincts, are nothing more than a liter-ary creation divorced from historical reality, or that a psalmist could speak of looking forward to praising God in a temple that was yet to be rebuilt. Hence the presence of this phrase points either to the period of the first temple (i.e., from its construction under Solomon to its destruction in 587) or to that of the second temple (i.e., ca. 520–515 onwards). The only period in the history of Israel and Second-Temple Judaism that is categorically excluded would thus be the exilic and early post-exilic periods, i.e., between 587 and 520. Which of these first-mentioned historical epochs best fits PsHez can only be determined by a consideration of other factors, in particular linguistic evidence.

B. Linguistic Evidence

Appeal to evidence drawn from linguistic features must be used cau-tiously in attempting to date ancient Hebrew biblical texts. On the one hand, if a certain passage appears to be very old, it may be that the ele-ments that mark it as ancient are actually archaisms rather than gen-uinely archaic features. On the other hand, even in the case of an apparently late text we must reckon with the possibility of an occa-sional later addition to what is in fact an early piece of writing. On bal-ance, however, linguistic features that appear to mark a text as late should be given more weight on the scales of evidence than those that appear to mark it as early. So, for example, while a sixth-century B.C. poet could in theory make use a lexeme that had passed out of general usage in the language several centuries earlier (even as poets in modern languages may include "archaic" terms in their poems), it is hardly

---

[19] See Seybold, *Das Gebet des Kranken*, 147: "Durch den Hinweis auf 'das Haus Jahwes' (V 20) fällt die Entstehung dieses Psalmes in den Zeitraum des Bestehens eines Jahwetempels, wobei es nicht möglich ist, diese weite Spanne, sei es durch stilistische, durch literaturgeschichtliche oder durch literarkritische Beobachtungen, einzugren-zen."

conceivable that a ninth-century author could make use of a lexeme or morpheme that demonstrably was not in usage until the fifth century (e.g., a Persian loanword). Second, there is a certain hierarchy to indicators of lateness. If we take three of the most common ones—morphology, vocabulary, and syntax—it is clear that vocabulary is the least important. This is so because in the case of a dead language, especially one preserved in a relatively small corpus like Biblical Hebrew, we can never be certain if a "late" Semitic word was part of the active vocabulary at an earlier stage of Hebrew but simply left no trace in the biblical record except for a single occurrence. Most important of the three would be morphological indicators. For example, the presence of Aramaic pronominal suffixes on certain words in Psalm 116 (vv. 7, 12) is stronger evidence of the lateness of this poem, specifically, of Aramaic influence, than the presence of Aramaic vocabulary.

1. Standard Biblical Hebrew versus Late Biblical Hebrew

In the past fifty years or so a great deal has been written on linguistic evidence for dating OT texts. Those who make use of this methodology discern two strata of Hebrew from the biblical through the Second Temple period: Standard Biblical Hebrew (SBH) and Late Biblical Hebrew (LBH). The former is generally equated with "pre-exilic" and the latter with "post-exilic" Hebrew. Certain lexemes, morphemes, and syntactical constructions are found only in indisputably late books (Ezra, Nehemia, 1–2 Chronicles, Song of Songs, Qoheleth, Daniel, and Esther). The most obvious "give-aways" are loanwords from Persian, such as *ʾiggeret*, "letter."[20] When these occur in sufficient quantity in a biblical passage outside of these books, the language of the book in which the loanword appears may be classified as LBH. Such a feature is especially significant if the lexeme in question replaces one that is known to be at home in SBH, as LBH *ʾiggeret* replaces SBH *sēper*.[21] The presence of so-called "Aramaisms" is also relevant to the issue of dating. In the following section I shall discuss lexemes, expressions, and syntactic constructions that are possible

---

[20] See A. Hurvitz, "The Historical Quest for 'Ancient Israel' and the Linguistic Evidence of the Hebrew Bible: Some Methodological Observations," *VT* 47 (1997) 311–13.

[21] Ibid., 312.

indications of LBH and others that point in the direction of SBH to see what light such data may shed on the date of PsHez—i.e., whether it is to be dated to the pre-exilic, exilic, or post-exilic era.

2. The Question of Aramaisms

In dating an ancient Hebrew composition, the presence of lexical or grammatical features that are demonstrably borrowed from Aramaic, Persian, or Greek constitute evidence for lateness. No one has (to my knowledge) argued for Persian or Greek linguistic influence in PsHez. But in his monograph Begrich, and later others, have argued for a late date based on the presence of what he identified as Aramaisms.[22] In the foregoing chapters I dealt with these individually and in detail. In this chapter I shall summarize the conclusions reached thus far and discuss their diagnostic relevance for the dating of this poem.

First, a word is in order on Aramaisms and the dating of the compositions in which they are believed to occur. One or even two Aramaisms in a text the size of PsHez does not in itself constitute sufficient evidence from which to conclude that the work is to be assigned a post-exilic date.[23] In a paper on this issue A. Hurvitz observes, "So called 'Aramaisms' appear sporadically in earlier texts of the Bible as well. This is particularly true in poetic texts."[24] Since Hebrew and Aramaic are cognate languages, and since we know only a fraction of the actual vocabulary of classical Hebrew from the OT and Hebrew epigraphy from the biblical period, it is possible that a term not found elsewhere in Hebrew but which does occur in Aramaic could simply be a rare term in the Hebrew vocabulary, which *by chance* appears only once or twice in the corpus of classical Hebrew literature. Those who argue for Aramaic influence and therefore for lateness, then, would

---

[22] Nyberg has voiced skepticism with regard to the so-called Aramaisms that Begrich claimed to find in PsHez and his consequent late dating of the psalm: "Der Psalm ist im Gegenteil sehr archäisch sowohl der Form wie dem Inhalte nach und gehört ohne jeden Zweifel der vorexilischen Zeit an. Man spricht von 'Aramäismen'; wo sind die?" ("Hiskias Danklied," 96).

[23] On the chronological significance of Aramaisms, see the points made by R. Polzin in his *Typology of Biblical Hebrew Prose: Toward an Historical Typology of Biblical Hebrew Prose* (HSM 12; Missoula, MT: Scholars Press, 1976) 11; A. Hurvitz, "The Chronological Significance of 'Aramaisms' in Biblical Hebrew," *IEJ* 18 (1968) 234–40.

[24] Hurvitz, "Chronological Significance," 234.

have to prove *a significant degree* of Aramaic features in the work under discussion. In a composition the size of PsHez this would probably mean establishing the presence of three or four Aramaisms in the poem together with other linguistic indications of lateness.[25]

From his study of the issue of Aramaisms in Biblical Hebrew, A. Hurvitz concludes, "One should be extremely cautious in utilizing the evidence of Aramaisms as a means of dating a given biblical text."[26] According to Hurvitz, one may classify an Aramaism as a criterion for lateness if it fulfills three conditions:

(1) Where each Aramaism both satisfies the requirements of "opposition"[27] and has an existence and continuity in the later strata of the Hebrew Language (biblical and/or extra-biblical).

(2) Where the Aramaisms in the text under investigation are by no means significantly isolated elements. It is the heavy concentration of Aramaisms—as well as other late elements—that characterizes Late Biblical Hebrew and distinguishes it from the classical Biblical Hebrew as we know it from pre-exilic compositions (prosaic and poetic alike).

(3) Where, despite the fulfillment of these two conditions, it is not plausible to assume any particular circumstances which may have given the text a peculiar and highly distinctive Aramaising character as early as the pre-exilic period (for instance, the possibility that a given text was coloured by the Northern dialect [Song of Songs], Wisdom phraseology [Job, Proverbs], or by a foreign language [2 Kings 6]).[28]

The procedure in this section will be first to consider terms, phrases, and syntactic constructions that are potential candidates as indicators of LBH, proceeding in the order of occurrence within the poem. After this, those that might point to SBH will be considered.

---

[25] ". . . One cannot prove a chronologically questionable text to be late simply on the evidence of Aramaisms alone. There must be a heavy concentration of late linguistic elements (non-Aramaic as well as Aramaic) in the text under investigation" (Polzin, *Late Biblical Hebrew*, 11).

[26] "Chronological Significance," 237.

[27] "An 'opposition' or 'contrast' must be established between the Aramaism which is said to reflect 'late (= post-exilic) Hebrew' and the standard Biblical Hebrew which reflects 'early (= pre-exilic) Hebrew'" (ibid., 238).

[28] Ibid., 239–40.

3. Possible Indications of LBH in PsHez

V. 10a: *ănî*. One of the linguistic features characteristic of LBH has to do with the form of of the 1st person sg. pronoun. In SBH the preferred form is *ănōkî*, whereas in LBH it is *ănî*. In fact the former never occurs in biblical books that are widely considered to be late and rarely in the Dead Sea Scrolls.[29] But while one may speak of *ănōkî* as the *preferred* form in SBH, *ănî* is also well attested in this period of Hebrew. So the single occurrence of this shorter form of the pronoun in this brief poem cannot be used to argue for the latter's lateness. Moreover, it is quite significant that in the entire MT *only* *ănî* occurs with *ămartî*, never *ănōkî*.[30] Hence the presence of *ănî* in PsHez is of no diagnostic value for determining its date.

V. 11e: *ḥāled* (MT: *ḥādel*). T. K. Cheyne, in his *Introduction to the Book of Isaiah*, lists this term as the first of "five decidedly late words" in PsHez that support a post-exilic date. In Biblical Hebrew it is used exclusively in poetry.[31] It does not appear in any of the indisputably late books (Ezra, Nehemia, 1–2 Chronicles, Song of Songs, Qoheleth, Daniel, and Esther). Apparently it is not attested in the Dead Sea Scrolls. It does not appear in Aramaic—so the issue of an Aramaism is out of the question. In conclusion, evidence for labeling *ḥāled* as an indicator of LBH is wanting.

V. 12a: *dôrî*. As we have seen, the majority of commentators and translators maintain that *dôr* must be translated "dwelling place" here. Cheyne lists this term as the second of the allegedly late words in PsHez. He includes this term because he too claims it bears this nuance.[32] But since such a meaning is not elsewhere attested for bibli-

---

[29] Polzin, *Late Biblical Hebrew*, 126; A. Hurvitz, *A Linguistic Study of the Relationship between the Priestly Source and the Book of Ezekiel: A New Approach to an Old Problem* (Paris: Gabalda, 1982) 169; M. F. Rooker, *Biblical Hebrew in Transition: The Language of the Book of Ezekiel* (JSOTSup 90; Sheffield: Sheffield Academic Press, 1990) 72–74; F. W. Dobbs-Allsopp, "Linguistic Evidence for the Date of Lamentations," *JANES* 26 (1998) 14.

[30] *ănî* *ămartî* occurs in Isa 49:4; Jer 5:4; 10:19; Jonah 2:5; Pss 30:7; 41:5; 116:11. In contrast, the two words are reversed in the occurrences of this phrase in Qoheleth (2:1; 3:17, 18; 9:16).

[31] The term means both "life span" (Pss 39:6; 89:48; Job 10:12, 20; 11:17) and "world" (Pss 17:14; 49:2), similar to Greek αἰών.

[32] T. K. Cheyne, *Introduction to the Book of Isaiah* (London: Adam and Charles Black, 1895) 225.

cal Hebrew *dôr* but is for its Aramaic cognate, Begrich concludes that this is an Aramaism in PsHez.[33] The matter is not so simple. As we have seen, the nature of the simile demands that in this passage the word denote "life span" exclusively. It argues against a complete identification of the tenor (*dôrî*) with the vehicle (*ʾōhel rōʿî*). In this case its meaning is in line with the standard sense of this term in Standard Biblical Hebrew, "(a) generation." All the ancient versions support a nuance connected with "generation." Therefore one cannot claim, as does Begrich, that one must turn to Aramaic to find the proper meaning of the word in this passage. The claim that *dôr* in v. 12a is an Aramaism therefore lacks solid foundation.[34]

V. 12c: *kʾrg*. The MT (and 1QIsaᵃ: *kʾwrg*) read this word as a participle—*ʾōrēg*, "weaver." Begrich contends that it should be repointed as a noun meaning "(a piece of) woven cloth" or the like and vocalizes it *ʾārīg*, which he terms "[an] Aramaic expression."[35] *ʾārīg* is known from Mishnaic Hebrew, where it denotes "something woven."[36] In Chapter 4 I argued that the term in question could just as well be vocalized as a segholate noun, *ʾereg*, which occurs elsewhere in the MT, where in at least one instance it plausibly means "web, that which is woven" (Job 7:6). Begrich may be correct insofar as *ʾārīg* may be the correct vocalization of the term in v. 12c, but it is Hebrew, not Aramaic.[37] Hence his claim that this term is an Aramaism in PsHez must be judged groundless.

V. 12e: *tašlîmēnî*. Begrich claims that none of the meanings of *š-l-m* (*hiphil*) attested in Biblical Hebrew fits in v. 12e.[38] He therefore claims the Hebrew verb bears the sense of its Aramaic cognate, which is used to denote the "handing over of (someone) to (someone/something)." The principal flaw in this thesis is that the Aramaic idiom requires the proposition *lĕ-*, "to," followed by an object, indicating to whom or to what one is handed over. Both are lacking in v. 12. Moreover, our investigation of this passage shows that here the verb bears one of the

---

[33] *Der Psalm des Hiskia*, 25.

[34] De Boer denies that *dôr* here should be classified as late Hebrew simply because it means "dwelling-place" ("Isaiah xxxviii 9–20," 180).

[35] *Der Psalm des Hiskia*, 31.

[36] See Jastrow, *Dictionary of the Targumim*, 119.

[37] See above., pp. 90–91.

[38] *Der Psalm des Hiskia*, 33.

meanings attested for it elsewhere in biblical Hebrew, namely, "to bring to an end."

V. 14d: *ᶜuššĕqâ* (MT: *ᶜāšĕqâ*). This is the third of Cheyne's five late words. As is evident from Ps 119:122, and as Wildberger has ably demonstrated, this root is—on the literal level—a technical financial term, whose opposite is *ᶜ-r-b*. Its usage is not confined to late books. Cheyne's reference here to Aramaic *ᶜ-s-q*, "to busy oneself with," is totally irrelevant. There is no evidence that *ᶜ-š-q* belongs to LBH.

V. 15c: *ʾeddĕdâ* (MT: *ʾeddaddeh*). Cheyne describes this word as late, but he is referring to the Masoretes' pointing of it as a derivative from the root *d-d-y*. I have argued in Chapter 5 that it derives from *n-d-d*, a view supported by 1QIsaᵃ and defended by Driver.

V. 18c: *yĕsapperû* (MT: *yĕśabberû*). Cheyne points to the fact that *ś-b-r* occurs almost exclusively in the demonstrably late books, and suggests that it is an Aramaism. Wildberger has argued the same.[39] They are probably correct on this point,[40] but in any case it is irrelevant to the dating of PsHez because, as I have argued in Chapter 6, *yĕśabberû* is a corruption of original *yĕsapperû* from *s-p-r* (*piel*), a root which is well established in the vocabulary of SBH.

To summarize at this point with regard to Cheyne's "five decidedly late words": two belong to roots other than those indicated by the Masoretes, one that he alleges to be an Aramaism is not, and as for the other two he fails to make a case for their being LBH.

V. 20a: *lĕhôšîᶜānî* (MT: *lĕhôšîᶜēnî*). As one of the indicators of LBH Polzin lists the emphatic *lamed* (*lĕ-*)—but only in a restricted usage. He notes that the Chronicler uses this morpheme with some frequency "before the last element in a list."[41] He makes it clear that the morpheme itself is not a late feature and cites passages where it is used in earlier books.[42] Since *lĕhôšîᶜānî* is not part of a list and in fact is the

---

[39] *Jesaja 28–39*, 1445. Here Wildberger follows Wagner, *Aramaismen*, #292 (p. 108), who lists *ś-b-r* as a possible Aramaism.

[40] This root is attested in the following passages in the MT: Ruth 1:13; Neh 2:13, 15 ("inspect"); Esth 9:1; Pss 104:27; 119:116, 166; 145:15; 146:5. While Nehemiah and Esther are known to be late books, the dating of Ruth is more problematic, and the dating of individual psalms even more so.

[41] Polzin, *Late Biblical Hebrew*, 66–67.

[42] Ibid., 67. See also G. A. Rendsburg's comments in "Late Biblical Hebrew and the Date of 'P'," *JANES* 12 (1980) 72.

first word in the verse, Polzin's observations on this point—even if they are correct—do not apply to this term. Hence there are no grounds for claiming that the emphatic *lamed* in this passage is an indication that the language of PsHez is LBH.

4. Possible Indications of SBH in PsHez

Now that we have considered features of PsHez that may be indications of a post-exilic date (LBH), we shall look at those words or expressions in the poem that might point in the opposite direction— i.e., to a pre-exilic date (SBH).

V. 10b: *ʾēlēkâ*. Among the indicators of LBH catalogued by Polzin he includes the rarity of the 1st person sg. cohortative (or lengthened imperfect) form ending in -*â*.[43] He claims that this form appears only once in the Chronicler. But he admits that it is standard in the Ezra memoirs and frequent in Nehemiah, and moreover that "these lengthened forms are ubiquitous at Qumran." He explains the situation in Chronicles and Ezra-Nehemiah by appealing to "a diversity of scribal traditions."[44] G. A. Rendsburg, however, appeals to the fact that "in the Hebrew diglossia of Greco-Roman times, written Hebrew (exemplified by Q[umran] H[ebrew]) used the long imperfect extensively but spoken Hebrew (exemplified by M[ishnaic] H[ebrew]) never used it."[45] Since Rendsburg's position is based on epigraphical data, whereas Polzin's is more hypothetical, the former would seem to be the more likely explanation of this phenomenon. If Polzin is right, the occurrence of the two cohortatives, *ʾēlēkâ* in v. 10b and *ʾeddĕdâ* in v. 15c, might point in the direction of SBH. But if Rendsburg is right, the frequency or infrequency of this phenomenon is of no diagnostic value in deciding whether PsHez is early or late.

V. 12b: *kĕʾōhel rōʿî*. There are two aspects of this phrase that might point to SBH rather than LBH.

(1) One feature of LBH that has been noted in recent discussions of this phenomenon is preference for plural over singular noun forms, and especially in construct phrases. Examples of this usage would be LBH *gibbôrê ḥăyālîm* (1 Chr 7:5) for SBH *gibbôrê ḥayil* (Josh 1:14),

---

[43] *Late Biblical Hebrew*, 54–55.
[44] Ibid., 55.
[45] "Late Biblical Hebrew and the Date of 'P'," 70.

wĕhārāšê ʿēṣîm (1 Chr 14:1) for *wĕhārāšê ʿēṣ* (2 Sam 5:11), *ḥsdy ʾlw[hym]* (4QShirShabbᵃ 1.2.20) for *ḥesed ʾĕlōhîm* (2 Sam 9:3; Ps 52:10), etc.[46] Given this tendency, if PsHez is a LBH composition, one would expect to find "a tent of shepherds" (*ʾōhel rōʿîm*) in v. 12b rather than "a shepherd's tent" (*ʾōhel rōʿî*). But the matter may be more complicated. S. Gevirtz has denied that the preference for plural forms in the *nomina recta* of construct phrases like these is a reliable indication of LBH.[47] As an example he points out that 1 Chronicles 7 has *gibbôrê ḥăyālîm* (with plural *nomen rectum*) four times but *gibbôrê ḥayil* (with singular *nomen rectum*) two times.[48] He further notes that Deut 9:2 has *bĕnê ʿănāqîm* and *bĕnê ʿānāq* in the same verse.[49] On balance, the use of the the *nomen rectum* in the singular in v. 12b does not clearly point to an early (i.e., pre-exilic) date for PsHez.

(2) A potentially more important datum is the form of the second word, *rōʿî*. In Chapter 4 I presented evidence from several psalm fragments from Qumran Cave 4 showing that this is an earlier form of the masculine participle of a *lamed-he* verb, actually predating the SBH form (*rōʿeh*). This evidence is significant; for while it is likely that later scribes "levelled through" archaic grammatical forms, conforming them to contemporary forms, it is less conceivable that a scribe would do the opposite, namely, replace current forms with archaic ones. Hence while one must be cautious in drawing conclusions from an isolated linguistic phenomenon with regards to date, the presence of *rōʿî* in PsHez may be an indicator of earliness.[50]

V. 15c: *ʾeddĕdâ* (MT: *ʾeddaddeh* See the discussion of *ʾēlēkâ* in v. 10b above.

V. 20b: *wĕniggantî naggēn* (MT: *ûnĕgînôtay nĕnaggēn*). Polzin argues that the *infrequency* of "the use of the infinitive absolute in

---

[46] See R. Polzin, *Late Biblical Hebrew*, 42; Rooker, *Biblical Hebrew in Transition*, 75–77; Dobbs-Allsopp, "The Date of Lamentations," 14–16.

[47] S. Gevirtz, "Of Syntax and Style in 'Late Biblical Hebrew'—'Old Canaanite' Connection," *JANES* 18 (1986) 28–29.

[48] Ibid., 28.

[49] Ibid.

[50] Qimron (*The Hebrew of the Dead Sea Scrolls*, §100.34 [p. 20]) observes that in the Hebrew of the Dead Sea Scrolls *yod* sometimes represents "final e." However, he qualifies this by saying that the "e" in such cases is *ṣere*, not *segol*. It is therefore not precisely correct to say that *rʿy* is a "Nebenform zu רֹעֶה" as von Legelshurst (*Die Hiskiaerzählungen*, 39) allows, unless one understands it as an earlier form.

immediate connection with a finite verb of the same stem" is a sign of LBH,[51] noting that that this feature is "rare in Esther, Nehemiah, and Chronicles."[52] The converse would be that the *presence* of such a feature, or rather its frequency, is characteristic of SBH.[53] Rendsburg disputes this criterion, but his objections seem to miss Polzin's point.[54] Polzin's criterion has to do not with the use of the infinitive absolute as such but with the use of the *cognate* infinitive construction. Rendsburg objects that "the book of Esther makes wide use of the infinitive absolute"[55] and gives 16 passages in Esther containing this infinitive. But he does not point out that *only two* of these are part of the cognate infinitive construction. Yet since this construction does occur, albeit very rarely, even in late books such as 1–2 Chronicles and Esther, the presence of such a construction in PsHez is hardly a reliable counter-indicator of LBH.

V. 20: *bêt-yhwh*. We saw above that the presence of the expression *bêt-yhwh*, "house/temple of Yhwh," in v. 20 could indicate a pre-exilic date because the hope of praising Yhwh for the rest of one's life "in front of the house of Yhwh" implies that the (first or second) temple was still standing when these words were written. But aside from this, the expression *bêt-yhwh* has diagnostic value in itself as a linguistic feature. This phrase is the standard designation of the Jerusalem temple in SBH. Its counterpart in LBH is *bêt 'ĕlōhîm*, "the house of God."[56]

The linguistic evidence reviewed in the foregoing survey shows that there is nothing in PsHez, as reconstructed here, that justifies its classification as LBH, i.e., post-exilic Hebrew. Cheyne's "five decidedly late words" do not pan out, and the "Aramaisms" it allegedly contains prove to be non-existent. In fact, PsHez contains a few features that point in the direction of SBH. The view articulated by Begrich and others which maintains that there is strong evidence in the poem for its

---

[51] *Late Biblical Hebrew*, 43–44.

[52] Ibid. Polzin says he can find this only in two passages in Chronicles: 1 Chr 4:10 and 2 Chr 28:10.

[53] Polzin, *Late Biblical Hebrew*, 43.

[54] "Late Biblical Hebrew and the Date of 'P,'" 67–68.

[55] Ibid., 67.

[56] Polzin, *Late Biblical Hebrew*, 130; Dobbs-Allsopp, "Linguistic Evidence for the Date of Lamentations," 22.

being composed during the post-exilic period is therefore not justified. May one then conclude that PsHez is pre-exilic? Before answering this question, one further observation should be made. The current discussion regarding SBH and LBH is concerned with larger literary works— i.e., entire books such as Lamentations, Ezra, Nehemiah, Daniel, or compositions that span several books such as 1–2 Chronicles and "P"—rather than with short pieces such as individual psalms or canticles. This fact seems to suggest that the methodology employed for dating cannot be expected to achieve the kind of solid results when dealing with smaller literary works that are possible with larger ones. Yet in the last analysis, because the linguistic evidence does not point to any LBH features and some of it points in the opposite direction, a pre-exilic date for PsHez is more likely that a post-exilic one.

Authorship

Was Hezekiah the author of this psalm? The foregoing section on the date of PsHez presents some evidence that it may date from the monarchical period. The reign of Hezekiah was situated within this time-frame. In other words, the date of composition does not absolutely militate against Hezekian authorship.

However, there are a number of considerations leading to the conclusion that the attribution of PsHez to Hezekiah is not based on historical reality. First, the practice of placing poems on the lips of major figures at key junctures is well attested in OT narratives: Gen 49:1–27 (Jacob); Exod 15:1–18, 32:1–43, and 33:1–29 (Moses); Judg 5:1–21 (Deborah and Barak); 1 Sam 2:1–10 (Hannah); 2 Sam 1:19–27, 22:1–51, 23:1–7 (David); and Jonah 2:1–10 (Jonah). Like several of the preceding poems, PsHez also comes significantly at the end of a book—here First Isaiah (followed only by the transitional chap. 39, a lead-in to the Babylonian Exile).[57] The scholarly consensus as regards these compositions is that, with rare exception, they were neither uttered nor written by the historical figures to whom they are ascribed. Second, one must also be aware of the tendency, evident in the OT and NT as well, to attribute utterances to figures highly esteemed by later tradition. Compare, for example, the various psalms attributed to David (not to

---

[57] 1QIsa^b skips a whole line between Isa 38:22 and 39:1.

mention two ascribed to Solomon and one to Moses), the wisdom works ascribed to Solomon, and the canticles ascribed to Zechariah, Mary, and Simeon in Luke 1–2. Similarly, the fact that PsHez was attributed to Hezekiah by the pre-Isaian editors of the psalm collection from which it was taken and inserted into Isaiah 38 may have been occasioned by the fact that he was considered one of the few ideal kings of ancient Judah, who, according to certain traditions, had nearly died from a serious illness. Several post-biblical psalms were also attributed to him.

The foregoing considerations counsel caution about concluding that PsHez goes back to the historical Hezekiah. Nevertheless, the OT attests to the fact that Israelites did compose thanksgiving psalms in return for divine deliverance from affliction. These appear to have been performed in some kind of liturgical setting. We know very little about the precise circumstances under which they were performed,[58] but if ordinary individuals could offer thanksgiving hymns to God in the temple precincts it would seem unreasonable to deny this possibility to kings as well. A number of ancient Near Eastern prayers (Hittite and Assyro-Babylonian) name the reigning king as the one uttering the prayer.[59] There can be little doubt that these are in fact prayers composed for (more likely than by) the monarchs of these lands and recited by them. The existence of texts like these is not surprising, given the fact that the king was viewed in the ancient Near East as an intermediary between the people and the gods. Hence his health, well-being, and proper relationship to the gods were of paramount importance not only for him but for the nation as well. One major difference between these prayers and PsHez is that the name of the speaker is not given in the case of the latter.

But even if we grant the possibility that psalm-like prayers may have been composed by or for some Judahite kings, how does one prove that a specific prayer is to be attributed to a particular king, in this case Hezekiah? Such a task is virtually impossible. One might attempt to do this by first trying to determine whether PsHez reveals any indication

---

[58] See Ps 66:13–15.

[59] See, for example, R. Lebrun, *Hymnes et prières hittites* (Homo Religiosus 4; Louvain-la-Neuve: Centre d'histoire des religions, 1980) 132–347; Seux, *Hymnes et prières aux dieux de Babylonie et d'Assyrie*, 489–526.

of being a royal psalm. Many psalms categorized as royal are so classi-fied solely because of their superscription. Others contain certain motifs that more specifically reflect royal interests. Some of these would be the allusion to the Davidic covenant, to Yhwh's *ḥesed* with the king or his dynasty, to the speaker in the psalm as ruler, to foreign enemies opposing him, etc. But none of this is present in PsHez. In point of fact, if it were not for the superscription and context of vv. 9–20 there would be no reason to classify this psalm as royal.

Another approach one might be tempted to employ would be to ascertain whether the sufferings indicated by the psalmist in PsHez match those that are said to afflict Hezekiah in the pericope about the king's sickness (2 Kgs 20:1–11 = Isa 38:1–8, 21–22). This approach, how-ever, is doomed to failure from the outset. It is based on two unsup-portable assumptions: (1) that one can actually determine the nature of the protagonist's suffering by examining the psalmist's description of his afflictions in the poem, and (2) that the narrative about the king's illness can really be mined for historical details. As regards (1), it is axiomatic that the language of ancient Near Eastern laments and prayers of thanksgiving is extremely stereotypical. Such language is also notoriously opaque as to the specific nature of the sufferings to which it alludes. Studies which have ignored this reality and have pro-posed historical reconstructions based on such data have failed to carry conviction.[60] Specifically, with regard to PsHez, none of the ref-erences to the psalmist's sufferings points to any specific physical or psychological ailment. As for (2), it is unwise in the extreme to attempt to mine historical information—especially medical information—from the stories about Hezekiah's illness in 2 Kgs 20:1–11 = Isa 38:1–8, 21–22. This narrative is almost certainly comprised of at least two indepen-dent tales about this event: 2 Kgs 20:1–7 and 8–11. The latter is con-cerned with the sign the prophet gives the king that he will indeed be healed. As for the former, we noted earlier, v. 7 should be read as nar-rating the king's cure, concluding the first healing story: "They brought one [a fig cake] and placed it upon the boil *and he recov-ered.*"[61] This story mentions that Hezekiah suffered from *šĕḥîn*, a type

---

[60] See my review of M. Goulder, *The Prayers of David (Psalms 51–72): Studies in the Psalter II* (JSOTSup 102; Sheffield: JSOT Press, 1990) in *JBL* 111 (1992) 527–28.

[61] Cogan and Tadmor, *II Kings*, 253, 255.

of inflammation of the skin.[62] But nothing can be found in PsHez that points specifically this disease or indeed to any type of skin ailment. As regards these healing stories, it is not clear to what extent—if any—we are in the realm of real historical memory rather than of pious fiction.

The very end of PsHez, i.e., the coda, may have some bearing on the identity of the author of this psalm. We have seen in Chapter 7 that v. 20 *could* be taken as referring to a temple musician. Some indications point in this direction. If so, the speaker in the psalm is not Hezekiah, and in fact not a king at all. But in the last analysis these do not provide enough evidence from which to make a strong case for this hypothesis.

In summary, there is nothing in PsHez that provides any clarity on the issue of authorship. It is possible that this psalm was written by or for a Judahite king, by a temple musician, or by a Judahite of no special status. But sufficient evidence is wanting to prove any of these possibilities.

---

[62] This term "embraces a wide category of skin diseases" (ibid., 255). It is to be distinguished from *šĕḥîn rāʿ* (Deut 28:35; Job 2:7; undoubtedly equivalent to *šḥynʾ b[yʾšʾ]* in the Prayer of Nabonidus [4QPrNab 6]). Unlike *šĕḥîn*, the latter was apparently regarded as incurable and should probably be translated "acute *šĕḥîn*-disease."

CHAPTER 8

The Psalm of Hezekiah
in the Context of Isaiah 36–38[1]

A. Introduction

In recent years a considerable amount of debate has been generated
with regard to Isaiah 36-39 and its parallel in 2 Kgs 18:13–20:19. The controversy touches a wide range of considerations such as source, textual, and redaction criticism, historicity, literary priority, to name the
predominant ones. One fact that is not subject to debate is the obvious
fact of how close the two complexes are to each other in their wording.
The unifying element consists of the focus on the two central charac-
ters: the prophet Isaiah and king Hezekiah. This material consists of
roughly three major sections: (1) the crisis of Sennacherib's invasion of
Judah and its resolution (Isaiah 36–37 = 2 Kgs 18:13–19:37), (2) Hezekiah's sickness and recovery (Isaiah 38 = 2 Kgs 20:1–11), and (3) the visi-
tation of the delegation from Merodach-baladan of Babylon to
Hezekiah (Isaiah 39 = 2 Kgs 20:12–19).[2] It is clear that these three complexes have been edited in such a way as to establish connections

---

[1] This chapter is a reworking of a paper read at the annual Catholic Biblical Association meeting, August 11, 1991, in Los Angeles.

[2] See, for example, Wildberger, *Jesaja 28–39*, 1374. I accept the view of the majority of
commentators who concur that the formulas used to introduce the second and third
complexes—viz., *bayyāmîm hāhēm* ("in those days": 2 Kgs 20:1; Isa 38:1) and *bāʿēt hāhîʾ*
("at that time": 2 Kgs 20:12; Isa 39:1)—indicate the beginning of an originally independent unit. See, for example, Sweeney, *Isaiah 1–39*, 506.

between them. The link between the first two (the Sennacherib crisis and Hezekiah's sickness) is particularly solid, to the point that some consider them a single tradition.[3] The editorial connection between the second and third, though clear, is effected mainly by the remark that the visit by the ambassadors from Merodach-baladan was occasioned by Hezekiah's recent illness.[4] In this chapter our concern will be limited to the first two of these major sections.

The text of Isaiah and 2 Kings agree to a remarkable degree in these chapters, although in all but a very few verses the Isaiah text is shorter than its parallel in 2 Kings 18–20.[5] The most notable differences are: (1) the account of Hezekiah's accepting an onerous tribute from Sennacherib, involving the despoliation of the temple (2 Kgs 18:14–16), lacking in the Isaiah version, and (2) PsHez (Isa 38:9–20), lacking in 2 Kings. Although a good deal of attention has been paid to the former passage, there has been relatively little discussion of the latter in this context, although this block of material represents the single greatest divergence of the two complexes. How does one explain the inclusion of this poem within the midst of the Isaian narrative? Or, how does it function in this literary context?

It is important to note that PsHez originally concluded chap. 38. It formed the climax to this chapter, and to the entire complex of chaps. 36–38. I agree with the common view that vv. 21–22 are a later addition to Isaiah 38, an attempt to harmonize it with the 2 Kings text. These

---

[3] A. Jepsen, *Nabi: Soziologische Studien zur alttestamentlichen Literatur und Religionsgeschichte* (Munich: Beck, 1934) 85; A. Laato, "Hezekiah and the Assyrian Crisis in 701 B.C.," *SJOT* 2 (1987) 54.

[4] The formulations in the two texts are different. 2 Kgs 20:12 reads: *kî šāmaʿ kî ḥālâ ḥizqiyyāhû*, "for he [Merodach-baladan] had heard that Hezekiah had become/been ill"; Isa 39:1, however, has: *wayyišmaʿ kî ḥālâ wayyeḥĕzāq*, "and [/for?] he had heard that he had been sick but had recovered his strength." Since *ḥ-z-q* with the meaning "to recover from sickness" is not attested elsewhere in Biblical or in post-biblical Hebrew, nor in the cognate languages, it is likely that *wyḥzq* in Isa 39:1 represents a misreading of *(y)ḥzqyhw* (as in the 2 Kings text). The variant reading in 1QIsaᵃ, *wyḥyh* ("but had got well"), may have been motivated by a sensitivity to the inappropriateness of *wyḥzq* in this context, and thus may represent a correction of the word.

[5] If one could assume that the Isaiah text is a redaction of 2 Kings, then perhaps it would be possible to speak of a *Tendenz* on the part of the Isaian editors in the direction of abbreviation. But the question of literary priority is complicated. In any case, the addition of a long piece of material such as PsHez is somewhat surprising given the fact that Isaiah 36–38 consistently gives a shorter text than 2 Kings 18–20.

verses fit poorly in their present context and are anti-climactic, almost an afterthought. They are not connected syntactically with the chapter, despite the attempts of the LXX and some modern translations to create a connection.[6] Most importantly, they are entirely lacking in the "first hand" of 1QIsaᵃ. Although theoretically this omission might be explained as the result of haplography, S. Talmon has argued persuasively that the first Isaiah scroll from Qumran represents a shorter text of Isaiah 38 at this point. For this reason he rightly criticizes the common practice of transposing vv. 21–22 after v. 6 in order to bring them into line with 2 Kings.[7]

I cannot agree with the view of de Boer that PsHez is merely a "poetical interlude" with no connection to the surrounding narrative.[8] Rather, I find myself in the camp of those who see such connections. One who has written on the question of how PsHez functions in its context is P. R. Ackroyd.[9] In his brief treatment of this topic he compares the inclusion of psalm passages in the narrative context at several points within the Deuteronomistic History: the song of Moses (Deut 32:1–43), the song of Hannah (1 Sam 2:1–10), and the two psalms associated with David at the end of 2 Samuel 22–23 (22:1–51; 23:1–7). The reason for including such poems is "to draw out the significance of the narrative by the use of poems which point to important elements which it is desired to underline." Similarly, PsHez is "a comment on the larger significance of [Hezekiah's] recovery in the context of the whole work."[10] Ackroyd sees the psalm's theme of deliverance from the pit and restoration to life, climaxing in the king's joining the community in praise and worship, as a kind of judgment and exile. This theme of restoration speaks to the exiled community and holds out such a hope to them.[11]

---

[6] Cf. *NJPSV*.

[7] The text is transposed by most modern translations (*NEB, NAB, JB, NJB, TEV*). According to S. Talmon ("The Textual Study of the Bible–A New Outlook," in *Qumran and the History of the Biblical Text* [ed. F. M. Cross and S. Talmon; Cambridge, MA: Harvard University Press, 1975] 332) such transposition "must be considered improper procedure, both from the viewpoint of structural and textual analysis." See also Blenkinsopp, *Isaiah 1–39*, 482.

[8] De Boer, "Isaiah xxxviii 9–20," 185.

[9] P. R. Ackroyd, "An Interpretation of the Babylonian Exile: A Study of 2 Kings 20, Isaiah 38-39," *SJOT* 27 (1974) 344–45; Williamson, "Hezekiah and the Temple," 47–52.

[10] Ackroyd, "An Interpretation of the Babylonian Exile," 345.

[11] Ibid., 345–46.

I agree with Ackroyd's observations but believe that there are other connections between PsHez and its context that could be explored. The remainder of this chapter will explore some of the ways in which PsHez develops or completes themes and plot-lines present in 36:1-38:8, which in turn may help explain why it was added to chap. 38.

Isaiah 36-38 contains three speeches: (1) 36:4–10, (2) 36:13–20, and (3) 37:10–13. The first and second are the words of Sennacherib, through the mouth of the Rabshakeh. The third may also be understood as the words of the Assyrian king[12] through his ambassadors (37:9).[13] After the second threatening speech Hezekiah sends word to Isaiah, who delivers an oracle foretelling Sennacherib's return to his land and his violent death there (37:5–7). After the third speech Hezekiah prays to Yhwh, who responds with another oracle delivered by Isaiah (37:21–35). This one is very long and complex from a source-critical view. But the bottom line is the prediction that the Assyrian king will return to his own land and die (37:29, 33–34) and that Yhwh will save and protect Jerusalem (37:35). Finally, the narrative concludes with an account of Sennacherib's death at the hands of two of his sons.[14]

There is more divergence between 2 Kings and Isaiah with regard to the tradition about Hezekiah's sickness and healing (2 Kgs 20:1–11; Isa 38:1–8).[15] Both texts begin by mentioning the onset of some mortal ill-

---

[12] The identification of the speaker in the third speech is more difficult to determine than in the case of the first two. Read in its present context, the subject of "when he heard (the report), he sent" in Isa 37:9b (= 2 Kgs 19:9b) is Sennacherib. But according to the prevailing source-critical approach to these chapters, this verse marks the beginning of a second source, "B²" (2 Kgs 19:9b–35). In this case, the subject could be the Rabshakeh. The problem with making Sennacherib the subject is that (1) the speech is not introduced by the royal messenger formula, as in the case of the first two speeches (2 Kgs 18:19 [first speech]; 18:28–29 [second speech]) and (2) references to the Assyrian king are all in the third person, in contradistinction to the first two speeches.

[13] The third speech, delivered by Sennacherib's ambassadors (37:9–10), was apparently also contained in the letter which the king took/received from them after it had been read to him (37:14).

[14] "His sons" appears in the Qere but not in the Kethib of the 2 Kings parallel (19:37). That at least one of Sennacherib's sons was involved in his murder has now been established as historically accurate; see S. Parpola, "The Murderer of Sennacherib," in *Death in Mesopotamia: Papers Read at the XXVIᵉ Rencontre assyriologique internationale* (= *Mesopotamia: Copenhagen Studies in Assyriology* 8) (ed. B. Alster; Copenhagen: Akademisk Forlag, 1980) 171–82.

[15] Childs, *Isaiah*, 282.

ness and Isaiah's prognosis that the king is going to die. Upon hearing this Hezekiah prays to Yhwh and weeps bitterly. The prophet then receives a revelation with the command to return to the king and announce that his lifetime will be lengthened (2 Kings explicitly mentions that Hezekiah would be cured soon and go to the temple, details lacking in Isaiah). To this is added a promise to deliver Hezekiah and the city from the king of Assyria. In 2 Kings this is followed by a second healing story (v. 7), according to which Isaiah prescribes a fig-poultice to be applied to the "skin disease" (*šĕḥîn*), and a question by the king as to what sign would indicate that he would be healed and go up to the temple. Both these details are missing in Isa 38:1-8, but the fig-poultice incident and the question as to the sign that the king would go up to the temple are contained in the secondary 38:21–22. Finally, both texts contain a third tradition about a miraculous sign, confirming Yhwh's promise of healing/deliverance (2 Kgs 20:8–11; Isa 38:7–8).

B. The Fulfillment of Prophecy in Chaps. 37–38

One important function of PsHez serves vis-à-vis the foregoing narrative is to fulfill something that is foretold but unfulfilled in the narrative. In chap. 37 Isaiah utters two *prophecies* concerning Sennacherib. In the first (37:7) he predicts that the king will hear a rumor, return to his land, and be killed there. As the narrative reads now, the first detail is fulfilled in 37:8–9. Isaiah's second oracle (37:22–35) underscores the detail about Sennacherib's return (vv. 29, 34), adding that he will not besiege or enter the city (v. 33). It concludes with Yhwh's promise to save and protect Jerusalem (v. 35). All of these prophecies find fulfillment in the denouement of the drama, 37:36–38. Yhwh, through his *malʾāk*, destroys the Assyrian army, and Sennacherib is forced to return to Nineveh, where he is killed.

Isa 38:1-8, the Isaian account of Hezekiah's illness, also contains an oracle of Isaiah promising a series of saving actions by Yhwh, viz., in v. 6 (2 Kgs 20:6):

> Behold, I will add fifteen years to your life. I will deliver you and this city out of the hand of the king of Assyria, and I will protect this city.

But these promises are not explicitly fulfilled in the course of this narrative. It is likely that originally Isaiah's words, "Behold, I will add fifteen years to your life," were to be understood as effecting the actual healing. Wildberger translates, "See, I am adding [i.e., here and now] fifteen years to your life."[16] But the expansion by means of the tradition about the sign, which immediately follows, makes the narrative read in such a way that the healing is deferred to some time in the future.

Within the complex of chaps. 37–38, only in PsHez is there any reference to the healing or deliverance of the king; only here does the prophecy find fulfillment. Even though the superscription (v. 9) presumes that the king had already been healed when he uttered the psalm, PsHez nevertheless contains its own "narrative" of his sickness and recovery. The divine deliverance is narrated in v. 17c–f and repeated dramatically in the climactic cry at the end of the poem, *yhwh lĕhôšî̔ānî*, "Yhwh has saved me!" Thus PsHez constitutes the third in a series of fulfillments of Yhwh's word in chaps. 37–38.

One should note the lexical connections between these prophecies in 38:5b–6 and PsHez, in which they find their fulfillment. First, in v. 5b Isaiah says, *hinnî yôsîp ̔al-yāmêkā hămēš ̔eśrēh šānâ*, lit., "Behold, I will add fifteen *years* to *your days*." Now we have seen that the chiastic distribution of the word-pair "(my) days" and "(my) years" is one of the most important structuring devices in PsHez. Moreover, the poet's concern about his lifetime (= "my days/years") and whether it will be ended or not is a dominant theme of the psalm. Second, *̔aṣṣîlĕkā* ("I will deliver you") is fulfilled by *lĕhôšî̔ānî* ("he has saved me!"), two verbs that form a word-pair.[17]

The fact that Isaiah's prophecy of Hezekiah's deliverance from sickness is fulfilled only in PsHez develops another characteristic of Isaiah 38 vis-à-vis 2 Kings 20. In the Isaiah recension the "miraculous" powers

---

[16] *Jesaja 28–39*, 1439. Similarly the tradition about the fig-poultice (in 2 Kgs 20:7 but lacking in Isaiah 38, though secondarily added in v. 21) originally narrated the healing itself and thus fulfilled the "prophecy" in 20:5bβ. Almost all translations assume that the entire verse (i.e., after "And Isaiah said") quotes the words of Isaiah—e.g., *RSV*: "And Isaiah said, 'Bring a cake of figs. And let them take and lay it on the boil, *that he may recover.*'" More likely, however, we are dealing here with an independent tradition about Isaiah as miraculous healer. One should therefore translate with M. Cogan and H. Tadmor, "Then Isaiah said, 'Fetch a fig cake.' They brought one and placed it [*wayyiqḥû wayyāśîmû*] upon the boil *and he recovered*" (Cogan and Tadmor, *II Kings*, 253, 255). See also Childs, *Isaiah*, 280.

[17] See Y. Avishur, *Word-Pairs*, 88, 225.

of Isaiah receive much less emphasis. This lack of emphasis on the miraculous highlights the fact that the deliverance is from Yhwh. In the 2 Kings parallel Isaiah not only prescribes a quasi-miraculous cure for the king's skin disease (the fig-poultice story) but even gives him his choice of several signs, one more miraculous than the other—details lacking in Isaiah 38.[18]

C. The Answer to Hezekiah's Prayer

The de-emphasis on the role of Isaiah as wonder-worker is at the service of another tendency in Isaiah 36–38, which also finds a kind of fulfillment in PsHez. Hezekiah's deliverance in Isaiah 38 is portrayed as a result not of any action on the part of the prophet but rather of the king's *prayer*. Whereas 2 Kgs 20:1–11 contains two verses in which the king addresses the prophet (vv. 8, 10), there is no parallel in Isa 38:1–8, so that Hezekiah is portrayed as *speaking only to God*—viz., in the short prayer in v. 3. This picture of Hezekiah as the pious king who prays directly to Yhwh in time of distress is consistent with the story of the Assyrian crisis at the end of chap. 37. After the Rabshakeh's second speech Hezekiah goes to the temple and from there sends word to Isaiah (37:1–4 = 2 Kgs 19:1–4) through messengers, asking him to pray for the deliverance of Judah. After the third speech he repairs to the temple for a second time, but this time he does not ask for the prophet's intercession; rather, he addresses Yhwh directly in prayer (37:15–20 = 2 Kgs 19:15–19). The motif of Yhwh answering Hezekiah's prayers in the narrative is analogous to that of the fulfillment of prophecy discussed above. PsHez forms the climax to this movement as the third in this series of prayers. As a result of his first prayer (37:15–20) Yhwh promises that Sennacherib will return to his own land and that Yhwh will protect his city. As a result of his second prayer (38:3) Isaiah's prognosis is reversed and Yhwh promises that the king will recover and that he and Jerusalem will be delivered. As a result of his third prayer (38:14d +16a–17b) Yhwh does not promise but actually restores Hezekiah to life (v. 17c–f) and saves him (v. 20).[19] In this con-

---

[18] I.e., assuming that vv. 21–22 are additions to the text.

[19] It is possible that the Isaian narrative emphasizes the theme that deliverance is the direct result of prayer more strongly than does the 2 Kings parallel. In 2 Kgs 19:20a–21a, Yhwh says to Hezekiah: "I have heard your prayer to me concerning King Sennacherib

nection it is also interesting to note that whereas in the 2 Kings narrative Yhwh promises Hezekiah that he will go up to the temple after his illness (20:5b), PsHez contains no such promise. Rather, it "narrates" the virtual fulfillment of this promise in v. 20, where the king resolves to praise God with music for the rest of his life *in the forecourt of the temple*. This is the third and final time the king goes up to the temple,[20] and it concludes the narrative of chaps. 36–38. Since this "visit" to the temple is the last "scene" in First Isaiah—i.e., before the addition of chap. 39—the book earlier concluded with a tableau in which the king is frozen in an eternal attitude of praise to Yhwh in his holy place.

One should also note a parallel between 38:3 and PsHez (v. 14c), one of the strongest links between the two compositions. The narrative relates that when Hezekiah heard Isaiah's prognosis that he was about to die, "he wept bitterly" (lit., "he wept with great weeping" [*wayyēbk . . . bĕkî gādôl*]). The phrase clearly denotes an extreme outpouring of emotion, i.e., loud and profuse weeping. Immediately after this God says to the king through Isaiah, "I have heard your prayer, I have seen your tears." As we noted earlier, Part I of PsHez concludes with a reference to the psalmist's profuse weeping (v. 14c: *kālû ʿênay*) followed by a short prayer (v. 14d). This prayer and weeping is not answered immediately in the poem, but only after his second prayer to Yhwh some verses later (vv. 16a-17b). Nevertheless, the implication of the divine deliverance immediately after this second prayer—though it is not explicitly stated in the poem—is that that God has heard his prayer and looked upon his tears.

D. The Contrast between Hezekiah and Other Kings

The larger context of the narrative 2 Kgs 18:13–20:19 = Isa 36–39 presents an adverse comparison of Hezekiah with two other kings. The

---

of Assyria. This is the word that Yhwh has spoken concerning him." The Isaian parallel, however, reads: "*Because* you have prayed to me concerning King Sennacherib of Assyria, this is the word that Yhwh has spoken concerning him." This syntax states more pointedly the fact that the oracle of deliverance is given as a direct result of the king's prayer.

[20] That Isa 38:20 constitutes a third visit to the temple within chaps. 36–38 has been pointed out by Coetzee, "The 'Song of Hezekiah'," 18.

first is with his father, Ahaz, whose name is mentioned in the narrative almost in passing.[21] The Assyrian army under the Rabshakeh stands precisely where Ahaz had stood in an earlier crisis with Assyria and refused to trust in Yhwh (Isa 7:3; 36:2). Through Isaiah Yhwh had offered to give Ahaz a sign that the prophet's words would come true, but the king declined (Isa 7:10–12). By way of contrast, in the 2 Kings version Hezekiah asks for a sign that he would be healed (20:8). Only three times in First Isaiah does God offer to give a sign to verify a prophecy: to Ahaz in Isaiah's confrontation with him (Isa 7:11, 14) and twice to Hezekiah in 37:30–32; 38:7–9.[22] The sign in Isa 37:30–32 is unbidden, as in the parallel 2 Kgs 19:29. But in the case of the third sign, Isa 38:7–9 = 2 Kgs 20:8–11, the accounts differ. The 2 Kings account has Hezekiah *ask* about a sign ("What will be the sign that . . .") whereas in Isaiah 38 Isaiah offers the sign with no prompting from the king. The effect is to present Hezekiah as not needing proofs in order to believe the word of Yhwh, thus portraying him as a paragon of faith vis-à-vis his faithless father. Finally, the glaring omission in the Isaiah narrative of the incident reported in 2 Kgs 18:14–16 also effects a contrast between Hezekiah and Ahaz. Two chapters earlier the 2 Kings narrative reports that in the face of the Assyrian threat Ahaz had declared himself a vassal of the king of Assyria. He removed gold from the temple treasury and his own royal coffers and sent them as a gift (*šôḥad*) to the king of Assyria, which was clearly a sign of accepting the latter's overlordship (2 Kgs 16:7–8). Similarly 2 Kgs 18:14–16 has Hezekiah sending the temple gold and the contents of the royal treasury to Sennacherib, though this is done in reaction to the Assyrian invasion of Judah (v. 13) and not as a "gift." But the Isaian parallel omits any mention whatsoever of Hezekiah's communicating with the Assyrian king or giving him anything, thereby portraying the Judahite king as one who does not yield an inch to the Assyrian monarch. Whereas Ahaz caved in and failed to show the proper trust in Yhwh in the face of the Assyrian

---

[21] Both versions of the narrative ironically mention "the dial of Ahaz" as the vehicle of the miraculous *sign* given to Hezekiah (2 Kgs 20:11; Isa 38:8).

[22] The fact that Isaiah had volunteered to give Hezekiah a sign in 2 Kgs 19:29–31 = Isa 37:30–32 may explain the particular wording of 2 Kgs 20:8: "What shall be the sign . . . ?" This is less direct than "Give me a sign" (which might have been thought presumptuous) and may indicate that since Isaiah had offered Hezekiah a sign earlier he had reason to expect that the prophet might do the same in this situation.

threat, Hezekiah is a model of the Isaian virtue of absolute trust in God.

Second, one can discern a number of contrasts in Isaiah 36-37 between Hezekiah and his nemesis, Sennacherib, who is portrayed as the diametric opposite of his Judahite counterpart. Both Isaian oracles in chap. 37 and the Rabshakeh's first and second speeches in chap. 36 are framed as "messages," i.e., they are introduced by the messenger formula, "Thus says X," followed by one or two epithets. In 36:4a it is "Thus says the great king, the king of Assyria"; and similarly in 36:13b–14a: "Hear the words of the great king, the king of Assyria. Thus says the king . . . ." Isaiah's oracle begins: "Thus says Yhwh, the god of Israel . . ." (37:21). Hence there is a suggestion that the utterances of Sennacherib have something of a "divine" character in these speeches, contrasting with the divine utterances of Yhwh. These details paint Sennacherib as a kind of "anti-god" vis-à-vis Yhwh, and thus a blasphemer of unprecedented arrogance. In 36:17 he goes so far as to promise to take the people away to a new "Promised Land," thus making himself an "anti-savior" in the place of the God of Israel.[23] But whereas the Assyrian king blasphemes against Yhwh by his arrogance and his virtual usurpation of Yhwh's role of savior with respect to Judah, Hezekiah is pictured as the pious king who trusts in Yhwh at every stage of the crisis. Each time the words of Sennacherib are related to him he makes no reply but responds by going to the temple (Isa 37:1,14) to pray to Yhwh. And each time he does not act on his own but waits for the word of Yhwh through the prophet (37:6–7, 21–35).

Yet there is another point of contrast between Sennacherib and Hezekiah which is suggested by the outcome of chap. 37 but not exploited in the narrative and which finds its resolution in PsHez. This has to do with the fate of the two kings. Isa 37:36–38 narrates that when Sennacherib returned to Nineveh, his capital, he was murdered by two of his sons as he was worshiping "in the house of Nisroch,[24] his

---

[23] See K. A. D. Smelik, "Distortion of Old Testament Prophecy: The Purpose of Isaiah 36 and 37," in *Crises and Perspectives: Studies in Ancient Near Eastern Polytheism, Biblical Theology, Palestinian Archaeology, and Intertestamental Literature: Papers Read at the Joint British-Dutch Old Testament Conference Held at Cambridge, U.K., 1985* (ed. J. C. De Moor et al.; OTS 24; Leiden: Brill, 1986) 80.

[24] The name "Nisroch" is a problem. No Assyro-Babylonian deity by this name is known, despite various attempts at identification. Recently K. van der Toorn and P. W.

god."[25] In the ancient Near East the temple was the place of safety and refuge par excellence. It was also the place where the life of the god(s) was imparted to the monarch in the form of "life" and "length of days,"[26] which he in turn dispensed to his subjects through his beneficent reign. Thus for the king to meet death—particularly a violent death—in the "house of life"[27] was the supreme irony and an unthinkable disaster both for himself and for his nation. This conclusion of the Sennacherib narrative contrasts sharply with the conclusion of PsHez with its blissful image of the king joyfully praising *his* god in Jerusalem, *his* capital city, in the safety of *Yhwh*'s temple precincts "all the days of [his] life" (38:20).[28] Moreover, the king's presence there is a sign of salvation not for him only but for all Jerusalem as well.

E. Assyrian Taunts, Divine Promises, and PsHez

Two especially important formulas in Isa 36–38 are 37:35 and 38:6, which are paralleled in 2 Kgs 19:34 and 20:6b:

37:35   *wĕgannôtî ʿal-hāʿîr hazzōʾt lĕhôšîʿāh lĕmaʿănî ûlĕmaʿan dāwīd ʿabdî*

> *And I will defend this city* and *save* it, for my sake and for the sake of my servant David.

---

van der Horst have claimed that *nsrk* "can hardly refer to any other than the god Ninurta" ("Nimrod Before and After the Bible," *HTR* 83 [1990] 14). See recently C. Uehlinger, "Nisroch נסרך," *DDD* (rev. ed.), 630–32.

[25] Assyrian sources give no clear evidence that the assassination took place in a temple. The widely disseminated view that Sennacherib was "perhaps crushed alive under a winged-bull colossus guarding the temple where he had been praying at the time of the murder" (mentioned by Parpola, "The Murderer of Sennacherib," 175), apparently influenced to some extent by Isa 37:38 // 2 Kgs 19:37 and based on a particular understanding of a passage in the king's annals, may be incorrect. See Cogan and Tadmor, *II Kings*, 240; *CAD* S, 160.

[26] Cf. Ps 21:5.

[27] A common temple-name in ancient Mesopotamia. A. R. George (*House Most High: The Temples of Ancient Mesopotamia* [Mesopotamian Civilizations 5; Winona Lake, IN: Eisenbrauns, 1993] 130-31) lists seven temples in ancient Mesopotamia that bore the name é.nam.ti.la, "the house of life."

[28] This contrast was also noted by Blenkinsopp, *Isaiah 1–39*, 483. Blenkinsopp believes that the juxtaposition of the two is deliberate, and results in the illogical placement of the account of the survival of Jerusalem *before* Hezekiah's recovery (ibid., 484).

38:6 *ûmikkap melek-ʾaššûr ʾaṣṣîlĕkā wĕʾēt hāʿîr hazzôʾt
wĕgannôtî ʿal-hāʿîr hazzōʾt*

> And I will *deliver* you and this city from the hand of the king
> of Assyria
> *and I will defend this city.*

The two sentences are connected by the identical phrase "I will defend
this city" (only here in chaps. 36–38) and by the word-pair *n-ṣ-l* and
y-š-ʿ. That they are key verses in chaps. 36–38 can be seen more clearly
from their 2 Kings parallels, namely 2 Kgs 19:34 and 20:6b respectively.
The wording in the 2 Kings and Isaiah versions is almost identical.[29] In
2 Kings each of these verses that promises divine protection and deliverance *is immediately followed by its fulfillment.* 2 Kgs 19:35–37 (and
also Isa 37:36–38) narrates the decimation of the Assyrian army by the
angel of the Lord, Sennacherib's departure, and his murder in Nineveh.
2 Kgs 20:6 is immediately followed by the report of the healing of
Isaiah's skin disease by the application of the fig-poultice. But as we
have seen, Isaiah 38 lacks this incident, except in the anticlimactic and
intrusive v. 21. The reader must look elsewhere to find the fulfillment of
this promise.

1. Assyrian Taunts Answered in 37:35

The three speeches of the Rabshakeh contain a number of taunts in
the form of mocking (rhetorical) questions by the Assyrian king. In
fact the first speech (36:4–10), addressed to Hezekiah, consists of a
series of questions at the beginning, middle, and end. The second
speech (36:13–20), addressed to the people on the city-wall, ends with a
series of five[30] questions (vv. 18b–20). The third "speech" (37:10–13),

---

[29] 2 Kgs 19:34 has *ʾel-hāʿîr* for the Isaian *ʿal-hāʿîr*, no doubt an example of the *ʾel/ʿal*
confusion (*ʿal* is the better reading here), and has the formula "for my sake and for the
sake of David my servant" after both verses. The Isaian parallel lacks this formula in
38:6.

[30] The parallel text in 2 Kgs 18:34 contains yet another question, according to the
reading of LXX[L]: καὶ ποῦ εἰσιν οἱ θεοὶ τῆς χώρας Σαμαρείας, "And where are the gods
of the land of Samaria?" Most recently this reading has been accepted by M. Cogan
and H. Tadmor in their commentary (*II Kings* [AB 11; New York: Doubleday, 1988] 224

delivered to Hezekiah via envoys, contains three questions (vv. 11b–13). None of these questions receives a response from those to whom it is addressed. The first speech is interrupted by the Judahite officials, who ask the Rabshakeh to speak in Aramaic rather than in Hebrew (36:11). After the second speech no answer is given to the Assyrian official because the people had been forbidden to do so by the king (36:21). In the case of Sennacherib's letter to Hezekiah—the third speech—again there is no response. Rather, the king of Judah goes up to the temple to pray (37:14–20). However, within the narrative at least some of these questions are answered, specifically the ones that appear at the conclusion of the three speeches.

The response to these questions is given not by the addressees but by Yhwh, in Isaiah's oracle at the end of the narrative (37:21–35). This oracle is the last "speech" material in the chapter—i.e., a speech of Yhwh spoken through his prophet.[31] It is followed by the account of the miraculous decimation of Sennacherib's army and his subsequent murder (37:36–38). In the present form of chaps. 36–37, it is clear that Yhwh literally has the "last word" on the fate of Jerusalem. To some extent this final "speech" in these chapters is to be read as a response to and refutation of the words of Sennacherib, especially the first speech.

In the *first speech*, in 36:10a, Sennacherib asks: *weʿattâ hămibbalʿădê yhwh ʿālîtî ʿal-hāʾāreṣ hazzōʾt lĕhašḥîtāh*, "Is it without (the cooperation of) Yhwh that I have come up against this land to destroy it?"[32] If we compare this to the last line of Isaiah's oracle (37:35), there is a strik-

---

and n. m.). It is interesting to note that in the annalistic description of his conquest of Samaria, Sargon II mentions deporting the "gods" of Samaria as well as its people and chariots; see M. Anbar, "Καὶ ποῦ εἰσιν οἱ θεοὶ τῆς χώρας Σαμαρείας, 'et où sont les dieux du pays de Samarie?'" *BN* 51 (1990) 7–8; H. Spieckermann, *Juda unter Assur in der Sargonidenzeit* (FRLANT 129; Göttingen: Vandenhoeck & Ruprecht, 1982) 349–50.

[31] Compare the fact that Sennacherib virtually speaks through his "prophet" or representative, the Rabshakeh.

[32] Statements like this, implying the cooperation of the local god(s) in the overthrow of their territories, are found elsewhere in Neo-Assyrian royal statements. Assurbanipal, for example, claims that the (chief) goddess of Arabia, angered with Hazail, king of Arabia, "handed him over to Sennacherib, my grandfather, and caused his defeat" (see M. Cogan, *Imperialism and Religion: Assyria, Judah and Israel in the Eighth and Seventh Centuries B.C.E.* (SBLMS 19; Missoula, MT: Scholars Press, 1974) 16, lines 2–3: *ina qātê Sin-aḫḫē-eriba ab abî bānīya tamnušu[ma ta]škuna abi[ktašu]*).

ing similarity of wording and structure: *wĕgannōtî ʿal-hāʿîr hazzōʾt lĕhôšîʿāh*,[33] "And I will defend this city to save it."[34] Each begins with a *qtl* verb in the 1st person sg. and ends with a *hiphil* infinitive. The opening verb is followed by a prepositional phrase introduced by *ʿal*, after which comes "this land"[35] or "this city." Though similar in form, the two statements contrast sharply on various levels. The final word of each clearly expresses the diametrically opposite intentions of the respective speakers: "to destroy" the land (in the case of Sennacherib) and "to save" the city (in the case of Yhwh).

The contrast also extends to the initial verbs, insofar as they likewise express what each has done or intends to do with regard to the area in question. Sennacherib says he has "come up" against the land. As a military term the verb could be translated "to advance" or even "make an expedition"[36] against a certain site. Nevertheless it does not completely lose its inherent sense of upward movement, for a military advance against a city involved literally "going up" the tell on which it stood.[37] Now the contrasting verb in the Isaiah oracle is the rare *g-n-n* II (*qal*).[38] In its present context the verb obviously denotes some protective or defensive action on the part of Yhwh "to save" his city. Accordingly *g-n-n* in the sense of "defend" creates a good contrast to "advance against, attack" in 36:10. However, the basic meaning of this verb appears to be "to descend upon" (originally in a neutral sense).[39]

---

[33] The words *ʾereṣ* and *ʿîr* form a word-pair (e.g., Jer 8:16; 46:8; 47:2; Ezek 19:7). See Avishur, *Word-Pairs*, 278.

[34] It is difficult to determine how v. 35 relates to the context. I tend to agree with those who judge it to be appended to the oracle in vv. 33–34. The main reasons for this are: (1) the subject of every verb in vv. 33–34 is Sennacherib, but this is not the case in v. 35; (2) the oracle in vv. 33–34 concludes with the formula *nĕʾum yhwh*, suggesting that what follows is not part of it; (3) the similarity of v. 35 to 38:6, which likewise appears to be an addition.

[35] 2 Kgs 18:25 has *hammāqôm hazzeh* ("this place") rather than *hāʾāreṣ hazzōʾt* ("this land").

[36] J. Gray, *I & II Kings* (2d ed.; OTL; London: SCM, 1970) 676.

[37] See G. Wehmeier, "עלה *ʿlh* hinaufgehen," *THAT*, 2. 275–77.

[38] Four of the biblical occurrences of this root occur in the Book of Isaiah (31:5[2x]; 37:35; 38:6). Two of the remaining four occurrences are in the 2 Kings passages parallel to Isaiah 36–38 (2 Kgs 19:34; 20:6).

[39] One should probably distinguish this root from *g-n-n* I meaning "enclose, surround." In Isa 31:5a, for example, I have maintained that it refers to Yhwh's "descending" or "alighting" upon Jerusalem as a carrion bird lights on its victim. This

Thus at their basic levels of meaning the first person verbs in the lines under discussion are direct, literal opposites—"to go up" *ʿal* and "to descend" *ʿal*. In 37:35, therefore, the Rabshakeh's mocking question receives an answer—from Yhwh himself. He implies that it was not by his will that Sennacherib "went up" against (= "attacked") the land, and counters by affirming that he will "descend" upon (= "over-shadow, protect") Jerusalem from Assyrian attack.

Sennacherib's *second speech* through the Rabshakeh (36:18b–20) ends with five questions, prefaced by the warning, "Beware lest Hezekiah deceive you saying, 'Yhwh will deliver us'":

> Has any of the gods of the nations delivered his land out of the hand of the king of Assyria? Where are the gods of Hamath and Arpad? Where are the gods of Sepharvaim? Have they delivered Samaria out of my hand? Who among all the gods of these countries have delivered their countries out of my hand, that Yhwh should deliver Jerusalem out of my hand?

The question, "Where are the gods of . . . ?" stands out because it is repeated here and also because it occurs in a slightly different form in the third speech, as we shall see. What is the import of this question? In theory it might be taken as rhetorical, viz., "Where were these gods when their people needed them?" (cf. Jer 2:28). Or the purpose of the question might be to mock these deities' inability to deliver their citizens from the Assyrian enemy. The verb "deliver," *n-ṣ-l* (*hiphil*), is prominent in this second speech of the Rabshakeh (seven times), indicating that the issue of divine deliverance is central.

But a third interpretation is possible: the question may not only intend to mock the enemies' gods, it may also intend to make the point that no national god did in fact come to the rescue of any of the lands conquered by Assyria. Several recent studies have interpreted the Rab-

---

interpretation of the verb is substantiated by the preceding lion simile in 31:4, where Yhwh is said to "descend" (*y-r-d*) upon Mount Zion, although in its present version (i.e., with the addition of v. 5b) this oracle is to be read in a positive sense vis-à-vis Jerusalem (see M. L. Barré, "Of Lions and Birds: A Note on Isaiah 31:4–5," in *Among the Prophets: Language, Image and Structure in the Prophetic Writings* [ed. P. R. Davies and D. J. A. Clines; JSOTSup 144; Sheffield: JSOT Press, 1993] 58). On the meaning "descend" for *g-n-n* in Syriac, see Payne Smith, *A Comprehensive Syriac Dictionary*, 73.

shakeh's words literally, understanding them as expressing the "divine abandonment" theme.[40] Divine abandonment was a standard topos of political propaganda in Neo-Assyrian royal inscriptions. Essentially, it claimed that the gods of the nations under siege by Assyria abandoned their dwelling-places, thus leaving their devotees at the mercy of the Assyrian conquerors. Occasionally the more extravagant claim was made that these gods not only abandoned their people but actually cast their lot with the Assyrian gods.[41] Thus the Rabshakeh's question, "Where are the gods of . . . ?" may have been meant literally, reflecting the belief that these deities had abandoned their dwelling-places in their native territories. If so, the import of his question could be that the god of Judah is no different from these other local deities and will likewise forsake his residence in Jerusalem, leaving its inhabitants at the mercy of the Assyrians.

But this taunt is also countered by Isa 37:35 (// 2 Kgs 19:34). Unlike other verbs for "protect, defend" (such as *š-m-r* and *n-ṣ-r*), *g-n-n* ʿal connotes the *immediate presence* of the one protecting, since it can mean "cover over" or even "overshadow."[42] The verb, at least in

---

[40] See Cogan, *Imperialism and Religion*, 111; Spieckermann, *Juda unter Assur in der Sargonidenzeit*, 346-47. These studies tie the divine abandonment theme specifically to 2 Kgs 18:25 = Isa 36:10. But R. Liwak sees it reflected in the Rabshakeh's questions in 2 Kgs 18:34 // Isa 36:19 ("Die Rettung Jerusalems im Jahr 701 v. Chr.: Zum Verhältnis und Verständnis historischer und theologischer Aussagen," *ZTK* 83 [1986] 151).

[41] For example, in his royal inscriptions Assurbanipal claims that the (chief) goddess of Arabia "decided not to dwell (any longer) with the people of Arabia (but) set out for Assyria" (Cogan, *Imperialism and Religion*, 16, line 4: *lā ašābša itti nīšē māt Aribi taqbû ana māt Aššur taṣba[ta ḫarrāna]* [lit., "she decreed her not-dwelling with the people of the land of Arabia (and) took the road to the land of Assyria"]). Here the expression is "not to *dwell*"; its equivalent, "abandon," appears in other texts containing this motif: "Its [i.e., Babylon's] gods and goddesses withdrew, *abandoned* their sanctuaries, and went up to heaven" (R. Borger, *Die Inschriften Asarhaddons Königs von Assyrien* [AfO Beiheft 9; Osnabrück: Biblio-Verlag, 1967]), 14, *Fassung* b: E, lines 12–14: *ilānišu u ištarātišu ipridû-ma kiṣṣīšunu ezibū-ma elû šamāmiš*). In both cases the implication is that the deities physically departed from their places of residence and went elsewhere. Cf. Yhwh's voluntary departure from his temple in Jerusalem described in Ezek 10:18–19; 11:22–23. But in this case the reason given is the sinful practices in the Jerusalem temple (chaps. 8-10).

[42] On the nuance "overshadow" for Aramaic/Syriac *g-n-n*, see S. P. Brock, *The Holy Spirit in the Syrian Baptismal Tradition* (Syrian Church Series 9; Poona: Anita, 1979) 7; idem, "An Early Interpretation of *pāsaḥ: ʾaggēn* in the Palestinian Targum," in *Interpreting the Hebrew Text: Essays in Honour of E. I. J. Rosenthal* (ed. J. A. Emerton and

Syriac, can also mean "to come to rest upon, dwell in."[43] Because *g-n-n ʿal* connotes the deity's immediate, protective presence "over" Jerusalem, this verse can be understood as Yhwh's response to the question raised in the Rabshekeh's second speech. Far from abandoning Zion, as the Assyrian's taunt implies, Yhwh will remain there, spreading his protective wings over the city and safeguarding it from harm. It is rather Sennacherib who will be forced to run away (Isa 37:33–34)! Yhwh's resolve to continue his protective presence in his city contrasts with the statement immediately following that Sennacherib "dwelt in Nineveh" (his newly rebuilt capital city), only to meet death there soon afterwards.

2. Assyrian Taunts Answered in 38:6

Several other taunting questions raised by the Assyrian enemy are answered by Yhwh in the parallel verse to Isa 37:35, namely 38:6.

Sennacherib's *third speech* (37:10–13) differs from the first two in several respects. Whereas the first two are spoken to—or at least within the hearing of—Judahite officials by the Rabshakeh, the third is communicated directly to the king, and to him alone, through Assyrian envoys. According to 37:14 it is not delivered to him as a "speech" but through the medium of a letter. Nevertheless, the contents of the letter are "read" to the reader in 37:10–13, so that the communication is clearly equivalent to a third "speech" by the Assyrian king. Hezekiah is a more central figure in the narrative containing this last speech. It too concludes with a set of questions which are quite similar in style to the questions at the end of the second. But here the Assyrian threat is hurled not only at Judah or Jerusalem *but directly at Hezekiah himself.* The verb "deliver" (*n-ṣ-l*) is again prominent here (cf. 36:18–20):

> Behold, you have heard what the kings of Assyria have done to all lands, destroying them utterly. *And shall you be delivered?* Have the gods of the nations *delivered* them . . . ? (37:11–12).

S. C. Reif; Cambridge: Cambridge University Press, 1982) 30. This also may be the nuance of the Hebrew verb in Zech 9:15, *yhwh ṣĕbāʾôt yāgēn ʿālêhem.* See the previous verse (*wĕyhwh ʿālêhem yērāʾeh*, "Yhwh shall appear over them"), where the locative force of the preposition is apparent.

[43] Payne Smith, *A Compendious Syriac Dictionary,* 73.

This taunt about Hezekiah's deliverance does not receive a response in chapter 37. Rather, it is not directly answered until 38:6: "And *I will deliver you* and this city from the hand of the king of Assyria, and I will protect this city." That this is a response to the questions in 37:11–12 could not be clearer. But this connection back to chap. 37 is, as many commentators have noted, quite artificial. Although the lifting of the siege of Jerusalem and Sennacherib's departure have already been narrated in 37:36–38, 38:6 appears to assume that the Assyrian crisis has not been resolved and that Jerusalem and the king are still in danger. But this artificiality makes the connection between 37:35 and 38:6 stand out all the more. 38:6 is the last occurrence of the verb *n-ṣ-l* in these chapters. Just as the parallel verse (37:35) constitutes Yhwh's response to Sennacherib's threat to destroy Judah, so 38:6 is the divine response to his threat against Hezekiah (and Jerusalem)[44] in 37:10–13, especially v. 11b. But it is a response in word only. The reader is forced to look elsewhere for its fulfillment.

The "Where are . . . ?" question in Isa 37:13 refers not to the deities of the conquered lands (as in 36:19) but to their kings: "Where are the king of Hamath, the king of Arpad, the king of the city of Sepharvaim, the king of Hena, or the king of Ivvah?" If the similar question in 36:19 implied that various foreign deities had abandoned their dwelling-places or had been "deported" to Assyria, "Where are the kings of . . ." may well have a similar import. The ignominious deportation of rebellious kings by the Assyrians is well known in Assyrian annals. Thus—at least on one level—the question would imply that Hezekiah, like his god, will also be removed from his royal city. But this taunt receives no direct response either in chapter 37 or in 38:1–8.

3. 37:35 and 38:6 Fulfilled in PsHez (38:20)

The decisive action by which Yhwh delivers Hezekiah is related only in PsHez, particularly in vv. 17c–f and 20, as noted above, where the deliverance/salvation is described as having actually occurred (*ḥāśaktā . . . hišlaktā yhwh lĕhôšîʿānî*).

As chapter 38 reads in its present form, the fulfillment of the promise

---

[44] Any threat against Hezekiah would automatically be a threat against Judah and its capital city, Jerusalem, as well.

of deliverance in 37:35 and 38:6 is situated in PsHez,[45] where the deliverance of the king is mentioned twice—in 38:16a-17b and especially in the climactic *yhwh lĕhôšîʿānî* of v. 20a. Moreover, the coda may be interpreted as offering a response to 37:11-12, which threatens deportation or even death for Hezekiah. Read in the context of chaps. 36–38, v. 20 expresses the king's conviction that Yhwh has indeed saved him from the fate of deportation and death. On the contrary, his destiny is to frequent the temple precincts where he may praise Yhwh "all the days of [his] life," forever free from threat or harm.[46]

This view is reinforced by a number of verbal associations between 37:35 and 38:6 on the one hand and 38:20 on the other. The rare verb *g-n-n* in the first two texts occurs only seven times in the MT, and four of these occurrences are in the 2 Kgs 18:13–20:19 // Isaiah 36–39 material.[47] The verb in 38:20 derives from its anagram, the likewise rare verb *n-g-n* (fifteen times in the MT).[48] In all three passages the verbs are 1st person sg. *waw*-prefixed forms: *wĕgannôtî* and *wĕniggantî*. Most frequently, *g-n-n* is followed by the preposition ʿ*al*[49] as it is in 37:35 and 38:6. In 38:20 *n-g-n* is also followed by ʿ*al*. Moreover, there is a connection between the terms that the preposition governs in these passages. In 37:35 and 38:6 it governs *hāʿîr hazzōʾt*, "this city" (i.e., Jerusalem). In 38:20 it governs *bêt yhwh*, "the house of Yhwh." Now ʿ*îr* and *bayit* form a parallel word-pair that is attested at least ten times in the MT.[50]

---

[45] It is true, as I noted above, that the fulfillment of 37:35 follows immediately after this verse, with the narrative of the angel of the Lord slaying 185,000 in the Assyrian camp, Sennacherib's hasty departure and return to Nineveh, and his subsequent murder in "the temple of his god." Yet 38:6 reads as if none of this has happened—the threat of "the king of Assyria" still hangs over Hezekiah and Jerusalem.

[46] One of the differences between the 2 Kings and the Isaiah narrative of Hezekiah's illness is that while the former contains a promise that the king will "go up to the temple on the third day (presumably = after he has been healed)" the latter makes no reference to the temple at all—*except in PsHez*. At the very least one can say that the image of the king's being in the temple courts praising God *for the rest of his life* (Isa 38:20) is much more powerful and dramatic than that of *a single trip* to the temple after his recovery (2 Kgs 20:5).

[47] 2 Kgs 19:34; 20:6; Isa 37:35; 38:6.

[48] 1 Sam 16:16(2x), 17, 18, 23; 18:10; 19:9; 2 Kgs 3:15 (3x); Pss 33:3; 68:26; Isa 23:16; 38:20; Ezek 33:32. Note that five of the occurrences appear in a single passage, 1 Samuel 16.

[49] It is followed by ʿ*al* in 2 Kgs 20:6; Isa 31:5; 37:35; 36:8; Zech 9:15. The exceptions are 2 Kgs 19:34, where it is followed by ʾ*el* (probably the ubiquitous ʾ*el*/ʿ*al* confusion), and Zech 12:8, where it is followed by *bĕʿad*.

[50] Deut 19:1; Isa 6:11; Jer 26:6, 9, 12; 38:17; Joel 2:9; Zech 14:2; Ps 127:11; Job 15:28.

In Jer 26:6, 9, 12 both terms are modified by "this" (as in Isa 37:35 and 38:6) and, as in those passages, "this city" refers to Jerusalem, while the "house" in question denotes the house of Yhwh. Finally, v. 20 contains links to the other two verbs in 37:35 and 38:6, *y-š-ᶜ* ("save") and *n-ṣ-l* ("deliver") respectively. That the editors intended a connection between the occurrences of *y-š-ᶜ* in 37:35 and 38:20 is suggested by the fact that this verb appears in chaps. 36-38 only in these two passages, in both cases governed by *lĕ-*: *lĕhôšîᶜāh* and *lĕhôšîᶜānî*. A connection between *n-ṣ-l* in 38:6 and *y-š-ᶜ* in 38:20 is likely from the fact that the two form a word-pair and that *n-ṣ-l* in 38:6 has Hezekiah as its object (*ᵓaṣṣîlĕkā*) just as he is the object of synonymous *y-š-ᶜ* in 38:20. Hence although it cannot be proved, it is hardly conceivable that this complex of associations is the result of mere coincidence. By means of them the editors of Isaiah meant the reader to make connections between the promissory texts 37:35 and 38:6 and their fulfillment in 38:20.

One might object that in context this verse refers only to the deliverance of the king himself—there is no mention of Jerusalem. But such a view ignores the symbolism of the king in ancient Near Eastern societies. His safety and well-being was inextricably connected with that of his royal city and his people as well. The positive image of divine protection of the city is matched by the equally positive and hopeful image of the king safe in the temple complex, giving unceasing thanks for his deliverance. Furthermore, the "Zion theology" forges a close connection between the David dynasty and Zion, so that the salvation of one is linked with that of the other. The theme of the Davidic dynasty is made explicit in 37:35: "for the sake of my servant David."[51] Thus 38:20 fulfills Yhwh's promise in 36:8 to defend Jerusalem and to save it and Hezekiah from harm. The later "democratization" of v. 20 into "*we* shall make music . . . all the days of *our* life," which can hardly have any other reference but those worshiping at the Jerusalem temple, complements this theme.

F. Conclusion

In this chapter I have tried to show some of the ways PsHez functions in its literary context. These may in turn give a partial explana-

---

[51] See Clements, *Isaiah 1-39*, 289-90.

tion to the question of why the editors of Isaiah 38 saw fit to append this psalm to the narrative of the healing of Hezekiah. The more important of these may be summarized as follows: (1) PsHez fulfills the oracle of Yhwh in 38:5–6, promising to heal and deliver the king. (2) In PsHez Hezekiah's plea for restoration to health is heard and his deliverance is explicitly stated in PsHez, continuing the theme of prayer and response in chap. 37. (3) The conclusion to PsHez (v. 20) effects an interesting contrast between Sennacherib and Hezekiah: the Assyrian king is murdered in the temple of his god, whereas Hezekiah is given life (38:16b) and allowed to dwell safely in Yhwh's temple "all the days of [his] life." (4) The coda also shows a close connection to the two key verses 37:35 and 38:6, each of which concludes Yhwh's word to Hezekiah through Isaiah, even as the coda concludes PsHez itself. Each of these verses contains the verb "save" or "deliver," the former occurring only here in Isaiah. Moreover, taken together the three show an increasing focus on Hezekiah. In 37:35 Yhwh promises to save/protect Jerusalem; in 38:6 he promises to deliver Jerusalem *and Hezekiah*; finally, 38:20 affirms that he has indeed saved the king, who will play music to him before his temple all his days. Thus the final verse of the prayer sounds the principal "theological" themes of chaps. 36–38 and brings them to conclusion.

CHAPTER 10

Summary

PsHez is a psalm of thanksgiving with a larger lament component than is usual in psalms belonging to this category. I base this judgment chiefly on the fact that the psalm relegates the psalmist's sufferings and petitions for divine aid to the past, while locating his expression of praise and thanksgiving unambiguously in the present (v. 19b: *kāmônî ḥayyôm.* "as I [give you thanks] this day") and the extended future (v. 20: *kol yĕmê ḥayyay,* "all the days of my life"). In line with this, *yhwh lhwšyʿny* in v. 20, far from being a petition for deliverance, the granting of which is also presented as past in v. 17c–f, is the joyous thankful cry of one who has experienced God's saving action: "Yhwh has saved me!"

The prevailing view, particularly since Begrich, that PsHez is a late (i.e., post-exilic) composition is largely based on the conviction that it contains a number of Aramaisms, which would tend to classify it as Late Biblical Hebrew. But, as I have argued in the foregoing pages, there is virtually nothing in the poem—as I have restored the text—whether in terms of vocabulary, syntax, or or other linguistic indicators, that warrants this conclusion. In fact, PsHez contains several features that argue for its classification as Standard Biblical Hebrew. Moreover, its conclusion that the psalmist looks forward to praising Yhwh for the rest of his life "before the house (i.e., temple) of Yhwh" seems to exclude the time-frame of exile as a date of composition. All told, these data suggest a *terminus a quo* some time in the (probably late) monarchical period for the origin of the poem.

Such a date leaves open the theoretical possibility of Hezekian authorship. While this cannot absolutely be ruled out, it is very unlikely. PsHez is one of a number of poems inserted by OT editors into narrative contexts at key junctures. Few scholars today would ascribe any of these compositions to the biblical figure on whose lips they are placed. Nor is there anything about this poem considered in itself—i.e., once one brackets it from its present context—that would point to Hezekiah or indeed any Judahite king as its author.

PsHez pre-existed the Book of Isaiah. The superscription (v. 9) indicates that it was not composed by the editors of Isaiah. Whoever placed PsHez into a now lost collection of psalms and supplied it with a superscription (v. 9) classified it as a *miktām*, a word whose meaning eludes us, but which is most probably a technical term that has to do with some aspect of its performance, probably relating to music. The fact that its later insertion into Isaiah 38 by the Isaian editors creates an awkward fit into the narrative context indicates that it was already attached to the poem and thus considered an integral part of it when it was introduced into chap. 38.

The Isaian editors inserted PsHez into the context of chaps. 36–38, where it serves as the conclusion to this unit and indeed to First Isaiah itself (before the transitional chap. 39). It picks up various threads laid down in these chapters dealing with the threat of Sennacherib's invasion and Hezekiah's illness (chaps. 36–38) and thus is securely integrated into this context. Various taunts voiced by Sennacherib through the Rabshakeh earlier in the narrative in the form of questions, as well as divine predictions and promises, find their resolution in PsHez. The righteous king Hezekiah turns to God in prayer at key moments of the Assyrian crisis, the climax of which is his last and longest prayer, PsHez. His fate as depicted in this prayer forms a stark contrast with that of his nemesis, Sennacherib: the latter returns to his capital city, where he is murdered in a temple, whereas Hezekiah is safe in his capital city, in the precincts of Yhwh's temple, praising him all the days of his life. The deliverance/healing of Hezekiah narrated in the poem also suggests the deliverance of Zion given the Zion theology, which intimately connects the Davidic dynasty and its stability/security with that of Zion.

One aim of the present work has been to present insofar as is possible at this stage of our expertise an accurate understanding and appreciation of PsHez as a piece of ancient Hebrew poetry. One could probably say that Begrich's monograph represented the best efforts of his day as regards Hebrew poetics, but our knowledge in this area has grown considerably since 1926. Some of the specific areas that might be mentioned are research into word-pairs, stylistic devices, structuring devices, etc. These have been brought to bear in the present study of PsHez. Moreover, in this work the attempt has been made to give the poetry of this composition its due recognition and to acknowledge the indispensability of taking the poetic aspects of this composition into consideration for the tasks of restoration and interpretation.

As regards structure, PsHez is a carefully balanced composition. As restored here, the body of the poem (vv. 10–19) divides into two equal halves (vv. 10–14, 15–19) of exactly sixty words each plus a coda of ten words. Part I is delimited as a separate unit from the following verses by: (1) the extra-long second colon v. 14d, (2) the inclusion built around the theme of "copious weeping" in v. 10d (*wĕmar šĕnôtāy*, "weeping bitterly for my years") and in v. 14c (*kālû ʿênay*, "I have cried my eyes out"), and the abrupt change of theme from lamentation in Part I to deliberation, prayer, deliverance in Part II A. One of the main connecting devices in the poem is the well attested word-pair *yôm // šānâ*, specifically in the suffixed plural form *yāmay // šĕnôtay*. This pair brackets the first subunit of the poem, Part I Aa (v. 10) and then functions as an inclusive device in Part II (vv. 15c and 20b)—only chiastically. One important conclusion as regards the content of PsHez that one may draw from the use of this word-pair is that the coda, v. 20, is an integral part of the poem, not a "liturgical addition" as was suggested by a number of earlier scholars.

As the poem opens, the psalmist is mourning and weeping over the prospect that his lifetime is about to end prematurely. He is so certain of this that he describes himself as already having been handed over to the netherworld (v. 10). He then voices the sense of loss he feels over the prospect of no longer being able to commune with his fellow human beings or with his God (v. 11). In the subsequent lines a series of similes drawn from the human professions of shepherding and textile production give expression to how the poet's life has suddenly been reduced to less than a day and is about to be taken away from him. He is certain that Yhwh will not let him see the next sunrise (vv. 12a–13a). Next comes a series of similes drawn from the animal world. Following on the heels of the accusation that God will shortly end his life is a bolder charge against Yhwh, namely that he is crushing his bones as a lion does with his prey (v. 13bc), a bitter parody of Yhwh as "the good shepherd" (Psalm 23). The silence of the psalmist up to this point is broken by a series of moaning sounds typical of certain birds that give some kind of inarticulate expression to the depth of his depression (v. 14ab). In the last verse of Part I he finally addresses God, asking the Almighty to "go surety" for him, still implying that God is the cause— even the unjust cause—of his suffering (v. 14cd).

At the beginning of Part II the poet realizes that his brief, somewhat accusatory prayer, has gained him nothing. He then deliberates as to whether it would do any good to address the Lord further, since God has already decided to bring this trouble upon him. But then he thinks of the alternative: to live the rest of his life in abject misery (v. 14a–d)— despite v. 12ef, he might live longer than a single day after all! And so he decides to make one final attempt to beseech God to heal him. In the beautiful prayer of v. 16a–17b, which appears without introduction, he humbly acknowledges Yhwh as the source of all life and happiness and in a dramatic threefold petition (vv. 16c–17a) entreats him to restore his strength, let him recover, and restore his well-being, adding as a motivating factor that his present lot is bitter indeed (v. 17b). The turning point of the psalm occurs in the two bicola that make up v. 17c–f. This is clearly the divine response to the psalmist's urgent plea in vv. 16c–17a. He is pulled back from the brink of the pit and his sins forgiven—images which allude in poetic terms to his deliverance and complete healing.

The final section of the body of PsHez, Part IIB, deals with the issue of who can and who cannot praise Yhwh (v. 18). The subtext here is to convince the deity to keep the poet and others like him alive so that the praise of Yhwh may continue to rise upward to heaven, and to grant them progeny to whom they might relate his saving deeds and who in turn may continue the chorus of praise in future generations (v. 19). Lastly, the coda (v. 20) recapitulates the themes of vv. 17c–19d by asserting emphatically the fact of God's healing and the poet's resolve to respond by life-long praise on stringed instruments in the forecourt of the temple.

Seen as a whole, PsHez moves from lamentation through deliverance to joyful thanksgiving, from the netherworld to the house of Yhwh, from past to future. This movement is virtually an *anabasis*, since among the ancient Israelites the netherworld was regarded as the nadir of the cosmos and the temple of Yhwh its zenith. It is at the same time, of course, a movement from sickness to health, from sin to forgiveness, from death to life. All these aspects of the poet's "journey" reach their destination precisely in the coda. Without this crucial verse these thematic threads within the poem are left dangling, for only here does the poet speak in his own name of rendering thanks to God, and only here is he said to enter the life-giving sphere of the temple. Toward the beginning of the poem the psalmist had bemoaned the prospect of never again "seeing" Yhwh "in the land of the living" or "the land of life" (v. 11bc). But at its conclusion he is able to rejoice confidently in the hope of praising the God of Israel in the temple, the "Land of Life" par excellence. In the context of chaps. 36-38, the reader is meant to see in this final verse of PsHez, and (what was perhaps originally) the final verse of First Isaiah, a timeless, quasi-eschatological tableau portraying the delivered king of Judah—and through him all of Zion—rejoicing and praising Yhwh at his temple all the days of its existence, i.e., until the end of time.

Emended Text and Translations

EMENDED TEXT

Superscription

9   *miktām lĕḥizqiyyāhû melek yĕhûdâ baḥălōtô wayḥî mēḥolyô*

Part I

10a	*ʾănî ʾāmartî*	**Aa**
b	*bĕdōm yāmay ʾēlēkâ*	
c	*bĕšaʿărê šĕʾôl puqqadtî*	
d	*wĕmar šĕnôtāy*	

11a	*ʾāmartî*	**Ab**
b	*lōʾ ʾerʾeh yāh yāh*	
c	*bĕʾereṣ ḥayyîm*	
d	*lōʾ ʾabbîṭ ʾādām ʿôd*	
e	*ʿim yôšĕbê ḥāled*	

12a	*dôrî nissaʿ wĕniglâ minnî*	**Ba**
b	*kĕʾōhel rōʿî*	

c   *quppadtî ḥayyay kĕʾereg*
d   *middallâ yĕbaṣṣĕʿennû*
e   *miyyôm ʿad laylâ tašlîmēnî*
13a   *sāpîtî ʿad bōqer*

b   *kāʾărî kēn yĕšabbēr*   **Bb**
c   *kol ʿaṣmôtāy*
d   {*miyyôm ʿad laylâ tašlîmēnî*}
14a   *kassas-ʿûgār kēn ʾăṣapṣēp*
b   *ʾehgeh kayyônâ*
c   *kālû ʿênay lammārôm*
d   *ʾădōnāy ʿuššĕqâ lî ʿorbēnî*

Part II

15a   *mâ ʾădabbēr wĕʾōmar lô*   **Aa**
b   *wĕhûʾ ʿāśâ*
c   *ʾeddĕdâ kol šĕnôtay*
d   *ʿal mar napšî*

16a   *ʾădōnāy ʿēlî hammaḥăyeh kol lēb*   **Ab**
b   *hammaḥăyeh rûaḥ*
c   *taḥălîmēnî wĕhaḥăyēnî* 17a *hanḥēl šālôm*
b   *mar lî mĕʾōd*

c   *wĕʾattâ ḥāśaktā napšî*   **Ac**
d   *miššaḥat bĕlî*
e   *kî hišlaktā ʾaḥărê gēwkā*
f   *kol ḥăṭāʾāy*

18a   *kî lōʾ šĕʾôl tôdekkā*   **Ba**
b   *māwet yĕhallĕlekkā*
c   *lōʾ yĕsappĕrû yôrĕdê bôr*
d   *ʾēl ḥasdekā*

19a   *ḥay ḥay hûʾ yôdekā*   **Bb**
b   *kāmônî hayyôm*

c   *ʾāb lĕbānîm yôdîaʿ*
d   *ʾēl ʾămittekkā*

Coda

20a   *yhwh lĕhôšîʿānî*
 b   *wĕniggantî naggēn kol yĕmê ḥayyāy*
 c   *ʿal bêt yhwh*

TECHNICAL TRANSLATION

Superscription

9   A *miktam* by Hezekiah, king of Judah,
(which he uttered/sang) after he had been sick
and had recovered from his sickness.

Part I

10a   (Once) I had thought: **Aa**
 b   Mourning for my days, I must depart;
 c   to the gates of the netherworld I have been
              consigned,
 d   weeping bitterly for my years.

11a   I had thought: **Ab**
 b   Never (again) shall I see Yah-Yah,
 c   in the land of the living/of life;
 d   Nevermore shall I behold (other) human beings
          among those who dwell in the world.

12a   My lifetime has been pulled up and taken away   **Ba**
          from me
 b   like a shepherd's tent.

c   I have/My life has been shrunk like a piece of cloth
d   after it has been cut from the thrum.
e   Between day(break) and night(fall) you will finish me off,
13a   by morning I shall have vanished.

b   Like a lion he crushes   **Bb**
c   all my bones.
14a Like a swallow I chirp (plaintively),
b   I moan like a dove.
c   I have cried my eyes out to the Most High (saying:)
d   "O Lord, I am oppressed! Be my surety!"

Part II

15a What (words) can I speak, what can I say to him,   **Aa**
b   since he has (already) acted?
c   Must I wander about (depressed) all my years
d   because of my despondency?

16a "O Lord Most High, you who give life to every heart,   **Ab**
b   who give life to every spirit—
c   Restore my strength, let me recover, 17a grant me
            health/peace,
b   (for) bitter indeed is my anguish!"

c   And then you pulled back my life   **Ac**
d   from the Pit of annihilation;
e   Yes, you cast behind your back
f   all my sins!

18a For it is not the Netherworld that gives you thankful   **Ba**
            praise,
b   nor Death that extols you;
c   Neither can those who go down into the Pit proclaim,
d   O God, your steadfast love.

19a It is each living person that gives you thankful praise   **Bb**
  b   as I do this day;
  c It is the father that makes known to (his) children,
  d   O God, your faithfulness.

Coda

20a Yhwh has saved me!
  b   And (so) I will play music (to him) all the days of my life
  c   before the house of Yhwh.

SIMPLIFIED TRANSLATION

The following is a non-technical translation of PsHez, i.e., without arcane terminology, dividing lines, slashes, or parentheses. It is slightly more periphrastic, and uses the familiar "Lord" instead of "Yhwh" or "Yah." It is intended not for study but for prayer and reflection.

Part I

10   I had thought to myself:
       As I mourn for my days that are no more I must go away;
          I have been consigned to the gates of the netherworld,
          as I weep bitterly for my years.

11   I had thought:
       Never again shall I behold the Lord
          in the land of the living;
       Nevermore shall I see my fellow human beings
          among those who live in this world.
12   What remains of my life has been pulled up and taken away
          from me
       like a shepherd's tent.

My life span has been shrunk like a woven cloth
    when it is cut from the loom.
Between daybreak and nightfall you will finish me off;
13   by morning, I shall have vanished.

Like a lion he crushes
    all my bones.
14 Like a swallow I chirp pathetically,
    I mourn like a dove.
I have cried my eyes out to the Most High, saying:
    "O Lord, I am oppressed! Be my security!"

Part II

15 But what words can I speak, what can I say to him,
    since he has taken action against me?
Must I wander about depressed all my remaining years
    because of my despondency?

16 "O Lord Most High, it is you who give life to every heart,
    you who give life to every spirit;
Restore my strength, let me recover, 17 grant me health and
    peace,
    for I am in bitter anguish!"

And then you pulled back my life
    from the pit of annihilation!
Yes, you cast behind your back
    all my sins!

18 For it is not the Netherworld that gives you thankful praise,
    nor Death that can praise you;
Neither can those who descend into the Grave proclaim,
    O God, your steadfast love.

19   Each living person—that is who can give you thankful praise,
        as I do this day;
    It is the father that makes known to his children,
        O God, your faithfulness.

20   The Lord has saved me!
        And so I shall make music to him all the days of my life,
        before the house of the Lord.

Bibliography

Ackroyd, P. R. "An Interpretation of the Babylonian Exile: A Study of 2 Kings 20, Isaiah 38-39." *SJOT* 27 (1974) 329–52.

Alcalay, R. *The Complete Hebrew-English Dictionary:* מילון עברי־ אנגלי שלם. Rev. ed. Bridgeport, CT: Prayer Book Press, 1974.

Alter, R. *The Art of Biblical Poetry*. New York: Basic Books, 1985.

Anbar, M. "Καὶ ποῦ εἰσιν οἱ θεοὶ τῆς χώρας Σαμαρείας, 'et où sont les dieux du pays de Samarie?'" *BN* 51 (1990) 7–8.

André, G. *Determining the Destiny: PQD in the Old Testament.* ConBOT Series 10. Gleerup: CWK, 1980.

Avishur, Y. *Stylistic Studies of Word-Pairs in Biblical and Ancient Semitic Literatures.* AOAT 210. Kevelaer: Butzon & Bercker; Neukirchen-Vluyn: Neukirchener Verlag, 1984.

Barr, J. *Comparative Philology and the Text of the Old Testament.* Oxford: Clarendon Press, 1968.

Barré, M. L. "ʾrṣ (h)ḥyym—'The Land of the Living'?" *JSOT* 41 (1988) 37–59.

———. "An Analysis of the Royal Blessing in the Karatepe Inscription." *Maarav* 3 (1982) 177–94.

———. "Bulluṭsa-rabi's Hymn to Gula and Hosea 6:1-2." *Or* 50 (1981) 241–45.

———. "The Crux of Psalm 22:17c: Solved at Long Last?" In *David and Zion: Biblical Studies in Honor of J. J. M. Roberts.* Ed. B. F.

Batto and K. L. Roberts. Winona Lake, IN: Eisenbrauns, 2004. 287–306.

———. "The Formulaic Pair חסד(ו) טוב in the Psalter." *ZAW* 98 (1986) 100–105.

———. "Hearts, Beds, and Repentance in Psalm 4,5 and Hosea 7,14." *Bib* 76 (1995) 53–62.

———. "The Meaning of *pršdn* in Judges iii 22." *VT* (1991) 1–11.

———. "Mesopotamian Light on the Idiom *nāśāʾ nepeš*." *CBQ* 52 (1990) 46–54.

———. "New Light on the Interpretation of Hosea vi 2." *VT* 28 (1978) 129–41.

———. "Of Lions and Birds: A Note on Isaiah 31:4–5." In *Among the Prophets: Language, Image and Structure in the Prophetic Writings*. Ed. P. R. Davies and D. J. A. Clines. JSOTSup 144. Sheffield: JSOT Press, 1993. 55–59.

———. "Psalm 116: Its Structure and Its Enigmas." *JBL* 109 (1990) 61–78.

———. "Restoring the 'Lost' Prayer of Hezekiah (Isaiah 38:16–17b)." *JBL* 114 (1995) 385–99.

———. "A Rhetorical-Critical Study of Isaiah 2:12-17." *CBQ* 65 (2003) 522–34.

———. "'Tarshish Has Perished': The Crux of Isaiah 23,10." *Bib* 85 (2004) 115–19.

———. "Textual and Rhetorical-critical Observations on the Last Servant Song (Isaiah 52:13–53:12)." CBA Presidential Address. *CBQ* 62 (2000) 1–27.

———. "'Wandering About' as a Topos of Depression in Ancient Near Eastern Literature and in the Bible." *JNES* 60 (2001) 177–87.

———. Review of M. Goulder, *The Prayers of David (Psalms 51–72): Studies in the Psalter II* (JSOTSup 102; Sheffield: JSOT Press, 1990). *JBL* 111 (1992) 527–28.

——— and J. S. Kselman. "New Exodus, Covenant, and Restoration in Psalm 23." In *The Word of the Lord Shall Go Forth: Essays in Honor of David Noel Freedman in Celebration of His Sixtieth Birthday*. Ed. C. L. Meyers and M. O'Connor. ASOR Special Volume Series 1. Winona Lake, IN: Eisenbrauns, 1983. 97–127.

Barth, C. "זמר *zmr*." *TDOT*, 4. 91–98.

Barthélemy, D., ed. *Critique Textuelle de l'Ancien Testament: Rapport final du Comité pour l'analyse textuelle de l'Ancien Testament hébreu institué par l'Alliance biblique universelle.* 3 vols. OBO 50. Fribourg: Éditions Universitaires. Göttingen: Vandenhoeck & Ruprecht, 1982–.

Bauer, H., and P. Leander. *Historische Grammatik der hebräischen Sprache des Alten Testaments: I.* Hildesheim: Georg Holms, 1965. Reprint of the 1922 edition.

Bauer, T. *Das Inschriftenwerk Assurbanipals.* 2 vols. Assyriologische Bibliothek (Neue Folge) 1–2. Leipzig: Hinrichs, 1933.

Baumgartner, W. et al., eds. *Hebräisches und aramäisches Wörterbuch zum Alten Testament.* Leiden: Brill, 1967–90.

Beeston, A. F. L. et al., eds. *Sabaic Dictionary (English-French-Arabic).* Louvain-la-Neuve: Éditions Peeters, 1982.

Begrich, J. *Der Psalm des Hiskia: Ein Beitrag zum Verständnis Jesaja 38 10–20.* (FRLANT [Neue Folge]) 25. Göttingen: Vandenhoeck & Ruprecht, 1926.

———, *Studien zu Deuterojesaja.* Ed. W. Zimmerli. TBü 20. Munich: Kaiser, 1963.

Berlin, A. *The Dynamics of Biblical Parallelism.* Bloomington, IN: Indiana University Press, 1985.

Biella, J. C. *Dictionary of Old South Arabic: Sabaean Dialect.* HSS 25. Chico, CA: Scholars Press, 1982.

Black, J., A. George, and N. Postgate, eds. *A Concise Dictionary of Akkadian.* SANTAG. Arbeiten und Untersuchungen zur Keilschriftkunde 5. Wiesbaden: Harrassowitz, 2000.

Blenkinsopp, J. *Isaiah 1–39.* AB 19. New York: Doubleday, 2000.

Borger, R. *Die Inschriften Asarhaddons Königs von Assyrien.* AfO Beiheft 9. Osnabrück: Biblio-Verlag, 1967.

Bredenkamp, C. J. *Der Prophet Jesaia.* Erlangen: Deichert, 1887.

Brock, S. P. "An Early Interpretation of *pāsaḥ: ʾaggēn* in the Palestinian Targum." In *Interpreting the Hebrew Text: Essays in Honour of E. I. J. Rosenthal.* Ed. J. A. Emerton and S. C. Reif. Cambridge: Cambridge University Press, 1982. 27–34.

———. *The Holy Spirit in the Syrian Baptismal Tradition.* Syrian Church Series 9. Poona: Anita, 1979.

———, ed. *The Old Testament in Syriac, according to the Peshitta Version: Part III Fascicle 1. Isaiah.* Leiden: Brill, 1987.

Brockelmann, K. *Lexicon Syriacum.* 2d ed. Halle: Straus & Cramer, 1928.

Brockington, L. H. *The Hebrew Text of the Old Testament: The Readings Adapted by the Translators of the New English Bible.* Oxford: Oxford University Press, 1973.

Brønno, E. *Studien über hebräische Morphologie und Vokalismus auf Grundlage der Mercatischen Fragmente der zweiten Kolumne der Hexapla des Origenes.* Abhandlungen für Kunde des Morgenlandes 28. Leipzig: Brockhaus, 1943.

Brown, F., S. R. Driver, and C. A. Briggs. *Hebrew and English Lexicon of the Old Testament.* Boston: Houghton, Mifflin, and Company, 1906.

Burrows, M. *The Dead Sea Scrolls of St. Mark's Monastery.* New Haven: American Schools of Oriental Research, 1950.

Castellino, G. R. "Lamentazioni individuali accadiche ed ebraiche." *Salesianum* 10 (1948) 145–62.

Charlesworth, J. H., and J. A. Sanders. "More Psalms of David (Third Century B.C.–First Century A.D.)." In *The Old Testament Pseudepigrapha: Volume 2: Expansions of the "Old Testament" and Legends, Wisdom and Philosophical Literature, Prayers, Psalms, and Odes, Fragments of Lost Judeo-Hellenistic Works.* Ed. J. H. Charlesworth. Garden City, NY: Doubleday, 1985. 609–24.

Cheyne, T. K. *Introduction to the Book of Isaiah.* London: Adam and Charles Black, 1895.

Childs, B. S. *Isaiah.* OTL. Louisville: Westminster/John Knox, 2001.

———. "Psalm Titles and Midrashic Exegesis." *JSS* 16 (1971) 137–50.

Chilton, B. D. *The Isaiah Targum.* The Aramaic Bible 11. Wilmington: Michael Glazier, 1987.

Clements, R. E. *Isaiah 1–39.* NCB. Grand Rapids: Eerdmans; London: Marshall, Morgan, & Scott, 1980.

Clines, D. J. A., ed. *The Dictionary of Classical Hebrew: Volume II:* ב–ו. Sheffield: Sheffield Academic Press, 1995.

Coetzee, J. H. "The 'Song of Hezekiah' (Isaiah 38:9–20): A Doxology of Judgement from the Exilic Period." *Old Testament Essays* (new series) 2 (1989) 13–26.

Cogan, M. *Imperialism and Religion: Assyria, Judah and Israel in the Eighth and Seventh Centuries B.C.E.* SBLMS 19. Missoula, MT: Scholars Press, 1974.

Cohen, C. "The Meaning of צלמות 'Darkness': A Study in Philological Method." In *Texts, Temples, and Traditions: A Tribute to Menahem Haran.* Ed. M. V. Fox et al. Winona Lake, IN: Eisenbrauns, 1996. 287–309.

Cohen, M. E. *Sumerian Hymnology: The Eršemma. HUCA* Supplements 2. Cincinnati: Ktav Press, 1981.

Collins, T. "The Physiology of Tears in the Old Testament (Part I)." *CBQ* 33 (1971) 18–38.

Comprehensive Aramaic Lexicon. <http://cal1.cn.huc.edu>.

Cooper, A. "Divine Names and Epithets in the Ugaritic Texts." In *Ras Shamra Parallels: The Texts from Ugarit and the Hebrew Bible: Vol. III.* Ed. S. Rummel. AnOr 51. Rome: Pontifical Biblical Institute, 1981. 333–469.

Cowley, A. *Aramaic Papyri of the Fifth Century B.C.* Osnabrück: Zeller, 1967. Reprint of the 1923 edition.

Cross, F. M. "The Cave Inscriptions from Khirbet Beit Lei." In *Near Eastern Archaeology in the Twentieth Century: Essays in Honor of Nelson Glueck.* Ed. J. A. Sanders. Garden City, NY: Doubleday, 1970. 299–306.

———. "The Development of the Jewish Scripts." In *The Bible and the Ancient Near East: Essays in Honor of William Foxwell Albright.* Ed. G. E. Wright. Garden City, NY: Doubleday, 1961. 133–202.

Dahood, M. "The Divine Name ᶜēlî in the Psalms." *TS* 14 (1953) 452–57.

———. "*ḥadel,* 'Cessation' in Isaiah 38:11." *Bib* 52 (1971) 215–16.

———. *Psalms I: 1–50.* AB 16. Garden City, NY: Doubleday, 1966.

———. "Textual Problems in Isaia." *CBQ* 22 (1960) 400–409.

Dalglish, E. R. *Psalm Fifty-One in Light of Ancient Near Eastern Patternism.* Leiden: Brill, 1962.

Dalman, G. H. *Aramäisch-Neuhebräisches Handwörterbuch zu Targum, Talmud und Midrasch.* Frankfurt am Main: Kaufmann, 1922.

———. *Arbeit und Sitte in Palästina: Band 5: Webstoff, Spinnen, Weben, Kleidung.* 7 vols. Beiträge zur Forderung christlicher Theologie, 2. Reihe: Sammlung wissenschaftlicher Monographien 36. Gütersloh: Bertelsmann, 1937.

De Boer, P. A. H. "Notes on Text and Meaning of Isaiah xxxviii 9–20." *OTS* 9 (1951) 170–86.

Delitzsch, F. *Assyrische Lesestücke mit den Elementen der Grammatik und vollständigem Glossar.* 5th ed. Assyriologische Bibliothek 16. Leipzig: Hinrichs, 1912.

———. *Die Lese- und Schreibfehler im Alten Testament.* Berlin/Leipzig: de Gruyter, 1920.

Del Olmo Lete, G., and J. Sanmartín. *A Dictionary of the Ugaritic Language in the Alphabetic Tradition.* Trans. W. G. E. Watson. HdO 67. Leiden/Boston: Brill, 2003.

Deutsch, R. "Lasting Impressions: New Bullae Reveal Egyptian-Style Emblems on Judah's Royal Seals." *BAR* 28 (2002) 42–52, 60–62.

Dillmann, A. *Lexicon Linguae Aethiopicae.* Leipzig: Weigel, 1865.

Dobbs-Allsopp, F. W. "Linguistic Evidence for the Date of Lamentations." *JANES* 26 (1998) 1–36.

Donner, H., and W. Röllig. *Kanaanäische und aramäische Inschriften.* 2d ed. 3 vols. Wiesbaden: Harrassowitz, 1968.

Driver, G. R. "Birds in the Old Testament: I: Birds in Law." *PEQ* 87 (1955) 5–20.

———. "Birds in the Old Testament: II: Birds in Life." *PEQ* 87 (1955) 129–40.

———. "Hebrew Notes." *JBL* 68 (1949) 57–59.

———. "Isaiah i–xxxix: Textual and Linguistic Problems." *JSS* 13 (1968) 36–57.

———. *The Judaean Scrolls: A Problem and a Solution.* Oxford: Blackwell, 1965.

———. "Two Forgotten Hebrew Words." *JTS* 28 (1927) 285–87.

Drower, E. S., and R. Machuch. *Mandaic Dictionary.* Oxford: Oxford University Press, 1963.

Duhm, B. *Das Buch Jesaja.* 4th ed. HKAT. Göttingen: Vandenhoeck & Ruprecht, 1922.

Ebeling, E. *Die akkadische Gebetsserie "Handerhebung."* Deutsche Akademie der Wissenschaft zu Berlin, Institut für Orientforschung 20. Berlin: Akademie Verlag, 1953.

———. *Tod und Leben nach den Vorstellungen der Babylonier.* Berlin: de Gruyter, 1931.

Ehrlich, W. *Randglossen zur hebräischen Bibel.* 7 vols. Leipzig: Hinrichs, 1908–14.

Eitan, I. "La particule emphatique 'la' dans la Bible." *REJ* 74 (1922) 1–16.

Erman, A., and H. Grapow. *Wörterbuch der aegyptischen Sprache.* 5 vols. Berlin: Akademie Verlag, 1961.

Fabry, H.-J. "דל *dal.*" *TDOT*, 3. 208–30.

———. "מרר *mrr.*" *TDOT*, 9. 15–19.

Field, F. *Origenis Hexaplorum Quae Supersunt.* 2 vols. Oxford: Clarendon Press, 1875.

Fisher, L. R., ed. *Ras Shamra Parallels: The Texts from Ugarit and the Hebrew Bible: Volume I.* AnOr 49. Rome: Pontifical Biblical Institute, 1972.

Fitzmyer, J. A. *The Aramaic Inscriptions of Sefire.* BibOr 19. Rome: Pontifical Biblical Institute, 1967.

Flint, P. W. *The Dead Sea Psalms Scrolls and the Book of Psalms.* STDJ 17. Leiden: Brill, 1997.

——— and A. E. Alvarez. "The Oldest of All the Psalms Scrolls: The Text and Translation of 4QPsª." In *The Scrolls and the Scriptures: Qumran Fifty Years After.* Ed. S. E. Porter and C. A. Evans. JSPSup 26. Sheffield: Sheffield University Press, 1997. 142–69 .

Fohrer, G. *Das Buch Jesaja.* 3 vols. ZBAT. 2d ed. Zurich/Stuttgart: Zwingli, 1960–67.

Foster, B. R. "Letters and Literature: A Ghost's Entreaty." In *The Tablet and the Scroll: Near Eastern Studies in Honor of William W. Hallo.* Ed. M. E. Cohen et al. Bethesda, MD: CLD Press, 1993. 98–102.

Freedman, D. N. "Deliberate Deviation from an Established Pattern of Repetition in Hebrew Poetry as a Literary Device." In *Divine Commitment and Human Obligation: Selected Writings of David Noel Freedman.* Ed. J. R. Huddlestun. 2 vols. Grand Rapids: Eerdmans, 1997. 2. 205–12.

———. "Divine Names and Titles in Early Hebrew Poetry." In *Pottery, Poetry, and Prophecy: Studies in Early Hebrew Poetry.* Winona Lake, IN: Eisenbrauns, 1980. 77–129.

——— and J. Lundbom. "דור *dôr.*" *TDOT,* 3. 169–81.

Friedländer, M. *The Commentary of Ibn Ezra on Isaiah.* 2 vols. New York: Feldheim, 1873.

Fuhs, H. F. "דכא *dākhāʾ.*" *TDOT,* 3. 195–208.

Gadegaard, N. H. "On the So-Called Burnt Offering Altar in the Old Testament." *PEQ* 110 (1978) 35–45.

Galling, K. "Altar." *IDB,* 1. 96–100.

García Martínez, F., and E. J. C. Tigchelaar, eds. *The Dead Sea Scrolls: Study Edition.* 2 vols. Leiden: Brill, 1997–98.

Garr, W. R. "The Grammar and Interpretation of Exodus 6:3." *JBL* 111 (1992) 385–408.

Gelb, I. et al., eds. *The Assyrian Dictionary of the Oriental Institute of the University of Chicago.* Chicago: Oriental Institute; Glückstadt: J. J. Augustin: 1956–.

Gerlemann, G. "שלם *šlm* genug haben." *THAT*, 2. cols. 919–35.

George, A. R. *House Most High: The Temples of Ancient Mesopotamia.* Mesopotamian Civilizations 5. Winona Lake, IN: Eisenbrauns, 1993.

Gevirtz, S. "Of Syntax and Style in 'Late Biblical Hebrew'—'Old Canaanite' Connection." *JANES* 18 (1986) 25–29.

Gibson, J. C. L. *Textbook of Syrian Semitic Inscriptions: Volume I: Hebrew and Moabite Inscriptions.* Oxford: Clarendon Press, 1971.

Ginsberg, H. L. "Psalms and Inscriptions of Petition and Acknowledgment." In *Louis Ginsberg Jubilee Volume.* Ed. A. Marx. New York: American Academy for Jewish Research, 1945. 159–71.

Goshen-Gottstein, M. H., ed. *The Book of Isaiah.* The Hebrew University Bible. Jerusalem: Magnes Press, 1995.

Gray, J. *I & II Kings.* 2d ed. OTL. London: SCM, 1970.

Greenberg, M. *Biblical Prose Prayer as a Window to the Popular Religion of Ancient Israel.* Berkeley: University of California Press, 1983.

———. *Ezekiel 21–37.* AB 22A. New York: Doubleday, 1997.

Greenfield, J. C. "Scripture and Inscription: The Literary and Rhetorical Element in Some Early Phoenician Inscriptions." In *Near Eastern Studies in Honor of William Foxwell Albright.* Ed. H. Goedicke. Baltimore: The Johns Hopkins University Press, 1971. 253–68.

Grelot, P. "La prière de Nabonide (4 Q Or Nab)." *RevQ* 9 (1978) 483–95.

Gruber, M. I. *Aspects of Nonverbal Communication in the Ancient Near East.* 2 vols. Studia Pohl 12. Rome: Pontifical Biblical Institute, 1980.

Gurney, O. R., and J. J. Finkelstein. *The Sultantepe Tablets I.* Occasional Publications of the British Institute of Archaeology at Ankara 3. London: British Institute of Archaeology at Ankara, 1957.

Haak, R. D. "Altar." *ABD*, 1. 162–67.

Habel, N. *The Book of Job: A Commentary.* OTL. Philadelphia: Westminster, 1985.

Hackett, J. A. *The Balaam Text from Deir ʿAllā.* HSM 31. Chico, CA: Scholars Press, 1980.

Hallo, W. H. "The Royal Correspondence of Larsa: I. A Sumerian Prototype for the Prayer of Hezekiah?" In *Kramer Anniversary Volume: Cuneiform Studies in Honor of Samuel Noah Kramer.* Ed. B. L. Eichler et al. AOAT 25. Kevelaer: Butzon & Bercker; Neukirchen-Vluyn: Neukirchener Verlag, 1976. 209–24.

Hava, J. G. *Arabic-English Lexicon.* Beirut: Catholic Press, 1951.

Held, M. "Pits and Pitfalls in Akkadian and Biblical Hebrew." *JANES* 5 (1973) 173–90.

Hiebert, T. *God of My Victory: The Ancient Hymn in Habakkuk 3.* HSM 38. Atlanta: Scholars Press, 1986.

Hillers, D. R. *Lamentations.* 2d ed. AB 7A. New York: Doubleday, 1992.

———. "The Roads to Zion Mourn." *Perspective* 12 (1971) 121–34.

Hodge, C. T. "Miktam." In *Semitic Studies in Honor of Wolf Leslau on the Occasion of his Eighty-fifth Birthday, November 14th, 1991.* 2 vols. Ed. A. S. Kaye. Wiesbaden: Harrassowitz, 1991. 1. 634–44.

Hoftijzer, J., and K. Jongeling. *Dictionary of the North-West Semitic Inscriptions.* 2 vols. HdO 21. Leiden: Brill, 1995.

Holladay, W. L. *A Concise Hebrew and Aramaic Lexicon of the Old Testament.* Grand Rapids: Eerdmans, 1988.

———. *Jeremiah 1: A Commentary on the Book of the Prophet Jeremiah Chapters 1–25.* Hermeneia. Philadelphia: Fortress, 1986.

Huehnergard, J. "Asseverative *la and Hypothetical *lu/law in Semitic." *JAOS* 103 (1983) 569–93.

Hurvitz, A. "The Chronological Significance of 'Aramaisms' in Biblical Hebrew." *IEJ* 18 (1968) 234–40.

———. "The Historical Quest for 'Ancient Israel' and the Linguistic Evidence of the Hebrew Bible: Some Methodological Observations." *VT* 47 (1997) 301–15.

———. *A Linguistic Study of the Relationship between the Priestly Source and the Book of Ezekiel: A New Approach to an Old Problem.* Paris: Gabalda, 1982.

Ibn Manẓūr, M. *Lisān al-ʿArab.* 20 vols. Beirut: Dār Beirut lil-Ṭibāʿa wal-Našr, 1955.

Jamme, A. *Sabaean Inscriptions from Maḥram Bilqîs (Mârib).* Baltimore: The Johns Hopkins University Press, 1962.

Jastrow, M. *Dictionary of the Targumim, Talmud Babli, Talmud Yerushalmi and Mishnaic Literature*. New York: Jastrow, 1967.

Jenni, E. *Das hebräische Pi'el: Syntaktisch-semasiologische Untersuchung einer Verbalform im Alten Testament*. Zurich: EVZ Verlag, 1968.

Jepsen, A. *Nabi: Soziologische Studien zur alttestamentlichen Literatur und Religionsgeschichte*. Munich: Beck, 1934.

Joüon, P., and T. Muraoka. *A Grammar of Biblical Hebrew*. 2 vols. Subsidia Biblica 14. Rome: Pontifical Biblical Institute, 1991.

Kaiser, O. *Isaiah 13–39*. OTL. Philadelphia: Westminster, 1974.

Kaltner, J. *The Use of Arabic in Biblical Hebrew Lexicography*. CBQMS 28. Washington: Catholic Biblical Association of America, 1996.

Kautzsch, E., and A. E. Cowley, eds. *Gesenius' Hebrew Grammar*. 2d ed. Oxford: Clarendon Press, 1910.

Kellermann, D. "בצע *bṣ'*." *TDOT*, 2. 205–8.

Kilmer, A. D. "The Musical Instruments from Ur and Ancient Mesopotamian Music." *Expedition* 40 (1998) 12–19.

King, L. W. *Babylonian Boundary-Stones and Memorial-Tablets in the British Museum*. London: British Museum, 1912.

King, P. J., and L. E. Stager. *Life in Biblical Israel*. Library of Ancient Israel. Louisville: Westminster John Knox, 2001.

Kittel, B. P. *The Hymns of Qumran: Translation and Commentary*. SBLDS 50. Chico, CA: Scholars Press, 1981.

Klostermann, A. "Lautverschiebung im Texte des Hiskia-Psalms (Jes. 38, 9–20)." *Theologische Studien und Kritiken* 57 (1884) 157–67.

Koehler, L., and W. Baumgartner, eds. *Lexicon in Veteris Testamenti Libros*. 2d ed. Leiden: Brill; Grand Rapids: Eerdmans, 1951–53.

Kraus, H.-J. *Psalms 1-59: A Commentary*. Minneapolis: Augsburg, 1988.

Kselman, J. S. "Design and Structure in Hebrew Poetry." In *SBL Seminar Papers 1980*. Ed. P. J. Achtemeier. *SBLSP 1980*. Chico, CA: Society of Biblical Literature, 1980. 1–16.

Kutscher, E. Y. *The Language and Linguistic Background of the Isaiah Scroll (1QIsaᵃ)*. Leiden: Brill, 1974.

Laato, A. "Hezekiah and the Assyrian Crisis in 701 B.C." *SJOT* 2 (1987) 49–68.

Lambert, W. G. E. *Babylonian Wisdom Literature*. Oxford: Clarendon Press, 1960.

———. "Dingir.šà.dib.ba Incantations." *JNES* 33 (1974) 267–322.

———. "Three Literary Prayers of the Babylonians." *AfO* 19 (1959–60) 47–66.

———. Review of *Eblaitica 3: Essays on the Ebla Archives and Eblaite Language. Volume 3* (ed. C. H. Gordon and Gary A. Rendsberg; Winona Lake, IN: Eisenbrauns, 1995). In *Bulletin of the School of Oriental and African Studies, University of London* 58 (1995) 348–50.

Lane, E. W. *Arabic-English Lexicon*. 8 vols. London: Williams and Norgate, 1863–1893. Reprint: 2 vols. Cambridge: Islamic Texts Society, 1984.

Lebrun, R. *Hymnes et prières hittites*. Homo Religiosus 4. Louvain-la-neuve: Centre d'Histoire des Religions, 1980.

Levine, B. A. "Silence, Sound, and the Phenomenology of Mourning in Biblical Israel." *JANES* 22 (1993) 89–106.

Levy, J. *Wörterbuch über die Talmudim und Midraschim*. 4 vols. 2d ed. Berlin/Vienna: Benjamin Harz, 1924.

Liddell, H. G., and R. Scott. *A Greek-English Lexicon*. Rev. by H. S. Jones. Oxford: Clarendon Press, 1968.

Lindenberger, J. M. *The Aramaic Proverbs of Ahiqar*. JHNES. Baltimore/London: The Johns Hopkins University Press, 1983.

Linder, J. "Textkritische und exegetische Studie zum Canticum Ezechiae (Is 38, 9-20)." *ZKT* 42 (1918) 46–73.

Lipiński, E. "ערב I *ʿārab*." *TDOT*, ii. 326–30.

Livingstone, A. *Court Poetry and Literary Miscellanea*. State Archives of Assyria 3. Helsinki: Helsinki University Press, 1989.

Liwak, R. "Die Rettung Jerusalems im Jahr 701 v. Chr.: Zum Verhältnis und Verständnis historischer und theologischer Aussagen." *ZTK* 83 (1986) 137–66.

Luckenbill, D. D., ed. *The Annals of Sennacherib*. OIP 2. Chicago: University of Chicago Press, 1924.

Lust, J. et al., eds. *A Greek–English Lexicon of the Septuagint*. 2 vols. Stuttgart: Deutsche Bibelgesellschaft, 1992–96.

Marcus, E. and M. Artzy. "A Loom Weight from Tel Nami with a Scarab Seal Impression." *IEJ* 45 (1995) 136–49.

Mayer, W. *Untersuchungen zur Formensprache der babylonischen "Gebetsbeschwörungen."* Studia Pohl: Series Maior 5. Rome: Biblical Institute, 1976.

McCarter, P. K., Jr. *1 Samuel*. AB 8. Garden City, NY: Doubleday, 1980.

———. "The Balaam Texts from Deir ʿAllā: The First Combination." *BASOR* 239 (1980) 49–60.

———. *Textual Criticism: Recovering the Text of the Hebrew Bible*. Philadelphia: Fortress, 1986.

Meyer, D. R. *Hebräische Grammatik*. 4 vols. Berlin: de Gruyter, 1972.

Miller, P. D. *They Cried to the Lord: The Form and Theology of Biblical Prayer*. Minneapolis: Fortress, 1994.

———. "Psalms and Inscriptions." In *Congress Volume: Vienna 1980*. Ed. J. A. Emerton. VTSup 32. Leiden: Brill, 1981. 311–32.

Muraoka, T. *Emphatic Words and Structures in Biblical Hebrew*. Jerusalem: Magnes; Leiden: Brill, 1985.

———. *Hebrew/Aramaic Index to the Septuagint: Keyed to the Hatch-Redpath Concordance*. Grand Rapids: Baker Books, 1998.

Myers, J. M. *II Chronicles*. AB 13. Garden City, NY: Doubleday, 1965.

Negoita, A. "הגה *hāgāh*." *TDOT*, 3. 321–24.

Nyberg, H. S. "Hiskias Danklied Jes. 38,9–20." *ASTI* 9 (1973) 85–97.

———. *Studien zum Hoseabuche: Zugleich ein Beitrag zur Klärung der alttestamentlichen Textkritik*. UUÅ 6. Uppsala: Almqvist & Wiksells, 1935.

Orlinsky, H. M. "Studies in the St. Mark's Isaiah Scroll, IV." *JQR* 43 (1952–53). 329–40.

Oswalt, J. N. *The Book of Isaiah: Chapters 1–39*. NICOT. Grand Rapids: Eerdmans, 1986.

Ottosson, M. "חלם *chālam*." *TDOT*, 4. 421–32.

Pardee, D. *Handbook of Ancient Hebrew Letters: A Study Edition*. SBLSBS 15. Chico, CA: Scholars Press, 1982.

———. *Ritual and Cult at Ugarit*. Writings from the Ancient World: Society of Biblical Literature 10. Atlanta: Scholars Press, 2002.

Parpola, S. "The Murderer of Sennacherib." In *Death in Mesopotamia: Papers Read at the XXVIᵉ Rencontre assyriologique internationale (= Mesopotamia: Copenhagen Studies in Assyriology 8)*. Ed. B. Alster. Copenhagen: Akademisk Forlag, 1980. 171–82.

——— and K. Watanabe. *Neo-Assyrian Treaties and Loyalty Oaths*. State Archives of Assyria 2. Helsinki: Helsinki University Press, 1988.

Parry, D. W., and E. Qimron. *The Great Isaiah Scroll (1QIsaᵃ): A New Edition*. STDJ 32. Leiden: Brill, 1999.

Payne Smith, J. *A Compendious Syriac Dictionary*. Oxford: Clarendon Press, 1903.

Payne Smith, R. *Thesaurus Syriacus*. Oxford: Clarendon Press, 1879–1901.

Polzin, R. *Typology of Biblical Hebrew Prose: Toward an Historical Typology of Biblical Hebrew Prose*. HSM 12; Missoula, MT: Scholars Press, 1976.

Pope, M. H. "A Resurvey of Some Ugaritic-Hebrew Connections." *Maarav* 7 (1991) 199–206.

———. *Job*. AB 15. 2d ed. Garden City, NY: Doubleday, 1973.

Qimron, E. *The Hebrew of the Dead Sea Scrolls*. HSS 29. Atlanta: Scholars Press, 1986.

Raabe, P. R. "Deliberate Ambiguity in the Psalter." *JBL* 110 (1991) 213–27.

Ravasi, G. *Il libro dei Salmi*. 3 vols. Bologna: Edizione Dehoniane, 1985.

Rendsburg, G. A. "Eblaite *sa-su-ga-lum* = Hebrew *ssᶜgr*." In *Eblaitica: Essays on the Ebla Archives and Eblaite Language: Volume 3*. Ed. C. H. Gordon and G. A. Rendsburg. Publications for the Center for Ebla Research at New York University 3. Winona Lake, IN: Eisenbrauns, 1992. 151–53.

———. "Late Biblical Hebrew and the Date of 'P'." *JANES* 12 (1980) 65–80.

Ricoeur, P. *The Rule of Metaphor: Multi-Disciplinary Studies of the Creation of Meaning in Language*. Toronto/Buffalo: University of Toronto Press, 1975.

Rimbach, J. "'Crushed Before the Moth' (Job 4:19)." *JBL* 100 (1981) 244–46.

Ringgren, H. "The Omitting of *kol* in Hebrew Parallelism." *VT* 32 (1982) 99–103.

Roberts, J. J. M. *Nahum, Habakkuk, and Zephaniah: A Commentary*. OTL. Louisville: Westminster/John Knox, 1991.

Rooker, M. F. *Biblical Hebrew in Transition: The Language of the Book of Ezekiel*. JSOTSup 90. Sheffield: Sheffield Academic Press, 1990.

Sawyer, J. F. A. "An Analysis of the Context and Meaning of the Psalm Headings." *Glasgow University Oriental Society Transactions* 22 (1970) 26–38.

Schmidt, B. "AL." *DDD* (Rev. ed.). 14–17.

Schmuttermayr, G. *Psalm 18 und 2 Samuel 22: Studien zu einem Doppeltext: Probleme der Textkritik und Übersetzung und das Psalterium Pianum.* SANT 25. Munich: Kösel, 1971.

Schuller, E. M. *Non-Canonical Psalms from Qumran: A Pseudepigraphic Collection.* HSS 28. Atlanta: Scholars Press, 1986.

Scott, R. B. Y. "Isaiah: Text, Exegesis, and Exposition, Chapters 1–39." *IB* 5. 165–381.

Segert, S. *A Basic Grammar of the Ugaritic Language.* Berkeley: University of California Press, 1984.

Segond, L. *La Sainte Bible: Traduite d'après originaux hébreu et grec.* Rev. ed. Paris: Alliance Biblique Universelle, 1998.

Seitz, C. R. *Zion's Final Destiny: The Development of the Book of Isaiah: A Reassessment of Isaiah 36–39.* Minneapolis: Fortress, 1991.

Seow, C. L. "Linguistic Evidence and the Dating of Qoheleth." *JBL* 115 (1996) 643–66.

Seux, M.-J. *Hymnes et prières aux dieux de Babylonie et d'Assyrie.* LAPO 8. Paris: Éditions du Cerf, 1976.

Seybold, K. *Das Gebet des Kranken im Alten Testament: Untersuchungen zur Bestimmung und Zuordnung der Krankheits- und Heilungspsalmen.* BWANT 99. Stuttgart: Kohlhammer, 1973.

Siegel, J. P. *The Severus Scroll and 1QIsa*[a]. SBLMasS 2. Missoula, MT: Scholars Press: 1975.

Simms, K. *Paul Ricoeur.* Routledge Critical Thinkers: Essential Guides for Literary Studies. London/New York: Routledge, 2003.

Skehan, P. W., and A. A. Di Lella. *The Wisdom of Ben Sira.* AB 39. Doubleday: New York, 1987.

Slanski, K. E. "Classification, Historiography, and Monumental Authority: The Babylonian Entitlement *narûs* (*kudurru*s)." *JCS* 52 (2000) 95–114.

Smelik, K. A. D. "Distortion of Old Testament Prophecy: The Purpose of Isaiah 36 and 37." In *Crises and Perspectives: Studies in Ancient Near Eastern Polytheism, Biblical Theology, Palestinian Archaeology, and Intertestamental Literature: Papers Read at the Joint British-Dutch Old Testament Conference Held at Cambridge, U.K., 1985.* Ed. J. C. De Moor et al. OTS 24. Leiden: Brill, 1986. 70–93.

Smith, W. G. "Fullo." In *A Dictionary of Greek and Roman Antiquities.* Ed. W. G. Smith. London: John Murray, 1875. 551–53.

Soggin, J. A. "Il 'Salmo di Ezechia' in *Isaia* 38,9–20." *BibOr* 16 (1974) 177–81.

Sokoloff, M. *A Dictionary of Jewish Palestinian Aramaic of the Byzantine Period.* Ramat-Gan: Bar Ilan University Press, 1990.

———. *A Dictionary of Jewish Babylonian Aramaic of the Talmudic and Geonic Periods.* Ramat-Gan: Bar Ilan University Press; Baltimore: The Johns Hopkins University Press, 2002.

Spieckermann, H. *Juda unter Assur in der Sargonidenzeit.* FRLANT 129. Göttingen: Vandenhoeck & Ruprecht, 1982.

Stähli, H.-P. "רום *rūm* hoch sein." *THAT*, 2. cols. 754–61.

Stenning, J. F. *The Targum of Isaiah.* Oxford: Clarendon Press, 1949.

Sweeney, M. A., *Isaiah 1–39.* FOTL 16. Grand Rapids: Eerdmans, 1996.

Szpek, H. M. "The Peshitta on Job 7:6: 'My Days Are Swifter Than an ארג'." *JBL* 113 (1994) 287–90.

Tal, A. *A Dictionary of Samaritan Aramaic.* HdO 50/1–2. Leiden: Brill, 2000.

Talmon, S. "The Ancient Hebrew Alphabet and Biblical Text Criticism." In *Mélanges Dominique Barthélemy: Études bibliques offertes à l'occasion de son 60e anniversaire.* Ed. P. Casetti et al. OBO 38. Fribourg: Éditions Universitaires, 1981. 497–538.

———. "The Ancient Hebrew Alphabet and Biblical Text Criticism." In *Mélanges bibliques et orientaux en l'honneur de M Mathias Delcor.* Ed. A. Caquot et al. AOAT 215. Kevelaer: Butzon & Bercker, 1985. 387–402.

———. "Aspects of the Textual Transmission of the Bible in Light of Qumran Manuscripts." In *Qumran and the History of the Biblical Text.* Ed. F. M. Cross and S. Talmon. Cambridge, MA: Harvard University Press, 1975. 226–63.

———. "The Textual Study of the Bible—A New Outlook." In *Qumran and the History of the Biblical Text.* Ed. F. M. Cross and S. Talmon. Cambridge, MA: Harvard University Press, 1975. 321–400.

Touzard, J. "De la conservation du text hébreu: Étude sur Isaïe, xxxvi–xxxix (Suite)." *RB* 8 (1899) 83–108.

Tov, E. "Renderings of Combinations of the Infinitive Absolute and Finite Verbs in the LXX–Their Nature and Distribution." In *Studien zur Septuaginta: Robert Hanhart zu ehren: aus Anlass seines 65. Geburtstages.* Ed. D. Fraenkel et al. Abhandlungen der

Akademie der Wissenschaften in Göttingen; Philologisch-historische Klasse, dritte Folge 190; Mitteilungen des Septuaginta-Unternehmens 20. Göttingen: Vandenhoeck & Ruprecht, 1990. 64–73.

———. *The Text-Critical Use of the Septuagint in Biblical Research.* Jerusalem Biblical Studies 3. Jerusalem: Simor, 1981.

———. *Textual Criticism of the Hebrew Bible.* Minneapolis: Fortress, 1992.

Trever, J. C. *Scrolls from Qumrân Cave I.* Jerusalem: The Albright Institute of Archaeological Research; The Shrine of the Book, 1972.

Tromp, N. J. *Primitive Conceptions of Death and the Nether World in the Old Testament.* BibOr 21. Rome: Pontifical Biblical Institute, 1969.

Uehlinger, C. "Nisroch נסרך." *DDD.* Rev. ed. 630–32.

Ulrich, E. *The Dead Sea Scrolls and the Origins of the Bible.* Studies in the Dead Sea Scrolls and Related Literature. Leiden: Brill; Grand Rapids: Eerdmans, 1999.

———. "The Developmental Composition of the Book of Isaiah: Light from 1QIsaᵃ on Additions in the MT." *DSD* 8 (2001) 288–305.

———. "The Text of the Hebrew Scriptures at the Time of Hillel and Jesus." In *Congress Volume: Basel 2001.* Ed. A. Lemaire. VTSup 92. Leiden: Brill, 2002. 85–108.

Van der Kooij, A. *Die alten Textzeugen des Jesajabuches: Ein Beitrag zur Textgeschichte des Alten Testaments.* OBO 35. Göttingen: Vandenhoeck & Ruprecht, 1981.

Van der Ploeg, J. "Fragments d'un manuscrit de psaumes de Qumran (11QPsᵇ)." *RB* 74 (1967) 408–12.

Van der Toorn, K., and P. W. van der Horst. "Nimrod Before and After the Bible." *HTR* 83 (1990) 1–29 .

Van der Westhuizen, J. P. "Isaiah 38:10–20: Literary Devices and Exegesis." In *Studies in Isaiah.* Ed. W. C. van Wyk. Ou-Testamentiese Werkgemeenskap in Suider Africa 22, 23. Hercules, South Africa: Nhw Press, 1982. 198–212.

Vogt, E. *Lexicon Linguae Aramaicae Veteris Testamenti.* Rome: Pontifical Biblical Institute, 1971.

Von Legelshurst, R. D. *Die Hiskiaerzählungen: Eine formgeschichtliche Untersuchung der Texte Js 36–39 und 2R 18–20.* Basel: Basileia Verlag, 1969.

Von Soden, W. *Akkadisches Handwörterbuch*. 3 vols. Wiesbaden: Harrassowitz: 1965– 1981.

Wagner, M. *Die lexikalischen und grammatikalischen Aramaismen im alttestamentlichen Hebräisch*. BZAW 96. Berlin: Töpelmann, 1966.

Waldman, N. M. "The Imagery of Clothing, Covering, and Overpowering." *JANES* 19 (1989) 161–70.

Waltke, B. K. "How We Got the Hebrew Bible: The Text and Canon of the Old Testament." In *The Bible at Qumran: Text, Shape, and Interpretation*. Ed. P. W. Flint and T. H. Kim. Studies in the Dead Sea Scrolls and Related Literature. Grand Rapids: Eerdmans, 2001. 27–50.

——— and M. O'Connor. *Introduction to Biblical Hebrew Syntax*. Winona Lake, IN: Eisenbrauns, 1990.

Watson, W. G. E. *Classical Hebrew Poetry: A Guide to Its Techniques*. JSOTSup 26. Sheffield: JSOT Press, 1984.

Watts, J. W. *Psalm and Story: Inset Hymns in Hebrew Narrative*. JSOTSup 139. Sheffield: Sheffield Academic Press, 1992.

Weber, R. et al., eds. *Biblia Sacra Iuxta Vulgatam Versionem*. Stuttgart: Deutsche Bibelgesellschaft, 1983.

Wehmeier, G. "עלה *ʿlh* hinaufgehen." *THAT*, 2. cols. 272–90.

Wehr, H. *A Dictionary of Modern Written Arabic*. Ed. J. M. Cowan. 3d ed. Ithaca, NY: Spoken Language Services, 1976.

Weinfeld, M. "Job and Its Mesopotamian Parallels—A Typological Analysis." In *Text and Context: Old Testament and Semitic Studies for F. C. Fensham*. Ed. W. Claassen. JSOTSup 48. Sheffield: JSOT/Sheffield Academic Press, 1988. 217–26.

Weiss, R. "Textual Notes." *Textus* 6. Ed. S. Talmon. Jerusalem: Magnes, 1968. 127–28.

Westenholz, J. G. *Legends of the Kings of Agade*. Winona Lake, IN: Eisenbrauns, 1997.

Westermann, C. *Praise and Lament in the Psalms*. Atlanta: John Knox, 1981.

———. "ידה *jdh* hi. preisen." *THAT*, 1. cols. 674–82.

Wildberger, H. *Jesaja: 3. Teilband: Jesaja 28–39: Das Buch, der Prophet, und seine Botschaft*. BKAT 10/3. Neukirchen-Vluyn: Neukirchener Verlag, 1982.

Williams, R. J. "The Passive *Qal* Theme in Hebrew." In *Essays on the Ancient Semitic World*. Ed. J. W. Wevers and D. B. Redford.

Toronto Semitic Texts and Studies. Toronto: University of Toronto Press, 1970. 43–50.

——. *Hebrew Syntax: An Outline.* 2d ed. Toronto/Buffalo: University of Toronto Press, 1976.

Williamson, H. G. M. "Hezekiah and the Temple." In *Texts, Temples, and Traditions: A Tribute to Menahem Haran.* Ed. M. V. Fox et al. Winona Lake, IN: Eisenbrauns, 1996. 47–52.

Wilson, G. H. *The Editing of the Hebrew Psalter.* SBLDS 76. Chico, CA: Scholars Press, 1985.

Würthwein, E. *The Text of the Old Testament: An Introduction to the Biblia Hebraica.* 2d ed. Grand Rapids: Eerdmans, 1995.

Xella, P. "Resheph רשׁף." *DDD.* Rev. ed. 700–703.

Yeivin, I. מבוא למסורה הטברנית: *Introduction to the Tiberian Masorah.* Trans./ed. E. J. Revell. SBLMasS 5. Chico, CA: Scholars Press, 1980.

Youngblood, R. "Divine Names in the Book of Psalms: Literary Structures and Number Patterns." *JANES* 19 (1995) 171–81.

Ziegler, J., ed. *Isaias.* Septuaginta: Vetus Testamentum Graecum Auctoritate Societatis Litterarum Göttingensis editum 14. Göttingen: Vandenhoeck & Ruprecht, 1939.

Zimmerli, W. *Ezekiel 1: A Commentary on the Book of the Prophet Ezekiel, Chapters 1–24.* Hermeneia. Philadelphia: Fortress, 1979.

Zorrell, F. *Lexicon Hebraicum et Aramaicum Veteris Testamenti.* Rome: Pontifical Biblical Institute, 1968.

Index of Scripture Passages

Italicized Psalms references give the Septuagint numeration of the psalm and verse.

Index of Authors